# DAILY LIFE IN

# RENAISSANCE ITALY

**The Greenwood Press "Daily Life Through History" Series**

# DAILY LIFE IN

# RENAISSANCE ITALY

## ELIZABETH S. COHEN AND THOMAS V. COHEN

The Greenwood Press "Daily Life Through History" Series

**GREENWOOD PRESS**
Westport, Connecticut • London

**Library of Congress Cataloging-in-Publication Data**

Cohen, Elizabeth Storr, 1946–
    Daily life in Renaissance Italy / Elizabeth S. Cohen and Thomas V. Cohen.
        p.   cm.—(The Greenwood Press "Daily life through history" series, ISSN 1080–4749)
    Includes bibliographical references and index.
    ISBN 0–313–30426–2 (alk. paper)
        1. Italy—Social life and customs—To 1500.   2. Renaissance—Italy.   I. Cohen,
    Thomas V. (Thomas Vance), 1942–  .   II. Title.   III. Series.
    DG445.C48 2001
    945'.05—dc21          00–069150

British Library Cataloguing in Publication Data is available.

Library of Congress Catalog Card Number: 00–069150
ISBN: 0–313–30426–2
ISSN: 1080–4749

First published in 2001

Greenwood Press, 88 Post Road West, Westport, CT 06881
An imprint of Greenwood Publishing Group, Inc.
www.greenwood.com

Printed in the United States of America

The paper used in this book complies with the
Permanent Paper Standard issued by the National
Information Standards Organization (Z39.48–1984).

10 9 8 7 6 5 4 3 2 1

## Copyright Acknowledgments

The authors and publisher gratefully acknowledge permission for the use of the following material:

Illustrations from Bertelli, *Diversarum Nationum Habitus* (Padua, 1594); Biringuccio, *Li Diece libri della Pirotechnia* (Venice, 1558); and Bartolomeo Scappi, *Opera* (Venice, 1605), from the collections of the Biblioteca Angelica, are reproduced with the concession of the Ministero per i Beni e le Attività Culturali. Reproduction or ulterior duplication for any purpose is prohibited.

Antonio Tempesta's woodcuts "Febbraio," "Aprile," "Caccia: frontespizio," "Caccia di cinghiale," "Aetas Enea" and "Vini e bavitori," from the collections of Gabinetto Nazionale delle Stampe, Roma–Istituto Nazionale per la Grafica, are reproduced by gracious concession of the Ministero per i Beni e le Attività Culturali.

Illustrations labeled Bertarelli—"Lucrezia, esemplare delle donne," "Forfanti," two sins (Avaritia and Gioco), and five "months" from *Missale romanum novissime impressum*—and four images from the woodcuts "Giugno" and "Dicembre" by Antonio Tempesta are reproduced with permission from the collections of the Civica Raccolta delle Stampe Achille Bertarelli–Milano.

# Contents

# Acknowledgments

Our thanks to many unnamed people on both sides of the Atlantic who, wittingly and not, have offered information and assistance for this book. We are grateful, in particular, to the direction of the Archivio di Stato di Roma for helping our own primary research in many ways and to the friendly staffs at the several libraries and collections where we gathered our illustrations: in Rome, the Biblioteca Angelica and the Gabinetto Nazionale delle Stampe, and in Milan, the Raccolta Civica Achille Bertarelli. (Illustration sources are given in the Copyright Acknowledgments on p. v.) We appreciate the advice of Rosamund Morley, Jane Couchman, and Barbara Sparti on sources for music and dance and of Annie Storr about museums and the Web. All errors and imprudent formulations are our own.

# Chronology

| 1465 | First Italian printing press at Subiaco |
| 1474 | Mantegna completes *Camera degli Sposi* at Mantua<br>Federico de Montefeltro, now formally titled duke of Urbino, continues embellishing his palace |
| 1478 | Pazzi conspiracy in Florence; Lorenzo de' Medici, the Magnificent, assumes power alone |
| 1482 | Botticelli paints *Primavera* |
| 1490 | Aldo Manuzio founds his humanist press at Venice<br>Isabella d'Este joins her husband's court at Mantua and begins a long career as patron of art and culture |
| 1494 | Charles IX of France invades, opening the Italian Wars |
| 1498 | Savonarola burned at the stake |
| 1499–1502 | Cesare Borgia, son of Pope Alexander, campaigns in Romagna and the Marches |
| 1503–13 | Papacy of Julius II, warrior and art patron |
| 1504 | Spanish viceroy established in Naples |
| 1506 | Leonardo da Vinci finishes *Mona Lisa* |
| 1507 | Foundations laid for the new St. Peter's Church |
| 1508–20 | Raphael paints at the Vatican |
| 1509 | Venetians, routed at the Battle of Agnadello, barely conserve their state |
| 1513 | Machiavelli writes *The Prince*<br>Michelangelo finishes frescoes in the Sistine Chapel ceiling |
| 1513–21 | Papacy of Leo X, patron of culture and target of Martin Luther |
| 1516 | Jews readmitted to Venice and ghetto established |
| 1525 | Imperial coalition defeats French at Battle of Pavia |
| 1527 | Sack of Rome by imperial troops |
| 1528 | Castiglione publishes *The Courtier* |
| 1530 | Charles V crowned Holy Roman Emperor in Bologna<br>Last Florentine republic falls; Medici installed as hereditary rulers |
| 1532 | Ariosto publishes his epic, *Orlando furioso* |
| 1535 | Spanish governor rules in Milan |

| | |
|---|---|
| 1540 | Bull of Foundation of the Jesuits<br>Death of St. Angela Merici, founder of teaching congregation at Brescia |
| 1541 | Michelangelo completes *Last Judgment* |
| 1542 | Roman Inquisition established |
| 1545 | Council of Trent opens |
| 1551 | Palestrina enters long career as papal composer |
| 1555–59 | Papacy of Paul IV, ferocious religious reformer |
| 1555 | Roman Jews enclosed in a ghetto; fifty-five Jewish apostates burned at Ancona<br>Florence conquers Siena |
| 1556 | St. Philip Neri initiates Oratory of Divine Love |
| 1559 | Peace of Cateau-Cambresis ends the Italian Wars and seals Spanish primacy in the peninsula<br>Roman Index of Prohibited Books published<br>Sofonisba Anguissola, portraitist from Cremona, goes to serve at the court of Spain |
| 1563 | Closing of the Council of Trent |
| 1571 | Much-feared Turkish fleet defeated near Lépanto (modern Nafpaktos) |
| 1576 | St. Carlo Borromeo, reforming archbishop of Milan, succors plague victims |
| 1580 | Court at Ferrara adorned with a novel "concerto" of women singers |
| 1582 | Gregory XIII reforms the calendar |
| 1585–90 | Papacy of Sixtus V, energetic religious reformer and urban renewer |
| 1586–96 | Hunger crises and associated waves of brigandage |
| 1590 | Dome closed on unfinished St. Peter's basilica |
| 1600 | Giordano Bruno, philosopher, executed for heresy<br>Posthumous publication of Moderata Fonte's *The Worth of Women* |

Italy in the Renaissance.

# 1

# Italy in the Renaissance

The daily life of any place and time is a fascinating subject. It is all the more so when the setting is so rich, varied, rambunctious, and inventive as Italy in the Renaissance. So central is Renaissance Italy to Western history, and so momentous are its achievements in complex ways for the rest of the globe, that hundreds of scholars have studied a wealth of details about its history. Much of this research bears, directly or at short remove, on the story of the daily life of Italians in that important time. We two historians who wrote this book thus belong to a long, lively tradition of inquiry and debate. Like any view, ours is partial, conditioned by our own research on Rome and its hinterland, our finite readings in an inexhaustible literature on other parts of Italy, and the habits of our scholarly world. Like any history, this is a work of interpretation.

Let us begin by defining the terrain of investigation—its subject matter, time, and place. What does the title mean? "Daily life" itself is a more complex subject than first meets the eye. The term covers, of course, the simple facts of existence: what people wore and ate, how they worked, played, rested, took sick and recovered, and how they prayed, mourned, and celebrated. In this sense, a history of daily life might be a long catalog of things and activities in a given time and place. In this book, we push further, to lay out the larger structures of social life and the cultural logic that made sense of them. How did Italians of the Renaissance experience both their surroundings and each other? And what effects did they see themselves having on their social and material environment?

## DAILY LIFE

Renaissance Italians shaped their daily lives. *Agency*, a term borrowed from the social sciences, offers a useful model for understanding any society, for it lays out persons' powers to make things happen. Agency is not the untrammeled freedom to do exactly what one wants. No one, in any social or natural world—not even the hermit in his cave—lives free of constraints. Agency is best understood as the capacity to make a difference under the particular conditions that inevitably hem one in. Italians in the Renaissance lived with restrictions, both internal and external, both human and natural, very different from those that constrain us moderns. There are few better ways to see both their kinship with us and their differences from us than to study their lives with an eye to the ploys and stratagems that men, women, and children used to make headway in their world. In some ways, this is a harder topic than material culture, for to study it, one must explore the minds, feelings, and senses of people now more than four centuries gone.

Historians can never resurrect the dead; the deeds and consciousness of past people are out of reach. Nevertheless, scholars can reconstruct a likeness, and here the Italians of the Renaissance left rich sources for later research. They expressed themselves profusely, in letters, diaries, memoirs, commentaries, poems, ambassadorial reports, trial depositions, and deathbed testaments. They also produced a rich imaginative literature—short stories, plays, epics, songs—full of details true to life. Alongside such literature, describing more or less accurately how people conducted themselves, Italians also penned and printed a mass of normative writing, saying what one ought to do: statutes, decrees, sermons, and instructions. These last also offer abundant clues, although laws and rules as often suggest infraction as obedience. All of these various papers survive in myriads. Despite Italy's eventful history, its archives, with a few tragic exceptions, have been spared many of the catastrophes wrought by modern history. They remain immensely rich and far from fully explored. Renaissance Italians left the materials for a detailed and colorful portrait.

Two kinds of sources offer especially precious access to the lives of Renaissance Italians. First are the accounts of outsiders, for, since the early Middle Ages, Italy has been a great destination of travelers. Men and women came to view the holy places and the awesome remains of ancient Rome, petition the papal court on legal matters, or seek the pontiff's blessing for their souls or their political ambitions. Artists and scholars crossed the Alps to admire, study, and imitate. Kings and armies came, bent on conquest. All this traffic left a rich literature on Italy by foreigners, who are useful to us precisely because they come from elsewhere. Travelers often note down what locals take for granted. The best observers among them, like the French philosopher Montaigne, left incomparable records of the little things—the taste of wine and food in the inns, the courtesies, songs, dances, games, and festivals that gave daily life its savor, sound, movement, and color. The second rich treasure of information comes from the graphic arts, especially from painting and book illustration. Renaissance Italians, pioneers of naturalism, skilled in depicting their surroundings, left abundant images of their countryside, streets, houses, furniture, implements, and clothing and of their labors, wars, and sacred or profane celebrations.

All such records of the Renaissance, be they words on parchment and paper or images of wood, metal, stone, pottery, and canvas, for all their clarity, eloquence, and immediacy, do not tell a transparent tale. Like any sources for the past, they need cautious, thoughtful interpretation. Doing history always involves subtle decoding, clever detective work, and seasoned intuition.

## RENAISSANCE

*Renaissance* is a famous term—not of its own time but of later date. It was coined in the nineteenth century by French literary historians to label a re-nascence, a re-birth, a stylistic revival that gave some fourteenth- and fifteenth-century Latin writings the polish of ancient Roman prose and poetry. After 1860, scholars generalized the word, applying it to all of high culture after the end of the Middle Ages. We thus now speak of Renaissance painting, sculpture, architecture, and decorative arts, where first Italians and then other Europeans adopted, adapted, and transformed the themes and motifs of ancient Greece and Rome. Literatures in the vernacular—in Italian, French, Spanish, Dutch, English, Polish, and other languages—are also said to have had their renaissances, marked, again, by the influence of classical models. The term stretches, for similar reasons, to cover contemporary European philosophy, theology, political theory, and natural sciences. Scholars have also pushed the term much further, into zones where it loses much of its initial, classicizing sense, as in coining "Renaissance monarchy," to label a more competent, more ambitious state neither re-born nor especially Roman. In this latter sense, *Renaissance* comes merely to designate a period in history. So we talk here of "Renaissance" society and mean social relations characteristic of the era of cultural rebirth. Yet we must keep in mind that most Italians of the time—shepherds, soldiers, wetnurses, washerwomen, weavers, merchants, notaries, and many others—spent little time either creating or observing Renaissance high art and literature, a refined product made for and often by elites. Common folk did see and hear and walk through Renaissance artifacts, but their everyday activities and social relations followed patterns having almost nothing to do with the rebirth of antiquity.

Thus, when it comes to daily life, *Renaissance* is a temporal tag that is not very informative. Nevertheless, since consensus among scholars has made the label stick and since historians of material and social life have come up with nothing better, we use it here.

Like most other historical periods, the Renaissance had fuzzy boundaries. It began sometime toward the middle of the 1300s and ended in the later 1500s, when the Catholic Reformation first censored cultural life. The Italians started the process; for some scholars, their Renaissance ended somewhat earlier. This book, a social history, explores the two centuries between 1400 and 1600, after which Italy entered the slow economic and political decline that long diminished its place in West European civilization.

## ITALY

**Geography**

"Italy," like "Renaissance," is largely a modern term, for the modern Italian state is only a mid-nineteenth-century creation. Renaissance Italians inhabited a political hodgepodge united by historical memory, geography, language, and a general shared culture, but not by government. Whatever common traits they possessed coexisted with startling diversity. *Italia*, in ancient times, had been a geographical designation first for a zone of allies gradually conquered by expansionist Rome and then for a province of the empire of the Caesars. In the central Middle Ages, the same term had attached for a while to a fragment of the broken empire of Charlemagne's successors. Otherwise there had never been an autonomous political entity called Italy. Nevertheless, Italians in 1400, when they spoke of Italy and Italians, knew what they meant.

Geographically, Italy was edged by clear boundaries. Visitors had no doubts about their arrival. Those who came by sea stepped gratefully onto the solid land of the peninsula or the islands; the quay, or beach, marked distinctly where Italy began. The many others—French, Germans, Netherlanders, Englishmen, and Central Europeans—who descended on the peninsula by land had to cross the formidable barrier of the Alps.

Once arrived, visitors who descended the length of the peninsula encountered an astonishing variety of terrain. Travelers trooping down the mountain passes would meet a linguistic frontier as the valleys widened, the climate softened, and the unfamiliar Mediterranean trees, fruits, and flowers first appeared on the terraced lower slopes. Passing the great subalpine lakes, they would emerge onto the fertile plains of Lombardy,

Landscape with wool
washing. [Tempesta]

thickly settled and strewn with cities and big towns. Then as now, the
change—in climate, terrain, economy, and culture—was dramatic. Early
modern Europeans detested mountains. Gratefully, they left the Alps at
their back and reveled in the lush flatlands that spread below. The mem-
oirist Thomas Coryate, back in England in 1611 after his north-Italian
travels, remembered:

Surely such is the fertility of this country, that I think no Region or Province
under the Sun may compare with it. For it is passing plentifully furnished with
all things, tending both to pleasure and profit, being the very Paradise, and
Canaan of Christendom. For, as Italy is the garden of the world, so is Lombardy
the garden of Italy, and Venice the garden of Lombardy. It is wholly plain, and
beautified with such abundance of goodly rivers, pleasant meadows, fruitful
vineyards, fat pastures, delectable gardens, orchards, woods, and what not, that
the first view thereof did even refocillate [revive] my spirits, and tickle my senses
with inward joy.[1]

The well-watered, intensely cultivated valley of the Po River and its
many snow-fed tributaries was not the only landscape that awaited voy-

agers who pushed farther south. Italy is long, more than 750 miles of mainland, with Sicily below, half-closing the narrow stretch of Mediterranean that separates Europe from North Africa. By European standards, 750 miles is a long way. By crow flight, Milan, just below the Alps, is far closer to Paris, Prague, and Berlin than it is to Palermo, the capital of Sicily. From Venice, it is as far to Rome as to Vienna. In the Renaissance, when roads were often bad and dangers, by land and sea, were many, those distances counted far more than they do today.

Italy was more than one long peninsula. There were three huge islands: Sicily to the south, and off the west coast, Sardinia and Corsica, the latter not yet French. They, and, in a sense, the bordering seas, the Tyrrhenian to the west, the Ionian at the instep of the boot, and the Adriatic to the east, all arms of the Mediterranean, were parts of a larger Italian whole. Italians used these waters to fish, travel, trade, and wage war. Italian control was always partial; it was challenged for decades by big Turkish fleets and lone North African slave raiders, and more peaceably by the merchant ships of other maritime nations. Still, all these familiar waters belonged to the Italian sphere.

Voyaging south, a traveler would meet sharp changes of landscape. The Lombard plains below the Alps are an exception, for little else is flat. Down the center of the peninsula runs a range of mountains, the Appennines, lower and drier than the Alps but cool and wet enough to offer summer pasture and rough enough to furnish little other wealth. They were ideal bandit and smuggler terrain. Flanking this range, especially to the west, are zones of hills and valleys, in Tuscany and Umbria, with tree-studded plots suitable for grain, vines, and olives. Ranging along the west coast, from Siena southward, is a series of volcanoes, all dead until one reaches rumbling Vesuvius near Naples, and many of them now filled with placid crater lakes. Below Vesuvius, the volcanic chain heads out to sea, reappearing at Stromboli, an island off Sicily, and at towering Etna, smoky and sulfurous on the east Sicilian coast. Much of the southeast of the peninsula, Apulia, is a plain, far drier than Lombardy, and much used in the Renaissance for winter pasture for vast flocks of sheep that summered in the Appennines. The whole peninsula is too narrow and too poorly watered to support many readily navigable rivers, except those that carry the meltwaters of the Alps; elsewhere they carried at most small craft and rafts of timber. Many small streams are mere seasonal torrents, shrinking to great gray streaks of dry boulders in summer. At the same time, in the premodern period many low-lying areas were swamp and marshland, precious to migrant waterfowl, but also hospitable to the mosquitoes that often carried the malaria so endemic in the Renaissance. The Maremma (the name means "swamp") of the Tuscan coast and the rolling Roman Campagna were particularly plagued and thus fairly empty of people. Economic geographers argue that for all this variety, Italy has three basic landscapes: plain (and valley bottom), hill, and mountain. Each had its products and its needs; the complementarity of these zones and their nearness to one another encouraged interzonal trade and economic interdependence.

To the eyes of Renaissance travelers, Italy was densely settled. Yet its population, though always high by European standards, fluctuated in the course of the Renaissance. The first great wave of bubonic plague, the famous Black Death of 1347, was for Italy, as for the rest of Europe, catastrophic. Modern commentators who glibly liken that swift epidemic to slow, insidious AIDS draw a false parallel. Plague, which killed within a week, raged through cities, killing a third or a half of the populace, or even more, in a month or two. Further bouts of plague undermined recovery. By 1400, Italy was down to 8 million, having lost 3 million in a century. For the next fifty years, numbers did not recover much; the Italy of the great Florentine Renaissance remained depopulated. Then, after 1450, although plague remained a danger, for reasons still little understood the numbers started to climb again. Throughout the sixteenth century, the Italian population rose steadily, reaching perhaps 13.5 million by 1600. Greater numbers did not always bring prosperity; on the contrary, in a world where most fertile land was under tillage and technology moved slowly, rising population could mean falling yields for land and labor and declining living standards. This indeed did happen; a population of 13.5 million strained resources, so in the last two decades of the sixteenth century, Italy knew severe food shortages and increasing poverty and vagabondage. By 1600, with a population only about a quarter of what lives there today, Italy was for its time overly full; the next century would see economic decline, low living standards, deurbanization, and a gradual fall in numbers. That sad story, however, lies outside our scope. Our Italy of the Renaissance remained generally prosperous; its manufactures were overall the best in Europe, its merchants and artists by far the most skilled. Travelers saw not dearth but abundance and wrote admiringly of the luxuries they encountered.

The Italian Renaissance landscape had characteristic settlement patterns. With the exception of the coastal Netherlands, nowhere else in Europe was so urban. Many Italians were city dwellers, and many others inhabited large commercial or administrative towns. This was particularly true of the North and Center, where cities in the Middle Ages had often won political independence and come to control the surrounding countryside. By modern standards, cities were modest in population. Naples, at 200,000 or more, was by far the biggest, followed by Venice, at 120,000. Florence in the time of the Medici had only 60,000 inhabitants. Many other urban centers were about half that size. South of Rome, despite the bulky regional capitals, Naples and Palermo, urbanization was much weaker, as were commerce and artisanal production. These two southern cities were big places, but they had few towns for company. This contrast between the South and the rest of Italy ran very deep and involved more than the size and number of cities. In many ways, it continues even today to mark the politics, economy, and culture of the peninsula. The North was then, and remains now, richer, less conservative, and much more tightly bound to the rest of Europe than the South and the three great islands of Sicily, Sardinia, and Corsica.

Although Italy was unusually urban for its time, some 75 percent of its people were rural. Of these country dwellers, relatively few lived on isolated family farms of the sort familiar to North Americans; instead, most were villagers. Their villages were often big, sometimes almost agro-towns. Many perched on hilltops or mountainsides, often several miles from their fields. Peasants therefore often had to commute to work, on foot or donkey back. These fortified villages to the casual eye look almost eternal; most in fact were founded in the early Middle Ages, as men and women abandoned the scattered villas of imperial Rome and gathered on higher ground for safety and sociability, at the cost of long trudges up and down. Villages were often close together. The traveler, casting his eye over the hills, might see many at once, with their encircling walls and bell towers.

The Italian landscape, more than any other in Europe except perhaps the Dutch, showed the mark of human hands, for Italy had a very long history of dense settlement and intense cultivation. Everywhere, the natural world bore the marks of intervention, much of it harmful. Although the fall of Rome had brought reforestation, the population growth of the central Middle Ages had reversed that process, so that by 1400, much of the original or recovered forest had been destroyed; what survived was under pressure from woodcutters, tillers, and herds. In some zones, the stable Mediterranean *macchia*, a succession plant community of tough herbs and woody bushes, had replaced the original trees. For reasons of climate, economics, and institutions, the farther south one went, the more fragile the cover of the slopes became. The fatal sequence of cutting, followed by downhill plowing and overgrazing sheep and goats, often produced catastrophic erosion. Today much of the mountain country of the South and Center is totally denuded of soil, a stark zone of deep environmental degradation. This process, well underway in the Middle Ages, accelerated in the Renaissance, thanks to the massive flocks of sheep that spent their summers in the high country of the South. Deforestation and erosion had many consequences; springs dried up, summer rains faltered, and runoff sped up, altering the flow and ecology of rivers, leaving them murky and more often slack or dry in summer. It also encouraged the alarming floods that often inundated riverside cities like Florence and Rome. The downwashed soil often found its way to the

Landscape with June activities. [Tempesta]

coast, silting the lagoon of Venice or extending the deltas of the Tiber and the Arno. By altering drainage, the eroded soil may also have fostered the spread of coastal marshes.

Other human interventions, somewhat less deleterious, aimed to expand cultivable land. Terracing made hillsides more fruitful. Generation after generation, patient, vigilant labor kept in place the stone walls that held soil to the slopes. Montaigne, traveling in the valley of Spoleto in 1581, marveled to see entire mountains terraced to their very summits, gray-green with olive trees.[2] Another form of land engineering important in the Renaissance was the systematic draining of swamps, often under princely auspices, to grow food and drive off malaria. Other projects included the irrigation of the fields near the river Po, the planning of aristocratic gardens and hunting preserves, and the planting of *pinete*, great groves of umbrella pines.

**Culture**    The Italians had a shared culture in which, despite regional diversities, common traits created affinity. Thus, with few exceptions, they all spoke versions of a common language descended from the Latin of the ancient Romans. In the Renaissance they seldom called this tongue "Italian," but rather Venetian, Milanese, Tuscan, Roman, Neapolitan, and so on. Their dialects were many and often mutually unintelligible. Nevertheless, with a little effort, most people could make themselves understood in a common speech, a peninsular amalgam that over the centuries, due to the cultural influence of Florence, took on more and more Tuscan coloration. This approximately national speech, with its local variations, was sometimes called *lingua cortigiana*, court language; thus, it had no home territory or place-based name.

Renaissance Italians also shared religious and moral systems. Aside from a Jewish minority, all were believing Catholics. Together they practiced a religion that offered a comprehensive vision of society, history, nature, and the universe, as well as a code of moral conduct, and a rich, complex set of rites and institutions that made contact with almost every aspect of daily life. At the same time, Italians, like many other Mediterranean peoples, ascribed to notions of honor. Honor provided its own ethics and a view of social and familial life sometimes sharply at odds with Christianity. Together, honor and religion combined to heighten Italians' senses of theater and ceremony. Furthermore, honor spurred a guarded, often anxious sense of rivalry. Competition at times set individuals at odds, but as often it mobilized the many solidarities, to which people attached themselves, for cities, families, neighborhoods, sodalities and guilds had their collective honor. Since men and women belonged to many groups at once, social life often required a delicate sense of balance as one strove to respect competing claims for loyal support. Renaissance values made for a sometimes violent, often edgy, and almost always intensely competitive social life. Religion and other lay ethics, so important to the nature of everyday life, will appear often in the chapters that follow.

**Politics**    Politics did not unite Renaissance Italians at all, for there was no central authority. Their political map was so complex that, especially in the North, a traveler met borders everywhere. The many states varied in size and in form of government. Ranging from monarchies to republics, Italian regimes had countless roads to power, from inheritance, to election, to assassination and stealthy coup d'état. Some states were fairly big, and others were mere sovereign fingernails of territory. The smallest were autonomous feudal lordships, nominally parts of the Holy Roman Empire. This body, despite its name, was an elective monarchy of the Germans that still asserted residual claims to northern Italy. Though legally subordinate to the emperor, these functionally independent lords might rule a clutch of villages, presiding over their own courts of justice and collecting fines and taxes. Somewhat larger were the self-governing cities, some, like Lucca, with modest territories a few dozen miles across, and others, like Florence, Ferrara, and Venice, capitals of fair-sized states with their own subject towns and cities. Some of these city-states were democratic, though suffrage was limited to elites, while others had fallen under the power of *signori*, lords who ruled in an autocratic spirit. Midway down the peninsula was a principality like none other, the State of the Church, centered on Rome and ruling a wide band that cut across the middle of the peninsula. The pope was therefore not only the head of Latin Christendom but also an elected temporal monarch, with his army and navy, his foreign policies and diplomats, his local governors, judges, and tax men. The southern third of mainland Italy, down to the heel and toe of the boot, and Sicily belonged to Italy's only kingdom, Naples.

Between 1400 and 1600, Italy's political fortunes changed radically. At the beginning of the period, transalpine powers were weak. In France, war with England convulsed the monarchy. And the German emperors, enfeebled, could not meddle, as traditionally, in peninsular affairs. In addition, the papacy, divided by schism, was torn between Rome and Avignon. In the resultant power vacuum, the middling states of Italy made shifting coalitions free of external interference. After 1440, with the pope back in command at Rome, a fairly stable system of five major states—Naples, the Papal State, Florence, Venice, and Milan—came to dominate political affairs. Since any three defenders could check two aggressors, no player could overwhelm the others. Italy knew, if not peace, at least a certain predictability. The end of the 1400s destroyed this stability as large, international powers—a revived France, a newly united Spain, and an ambitious German emperor—made Italy their chosen battleground and goal of conquest. For sixty-five years after 1494, France and Spain, whose Hapsburg king from 1519 also ruled the German Empire, fought "the Italian Wars" up and down the peninsula. The Italian states strove to play the two combatants off but were too weak to determine the outcome. In the end, after 1560, the French, falling into four decades of civil war, gave up their Italian ambitions, leaving Sicily, Naples, and Milan in Spanish hands until the early eighteenth century. Not even the papacy escaped Spain's influence, and the entire peninsula felt the effects of Iberian hegemony.

The political institutions of so richly mixed a scene do not summarize easily. Nevertheless, a few typical features are discernible. First comes sophistication. Renaissance Italy pioneered in statecraft. The origins of modern diplomacy, and espionage, seldom far apart, owe much to Italian ingenuity. The medieval visiting emissary gradually evolved into the resident ambassador, with his chancery and his diplomatic immunities. The brilliant reports from Italy and beyond by the ambassadors of Milan, Florence, and Venice, or by the papal nuncios, with their sharp eye for local detail, were precious sources of data for both the regimes that paid their wages and modern historians. Italian regimes were precociously literate and, by continental standards, complex and ambitious. States and cities devised various clever ways of financing their operations—military, judicial, and administrative. They legislated with an eye to regulating the economy, the environment, urban spaces, public health, and private morality. On the other hand, one should not overstate their modernity, for many states' ambitions outran their powers of coercion. Early modern statecraft was a dialogue between an ambitious center and a recalcitrant periphery. Subject territories, remote districts, and privileged groups and persons all strove, sometimes successfully, to balk the will of governments. A mark of weakness was that governments compromised, granting and selling exemptions from the rules, to the point that it sometimes seemed that Italian states ruled as much by exceptions as by decrees and laws.

Participation in power varied greatly. Some regimes were tightly held, others surprisingly open. In general, in states and towns of all shapes and sizes, political participation was much sought after, by both elites and those of middling station. This desire held as true for villagers as for city dwellers. Some positions came by appointment, others by ballot. Wherever elected councils sat, there were complex routines of nomination, election, and choice by lottery for offices of surprisingly short duration—perhaps three months, perhaps a year, seldom longer. The rapid circulation of council members was meant to spread the fruits of power and block anyone from becoming overly mighty; the subtle electoral machinery, with its element of chance, was designed to forestall alliances, connivance, influence peddling, and party faction. Alongside local councils, there were independent judges, almost always from some other place—for locals were thought to play favorites—and a corps of secretaries, notaries, and other lettered functionaries. In all regimes, from autocratic to democratic, power was unevenly distributed. Women, the young, the poor, and even the less wealthy working classes had no formal role. In general, even in democratic regimes, the rich amassed the lion's share of seats, thanks either to the rules, often made by them, or to their social influence. As the Renaissance went on, in many places, the base of power narrowed, in a process of aristocratization of elites.

Princely regimes increasingly developed courts. A court is a social world gathered around a monarch, where his friends and friends of friends battened off his wealth and power. There the ruler exchanged patronage for the submission and loyalty of his more privileged subjects. The richer the state, the more lucrative, though dangerous, courtly life could be. Courtiers, brokers of news and influence, traded in secrets, gifts, commissions, appointments, introductions, invitations, privileges, and other perquisites of power to build their own careers and to advance their kinsmen and friends. The court favored those who possessed tact, subtlety, and an exquisite sense of timing. It was a competitive, sometimes cutthroat place where the mastery of appearances, self-control, and smooth social graces were prize assets. There was little in common between the blunt public discussions of a republic's elected council and the veiled innuendo of much courtly talk.

With the usual regional variants, a lively economy sustained the states of Italy and fed, clothed, furnished, and **Economy** housed their people. Renaissance Italy was commercially more advanced than most of Europe. Mercantile practices and banking methods were more sophisticated. A diaspora of men and talents had scattered merchants, bankers, artisans, and artists to all urban corners of Europe and many parts of the Middle East. These Italians abroad helped sustain networks of commerce from Russia to Norway, Spain, and Egypt. Until, in 1498, the Portuguese sailed around Africa to India, Italy was the only conduit for the silks and spices of Asia. Even after they lost their monopoly, Italians remained important in East-West commerce into the seventeenth century and in general served as a point of contact between northern and central Europe, on the one hand, and the Middle East and North Africa, on the other. Their economy also produced successfully for both international export and home consumption. In scope, the most important industrial activity was the manufacture of cloth, wool, silk, linen, both plain and very fancy, for much of the nation's wealth was worn on its backs. Also important were the building trades and the production of glass, leather, and metal goods, including weapons. The other great zone of production, one that involved both the peasantry and all sorts of specialized trades, was providing food and drink.

What did it mean to live in such a landscape, culture, political order, and economy? How did it feel to be a Re- **Experience** naissance Italian? Much depended on who and where one **of Life** was. Unlike modern North Americans and Europeans, Renaissance Italians did not think of themselves as citizens of a large country, members of a national group. Rather, their loyalties were intensely local, pinned to family, neighborhood, guild, town, and region. Men and women took much of their identities from these alliances and associations. These group memberships, in turn, shaped their experience of self.

The Renaissance self was thus a product of both group affiliations and individual impetus. A famous cliché posits that the Italian Renaissance saw the birth of individualism—meaning that in the arts and politics,

Rider in the winter rain. [Bertelli]

men began to act on their own, untrammeled by custom and social ties, and to cultivate their singular genius. The cliché is an overstatement. Such an autonomous mind-set and sense of self did not fit the psychology of everyday Italian life. Rather, most people were so enmeshed in complex social relations that defined their values and their natures that they spent little time and energy on self-analysis or self-description. At the same time, in an intensely sociable world that had no word for privacy, they were often assertive, canny, and articulate in both self-presentation and the description of those around them. Italian social life required intense bargaining. Commerce, politics, courtship, play, and sociability all demanded acute negotiating skills. Accordingly, self-mastery, the control of appearances, self-declaration, and the decoding of the theatrics of others were precious abilities. All the alliances and solidarities, with other men and women and with the saints, Mary, and Jesus, served as bulwarks against the many dangers and insecurities that stalked the world. For many Italians, no one, not even a holy figure, was altogether reliable. It paid to be wary.

How did Italians conceive their personal goals in a society so defined and circumscribed by hierarchy and by tight social relations? The modern notion of getting ahead made little sense, for much of status was inherited. Nevertheless, with luck and pluck, one could better one's position. Still, in a volatile economy that as a whole grew slowly, if at all, descent was as likely as ascent. Beset by a realistic sense of pervasive scarcity and risk and unable to fall back on a reliable state or strong institutions of social welfare, Italians spent a lot of energy securing and defending themselves. Much effort went into finding protectors, both human and divine. Because much of one's security came from one's allies, one strove to advance and to protect not only oneself, but also one's associates, especially one's family. Agency, action in the presence of so much constraint, aimed at survival and safety, as well as pleasure and prosperity in this world, and salvation in the next.

One aspect of self-experience was sensation. Here, premodern Italian life was different from our own. Consider sight. We moderns almost never see deep darkness, for our electricity has diluted night. Aside from a few flickering torches on palaces or from the flambeaux and lanterns carried by some walkers, Italian towns were dark once the sun went down. Yet in good weather, stars were bright, and several days a month the light of the full moon helped peasants, soldiers, and bandits to move around at night. In the daytime, colors were often far brighter and sharper than they are today under Italy's often dismally polluted skies. Sound too was different, for there was no roar and rumble of internal combustion to drown out the human voices, the sharp cry of summer swallows, the hypnotic, rasping click of the Mediterranean cicada, the shrill chatter of the millions of winter starlings, the sounds of livestock, and the pervasive clangor of church bells. In the absence of raucous machines, Italians filled their streets and piazzas with social talk, calling and chiding children, greeting friends, hurling comments, insults, and challenges. From inside the house, the ears could monitor the social world of the street; noise of a fight would bring neighbors to the windows. There was also a great deal of music; peasants sang while working in the fields, friends played lutes and guitars on a summer evening, ambassadors arrived to the thump of drums and the blare of trumpets, holy processions sang psalms as they marched. The Renaissance nose, too, had its sharp experiences. The world was full of smells we moderns have banished. Seldom-washed human bodies carried acrid sweat and the gentler scent of hair, unmasked by deodorants and shampoo, though the affluent sometimes applied scented oils or perfumes. The warm odors of baking bread and cooking often filled the air and, wafting through open windows, competed with the pungent reek of stale blood at the butcher's shop, of garbage, and of animal and human excrement. The skin's sense of touch had to suffer the itch of fleas, lice, and bedbugs. It put up with a good deal of cold, without benefit of central heating, and with stifling summer heat, unrelieved by air-conditioning.

Daily life in Renaissance Italy thus had its geographic, political, and cultural setting. The actions of ordinary men, women, and young people were carried out against the handsome backdrop of a lovely countryside often still visible today, despite some frenzied overbuilding. The towns and villages, too, not rarely afforded a dramatic stage for work, play, and social life. The many institutions they housed, large and small, jostled one another for authority; Italians were adroit at using them and playing them off one another for leverage and protection. Society as a whole was very "face-to-face," to use a sociological term; most transactions felt personal, and emotions readily entered into play. Life was often neither comfortable nor easy, but even where tense or painful, it was seldom lonely. Existence, as a consequence, was at once very sociable and often intensely political. We will return to all these themes as we take up the many facets of the everyday life of Renaissance Italians.

## NOTES

Besides identifying sources for direct quotations, primarily these notes direct readers to further information. As much as possible, we cite works accessible to English-language readers. Our references are heavy on Florence and Venice; studies in Italian describe a wider range of places.

1. Thomas Coryate, *Coryat's Crudities*, v. 1 (Glasgow: James MacLehose and Sons, 1905), 238. (Spelling modernized.)

2. Michel de Montaigne, "Travel Journal," in *Complete Works: Essays, Travel Journal, Letters*, trans. D. Frame (Stanford: Stanford University Press, 1958), 967.

# 2

# Society: Who Was Who

In Renaissance Italy, as in other premodern European societies, people's life experiences varied according to rank, age, gender, and, especially for women, marital status. Thus, to be a child, an adult, or an old person affected what one must, could, could not, should not, or need not do. For women, the status of wife was in important ways the most constrained stage of life; widowhood offered more independence, though also greater vulnerability.[1] Differences also followed from how and where people made their livings. When Italians met—to talk, do business, play, fight, pray—all these social traits, most of them readily visible in body and clothing, governed expectations and options. Access to resources—not only material and economic goods like food or tools, but also political and social boons like good connections or legal privileges—strongly shaped daily life. What one had to work with depended heavily on the family to which one was born, for property and status passed mostly along lines of kinship. Nevertheless, such inherited assets did not wholly determine a person's place. Less predictable attributes, including personal talents and plain luck—what Renaissance Italians called Fortune—also helped determine where somebody fit into society.

In order to visualize a cast of characters for this book's panorama of daily life, it is useful to catalog the rich array of social roles or niches in which Renaissance Italians might play out their lives. Describing some of the commonest types lets us organize the welter of men and women, rich and poor, literate and illiterate, dominant and subordinate, urban and rural, worldly and otherworldly, into a workable model of a social structure. Helpful as this picture may be, however, we risk distorting actual Renaissance experience with too neat a scheme. Therefore, we offer some historical examples to show how people could fit the types, but imperfectly and with plenty of quirky distinctness.

In a hierarchical society such as Renaissance Italy, social roles were typically understood as standing higher or lower on a pyramid of prestige. In the same spirit, our portrait, like most other historical descriptions, will begin at the top and work down. We need to be wary, however, as we seek to understand common experience, for the most powerful and visible were also few. Their daily lives differed significantly from those lived by the much more populous lower classes. Furthermore, many traits made up a person's place in society, and there were many intersecting hierarchies. We need to imagine this social structure not as a simple, linear ladder but as a multidimensional complex.

In this chapter we survey Italian society status by status, beginning with the clergy, a social order with its own divisions and hierarchy that ministered to the Christian flock. Next we turn to the countryside, where dwelled the vast majority of this quite urbanized people. In rural areas lived a spectrum of social types, from privileged landowners through hard-working peasants to landless shepherds and bandits. Then we move on to urban society. Cities, the site of prosperous commerce, artisanal production, and princely courts, supported a wide range of activities and ways of life. Finally, we glance at a variety of colorful outsiders—people who occupied the margins of Renaissance society—and in particular, at soldiers, Jews, and prostitutes.

## CLERGY

The Christian clergy evolved through the Middle Ages as a separate order of society, committed only to the service of God. Its special and sacred task was to help all Christians, high and low, city and country, conform their lives to divine will and achieve salvation. The clergy constituted a separate jurisdiction, and, for most purposes, its members were answerable to church authorities, not to local rulers. Furthermore, becoming a cleric represented at least a theoretical break with family and those other ties that linked a person to worldly status. By the Renaissance, the clergy, both male and female, were vowed to celibacy; they could not marry. Besides the spiritual rewards of renouncing fleshly appetites, there were considerations of wholehearted service. In order that the church minister to all Christians alike, its clerics had to be free of special earthly ties to children and other claimants. This universal and godly mission not only set them apart from the rest of society, but also earned them a conceptual primacy in the earthly hierarchy.[2]

Within this distinct order, however, were many sorts of clerics with different powers, obligations, and lifestyles. The all-male, secular clergy was responsible for the care of the souls of the laity. That awesome burden required it to provide sacraments and other rituals, teach doctrine, offer moral counsel, support charitable works, and judge infractions of church law, as well as to administer the economic assets and physical plant that sustained all those activities. The secular clergy carried out this massive task through an elaborate institutional hierarchy that descended from the pope through the cardinals, archbishops, and bishops, and on down to local parish priests. At the bottom were numbers of students who took the lowest holy orders; these they could, and not infrequently did later renounce. Clerical status in the meantime entitled them to church benefices and exempted them from harassment for petty crimes. Great differences in power and affluence distinguished the many layers of this organization. The beneficiary of centuries of pious donations intended to support God's work, the church owned great wealth. The prelates at the top, the chief administrators of this great patrimony, had vast resources at their disposal. During the Renaissance, they were known often, though not always, for lavish lifestyles. The lower ranks of the clergy, on the other hand, generally lived quite modestly, though few faced the sharp economic hardships that periodically devastated their parishioners.

Besides these pastoral clerics, the church also relied on the efforts of clergy of another sort: men and women who belonged to religious orders and lived in obedience, under a special rule. Some of these, the traditional monks and nuns, dwelled in communities walled away from the distractions of the world, devoted to prayer, study, and good works. Others of the regular clergy, especially friars like the Franciscans and Dominicans, carried their work to ordinary people and sought, through preaching and counseling, to bring Christ's aid to the poor, wayward, and desperate. So popular did these medieval orders become with their novel kind of Christian social work that the church soon put them to use in other ways. During the Renaissance, friars were everywhere, preaching moral reform, acting as confessors to both commoners and patricians, lecturing in universities, and even, with the Florentine Dominican Savonarola, directing an attempted revolution in city government. The very ubiquity and prominence of the friars nevertheless made them the choice target of more and less good-humored anticlerical criticism, as in the stories of Boccaccio's *Decameron*.

Women clergy could not readily imitate the lifestyle of the friars, whose work led them to move about the world and, by the Renaissance, often included administering sacraments. Although houses of female Franciscans and Dominicans did exist, like the older orders of nuns, they practiced cloister. Yet many spiritually zealous women felt the impulse to serve God's poor directly. Some found a way to pursue their holy ambitions in the role of tertiary. Tertiaries were laypeople who took vows to live piously in the world, where they devoted themselves to helping the sick, prisoners, and others in pain. They often adopted formal ties with the orders of friars, but they had imitators who preferred autonomy. Some of these self-appointed holy people enjoyed the admiring support of their neighbors; others endured stinging attacks on their reputations. Devout women who chose independence, in particular, invited slander.

The Italian clergy had much in common with those of the rest of western Europe before the Reformation. Nevertheless, Italy was distinct, in part because the historic center of Catholicism was in Rome. Although in the early fourteenth century the papacy had removed to Avignon in southern France, in 1378 it returned to its traditional Roman seat. Despite several more decades of schism, when two rival popes sparred across the Alps, Italy reclaimed the focus of church politics, though a contested one. With the division resolved in 1417, the reunited papacy gradually made Rome once again a powerful magnet for all those who sought spiritual uplift at its holy sites or had business with the head of the church. In addition, as landlord over vast properties, especially in the southern half of the peninsula, the church played a major role in temporal affairs. Therefore, although never more than a small fraction of the total population, the clergy were very prominent in Italian life. Powerful churchmen—bishops, cardinals, heads of religious orders, and their agents—were numerous and influential.

---

## PROFILE: CARDINAL FRANCESCO GONZAGA

Cardinal Francesco Gonzaga (1444–83), son of the ruler of Mantua, was one of the worldly prelates who served the pre-Reformation papacy. He received a cardinal's red hat at the precocious age of seventeen while a student at the university at Pavia. According to many art historians, the Gonzaga family celebrated this great coup by having Andrea Mantegna fresco a collective court portrait on the walls of the famous Camera degli Sposi, in the ducal palace. Though not a priest, Francesco acquired through his career a number of benefices whose income was necessary, though ultimately insufficient, to sustain the heavy expenses incumbent upon a cardinal. These included maintaining a large household (in the first year of his appointment, Francesco's already contained eighty-two persons and fifty-four animals) and providing fittingly honorable accommodations for them in Rome and elsewhere. Pope Pius II, who had raised Gonzaga to the cardinalate, pressured him also to build a palace in the new summer capital at the tiny papal hometown renamed Pienza. When made bishop in his native Mantua in 1466, the cardinal faced squarely the inherent tensions of his position; his family wanted him to reside in his see and attend to the family's local interests, while his superior, the pope, demanded his service in the larger church domain, as in his posting as legate to Bologna. Like some other prelates of his era, he forewent clerical celibacy. His illegitimate son, known later as the "Cardinalino," was raised comfortably in Mantua under the eye of Francesco's mother.[3]

---

### PROFILE: ANGELA MERICI, FOUNDER OF A RELIGIOUS CONGREGATION

Saint Angela Merici (1474–1540), a mystic, founded the Ursulines, the first religious order devoted to educating poor girls. Born of modest parents in a small town on the shores of Lake Garda in Lombardy, she became an orphan at age ten; her older sister died three years later, suddenly and without last rites. According to Angela's hagiography, the first of her many visions occurred then; it reassured her anxiety over her sibling's salvation. Gratefully, she dedicated herself yet more fully to God, practiced great austerity, and lived a virgin in the habit of a Franciscan tertiary. Leading a cluster of like-minded young women, she began work with the local needy, a novel form of charitable service impossible for traditionally cloistered nuns. Her special project was to bring religious education to the neglected daughters of the poor. In Brescia, Merici oversaw the growth of a new kind of institution for religious women, dedicated to teaching, under the patronage of Saint Ursula. Its members worshipped and worked together but did not take vows or live communally. Merici and her institute attracted support from powerful and devout admirers. The company received formal papal approval four years after her death.[4]

---

## RURAL SOCIETY

The economic base of rural society was agriculture, and land was its key resource. Many Italians owned land, but, in much of the countryside, most of it belonged to small numbers of large landholders. Typically, rural society divided sharply into those few who owned the bulk of the land and other productive resources and the many who did the work.[5]

Big landlords gathered their income from several sources. A major portion came from collecting rent or a share of the crop that their properties yielded. Many landowners also held the legal status of *signori* (lords), a feudal rank that entitled them to intervene in customary ways in the lives of their dependent peasants and to take compensation for those activities. As *signori* they administered justice, provided facilities such as mills, presses and ovens, controlled hunting and fishing and other uses of their domains, and commandeered labor for public projects. For revenue the *signore* collected fees and fines from those who brought suits or were convicted by his courts. He (or occasionally she) rented out the monopolies on the mill, the wine presses, the bakery, the inn, and the store. And if he did not want exclusive use of his woods and streams for himself, he sold licenses to others. Some lords also bought from the

**Landlords and Signori**

government the option to collect state taxes. Or the lord might encroach on the rights and revenues of the local churches and lay confraternities. Thus, the lords relied for their well-being on wealth exacted from the less advantaged rural majority. In theory, elite privileges entailed responsibility, and Christian duty urged charitable benevolence toward dependents and the needy. Lords and tenants on occasion did look out for one another's welfare. Yet the financial chasm between landlords and workers and the fundamental contradiction between their interests shaped more or less overtly antagonistic social relations in the countryside.

Large landowners often held a number of properties. While these lands might be scattered, estates typically had their center in one of the densely settled villages. There the lord had a residence. In the hills and mountains that characterized much of the peninsula, it often was some form of castle, built originally as a place of defense against the endemic local violence of the Middle Ages. By village standards, it was a massive building that provided not only housing for the landlord, his family, retainers, officials, and guests, but also secure storage for cash, administrative papers, equipment, grain, wine, oil, produce, animals, and the weapons to protect them. Often there was a lock-up. Gradually, over the course of the fifteenth and sixteenth centuries, especially in states more successful in imposing order, these elite residences lost some of their military functions and were modified for greater comfort and pleasure, acquiring handsome big windows and columned porches called loggias to take in the view. In northern and central Italy, near some of the most civilized Renaissance cities, a few landowners put up new country homes, or villas, pleasure domes whose principal purpose was neither economic nor political, but aesthetic and even intellectual. In most places, however, the lord's house continued to serve less refined needs. Although violence declined during the Renaissance, in the countryside of the Center and South and in frontier zones like Friuli, physical disorder persisted as a reality of life. The local big men had to be tough to fend off incursions from aggressive neighbors, ambitious central governments, and restive dependents. Private wars were still the pastime of some *signori*.

Landowners were of different sorts. Families or individual men and women held much of the land, but so did religious or secular institutions. The churchmen's interests as estate holders did not always line up easily with the ideological imperatives of Christian benevolence. Some landowners enjoyed the titles and prestige of formal noble status, while others only "lived nobly," claiming respect through lifestyle rather than the law. Still others were commoners whose prosperity or tastes did not allow them aristocratic pretensions. Furthermore, landowners, noble and commoner alike, did not always live in the country. Increasingly, rural properties belonged to town dwellers. Owners whose careers focused on cities or courts often shared the country environment of their tenants and dependents for at best only part of the year. They might leave the running of their rural properties to hired estate agents or rent out their lands for months or years to capitalist enterprises that tilled and grazed the estate.

---

### PROFILE: GIULIANO CESARINI, BARON

Giuliano Cesarini (d. 1567), a proud man with a hot temper, pursued the lordly ambitions embraced by his forebears, a rising clan of wealthy barons. Over some hundred years, thanks to a series of Cesarini cardinals and some strategic marriages, the family had assembled villages and estates in the coastal lowlands near Rome, in the nearby mountains, and, finally, in the Marches of the Adriatic coast. The Cesarini had also acquired a prestigious sinecure, the largely ceremonial post of Standard-bearer of the Roman People. Flaunting this title, Giuliano paraded at civic festivals in gorgeous costumes studded with precious gems. His two palaces in Rome featured famous gardens adorned with antique statuary collected by his cardinal predecessors. His stable was full of fine horses, and, delighting in the hunt, he kept many dogs. Giuliano ruled his lands in absentia. A harsh but inattentive lord, he knew few of his tenants by name and had little knowledge of their needs and histories. His policy was to squeeze them hard through his paid agents, laying on new feudal obligations, and amassing peasant lands defaulted due to debts and fines. He was also an ambitious castle builder, using unpaid village labor for construction. By these ploys he financed his comforts and his public life, a series of governorships and high military commands in the Papal State. His tenants detested him, and several of his villages rebelled.[6]

---

Running estates and villages, especially where landlords were routinely absent, fell to a local elite who mediated between the residents and the larger outside world. **Village Elites** Agents, employed by the owners, managed the land, oversaw work on the lord's personal domains, and collected rents and dues. These deputies juggled contradictory sets of demands: to serve their employer's interests, make their own way, and live among the often impoverished or resentful tenants who had to pay out. The village elite also included professionals who came from elsewhere or had ties to external institutional networks. Among these, priests, though often not highly educated, were men of influence. A council of senior villagers, a small version of the communal assemblies in the cities, formed part of local government. But the central official, often called the *podestà* or *vicario*, was an outsider appointed by the feudal lord or the rulers of the state. Commonly, assisting these administrators, even in the country, were notaries, who wrote and preserved contracts and other documents. Their outside origins, professional ties, and official power tended to separate them from the rest of the rural community. Certainly local officials could demand and punish in the name of external authority. At the same time, they mediated conflicts between the village and the larger world and between contentious locals.

**Peasants**    Peasants were the most numerous group of Renaissance Italians. In families they lived on and worked the land. Some peasants owned land, but mostly it belonged to landlords or, in rougher country, was commons. For access to land, peasants normally paid money rent or delivered a share of their yield to the owner. They might also enter contracts to secure livestock and tools and equipment to work their farms. Furthermore, many of them owed various seigniorial dues in money, in kind, or in labor. They paid tithes to the church and, sometimes, taxes to the state. And, when times were hard, they often took on debt to pay their obligations. Feudal and economic dependency restricted peasants' options. Commonly, they had to piece together a livelihood from a medley of rural activities, in the home village or elsewhere. Theirs was not a closed world; economic necessity spurred much migration in search of income. Peasants consumed part of what they grew, but, for most, some of their produce, directly or via the landlord, made its way to market.

The organization of agriculture differed by locale, with varied patterns of family and residence. Peasant livelihood derived largely from family labor, supplemented where useful by hired workers. The most productive size and form of the residential group depended on the crops, holdings size, and tenure customs of a region. Thus, smaller nuclear families were better adapted to the less labor-intensive pastoralism of the mountain regions or to specialized farming with highly seasonal demands for workers. Larger, more extended family groups—whether built of three generations or of adult siblings—fitted well on the sharecropped, middle-sized farms of the arable North and Center that could make use of a substantial supply of labor through much of the year. The lands a peasant household worked, especially in zones of mixed farming, were seldom contiguous and compact. Rather, the family might cultivate flax in one place, vegetables in another, and olives yet somewhere else.

Besides relying on family, peasants also used networks of assistance among their peers. Villagers enlisted one another's cooperation at the well and the washing place, in collective work, at religious festivals, in local government, and in collaborative lawsuits. These associations, though not always harmonious, extended peasants' capacity to cope. In dispersed settlements, such social exchanges, though probably scanter than in villages, were still crucial to sustaining peasant families.

Peasants' prosperity was unpredictable. Many factors shaped their fortune. It depended on the fertility of the land and on the weather. It shifted with the succession of good years, when prices favored the peas-

Paduan peasant girl. [Bertelli]

ants, and bad years, when debts accumulated. When, in the later Renaissance, the population rose, the imbalance between scarce lands to work and many mouths to feed pressed on the peasantry as a whole. Yet some families fared better than others, whether through richer holdings, harder work, less greedy landlords, more fortunate timing of births and deaths, or just plain luck. Some peasants lived well, expanded their resources, and hired hands to boost their yield. Many others scraped by, improvising to keep the debt collector at bay and to hold on to their lands and goods.

---

### PROFILE: GIACOBO CAPONERO, RICH PEASANT

By the age of sixty-two, Giacobo di Giuliano, alias Caponero (Black Head), of Rocca Sinibalda had in 1556 probably gone gray or bald, but the old nickname stuck. He and Tomassa, his wife, had just married off a son. A rich peasant, literate and careful with numbers, he belonged to the village elite. He was then a very active *massaro*, an alderman, one of four who directed local government, and had also served as one of the *santesi*, the officers who raised and administered parish and confraternity funds. Caponero's economic enterprises were diverse. He owned land for growing hemp, a plot for trapping birds, woods, meadows, and vineyards, cattle, and a mule and donkey with which, as a feudal service, he carried bricks for the castle his lord was building. In addition, the peasant had leased from his lord rights to run the village mill; having lost badly on the contract, he had sold some of his real estate to pay back his debts. He had also held the monopoly on the local sale of cheeses and other foodstuffs, and at times he wholesaled salted pork and pigeons preserved in oil. He remembered hard times: of famine when, two decades back, his mother had brought bread and acorns to starving prisoners in the castle; of war and sack, when armies had cut his vines and driven off his cattle. Yet he had succeeded in recovering some of his prosperity.[7]

---

Some rural people lacked access to land at all.
**Landless Workers**    Sharply disadvantaged, the landless were among the
poorest in the community. There were, however,
ways they—or surplus workers from landed peasant families—could
earn a living. In some regions, instead of renting out parcels to families
landowners paid laborers to work their large estates. This pattern pre-
vailed on the grain lands of the Southeast and of Sicily. Elsewhere, harvesting and other labor-intensive seasonal tasks in agriculture provided
at least temporary employment. And in many areas herding, woodcut-
ting, and carting needed to be done. These activities often required workers to leave their home villages and move about the countryside. In some
places, rural industry offered opportunities. Making bricks was country
work. At a few sites workers extracted minerals: marble at the quarries
near Carrara, iron in parts of Lombardy, and, from the 1460s, alum, used
for fixing dyes in textiles, at the pope's mines at Tolfa. Elsewhere, the
textile industries in wool, linen, and silk, though usually organized from
cities, gave homework—spinning, weaving, fulling—to women and men
in the countryside. Because such work was often only part-time, it often
failed to provide a regular living. Especially in hard times, another option was to migrate, to seek work as a servant in the city or as a soldier
abroad or as a bandit in the hills. The sharp insecurities that the landless
faced meant that families tended to fragment as they scrambled to survive.[8]

## URBAN SOCIETY

City life differed sharply from country life in scale and tempo. Density
did not make the difference, for villages were, like cities, often closely
packed. Rather, urban centers were big, teeming, and diverse in ways of
life. Many cities owed their medieval origin or revival to commerce. As
they prospered, political, administrative, and cultural activities grew up
around their markets and warehouses. Urban society reflected these different functions. In combination, occupations and professions, wealth,
legal status, and education generated and defined an urban social hierarchy. The elite included a wealthy, politically active aristocracy and
a stratum of affluent citizens, many of them large-scale merchants and
entrepreneurs, plus a cohort of lettered professionals and bureaucrats.
In the middle was a diverse assortment of skilled artisans. Further down
the scale of workers came the semiskilled and unskilled, including, notably, servants. At the bottom struggled the deeply impoverished, many of
them sick or physically or mentally disabled, probably disproportionately
female, often capable only of begging and getting by at the whim of charity.

Patrician lady. [Bertelli]

The aristocracies of Renaissance Italian cities varied in origins and evolution. Depending on the place, this class **Patricians and** might include urban-dwelling members of the rural, feu- **Nobles** dal nobility. In the Middle Ages, some cities, such as Florence, greatly feared the power of these magnates and succeeded in excluding them from political office; elsewhere they made up part of the governing class. Even where these old-style nobles held power, they had to share it with a new, politically prominent group of rich families emerging out of international commerce, banking, and manufacturing. A new urban upper class that we call patricians emerged from the coalescence of these two groups: noble and mercantile. During the Renaissance, these patricians worked to consolidate their position, limiting political competition from other city constituencies and hindering social ascent into their caste. This group rewrote municipal statutes and constitutions to define their privileges and monopolize important public offices. In some cities, the restrictions on mobility were very stringent. There, patrician pretension could more readily acquire a legal status that passed from generation to generation and withstood financial ups and downs. To reinforce their distinctness, these families also pursued careful marriage strategies within their group. Nevertheless, not all was peaceful within patriciates. Rival insiders—individuals, families, or factions—jostled energetically, sometimes using political manipulation, judicial repression, and even violence.[9]

Many of the greatest cultural achievements of Renaissance Italy involved these patriciates, as both producers and patrons. Especially in the cities of the North, this social group committed itself early to the new educational and intellectual program of humanism, based in renewed use of the ancient Roman and Greek heritage. These men saw classical works as a means to enrich and validate civic political culture. This elite also supported the efforts of visual artists, whose work wedded models from the classical past to new technologies of building and painting. All this high culture enhanced and legitimated patrician superiority. In the sixteenth century, many patricians waxed aristocratic in tastes and values; more and more their culture took on a courtly cast.

---

### PROFILE: ALESSANDRA MACINGHI NEGLI STROZZI, PATRICIAN WIFE

Alessandra Macinghi (c. 1408–71), the daughter of Florentine patricians, at age fourteen married twenty-five-year-old Matteo, of the large, prestigious lineage of the Strozzi. Over ten years she bore eight children. Political struggles between factions inside the city government banned from Florence her husband and other males of his family. Alessandra joined her husband in exile until his death, about a year later; around the same time, three of their children died of plague. She then returned to Florence, where she lived her remaining forty-five years as a widow. Alessandra dedicated her life to protecting and advancing her children and their patrimony, especially through attentive play of local contacts and Strozzi family networks. While her exiled sons spent many years pursuing business outside Florence, she penned them an extended series of letters full of worries, counsel, and practical information.[10]

---

**Merchants and Businessmen**

The stratum of merchants and entrepreneurs spanned a wide range of stations in life. Fortunes were volatile in Renaissance Italy. One could get rich quickly, but could also fall fast. At the top of this group were very rich men who had everything in common with the patricians except the timing of their success. Theirs was new money. Profits came from sources much like those that had made the old guard prosper a generation or two before. Yet the tightening of rules for entry into the governing class often kept newcomers from political roles commensurate with their economic clout. They did enjoy legal rights as citizens and sometimes had access to less prominent offices. And they lived well, gaining and spending with some of the best. Of course, not all merchants became or remained so affluent. While the wealth and skills of Italian businessmen made them visible throughout Europe, many could not aspire to international markets. Among those who bought and sold for a living were quite modest dealers in local trade and even itinerant peddlers. The old-clothes seller was a more common, if less imposing, figure than a banker of Medici stature. The lifestyle of such small-scale entrepreneurs had much in common with that of their economic peers among the artisans. Prosperous merchants' wives do not appear to have engaged directly in the family business. Some widows, though, with control over assets, invested in their own or others' commercial ventures. And, in modest concerns, women at times worked on their own as retailers.

Those who lived from commerce and business had their own lively culture. They admired curiosity, ambition, prudence, and a propensity for calculated risk taking, all traits that served them well in their work. They also valued education, though of a practical sort. They supplemented their ability to keep records and reckon accounts with knowledge of applied geometry, geography, current affairs, foreign tastes and customs, prices, currencies and exchange rates, and commercial law.

---

### PROFILE: GREGORIO DATI, WEALTHY MERCHANT

Gregorio Dati (1362–1435) was a successful Florentine merchant, who entered into many profitable partnerships dealing in wool, silk, and other merchandise. His career, however, especially early on, knew the vicissitudes characteristic of Renaissance business. For example, while he was en route to Spain as his enterprise's traveling partner, a role typical for young men, pirates robbed him of all his goods, including a consignment of pearls, and of his own clothes. His recovery from such losses followed in part from helpful infusions of capital in the form of dowries from four successive marriages. Later in life, he was honored to serve a number of posts in the city government; his election to the prestigious office of Standard-Bearer of Justice marked the peak of his career. Over the years he wrote a "diary," actually an occasional record in which he kept accounts of his commercial and family life. Men of his kind pioneered this form of writing about the public and private self.[11] (See also Chapter 11.)

---

In medieval and Renaissance Italy, the demand for literate public servants prompted the rise of a new elite group whose distinction derived from their education. The work demanded facility in reading and writing classical Latin, skills more accessible to those with some family means to pay for the schooling. Yet here was one avenue by which more modest men could rise.

**Lettered Professionals and Bureaucrats**

Lettered professionals worked in several venues. Physicians and teachers belonged in this category, but their numbers were relatively few. High demand for literate employees came rather with the elaboration of government and associated public institutions. The tastes of the politically dominant groups favored those adept in the new culture of humanism. More and more, records needed keeping, negotiations with other bodies needed undertaking, speeches and letters of praise and persuasion needed writing. The appetite for lawyers, magistrates, administrators, secretaries, and notaries was sharp. Earlier in the Middle Ages, this kind of literacy and the work it led to belonged primarily to the church. Many Renaissance men who pursued careers in the expanding bureaucracies continued to find their way there by taking orders as celibate clerics. It became more common, however, for men to combine such work with marriage and family. In some cities, by the sixteenth century, the reproductive success of the lettered class contributed to its transformation into a closed, hereditary caste; only members' sons could apply to join.

---

### PROFILE: LEONARDO BRUNI, CIVIL SERVANT AND SCHOLAR

Leonardo Bruni (1369–1444) was born in Arezzo, a Tuscan town then under Florentine rule. He migrated to Florence to study law and entered the intellectual circle of a prominent humanist scholar. Through this connection came the offer of a position as a secretary in the papal court. After a lucrative decade in that role, he returned to Florence, where he divided his energies between the "active" life in public office and the "contemplative" life of scholarship. He served his adopted city in a variety of civil service posts, culminating in his appointment as chancellor, a prestigious officer in charge of ceremonial speeches, diplomatic correspondence, and government paperwork. At the same time he dedicated himself to translating Greek classics like Plutarch and Aristotle and writing the *History of the Florentine People*.[12]

---

**Courtiers**
In the course of the Renaissance, princes ruled more and more Italian states. They arrived by different routes, but many traced their power to military prowess and more or less coercive takeover. Once in place, they tried to consolidate their authority and establish dynasties where rule would pass by heredity within the family. One strategy was to establish a court. Its site was normally a city, albeit sometimes a small one such as Urbino. The function of a medieval court was to guard the king and his government and to secure advice from powerful dependents, whom the ruler bound to his person with hospitality and largesse. While the Renaissance Italian court retained these military and political functions, its social and cultural role blossomed. It became a lively center of artistic display and entertainment. Dispensing patronage and fostering art and festivities to bolster their legitimacy, princes and their families attracted a prestigious entourage that mixed the well-born, the beautiful, and the talented. A famous book called *The Courtier* set the model: a gentleman accomplished in military skills, graceful in body, elegant in manners, sage in conduct, knowledgeable in letters, and appreciative of the arts. He was to serve the prince as a soldier, adviser, and diplomat. This male paragon had his counterpart in a lady also beautiful in both body and soul, pleasing in bearing and conversation, clever, discreet, and wise. Besides those nobly born, courts welcomed men and women of unusual artistic and intellec-

tual gifts: musicians, singers, dancers, poets, architects, painters, philosophers. Their achievements and company gave pleasure to the prince and his guests and allure to his regime.

---

## PROFILE: BALDASSARE CASTIGLIONE, COURTIER AND WRITER

Baldassare Castiglione (1478–1529), author of *The Courtier*, wrote from his own experience. He was born near the middling northern city of Mantua, where his father served in the court of the ruling Gonzaga family. Educated in both humanist letters and the social and military skills of the family calling, he served princes in Milan, Mantua, and Urbino as a soldier and, especially, a diplomat. Later, this career led him to enter the church, where he worked for the pope and was appointed bishop of Avila in Spain. The artist Raphael painted Castiglione's portrait in the rich, but elegantly restrained garb that suited his ideal of the courtier.[13]

---

## PROFILE: LAURA PEVERARA, COURT SINGER

Laura Peverara (flourished 1580s) was one of the earliest representatives of a late Renaissance novelty, the female court musician. Passionate about music and poetry, Duke Alfonso wanted to entertain his court at Ferrara, a middle-sized northern center, and to attract international attention, so he set out to create an unusual musical ensemble. Although women did not then perform professionally, he recruited Peverara from her home in Mantua as a lady-in-waiting. She was described at the time as "rather beautiful" and as "singing and playing excellently." She was soon joined by other women singers, who performed to great acclaim. Unmarried when she went to Ferrara, Peverara wed three years later, with a huge dowry supplied by the duke and the promise of fat annuities to be paid to herself, her husband, and her mother. The family occupied a large suite of rooms in the ducal palace.[14]

---

**Artisans**

The productive core of urban society were artisans and their families. The workers of this group made and sold goods for both local consumption and external markets. Typically artisans worked with considerable independence, acquiring raw materials, working them, and then selling directly to consumers. Some routine goods were produced for general sale, but many, more specialized products were made on commission to a buyer's specifications. Artisans made things to fill the whole spectrum of Renaissance daily needs. Masons and carpenters carried on the skilled tasks of construction. Many artisans processed food, including bakers, cooks, and brewers. Others made hides into leather and leather into shoes, pouches, wall coverings, bookbindings, saddles, and harnesses. Woodworkers made barrels and furniture.

Soap, candles, paper, baskets, bird cages, musical instruments, ceramic and metal containers, weapons, jewelry, playing cards, books, and countless other objects all were produced in artisan workshops. The manufacture of textiles occupied many workers, especially in a city like Florence, which specialized in high-end merchandise for international trade. There, some of the most complexly organized of Renaissance enterprises coordinated the efforts of carders, spinners, weavers, dyers, and fullers. The tight vertical integration of this major industry gave workers less autonomy than many other artisans exercised. The cutting and sewing of clothing and the confection of special decorations like gold thread and lace occupied numbers of hands. In some cities artisans produced specialties for luxury consumption throughout Europe, as did the glassworkers of the Venetian lagoon and the armorers of Milan and Brescia. Much of the art that makes Renaissance Italy famous—rendered by jewelers, metalsmiths, majolica makers, and printers as well as painters and sculptors—was produced by men who functioned economically as artisans. As with other social types, artisans varied in their honor and prosperity. For example, workers in precious metals had more prestige than butchers and tanners, who handled carcasses and blood. The executioner was among the lowest of all. Also, within any craft, some men, more talented, ambitious, or hard working, succeeded better than their fellows.

The basic unit of artisan production was the household. Residence and workplace often occupied the same or adjacent premises. The master craftsman typically led the work of family members, assistants, and apprentices who were learning the trade. His wife frequently played an active role in the family's business; more rarely, she had a trade of her own, typically spinning or weaving. Many cities had corporations, or guilds, of artisans who shared a particular craft. These bodies oversaw the work, regulating quality and conditions and supervising entry into the occupation. Often they, or associated confraternities, also provided welfare services for members and their families. While some guilds claimed political roles, artisans were increasingly excluded from participation in government. (See also Chapter 15.)

---

### PROFILE: BENVENUTO CELLINI, GOLDSMITH, SCULPTOR

Benvenuto Cellini (1500–71) was a Florentine-born goldsmith. His father, a mason, hoped his son would become a cornetto player, but bent to the boy's artistic drives and apprenticed him to learn fine metalwork. Adventuresome and eager to perfect his art through observation of models from the ancient world, Cellini as a young man traveled to Rome. There, if one believes his colorful, if self-inflating, *Autobiography*, he worked in the shops of several masters and in due course received his own commissions from exalted patrons, including the pope. Anxious to display his artistic prowess, he undertook to make medals and even large sculptures, projects requiring skills beyond those in which he had trained. Also, when the imperial army sacked Rome in 1527, he turned his hand—most successfully, he claimed—to soldiery, killing one of the enemy leaders with a brilliant cannon shot from the Castel Sant'Angelo. His career as an artisan later took him abroad to create for the king of France.[15]

---

### PROFILE: GINEVRA ROSSI, WIFE AND CANDY MAKER

Ginevra (d. 1608), wife of Guglielmo Rossi, learned candy making from her husband. Together they developed a prosperous business in Rome and had five children. So successful were they that, according to Guglielmo, they attracted the envy of local competitors, who instigated an inspection by guild officials. The consuls barged into the shop during the Christmas rush and obliged Ginevra, then six months pregnant, to hurry about, hauling out boxes and climbing up and down stairs, to show their goods. Several days later, the woman miscarried and shortly after died. Her husband, blaming the stress caused by the inspectors, took them to court. He itemized his injuries, including the loss of the child and of Christmas business and the dishonor to his good name. The largest claims he made were for the loss of his wife's work caring for the children and overseeing the shop (500 scudi), of her expertise as a candy maker (2,000 scudi), and for her beloved companionship (4,000 scudi). Ginevra's centrality to this artisan family's livelihood was clear.[16]

---

**Semi- and Unskilled Workers/ Servants**

Renaissance cities depended on the efforts of workers who offered brawn and patience but only mediocre skills. To migrants from the countryside, such employment was the most accessible. Probably the most common form was domestic service. Where workplace and home merged, servants might participate in the economic activities of their masters as well as keep their houses. Even quite rich families seldom had more than one or two servants, although the numbers rose in the sixteenth century; the more aristocratic lifestyles of the later Renaissance called for more domestic support. Servants typically worked on contract, receiving board, shelter, sometimes clothing, and either a salary paid periodically or a lump sum at the end. Sometimes, loyal servants, through long service, earned their master's lasting affection and protection. Nevertheless, rapid turnover was normal. Accordingly, in the literature of the period, old family retainers are less common figures than the tricky or deceitful servants who exploit their intimate knowledge of the household goings-on to please a grateful master or embarrass a resented one. Both males and females worked as domestic servants, with women increasingly outnumbering men later in the Renaissance. For both sexes, service was often work for the young—sometimes children from age seven, but mostly those in their teens and early twenties. Girls, in particular, hoped to lay up wages toward a dowry. Many left domestic work when they married, but some remained or returned. Married female servants had more status and security. Some servants were elderly; employers occasionally described keeping an aged servant as a work of charity.

---

### PROFILE: CAMILLA OF PARMA, DOMESTIC SERVANT

By 1559 Camilla of Parma had been a servant in the house of Roman notary Girolamo and his young wife, Giulia, for more than a year. Probably middle aged, Camilla had to support herself; the husband she may once have had was no longer part of her life. Her daughter lived in a local monastery, where Camilla sent her gifts of food scrounged from Giulia. While the servant had a room upstairs that locked with a key, she passed much of her day in the company of her mistress. They shared work, such as organizing linens and clothing and sending old items out to be sold by Jewish second-hand dealers. Camilla also ran errands and carried messages, for Girolamo did not allow Giulia to circulate in the streets and even locked her in the house. The servant's activities served recreation as well as work. Camilla encouraged and perhaps even initiated an amorous intrigue between her mistress and a gentleman neighbor, who came calling secretly through a hole in the upstairs ceiling. The servant also showed Giulia how to do magic with beans in order to secure her lover's devotion and keep her husband under her control. The spell failed, however. Girolamo soon caught on, and Camilla ended up arrested and jailed.[17]

---

A minority of servants were slaves. Renaissance Italian practice had little in common with the plantation slavery of the Americas. Rather than labor in the fields, nearly all slaves in fourteenth- and fifteenth-century Italy, most of whom were women, worked as domestic servants. More common in some cities than others but seldom numerous, they had traveled farther than other migrants. Because Christians were supposed not to enslave fellow believers, many came from the infidel lands: some from northern or sub-Saharan Africa, others from the domains of the Ottoman Empire, especially in the Balkans and around the Black Sea. One trans-Adriatic route had backcountry girls enter Dubrovnik households as slaves, train in domestic service, and then, sold to traders, cross to the Italian market. Uprooted from their own cultures and set apart from Italians by their legal bondage yet thrust into the core of family life, these slaves occupied a highly contradictory place. By the sixteenth century the slave trade had changed; most slaves were then men, taken as prisoners of war and put to rowing Italian galleys.[18]

Besides domestic service, the city offered other forms of semiskilled and unskilled work, usually at day or piece rates. Transport and haulage was one important area. Workers were needed to handle loads of goods entering and leaving the city, to shift earth and stone at building sites, and, in bigger cities, to deliver drinking water. Others had to remove garbage and sewage from the streets and latrines. Such jobs fell mostly to men, but women also worked in this little prestigious and poorly paid sector of the urban workforce. Almost any female, for example, could nurse the sick, although particular experience or gifts might single some out.

Italian Renaissance city life also drew diversity and color from the presence of kinds of people who did not fit into the social structure we have just described. These included many foreigners and wanderers who for one or another reason found themselves in town. For a few, the motives were political; exiles, ordered banished from their homeplaces due to factional struggles, took refuge in other cities. So might banished criminals. Pilgrims traveled to fulfill a vow, to show gratitude, or to seek forgiveness, a cure, or some other manifestation of holiness. Many people came and went on business, more or less legitimate. Foreign merchants stopped to make connections and deals. Itinerant peddlers displayed their wares and then packed up and moved on. Mountebanks set up platforms from which to hawk cures for common ills, competing with musicians and actors of the *commedia dell'arte* for the ears and coins of local residents. Panhandlers and hucksters, likewise, clamored for attention, while thieves tried to stay out of sight. All these negotiated, wheedled, or grasped their living by traveling from town to town. Also nomadic were bands of gypsies, who appeared in Italy in the fifteenth century; they made a tenuous livelihood on the edges of the economy, trading in horses and other merchandise, picking up odd jobs, sometimes stealing and fencing goods, sometimes picking up loose coin by telling fortunes, playing music, and begging. Although some of these outsiders enjoyed good wealth and the status they brought with them, others flitted at the margins of respectability. Many, both high and low, compensated for their marginality by entering into local solidarities with their peers. Therefore, cities had their communities of, for example, Spaniards or Greeks, and their subcultures of entertainers, beggars, and thieves.

**Wanderers and Outsiders**

Three categories of outsiders—soldiers, Jews, and prostitutes—merit further comment. Soldiers were numerous in Italy, and highly mobile. Italian states relied heavily on mercenaries, often recruited by professional captains, or *condottieri*, who contracted at a price to supply military men for a fixed time. Soldiers moved from job to job, rarely serving in their own home territories. Many were not even Italian. When unemployed or unpaid, they were inclined to take what they wanted, not always gently, from their surroundings. Not a comfortable, steady, or domestic life, soldiering did not make for close bonds with the host community. The men often fell back on their fellows for companionship.

## PROFILE: JUAN GOMEZ, SOLDIER AND THIEF

Juan Gomez (active 1550s), a veteran Spanish soldier, found his way to North Italy and in 1551 enlisted to fight for his king against the French. Condemned for thefts and brawling in camp, he rowed as galley slave until, in 1555, two Spanish friends bailed him out and brought him penniless to Rome. The three companions took lodgings and, one Saturday, picked pockets. The next afternoon, Juan stood guard while his companions snatched from a house fine silver trays and bowls. At dusk, the trio buried their loot in ruins in the ancient Forum. On Monday, they unloaded half their treasure to a fence, but, returning to their stash, found the rest was gone. Suspecting one another, the thieves quarreled and sulked. On Tuesday, the police collared two of them, betrayed by the third or by the fence. The court, keen to trace the still missing silver, tortured Juan with fire to his feet. We last see him in the documents, in agony, protesting his innocence.[19]

Jews were outsiders because they did not share the faith that underpinned the culture of Christian Europe. This difference in beliefs sometimes sparked interreligious violence in which the Jews, outnumbered and disenfranchised, almost always came out the worse. Nevertheless, though few and often persecuted, they occupied a key place in the economy. A few wealthy ones acted as creditors to princes, but most were far from rich and worked as small-scale moneylenders and businesspeople. Before the end of the fifteenth century, Italian Jews lived scattered across small towns and cities—a few families here and there—with about half their population concentrated in Sicily. After the expulsions from Spain and Portugal in the 1490s, many Iberian Jews migrated to and through Italy in their search for a new home. These disruptions and their echoes elsewhere in Europe triggered great mobility and new settlement patterns. The sixteenth century was especially harsh toward Jews. Counter-Reformation legislation excluded Jews from many economic and social activities that they had once shared with the Christian majority. Those in Italy increasingly assembled in a few larger communities sited in principal cities. There they were often made to live in the first formally instituted ghettos, where at curfew they were locked inside. At times their religious life suffered persecution: book burnings, forced conversions, and Inquisitorial pressures, especially against apostates. By the end of the Renaissance, Jews were weaker, more segregated and straitened than before.[20]

Another group on the outside of the social scheme were the prostitutes. Their marginality, neither ethnic, geographic, nor economic, was moral. Prostitutes were conceptually excluded from the ranks of society by the tainted source of their livelihood. They became the emblem of

Jewish peddler. [Bertelli]

social contamination, the marker of what was wrong, particularly as the religious reform movements, Catholic as well as Protestant, heated up. This sixteenth-century view represented a shift from earlier Renaissance opinion where prostitutes were deemed a necessary lesser evil that prevented worse impropriety. Thus, governments had authorized them as an acceptable outlet for sexual appetites that, unsated, might cause affronts to respectable women. Even under the later moral climate, when prostitutes were castigated and restrictive laws curbed their trade and residence, these services remained a common way for women on their own to earn a living. As companions and neighbors, prostitutes often took part in urban social life; their prescribed segregation in practice remained only partial.[21]

## CONCLUSION

Many sorts of people inhabited the Italian peninsula and islands during the Renaissance. While their variety was great, especially in the vibrant cities, most fell into one or another of the types described here. These categories—patrician, courtier, artisan, servant, peasant, soldier, and so on—allow us to recognize important differences among the ways of life of diverse social groups. At the same time, it is important to remember that Italians of whatever status did not live only with their own kind. Renaissance Italy was at once sharply divided and socially promiscuous; across social boundary lines, there were frequent, routine exchanges and complex human relationships.

## NOTES

1. For a broad survey of premodern European society, see George Huppert, *After the Black Death: A Social History of Early Modern Europe*, 2d ed. (Bloomington:

Indiana University Press, 1998), or Henry Kamen, *Early Modern European Society* (New York: Routledge, 2000). For society in specific Italian cities, see, for example, Gene Brucker, *Renaissance Florence* (Berkeley: University of California Press, 1983), or Dennis Romano, *Patricians and Popolani: The Social Foundations of the Venetian Renaissance State* (Baltimore: Johns Hopkins University Press, 1987), chap. 2. On the role of women, for a pessimistic view, see Joan Kelly, "Did Women Have a Renaissance?" in *Becoming Visible*, ed. R. Bridenthal and C. Koonz (Boston: Houghton Mifflin, 1977), and Margaret King, *Women of the Renaissance* (Chicago: University of Chicago Press, 1991).

2. On the clergy, a compact introduction is Denys Hay and John Law, *Italy in the Age of the Renaissance, 1380–1530* (London: Longman, 1989), chap. 7.

3. D. S. Chambers, *Renaissance Cardinals and Their Worldly Problems* (Aldershot: Variorum, 1997).

4. *Butler's Lives of the Saints, Concise Edition*, ed. M. Walsh (New York: HarperCollins, 1991), 26–28.

5. On rural society, a very brief account is Hay and Law, *Italy in the Age of the Renaissance*, chap. 4. A fuller, regional example is Frank McArdle, *Altopascio: A Study in Tuscan Rural Society, 1587–1784* (Cambridge: Cambridge University Press, 1978). Notable from the much richer scholarship in Italian is Giovanni Cherubini, *L'Italia rurale del Basso Medioevo* (Rome: Laterza, 1984).

6. Archivio di Stato di Roma (ASR): Governatore, Tribunale Criminale: Processi, sixteenth century, b. 25 (1556); Processi, sixteenth century, b. 34 (1557); Processi, sixteenth century, b. 35 (1557); also, Sforza/Cesarini, Busta 89, document 12: Cecarelli, "Della Historia di Casa Cesarina libri due (1579)," 57v-58r.

7. ASR, Governatore, Tribunale Criminale: Processi, sixteenth century, b. 25 (1556); Processi, sixteenth century, b. 34 (1557); Processi, sixteenth century, b. 35 (1557), passim.

8. On the poor, see Brian Pullan, "Town Poor, Country Poor: The Province of Bergamo from the Sixteenth to the Eighteenth Century," in *Medieval and Renaissance Venice*, ed. E. Kittell and T. Madden (Urbana: University of Illinois Press, 1999), 213–236.

9. On urban patricians, from among many studies, see, for example, Donald Queller, *The Venetian Patriciate: Reality vs. Myth* (Urbana: University of Illinois Press, 1986); Joanne Ferraro, *Family and Public Life in Brescia, 1580–1650* (Cambridge: Cambridge University Press, 1993); Francis Kent, *Household and Lineage in Renaissance Florence: The Family Life of the Capponi, Ginori, and Rucellai* (Princeton: Princeton University Press, 1977).

10. Heather Gregory, ed., *Selected Letters of Alessandra Strozzi* (Berkeley: University of California Press, 1997).

11. "Diary of Gregorio Dati," in Gene Brucker, ed., *Two Memoirs of Renaissance Florence* (Prospect Heights, IL: Waveland Press, 1991), 107–141. On merchants, see also Iris Origo, *The Merchant of Prato* (Harmondsworth: Penguin, 1963); for a brief portrait of this merchant's wife, see Carole Levin, "Women in the Renaissance," in *Becoming Visible*, ed. Bridenthal and Koonz, 160–161.

12. Gordon Griffiths et al., eds., *Humanism of Leonardo Bruni: Selected Texts* (Binghamton: Medieval and Renaissance Texts and Studies, 1987), 21–42.

13. Baldesar Castiglione, *Book of the Courtier* (Harmondsworth: Penguin, 1967). On court life, see also David Herlihy, "Society, Court and Culture in Sixteenth-

Century Mantua," in *Women, Family and Society in Medieval Europe* (Providence, RI: Berghahn Books, 1995), 279–295; Sergio Bertelli et al., *Courts of the Italian Renaissance* (New York: Facts on File Publications, 1986); Gregory Lubkin, *A Renaissance Court: Milan under Galeazzo Maria Sforza* (Berkeley: University of California Press, 1994), chap. 5 and passim.

14. Anthony Newcomb, "Courtesans, Muses, or Musicians? Professional Women Musicians in Sixteenth-Century Italy," in *Women Making Music: The Western Art Tradition, 1150–1950*, ed. J. Bowers and J. Tick (Urbana: University of Illinois Press, 1986), 94–96.

15. Benvenuto Cellini, *Autobiography*, trans. G. Bull, rev. ed. (Harmondsworth: Penguin, 1998). On artisans' social world, see Dennis Romano, *Housecraft and Statecraft: Domestic Service in Renaissance Venice, 1400–1600* (Baltimore: Johns Hopkins University Press, 1996), chap. 4.

16. ASR, Tribunale Criminale, Processi 1600–19, b. 74, 138–79.

17. Thomas V. Cohen and Elizabeth S. Cohen, *Words and Deeds in Renaissance Rome: Trials before the Papal Magistrates* (Toronto: University of Toronto Press, 1993), 159–187. On servants, see also Christiane Klapisch-Zuber, "Women Servants in Florence during the Fourteenth and Fifteenth Centuries," in *Women and Work in Preindustrial Europe*, ed. B. Hanawalt (Bloomington: Indiana University Press, 1986), 56–93, and Romano, *Housecraft*.

18. On slaves, see Susan Stuard, "Ancillary Evidence for the Decline of Medieval Slavery," *Past and Present*, no. 149 (November 1995), 3–28, and Steven Epstein, *Genoa and the Genoese, 958–1528* (Chapel Hill: University of North Carolina Press, 1996), 266–269.

19. Thomas V. Cohen, "Three Forms of Jeopardy: Honor, Pain, and Truth-Telling in a Sixteenth-Century Italian Courtroom," *Sixteenth Century Journal* 29:4 (1998), 975–998.

20. On Jews, see Ariel Toaff, *Love, Work and Death: Jewish Life in Medieval Umbria* (London: Littmann Library of Jewish Civilization, 1996). Pictures from the life of Renaissance Italian Jews are scattered through Thérèse and Mendel Metzger, *Jewish Life in the Middle Ages* (Secaucus, NJ: Chartwell Books, 1982).

21. On prostitutes, see Richard Trexler, "Florentine Prostitution in the Fifteenth Century," in *Power and Dependence in Renaissance Florence*, v. 2 (Binghamton: Medieval and Renaissance Texts and Studies, 1993), 31–65. On the very few women who became celebrated courtesans, see Georgina Masson, *Courtesans of the Italian Renaissance* (New York: St. Martin's Press, 1975).

# 3

# Dangers

No society knows boundless security. Our own early twenty-first-century world lives with the memory of disastrous global wars and the unsettling facts of nuclear weapons and environmental degradation, both local and planetary. Our febrile media inform us daily of earthquakes, eruptions, tidal waves, conflagrations, and frightful outbreaks of new diseases in all corners of the earth. And, for thrills, we flock to films about unlikely asteroids of doom and other celestial threats. Nevertheless, despite these real and imaginary alarms, those of us who today live in the wealthy countries of the globe collectively enjoy unprecedented physical security. That fact does not rule out individual griefs and tragedies: traffic accidents, violent crimes, and the few still-unconquered diseases take their toll. But they do not haunt us as did the dangers faced by the men, women, and young folk of premodern Europe. Thus, to penetrate the minds and daily experiences of Renaissance Italians, it helps to scan the structural and cultural differences that made their world feel so much less safe than ours.

The dangers that stalked Renaissance Italians were several. Some stemmed from a natural world not easily controlled. Others, to premodern eyes, had supernatural origins. Some perils, as we shall see, had a double source, at once natural and supernatural, for God and the devil had a presumptive hand in storms, floods, fires, plagues, and earthquakes. A third set were human—the result of the political and social organization of the Renaissance world. In the face of all these perils, men and women took steps to secure themselves. This chapter explores the threats—supernatural, natural, and human—that menaced Italians and traces their attempts to ward them off. Before delving, let us first survey all three.

## THE SUPERNATURAL

God, for all his benevolence toward humankind, could also deal out harm. He, his saints, and, of course, the arch enemy, the devil, could be unpredictable and dangerous. In its anxiety in the face of God, premodern Christianity differed sharply from most modern versions of the faith. To Renaissance Catholic eyes, the earth, although of God's making, was no happy place. Rather, the true domain of peace, order, and good government lay outside this temporal world, in eternity, in another, nonterrestrial realm: heaven. From late antiquity and the Middle Ages, Christianity had inherited a strand of bleak antiworldliness. Woven across this theme was a lesser, contrasting thread that praised the beauty of God's creation. Nevertheless, preachers and moralists were quick to remind their flocks of the many dangers to body and soul that stalked the world. Fear the vanities of earthly hope, they warned, and stake all on the afterlife! One message of the world's imperfections therefore was to aspire to heaven. Spliced to it was a second admonition: flee sin to ward off disaster here on earth!

This double reading of terrestrial life reflected the Christian's two main goals: salvation and providence. The first was otherworldly, the second this-worldly. Salvation was the sin-bound soul's eventual redemption. Earthly traps meant that not everyone won this heavenly prize. For those who lost it, there was hell, which the Renaissance took dead seriously. Hell was no mere metaphor, but an agonizing reality of flames, molten metal, sucking toads, and biting snakes. People saw lively images of its gaping jaws and gleeful, eager devils in countless paintings, frescoes, and sculptures. Purgatory, too, was a real, but extraterrestrial place, a cleansing painful suburb of the true inferno, the temporary abode, en route to heaven, of all but the purest souls. Salvation therefore was serious work, an individual but also a collective endeavor that absorbed the energies of the clergy, who prayed and preached, and not a little of the wealth of the laity, who invested heavily in masses for themselves, their kinfolk, and other allies. Unlike most kinds of modern Christianity, where God's love and mercy hold center stage, the premodern version was bleaker about a soul's chances. Preachers, confessors, and devout books urged a life of anxious, vigilant self-control, to master sin. Hope there was, but tempered with a darker vision of the moral cosmos.

The second goal of Christian life, providence, much concerns us here, for, as a concept of the world's working, it heightened the pervasive premodern sense of insecurity. A notion far more central to earlier Chris-

Soul in danger: devils attack a miser, as a hell-mouth gapes.
[Bertarelli: Avarita]

tian thought than now, providence is God's justice wrought on earth.
With an eye to fairness and to instruction, he and his saints keep a firm
hand on the terrestrial tiller. Why did it hail on our crops? It must be
our sins! And why did the fleet go down? We blasphemed! We neglected
the sacraments! And why did our affairs prosper? Virtue rewarded! This
notion of divine providence shaped worship and colored the worldview
of the time. There was a double message: first, that catastrophes are a
divine chastisement integral to the ordained scheme of things, so that
we must expect them, for we all are sinners; second, and less bleak, that
all our scourges are neither meaningless nor entirely beyond human control. Plagues and earthquakes, locusts and wars invited moral actions—
rectitude, charity, chastity, and such devotions as fasting and prayer; a
virtuous and pious response might sometimes buy or beg them off. Not
only individuals, but states, towns, and villages therefore at times of
crisis looked to providence—to God, Mary, and the saints. People turned
to specialist saints, like Saint Rocco, good against plague, or Saint Nicholas, for safety on the seas. Whole communities sought help at local cult
sites, praying, for example, to the many black Madonnas deemed especially potent and holy. Collective vows, pilgrimages, and processions
with wonder-working images aimed to stave off disaster.[1]

God's creation, nature, was often perilously out of hand. Not that it
was even more potent than today; rather, people of the time faced the
world with technologies far feebler than our own. True, the Renaissance
gave birth to modern science; it was a time of lively experimentation and
avid investigation of the natural world. Nevertheless, in practical matters, progress was by modern standards slow. Italians of the fifteenth
and sixteenth centuries had nothing like our present upper hand over
matter and energy, over the landscape, its crops and animals, and over
pain and sickness. Moreover, natural science was the dispersed activity

of a few rather than a pervasive culture, set of institutions, and state of mind. In the popular imagination, it had no name and no fixed identity. Therefore, no concept of science was available as an antidote to anxiety. One could not say, "Surely science will find a way," for neither was such robust, agile science yet at hand, nor could the very thought be thought. As a consequence, to Italian eyes, it was not human sway and masterful response, but natural power, unpredictable and dangerous, that caught the fancy and stirred the feelings.

As for the threats of human origin, some were political, others social. As we shall see, states themselves were sometimes harsh or violent, and sometimes just inadequate. Their warfare and cruel justice caused much hardship. Alongside this public sphere of violence was an ample private one, not easily suppressed. In country and city alike, rather than wait for official justice, Italians readily took into their own hands the settling of accounts. The result, often, was bloody mayhem.

## NATURAL DANGERS

For all that it seemed to travelers' eyes a balmy garden, Italy, like any Mediterranean terrain, was often a dangerous land. The sharp swings of climate could work havoc, as could a restless tectonic underground. Trouble was a complex phenomenon; as always, human consequences of natural events hung on human environmental tamperings.

**Floods**  One feared natural force was flooding. The heavy rains of fall and spring often pushed rivers over their banks, and heavy deforestation made matters worse. A famous passage in Machiavelli's *Prince* likens "fortune," as he calls the force of chance in human affairs, to a river: "I compare fortune to one of those violent rivers which, when they are enraged, flood the plains, tear down trees and buildings, wash soil from one place to deposit it in another. Everyone flees before them, everybody yields to their impetus, there is no possibility of resistance."[2] The force of raging waters caught the Italian imagination. Leonardo da Vinci, as artist and engineer, was entranced by the swirling power of rushing waters. The same was true of less educated folk; Romans often pegged memories to the city's floods: "That was when the river grew."[3]

Floods also stirred up Christian anxieties, for they had a biblical resonance. There were moral implications. In Italian, as preachers and ballad singers liked to remind their audience, little distinguished an ordinary flood (*alluvione*) from Noah's deluge (*diluvio*). Raging waters therefore often seemed a sign, for they expressed aptly God's wrath against sin. Prayer and contrition might help keep the waters at bay. However, Machiavelli went on, in the same passage, "Yet such is [the rivers'] nature, it does not follow that when they are flowing quietly one cannot take precautions, constructing dikes and embankments so that when the river is in flood it runs into a canal or else its impetus is less wild and dangerous." As a Florentine official who had himself helped organize a failed military campaign to divert the river Arno, in hopes of retaking rebellious Pisa, Machiavelli wrote this passage mindful of his frustrated hydraulic engineering. Especially in the North, by long tradition, Italians built and repaired dams, dikes, and sluices for the control of raging waters. As with Machiavelli's "fortune," foresight sometimes helped a bit, but floods remained a problem.

Earthquakes were another menace, harder than flooding to corral. Almost the whole of Italy, from the Alps to Sicily, is seismically active, and many zones are prone to cata- **Earthquakes** strophic quakes. Scholars have tallied more than four hundred reported earthquakes for the seventeenth century, though only twenty-eight of these were grave enough to leave their mark in the incipient journalism of the age. Like floods, earthquakes could be read as portents of God's semiscrutable will. The Venetian diarist Marin Sanudo drew surprising comfort from some of the lucky accidents of a disastrous quake that in 1511 rattled Venice:

First there fell four marble kings that before had stood over the façade of the church of St. Mark. . . . There fell a woman in marble who represented Prudence, even though she was standing among other virtues. . . . The upper portion of the decorations over the great balcony of the Great Hall of the Major Council, which was high, fell, [along] with a Justice that was there, but a marble St. Mark [the patron saint of Venice] held firm and did not fall. . . . A marble merlon [a piece of a parapet] decorated with a plaster seal bearing a lily blossom fell, and many held this to be a good sign, because the lily, which is the crest of France, will fall and come to ruin, which is what God wants for the good of Italy, sorely tried by barbarians. . . . And I saw the holy Mark, who remained intact on top of a palace. . . . Thus this city will be the savior of Italy and of the faith of Christ by chasing the barbarians [i.e., the foreigners] from Italy.[4]

Venice at the time was struggling to recover from a stinging military defeat that had come close to annihilating its mainland domain. Public opinion thus readily linked the shaking earth to the day's tumultuous politics.

Such earthquakes and floods, as prodigies of nature, were divine signs that stimulated speculation, much of it anxious. **Omens** The same was true of the natural realm's less damaging surprises: unusual rainbows, falling meteorites, and even an unusual swarm of red butterflies. The birth of what the age called "monsters," deformed animals and humans—a four-legged chicken, a two-headed child, for instance—could stir both excited commentary and the same sort of anxious symbol reading as Sanudo and his fellow Venetians applied to the earthquake damage on their monuments.

**Hunger**  One scourge to which Italians devoted a great deal of energy and prudent attention was famine.[5] Hunger haunted premodern Europe. Unlike earthquakes or floods, a famine was not a simple act of God, a natural event perhaps made worse by imprudent architecture. Rather, it was the product of a complex interaction between humans and their surroundings. Nevertheless, almost always, nature contributed by delivering too much water, or too little, or excessive heat, or unseasonable frost, damaging the harvest, so that a district could not feed itself. Nevertheless, there was often more to it; war could disrupt production, driving off the peasants or impeding the movement of supplies. A siege could starve a city. International politics could block shipments. As in all premodern Europe, there was a strong link between hunger and demography. Where population rose, peasants crowded the terrain, dividing their lands among their heirs, so that from generation to generation, the average family had less and less to till. At the same time, in the absence of swift technological advance, population pressure fostered more precarious forms of cultivation. Peasants cleared marginal lands unsuitable for sustained agriculture. In the hungry search for plowland for grain, they colonized steeper slopes and marshy plains, destroying forests and driving out wildlife. They also encroached on pastureland, for, when food is scarce, animals and meat are luxuries. Thus, denizens of a crowded landscape were far more vulnerable to vagaries of climate. In the fairly empty Italy of the fifteenth century, meat was agreeably abundant, grain cheap, and famine a rarity. As the population rose, however, hunger became an ever graver threat, especially in the last two decades of the sixteenth century. Low yield-ratios of grain to seed (six or eight to one) and inefficient transport made things worse. Toward the century's end, the pressure on resources caused a general impoverishment of the peasantry and finally produced famines so widespread that the resources of the whole Mediterranean basin no longer sufficed. The early 1590s saw grave shortages, often the result of rain that rotted crops. Merchants and anxious state agents organized massive, costly shipments of Polish grain, carried by sea from the Baltic to Italy.

Italians knew keenly of the danger of scarcity of grain, their primary foodstuff. Prosperous individuals stockpiled in their houses enough for many months, sometimes hoarding the precious seeds in chests in their bedrooms. Cities had their major granaries and often closely regulated bread's price, weight, and composition, both to secure the welfare and survival of the poorer classes and to discourage riots. The Roman grain office, for instance, furnished its stored grain to the city's bakers.[6] As an organ of papal administration, it sold the importation rights to political

Open fires in an outdoor kitchen. [Scappi]

favorites in ways often tinged with graft. This cozy system could bring merchants huge profits, at the expense of the hungry populace. Villages too had their public grain hoards and their systems of emergency relief. But, in general, the cities, politically stronger, espoused grain policies that fed their urban inhabitants at the expense of the countryside. To the annoyance of landlords and peasants, they arrogated to themselves rights of purchase. A producer was supposed to sell to the capital, through its agents, even if he could make better profit shipping his grain to a hungrier market in another territory. Often, as with such rules, the growers retaliated by smuggling.

The other great natural scourge of premodern Italy was disease. Illness was something no one could readily prevent, es-    **Disease**
cape, or ignore. A phenomenon so vast and so profound in its
consequences deserves a chapter of its own. (See Chapter 14.)

## MAN-MADE VIOLENCE AND HARDSHIPS

Many threats to bodily safety and property were
social in origin.[7] Violence was common and much felt,    **Personal Violence**
by both travelers and resident Italians. Some violence    **and Crime**
was linked to quarrels, some to theft. Bloodshed var-
ied with the territory; some city-states were fairly well policed. But, in
most of Italy, everyday life was often combative. There was a culture of
violence, closely linked to notions of masculinity, though women too
could at times be rough. Men were quick to draw the knives they always
carried, or their swords where those were allowed, and to pursue longer
quarrels with all sorts of weapons, including clubs, torches, pikes, battle-

Boar beating, a risky
sport. [Bertelli]

axes, firearms, and poison. Simmering vendettas and sudden brawls, often over trifles, flared with little warning to take their toll in life and
limb. Surveying the record books of the barber surgeons, who had to
report all wounds they treated, a historian has calculated that sixteenth-
century Rome was much more dangerous than the cities of the United
States today.[8] Rome, in the late sixteenth century, with a population one-
hundredth New York's now, had ten serious woundings a day and about
thirty-five murders a year. At Rome's rate, modern New York would see
a thousand daily woundings and ten murders. Rome's homicide rate was
thus three to five times New York's in recent years. Most of this carnage
was probably linked to honor. Thus, men, especially younger men, if
peaceable, had to be on their toes and to mind their words, gestures,
and business dealings, lest they provoke an unwanted fight. Those many
who had a quarrel on their hands had to be alert against sudden attack
by enemies or hired thugs. Yet another of the many social risks of premodern Italy was that of damage to reputation. This is a matter to which
we return at length when discussing the complexities of Italian honor.

(See Chapter 6.) We will see that, because the pursuit of honor was highly competitive, men and women had to be on their toes to prevent slights and blots on their good name. Everyday social life demanded vigilance.

Some property crime threatened life and limb. In the cities there were muggings. Englishmen reported on the Venetian bravoes who attacked strollers in the depth of night, dispatched them, robbed them, and rolled the corpses into the nearest canal. In the countryside, banditry was a serious problem throughout the Renaissance. This brigandage flourished in the worse-governed states, in rough terrain, and along frontiers. In the sixteenth century, Tuscany, for instance, reasonably well ruled, was reputed safe, while the mountainous country behind Genoa and much of the Papal State, especially the Adriatic coast and the mountainous and wooded Neapolitan frontier, were notorious, as was Calabria. To avoid the bandits' depredations, travelers often went in large, armed groups. Another recourse was to disguise one's wealth, dressing in ragged garments, and to carry gold, easier to hide than silver because it was more precious for its weight. One sewed one's coins in unlikely secret places— inside the soles of shoes or in the lining of a jacket—or hid them deep in baggage. These stratagems did not always work, for the highway robbers were hard to fool. Nevertheless, a Polish gentleman in 1595 had the following lucky scrape:

I was going along, and, towards evening, when the sun was already setting behind the bushes, before Spaccafurno, out jumped two robbers who, after giving me a really thorough working over, having found nothing on me, went away into the woods, one of them first giving me two *testoni*, worth 20 *grossi* [Polish coins] or more, presumably out of great pity (for I had indeed pleaded with them a good deal) in compensation for having molested me in hopes of booty. Even though they had given me a good shaking over, everywhere: the cape, the jacket. I don't know if I would have gotten out of it safe and sound. But divine grace was my guardian, for in truth I had sewn into the soles of the cloth stockings in which I was walking 80 Hungarian florins, and over these I had shoes in rags, and the hose were of simple cloth and then it was difficult to guess by looking at me, because of my bad shoes and because I was traveling on foot.[9]

One recourse, in bandit country, was to hire a carrier, called a *vetturino*, who took charge of the travel arrangements: pack animals, wagons, and inns. In some zones, these ancestral travel agents and guides were widely believed to be in cahoots with the bandits; one paid them well for safety's sake. Even if honest, the *vetturini* thus profited from their bad reputation.

Travel at sea had its own risks, both natural and human. Even summer seas could be churned by sudden blasts of down-rushing alpine air, furious cold-front winds called *tramontana* on the west coast and *bora* on the east. Wrecks took their toll in lives and goods. In the sixteenth century, piracy grew more dangerous, partly due to Dalmatian adventurers but mainly because of Muslim raiders—large fleets and solitary pirate ships that scoured the seas and coasts for loot and captives. It was a predatory brand of commerce. The corsairs ransomed some prisoners on the spot and took thousands more away to enslave them on land or in the galleys, or to sell them back at a handsome profit. It is fair to remind ourselves that Christians, especially the Maltese knights, plied the same cruel and cynical trade on the opposing shore.

**State Violence**    Another source of insecurity, alongside the private violence of criminals and enemies, was the public violence of the state. This took two forms: warfare and judicial force. Warfare was not too burdensome in the fifteenth century, when small armies waged war for limited objectives. The sixty-five years between the French invasion of 1494 and the French-Spanish treaty of 1559, however, saw Italy as theater of operations for dynastic struggles that convulsed much of western Europe. The forces were now larger, the battles bloodier, and civilian damage greater. In 1527, a mutinous army starved for unpaid wages sacked Rome hideously for weeks. The city's physical fabric, population, and artistic culture needed several decades to recover. In the last forty years of the sixteenth century, on the other hand, Italy, though bedeviled by banditry, saw little warfare.

Armies did harm not only by killing, maiming, and ransacking their enemies. They also looted and raped and bullied their supposed allies and neutrals who had the bad luck to be in the way. Premodern armies had very primitive systems of supply and therefore tended to live off the land. Their soldiers were usually not local citizens, but mercenaries, often rough backcountry types from places like Switzerland, Germany, and the wilds of Scotland, Corsica, and Albania. Outsiders unchained by local ties, armed, and inured to theft and violence, they were dangerous even when demobilized; when a war stopped, the veterans easily descended into theft and banditry. Furthermore, crowded and unsanitary, armies often left a trail of disease in their wake.

Owing to its flaws, Renaissance government itself provoked anxiety. We moderns in the richer countries have become accustomed to the protection of a large, efficient, generally fair state, restrained by its own laws. Political debates in recent years have turned on just how big and how intrusive such a state should be, but few doubt the general utility of government. Advanced states today keep order, set ground rules for the marketplace, and look after the health, education, and welfare of the populace. Ideally, and often in fact as well, they treat their citizens even-handedly. Without denying the inefficiencies, blunders, and cruelties of which modern governments are capable, in the large, they guarantee stability and well-being. The situation in Renaissance Italy was often much less comfortable. Regimes could be capricious or callous. Also, their ambitions to regulate often overreached their capacity to enforce. It is hard to generalize, so diverse were they in structure, ambition, motivation, and competence. In some ways, Italian city-states and principalities anticipated our age, for they were zealous legislators of public and private behavior. Nevertheless, one should not read their laws and rules as banishing disorder from civic life.

This last point needs underlining. Despite a modern-looking zeal to legislate, Italian governments at the same time often seemed disconcertingly arbitrary. Thus, the state itself did not altogether master its territory. Its authority tended to protect the elites, though sometimes one at the expense of another, and its decrees often served less as controls than as inducements to buy exemptions. The ideal of equal treatment was tempered by the habit of exceptions, to the point that Italy was a quilt of special arrangements and privileges sold, granted, or appropriated. Inhabitants less powerful or privileged could not easily parry the state's financial and physical intrusions into their lives. Thus, government itself became a source of danger to pocket and to person.

Consider the matter of passing through customs. In northern Italy, where states were many, borders were ubiquitous. Merchants and other travelers therefore, again and again, had to make their way past customs officers. Since cities and states made ready money by taxing the goods that passed, the guards wanted to find what the wayfarers preferred to hide. The English traveler Fynes Moryson reported his dilemma: if you showed your valuables, the guards taxed you; if you hid them and they ransacked your baggage, they confiscated what they found. Then you had to bribe it back. The regulations themselves produced not clarity and certainty, but occasions for bargaining, with unpredictable results.

Justice itself was menacing. Take the police. The constabulary of many Italian cities was little better than the thieves it chased. The police, a device for civic safety, were themselves a frequent menace. The judiciary could also frighten. The law had its imposing majesty, and its arcane codes, books, and formulae. Although it upheld an ideal of impartial justice, reality was, however, far more nuanced. For one thing, regimes looked to the courts for income. Every procedure and every piece of legal paper had its fee. Criminal courts followed procedures very steeply tilted against the accused. Suspects were arraigned in isolation, interrogated without counsel by magistrates who did not have to reveal their evidence. Often, at the start of an interrogation, one did not even know the reasons for arrest. Thus, the apparatus of order itself, arbitrary and highhanded, sowed a degree of disorder. Courts tortured to gather evidence and punished with the whip, the jerking rope (*strappado*), and a medley of cruel capital punishments. The courts were also hard on property, for fines and confiscations were legion. To a degree, such official violence and rapine countered widespread disorder. At the same time, the courts gave individual Italians a means to battle their private enemies. All in all, for many, especially ordinary, people the judicial system, with its political vagaries and its penal ferocity, was a very mixed blessing. (See also Chapter 7.)

## CONCLUSION

All sorts of forces combined to foster anxiety and fear. Some were economic, and others political, medical, social, natural, or divine. This state of affairs did not at all reduce Renaissance Italians to quivering psychological jelly. What it did, however, was alert them to the need to take steps as best they could to protect themselves from risks on several fronts. In their relations with their fellow humans and with the saints, the Madonna, and God himself, they took care to secure themselves against all sorts of troubles. How they did this is the subject of later chapters.

## NOTES

1. On prophecy and religious sensibility, see Ottavia Niccoli, *Prophecy and People in Renaissance Italy*, trans. L. Cochrane (Princeton: Princeton University Press, 1990), and Cynthia L. Polecritti, *Preaching Peace in Renaissance Italy: Bernardino of Siena and His Audience* (Washington, DC: Catholic University Press, 2000).

2. Niccolò Machiavelli, *The Prince*, trans. George Bull (Harmondsworth: Penguin, 1961), 130.

3. Archivio di Stato di Roma, Governatore, Tribunale Criminale, Processi sixteenth century, b. 48, case 13, 19v (1559).

4. Quoted in Niccoli, *Prophecy and People*, 31.

5. On demography and food supply, see Fernand Braudel, *The Mediterranean and the Mediterranean World*, v. 1, part III, chapter 2 (Berkeley: University of California Press, 1995), and Massimo Montanari, *The Culture of Food*, trans. C. Ipsen (Oxford: Blackwell, 1994).

6. On food supplies, see Melissa Bullard, "Grain Supply and Urban Unrest in Renaissance Rome: The Crisis of 1533–34," in *Rome in the Renaissance: The City and the Myth*. ed. P. A. Ramsey (Binghamton: Center for Medieval and Early Renaissance Studies, 1982), 278–292.

7. On crime and punishment, see Trevor Dean and K. J. P. Lowe, eds., *Crime, Society and the Law in Renaissance Italy* (Cambridge: Cambridge University Press, 1994).

8. Peter Blastenbrei, *Kriminalität in Rom* (Tübingen: Karl Niemeyer Verlag, 1995), 70ff.

9. Antoni Maczak, *Viaggi e viaggiatori nell'Europa moderna* (Rome: 1994), 243–44. Our translation.

# 4

# Family and Other Solidarities

Renaissance people faced lives full of dangers and insecurities. To cope with these and get on in the world as best they could, they depended heavily on relationships with other people—in particular, on belonging to a variety of networks and groups. The most important was family, but webs of patronage, brotherhoods, and alliances based on shared neighborhood or regional origins also gave support. Furthermore, men and women built their very social identities by compiling such group associations. These personal affiliations were crucial in a time when public institutions had only begun to evolve toward their modern competence and strength and when the universal assistance programs that twenty-first-century North Americans and Europeans rely on did not exist. The Renaissance state, though expanding its powers and concerns, could neither quell violence in all its territories nor stave off famine, plague, and the other catastrophes. (See Chapter 3.) Hospitals had few beds and little capacity to treat most illnesses. Schools were small and taught very largely boys whose families could afford to pay. Charity helped some of the poor and disabled, but no modern arrangements, public or private, such as health, unemployment, or life insurance, buffered the hard times that swept across Renaissance lives with frequency and vehemence. When, as often, people needed help, they fell back on less public solidarities.

The nature of these affiliations varied. Some associations were loose and others very formal. Some brought people together more or less as equals, and others supplied vertical ties that linked people up and down the social hierarchy. In some cases, as most obviously with family, birth determined group membership, and no choice was possible. In other settings, birth, and the place in society that followed from it, might position a person to adopt a particular affiliation, but it was up to the individual to do so. Other connections were purely voluntary. Frequently these associations bound someone to other persons, but institutions too could enter into bonds with individuals. All such relationships can be viewed as exchanges, with benefits and obligations accruing to both parties. Although there was always reciprocity of some sort, the repayment was not always direct or the same in kind. Thus, a client might convey a rich gift to his patron, who would respond with goodwill and good words dropped in the ear of an ally who could offer the client's nephew a job. Nor did the exchange necessarily occur immediately; a service now might well be returned only later. Renaissance Italians never knew when they would need a favor. They thus found it prudent to cultivate connections and store up claims against the next opportunity or misfortune. In some circumstances, the law defined the nature of affiliations and their obligations, but typically these exchanges lacked the precision and the guarantees of formal contract. Indeed, one strength of this way of dealing was its flexibility. Yet these solidarities were vulnerable as well as important. Therefore, one invested not only effort and material assets, but also feelings. As people pursued their practical ends, they also expressed their commitments, bolstered their claims, or veiled their self-interest in the language of strongly felt loyalty and love.[1]

## FAMILIES

Family was the primary solidarity. One was born into a family; one could not choose to join or opt out. Family must be understood both as a general institution, hedged by laws and customs that gave it common features, and as particular groupings of people, whose configurations and dealings with one another varied hugely. In an environment where few could make their way from rags to riches on their own and public institutions offered little consistent support, people had to rely heavily on their families for the means to survive, get on in the world, and defend themselves from physical or other assault. More than in modern society, the Renaissance family met a comprehensive array of human needs: material and economic, social and political, personal and psychological.[2]

As the central structure that mediated between people and the larger world, the family both provided essential benefits and made heavy demands. On the one hand, family was the major conduit for life-sustaining resources of many kinds. It controlled the property that purchased shelter, food, and other necessities and provided the capital underpinning economic activity. For many, the family also taught the skills on which a living depended. Social status, reputation, and connections passed through the family, as did political rights and alliances. On the other hand, family could deliver these goods and services only with the compliance of its members. Thus, people had to subordinate themselves to the group and to obey and cooperate with its leadership. They had to accept responsibility for others, often at the expense of their own appetites or inclinations. Like its modern counterpart, but with its possibilities and circumstances set very differently, the Renaissance family was the site of complex, subtle negotiations to balance the needs of each member against the stability of the whole.

In this environment where family loomed larger than most other institutions, it mattered that bigger and more powerful families had greater worldly assets. A family with many resources—material, social, political, educational, and honorific—had more to give its members, and they in turn had stronger motives to maintain their ties. For the same reason, that family could make heavier demands, impose stronger discipline, and mobilize more effort to enhance the collective well-being. Thus, it was among the rich, and especially among nobles and patricians, that one finds the great, many-branched families that figure prominently in Italian politics and culture of the period. Such families could sustain the cohesion necessary to carry on the factional struggles that consumed many cities in the early Renaissance.

Further down the scale of privilege and wealth, fewer assets meant more vulnerability and typically smaller and often fragmented families. Death often came sooner and more disruptively to families that were economically fragile. Even short of death, too little land or food to provide for everyone was more likely to break up families of the poor, through migration and abandonment. Nevertheless, among ordinary country folk, circumstances might keep some families working in bigger groups. Some larger peasant households held together because their capacity to deliver a lot of labor improved their opportunities to secure contracts for land. Elsewhere, self-defense during feuds reinforced the need for kin solidarity.

In Renaissance Italy, many families were highly self-conscious about their collective, public face. They in-    **Family Identities** vested heavily in marking themselves out and in cultivating the respect of others. While the elite were especially energetic in this domain and had more means to dedicate to the project, the less privileged were also keen to protect familial honor. In public dealings, families identified themselves to the ear and the eye. The family names that in modern European cultures routinely pass from generation to generation were current only in some parts of Renaissance society. Lineages of nobles and patricians proudly called themselves by these collec-

tive names, often, though not always, ending in the "i" of the Italian
plural: Grimaldi, Medici, Orsini, Contarini, but also Sforza, Doria,
Caracciolo. Many ordinary Italians, however, continued to use either patronymics or tags built on occupation, place of origin, or nicknames. Thus,
in daily life the many men called "Giovanni" were distinguished by
phrases like, "son of Bernardo" or "the tailor" or "the Neapolitan" or
"the Left-handed." Married women were generally known as the "wife
of So-and-so" (see Chapter 11). Yet, although such names did not em-
phasize collective family identities, people knew where they and others
belonged.

Families also marked their identities in public space. Family was
closely linked to the properties it owned and occupied. In the city, the
house, or *casa*, with its facade on the street was a highly visible site of
family honor. Wealthy families would also reach out into other spaces
to claim recognition. The decoration of a tomb or chapel in the local
church was a favored investment. Other charitable endowments for public use, such as fountains, might bear a family name or shield. Those
with truly aristocratic ambitions sometimes sent their liveried servants
about town, trumpeting the family colors on their bodies.

**Who Is Family?**   *Family* was a term with many meanings—some stretching quite far across space and time—and the compo-
sition of a family depended on which sense of the term
was in play. On the one hand, *family* denoted groups of people bound
by chains of biological continuity, described metaphorically as blood,
and by marriage. These ties defined kin. On the other hand, *famiglia* in
Renaissance Italian also referred to a household or group that lived, and
often worked, together. In this meaning, servants, dependent workers,
or a powerful man's entourage, even where they bore no kinship to their
master, were also members of the "family." Thus, in spatial terms, *family*
might mean, quite narrowly, all those who shared a residence or, very
broadly, those linked by kinship but living in many different places. For
many purposes, the family that mattered for everyday life was the group
that lived together. But from time to time, a ceremony, a tragedy, an
ambition would lead Italians to call on the more scattered family to observe or assist.

The co-resident family could take a number of forms. Many people
lived in a nuclear family, the basic unit of a married couple and their
children. This simple unit nonetheless varied greatly, as the life cycle
and high mortality did their work. A married couple lived alone before
children were born and after they had moved out or died. Or one widowed parent carried on raising the offspring. Often servants and sometimes an unattached relative or boarder filled out a nuclear household.
There were also households structured on a more complex core of kin.
Families where several generations lived together did occur, although

the heavy death toll made this fairly brief and rare. In the city, for example, aging parents often lodged with one of their adult children. In the country, patterns of land tenure reinforced this practice. The benefits of consolidating agricultural labor also underlay another sort of extended household, in which siblings, generally brothers, would co-reside with their wives and children. Demographic and economic circumstances could cause a family's resident composition to shift over time between nuclear and extended forms.

Such large and complex families were most characteristic among the upper ranks of society. Patricians often created elaborate households extending both vertically across generations and laterally among siblings and incorporating even some more distant relatives without homes of their own. In cities such as Genoa, Florence, and Naples, networks of such households with shared lineage would occupy nearby buildings and dominate the neighborhood. Keeping these complicated families going cost money and effort, but the economic and political advantages paid off. Note, though, that these powerful families did not mirror the strategies of most people of the time.

Family also meant people linked through time, to past and future. A family had its own life cycle; its living membership changed as the parental generation aged and died and as the children matured and in turn produced their own offspring. As souls and memories, the dead remained part of the family, acknowledged in memorial rites and invoked by the living as they plotted family strategies. This sense of family underlay lineage, the institution that linked people, especially males, across generations. Thus, for Renaissance Italians, name, property, and reputation passed from ancestors (including, not infrequently, imaginary ones) to grandfather to father to son and on down. Men claimed the achievements of their ancestors to enhance their own honor and enjoined their descendants to remember, preserve, and live up to the family's tradition. So, too, disgrace marred not just an individual's reputation but that of his sons. The family memoirs, or *ricordanze*, written by Renaissance Florentines and others reflected the potent impulse to create such a sense of family history. So did the half-fantastical genealogies that claimed to trace a bloodline back to the Caesars or the Trojan War. These attitudes flourished among the well-born, those who had most to crow about, but even ordinary Italian men knew they belonged to a line. Thus, some trailed a chain of patronymics three or four generations long. "I, Giorgio di Pietro di Antonio di Pietro," might begin a legal deposition.[3]

Because it provided essential resources and protection, the family played host to many of the key power relations in life. Each household had a head, usually the senior male, cast in the roles of husband, father, and master. When no adult man was available, women sometimes stepped in. The head

**Family Dynamics**

enjoyed full authority over all the household's dependents: younger men, women, children, servants, and any others there. The law did place some curbs. If a man's wife failed in her duties or proper submission, for example, he could beat her—but not too much. With this legitimate power came responsibility—the obligation to care for the moral and economic well-being of all family members. The head had to administer property and other assets so that everyone got his or her present and future due. Children were entitled not only to food and shelter, but also to training and a start in life. For city boys, that might mean an apprenticeship, a role in the family business, or start-up capital for their own enterprise; in the country, land was the key. For a girl, parents had to pay out a dowry so she could marry or enter a nunnery, or, if they could not, at least to help her to find a place in, for example, domestic service, to earn money toward her future. Widowed wives were owed their dowries back, to pay their keep. Decisions to attain these goals belonged to the head of the family, but he had to balance many competing interests, as all the others lobbied for their own concerns.

Central to family dynamics was property—its administration and distribution. A family's material assets, fundamental to the well-being of all members, passed from generation to generation through legal and customary arrangements. The bulk of property followed blood, but will makers could make some bequests according to their own judgments and affections. By Italian law, inheritance was partible, that is, divided among all eligible descendants, and not concentrated in the hands of a single heir, as was the practice in some other countries at the time. This pattern recognized the claims of all offspring but risked fragmenting resources so that nobody got enough to live on. Families therefore developed strategies aimed at balancing two imperatives: providing something for everyone and keeping together a patrimony capable of sustaining position and honor.

A principal focus of these calculations was marriage. From the perspective of the family's property and reputation, marriage of offspring had both great benefits and substantial costs. First, marriage was the only legitimate means to secure women's honor and extend the family into the next generation. But successful reproduction multiplied claims on family resources. Second, marriage created links with other families through which to consolidate assets, both property and social and political connections. But such links went both ways, and families expected not only to receive but also to pay out. To make a match, both families had to commit material resources, so that the new couple had a base for supporting themselves and their soon-anticipated children. In supplying the dowry, however, the bride's family made the larger outlay (see Chapter 11). Daughters therefore were seen as a burden, since the assets they carried away were hefty and went to benefit another lineage. Incompletely symmetrical, marital exchanges were also slow to balance, because transmission of property to sons and to daughters had different timing in the life cycle: dowry coincided with a girl's marriage and a son's inheritance only with his father's death. Legal doctrine said that dowered women had no further claim on their fathers' estates. But the family who had children of both genders to marry off could expect a flow both out and in. Marrying off children thus extended the family's connections and secured its honor, but at a price.[4]

A family that felt financially pressed, as many did, tried to find cheaper ways to provide for some of their children, both daughters and sons. Parents wanted alternatives to the expenses of marriage. For the well-off, the church provided one outlet. Convents did require dowries, but smaller ones. Many surplus daughters went off to live as nuns. Some communities became little more than respectable repositories for not especially pious women, who did not want to be there. Other girls, however, particularly those socialized from childhood in convents, chose the religious life willingly. A few even knew profound spiritual vocations. Rather than being forced to take the veil, daughters described in saints' lives sometimes fought their families for permission to take Christ as their bridegroom. Sons could make useful and occasionally brilliant careers as clerics; to aim for the ecclesiastical top, however, usually required a heavy investment. Similar money problems troubled less affluent families, who also sent their children off, usually unmarried, to find work for themselves. Clearly, when, how, and in what form family members were to take their share of the patrimony were questions crucial to family dynamics. Decisions about who would marry and who would not flowed from the overall strategy for the family as a group. Nevertheless, dependents could lobby the family's head to try to shape their fate. Competing requests, pleas, suggestions, and resistances in response to plans about property and the future were central to family life.

Renaissance Italians' preoccupation with property in family relations seems foreign, indeed mercenary, to modern observers taught to see romance as the core of marriage and love as the great domestic bond. Italian habits of expression about family seem often to confirm this impression that they lacked sentiment. For example, the diary of the Florentine merchant, Gregorio Dati, recorded births, deaths, commercial investments, and amounts of dowries, but spent few words on his affection for his twenty-six children. The quality of parental love for children, in particular, has been the subject of much historical debate (see Chapter 11). In courtship, with survival at stake, couples probably did have to put material needs first. Certainly the psychological climate of Renaissance families differed from our own. Weaker control over many aspects of the environment must have influenced the culture and values of the times. Nevertheless, the divergence between their emotional expectations and ours probably amounted more to an altered balance of concerns than to a radical difference in kinds of feelings. We too pick our spouses with attention to social status and economic prospects, even though that is not what we talk most about. And Renaissance people clearly felt love and loyalty toward their families, even though the language of affection did not usually predominate. And a host of other feelings—jealousy, gratitude, anger, delight, anxiety, and so on—also colored familial relations. All in all, because emotions are hard to trace, we should take care not to underestimate their role in everyday Renaissance lives.

**Family Relationships**

A closer look at the central family relationships—of husbands and wives, and of parents and children—illustrates their complexity. Husbands wielded undisputed authority over their spouses, as over children and servants. Commentaries on optimal family life, written by elite men, placed obedience and artful submission among the primary virtues of married women. The fifteenth-century Venetian patrician Francesco Barbaro, for example, wrote in the humanist tradition a book, *On Wifely Duties*; although admired perhaps more for its style, replete with classical examples, than for its rather abstract content, this treatise was widely read. In it Barbaro laid much responsibility for marital harmony on wives' docility, although he also acknowledged the frequent hardships of their lot:

Therefore, there are three things that, if they are diligently observed by a wife, will make a marriage praiseworthy and admirable: love for her husband, modesty of life, and diligent and complete care in domestic matters. . . . I want to say something about the faculty of obedience, which is her master and companion, because nothing is more important, nothing greater can be demanded of a wife than this. . . .

Cyrus, that great man and emperor, used to tell his troops that if the enemy advanced making a great noise, they should withstand the assault in silence, but if the enemy approached silently, then his men should go into battle with great noise and clamor. I would give the same advice to wives. If a husband, excited to anger, should scold you more than your ears are accustomed to hear, tolerate his wrath silently. But if he had been struck silent by a fit of depression, you should address him with sweet and suitable words, encourage, console, amuse, and humor him. Those who work with elephants do not wear white clothes, and those who work with wild bulls are right not to wear red; for those beasts are made ever more ferocious by those colors. . . . Wives ought to observe the same thing; if, indeed, a particular dress is offensive to a husband, then we advise them not to wear it, so that they do not give affront to their husbands, with whom they ought to live peacefully and pleasantly. I think that ear guards . . . are far more necessary for wives than for wrestlers, for the ears of the latter are subject only to blows, but indeed the former are subject to bills of repudiation accompanied by deep humiliation.[5]

Gathering at the hearth. [Bertarelli: Missale]

This prescriptive literature on marriage urged the well-born husband to teach his new wife how to manage the household and to please him. In the Florentine Leon Battista Alberti's famous dialogue *On the Family*, one fictional character gave this account of his experience:

After my wife had been settled in my house for a few days, and after her first pangs of longing for her mother and family began to fade, I took her by the hand and showed her around the whole house. I explained that the loft was the place for grain and that the stores of wine and wood were kept in the cellar. I showed her where things needed for the table were kept, and so on through the whole house. . . . Then we returned to my room and, having locked the door, I showed her my treasures, silver, tapestry, garments, jewels, and where each thing had its place. . . . I wanted none of my precious things to be hidden from my wife. I opened to her all my household treasures, unfolded them, and showed them to her. Only my books and records [documents] and those of my ancestors did I determine to keep well sealed both then and thereafter. These my wife not only could not read, she could not even lay hands on them.

. . . I made it a rule never to speak with her of anything but household matters or questions of conduct, or of the children. Of these matters I spoke a good deal to her. From what I said, and by answering me and discussing with me, she learned the principles she required and how to apply them. I did this . . . in order to make it impossible for her to enter into discussion with me concerning my more important and private affairs.[6]

We must remember that these colorful descriptions portray some men's self-comforting ideals, not the loose ends of untidy reality. Nevertheless, in such families, husbands and wives evidently lived quite separate lives. This image of the man's molding the woman as fresh clay must have seemed especially credible when, as among the Florentine patricians, older men wed quite young women. The age gap reinforced the legal and customary hierarchy of marital relations.

Not only was the wife subordinate; she was also insecure for, especially among high-ranking families, as the daughter of another lineage, she was a perpetual outsider in her husband's home. Tension about where, in the crunch, her loyalties lay could haunt a marriage. On the other hand, testamentary evidence of husbands' appointing their wives to execute their wills and oversee the children and the inheritance suggests a strong sense of common goals and mutual confidence. A careful, thoughtful woman could acquire respect and influence in her household. A matron who carried out her housewifely duties, bore children, lived honorably and discreetly, and attended to the interests of her husband's family deserved her spouse's ear. Furthermore, the dowry she had brought and her links to her natal family, especially where both were weighty, added to her credibility. The ideal for marital relations did not call for cozy companionship; still, inequalities were softened by mutual responsibility and common concern.

Further down the social scale, it is much harder to see clearly how spouses dealt with one another. While, among the working classes, male and female domains of activity were distinct, both members of the couple shared an interest in the smooth running of the family and often also of its collective enterprise. Work more often shared and a smaller age gap between husbands and wives may have fostered less distant, more symmetrical relationships.

Relations between parents and children were also strongly hierarchical. Sons and daughters owed deference as youngsters and even as adults. Fathers enforced their authority through their open or niggardly hand on the property on which the offspring depended for their futures. Women, when distributing property, as through wills, did the same, although they might be more generous to dependents disadvantaged by patrilineal claims. Poor parents who had little to pass on had less control; their children were likely to head off into the world to fend for themselves. Yet all this maneuvering around money and goods did not preclude deep sentimental ties as well. To the Renaissance mind, the fear and obedience that progeny owed their parents did not inhibit filial love. And fathers and mothers reciprocated. Their emotions most often become visible in expressions of grief over the death of a beloved child. Parents did not, however, share the modern obligation to love all their children equally. Favoritism was indeed for them a mark of authentic feelings.

Although, in a sense, families shed their excess daughters into nunneries, this step did not amount to abandonment. As with marriage, here too a daughter's persistent sense of lineage loyalty was often strong. This interest was reciprocated; although a nun remained enclosed for life, her kin could visit her, and often did, passing news and gifts of food and clothing through the cloister grill in the parlor. Wealthy families often patronized favorite religious houses, regularly depositing their women there as nuns or pensioners, befriending other sisters, leaving legacies, storing valuables in the house, and hoping to have an abbess in the family. The nuns themselves remembered their own ties and often followed affairs of kin with keen interest. At the same time, the nunnery took on some of the traits of a surrogate family for all its denizens; the abbess functioned as a "mother (superior)" for her "daughters," the "sisters" in the house. While male monasteries did not so regularly serve as honorable depositories for extra sons, these institutions used the same familial vocabulary and ideology.[7]

Family relationships thus were tenacious. So central was family to the structure of society that Italians often remembered and respected its claims no matter where their lives took them. Nevertheless, they had to balance their obligations to their kin with those to other groups.

## PATRONS AND CLIENTS

Another solidarity, of lesser impact than family, that helped Renaissance people live their lives were bonds between patrons and clients. Patrons had resources that enabled them to offer protection and assistance to less advantaged people, their clients, in return for services and loyalty. Like family, this alliance was built on both hierarchy and reciprocity of obligations. Unlike family, it was voluntary. While long habits, even lasting decades, sometimes linked patrons and clients over generations, it took choice by individuals—or by institutions—to enter into and sustain this kind of relationship. Although patrons and clients might draw up legal papers for specific projects, these associations were not contractual. Rather, they were typically couched in periodic, often flamboyant protestations of mutual loyalty and concern.

Patron-client ties were conveniently flexible. The two parties cultivated the relationship expecting eventual but imprecise mutual benefit. Often a continuing connection might vary in intensity as needs came and went. Both sides would gain, but not necessarily at the same moment. Reciprocation could come later, and in different form. Furthermore, these alliances were not exclusive. Not only might a patron have many clients, but one client might well serve several patrons. Informal networks sometimes arose, for one person's client might be another's patron, and co-clients could make common cause. At the same time these alliances were fluid and liable to rivalry and rupture. Thus, it was important to nurture those bonds that one wanted to maintain; they could not be taken for granted.

The core was an exchange between a well-placed patron and a more lowly client. The hierarchical difference was relative. The privileged could be clients of their own superiors, and rather modest folk could patronize those even further below. The advantages for the client were obvious; these vertical ties provided access to protection, help with problems, and opportunities for work and preferment. Less evident to modern eyes than to the patron were the gifts, skills, labor, solicitude, admiration, and support that the client had to offer. Some clients provided a reservoir of political or military force that a patron could rally when needed. Others supplied useful gifts or money for spendthrift patrons strapped for cash. Still others had connections in corners of society that an elite man could not know. In other ways clients enhanced the prestige of their patrons. To have as clients men and women who earned honor by their own achievements flattered the vanity of their superiors. Likewise, being seen to do service to one's deserving dependents reflected well on one. Thus, for both parties, such vertical bonds enlarged the resources at hand.

Up and down the social scale, patron-client relationships had a variety of goals. One was to promote business arrangements inside ongoing patronage links. For example, patrons commissioned works from artists and architects. There might be a detailed contract spelling out what the creator would make, with what materials, how soon, and for what pay. This agreement often formed only part of a broader alliance between the two in which the artist visited, advised, and flattered the patron, while the patron entertained, encouraged, chided, defended, as well as paid his protégé. Many other relationships might assume something of this model. Thus, an army was a veritable pyramid of patronage, where men served loyally not the state, but the persons of their leaders. Commanders advanced their favorite captains, and captains courted loyal officers with gifts and protection, feeding them well at table and, not rarely, conniving with them to defraud the state of pay to phantom infantry on their padded muster rolls. Patronage also appeared in the realm of charity and worship. Institutions serving the needy dealt with their charges— the sick, orphans, dowerless girls—as clients and expected reciprocation in prayers and gratitude. And, very commonly, people alone or in groups went as clients to propitiate and beg aid from patron saints. The suppliants petitioned particular holy protectors, with whom they cultivated personal ties, for help in exchange for gifts, praise, and thanks.[8]

## OTHER SOLIDARITIES

**Friends and Enemies**
Alongside the hierarchical relationships of family and patronage, Renaissance people used a range of other, more egalitarian solidarities. Friendship, especially for high-status Italian men, produced an ambiguous tension between idealistic altruism and pragmatic interest. In humanist writing echoing the values of the ancients, friendships between adult men were

sometimes hailed as the most reliable and candid of human ties. At the same time, friendships often linked more and less powerful men, sometimes older and younger men, in ways that served mutually beneficial social aims. So, a patrician Florentine, Giovanni Morelli, writing instructions for his sons advocated the careful cultivation of "friends" as a defense against the hazards of public life. There friendship looked not so different from clientage, but preserved a more egalitarian ethos.

For most ordinary people, however, friendship was one of the looser of peer alliances. These connections were more modest in their claims and benefits, but at critical moments their support could be valuable. Friendship frequently grew out of proximity and common experience. Among the often mobile population of cities, friends were not necessarily of long standing. While intellectuals wrote of friendship as a high philosophical or spiritual meeting of minds, for most ordinary Italians a friend was someone whom you worked or lived beside, with whom you sometimes shared the routines of daily life (meals, chat, recreation, even beds), and on whom you called for occasional service. Friends might stand you to food or drink, lend you clothing, or store goods; they might take you in if the police were chasing you or your husband had thrown you out. Before the law, they might bear witness to your contracts, stand surety for your obligations, or baldly perjure themselves on your behalf in court. In the street they might stand up for you in a fight or counter nasty gossip. Nevertheless, there was no clear code defining what friends ought to do for one another. In the world where disorder was endemic, family fragile, and governance erratic, friends often were the people who were there. You hoped they would come through when you needed them.[9]

Although friendship imposed no specific obligations, enmity, its recognized opposite, had sharper boundaries and better-defined rituals. It constituted a kind of antisolidarity. An enemy was someone with whom you shared nothing, not even words. Not to be literally on speaking terms was one of the characteristic, more benign expressions of antagonism. More generally, enemies could be expected to do you harm whenever possible. All the while they were not speaking to you, their words did injury as they bad-mouthed you to all and sundry and tattled to the authorities on your spied-out lapses. At other times, enemies engaged in slanging matches, which often sparked violence. Men lashed out with rocks, knives, swords, and guns. Women scratched, pulled hair, and wielded broomsticks. Sometimes such hostilities persisted for months or years, as feuds. Enmity was costly, however, and means of resolution were available. With time, as courts became more accessible, a lawsuit was one recourse; in less institutionalized settings, the private negotiation of a peace was a recognized way to reconcile enemies. Sealed with a kiss, and wine or cake or a common meal and sometimes with a no-

Party in a wine cellar. [Tempesta]

tarized document, a peace ritually marked the end of the exchange of injuries.

The same associative habits that sustained family, patronage, friendship, and enmity also fostered militant networks we call factions. In some cities, such coalitions arose, to struggle by fair means and foul for dominance. At times, their conflicts could reduce a town to endemic civil war or end in the exile of whole alliances. At other times, factions functioned more benignly as semilegitimate political parties and benevolent associations.

**Compatriots and Neighbors**
The choice of friends was often the work of happenstance, as the accidents of life and work threw people together. Other alliances grew out of shared geography. Thus, common birthplace or residence created another sort of loose, structurally egalitarian association to which Italians might turn for support. Ties to region, city, or neighborhood, generally informal, did not obligate compatriots to demanding mutual service. But sometimes these links did shape behavior. In particular, people felt and used geographical bonds when away from home. Thus, migrants would often form communities with their *paesani* (fellow townsmen), and travelers, in a foreign town, would seek them out for lodgings, company,

and help. Thus, in Italy or abroad, Genoese or Neapolitans would band together to live, socialize, do business, and defend themselves. As in the goldsmith Benvenuto Cellini's experience, an attack on a Florentine in Rome rallied other Florentines to fight. Boundaries between territories also invited dramatic enactments of local patriotism. Wars to expand borders were the most serious such expressions. These were mirrored in less harmful ritualized competitions such as the district-based horse races of the Palio in Siena or the massed battles between the youths of different neighborhoods in Venice, Pisa, and other towns.

Among the solidarities of peers available to Renaissance Italians, the most institutionalized were corporate **Confraternities** brotherhoods. Guilds of merchants or artisans in a given trade, such as silk dealers or shoemakers, were one sort. Typically these had a formal structure, with foundation statute, by-laws, and governing board selected from the membership. To practice a guild trade in a town, one had to be admitted to the brotherhood. Entry depended on qualification and a vote of admission. Once admitted, brothers expected to treat one another more or less as equals. The guilds promoted good business; they worked to ensure fair practices and good standards, defended against outside competition, and assisted members and their families.

Confraternities were similar in structure but with a religious focus. Such congregations gathered laity and clergy. Many were male, some female or mixed. These organizations sometimes assembled age-mates, as did the boys' confraternities in Florence (see Chapter 11). Membership in brotherhoods was voluntary, although there might be social pressure. Some confraternities paralleled guilds, drawing their membership from a trade; others assembled people who shared a parish or a particular devotion. Characteristically, confraternities sponsored regular gatherings for prayer and, on suitable occasions, processions and special celebrations. They also often devoted themselves to holy charity, ministering to the welfare of needy members or outsiders. Confraternities multiplied in Renaissance cities, drawing their support from a broad spectrum of society. Among the most flamboyant were the hooded flagellants who on Good Friday and other holidays beat themselves through the streets as penance on behalf of all sinners. Many confraternities expressed their religious fervor in less gory fashion by singing psalm cycles.[10]

Those who lived on the margins of society had fewer opportunities to join solidarities. Strolling players, pros- **Solidarities on** titutes, vagabonds, thieves, rural brigands, hit-men, and **the Margins of** their like haunted the social edges because of mobility, **Society** poverty, ill repute, and legal persecution. For all these reasons, their families were often fragmented and far. Such persons lacked the trade, money, respectability, juridical rights, or stable local ties to join most formal organizations. They could sometimes enter into clientele relationships, but what they had to offer to patrons, whether delightful or sinister, usually had to be discreetly veiled. Exposure threw them back on one another; common vulnerability urged cooperation. They relied on their own subcultures, convening with their peers over food and wine to share jokes, lore, news, and support. As outsiders and, sometimes, criminals, such persons could seldom use the state with its courts and contracts to arbitrate and monitor their dealings. Instead, solemn oaths of loyalty, gift giving, reciprocal debt, and shared risks and secrets were their only bond. In the absence of a stable internal polity, these devices were fallible; betrayal was a constant danger.

## CONCLUSION

Renaissance Italians had a range of solidarities on whom they depended for the support that public institutions and private enterprise did not provide. Some, notably the all-important family, were not a matter of choice. Most others, however, whether hierarchical or egalitarian, because elective, required cultivation. Most Italians belonged to several such groups, for diverse purposes. Membership was far from random, for solidarities often lined up and reinforced one another. Two kinsmen might well belong to the same guild, confraternity, religious house, or outlaw band. Italians were often asked to serve as godparents to their clients, neighbors, or other allies. Thus, each solidarity easily intersected many others. For each Renaissance person, living meant negotiating a path through the sometimes convergent, sometimes competing claims of many solidarities. All transactions required nimble, conscious calculations about the obligations, needs, and risks of family, patrons, friends, faction members, neighbors, ritual kin, and other associates. Renaissance individualism, such as it was, was trammeled in collective obligations.

## NOTES

1. Studies that highlight various solidarities include Richard C. Trexler, *Public Life in Renaissance Florence* (New York: Academic Press, 1980) and Dennis Romano, *Patricians and Popolani* (Baltimore: Johns Hopkins University Press, 1987).

2. On family in general, see, for example, besides works in note 1: Stanley Chojnacki, *Women and Men in Renaissance Venice* (Baltimore: Johns Hopkins University Press, 2000); David Herlihy and Christiane Klapisch-Zuber, *Tuscans and Their Families* (New Haven: Yale University Press, 1985); Francis Kent, *Household and Lineage in Renaissance Florence* (Princeton: Princeton University Press, 1977); James Grubb, *Provincial Families of the Renaissance: Private and Public Life in the Veneto* (Baltimore: Johns Hopkins University Press, 1996); Francesco Benigno, "The Southern Italian Family in the Early Modern Period," *Continuity and Change* 4:1 (1989), 165–194. For a famous Renaissance treatise, see Leon Battista Alberti,

*The Family in Renaissance Florence*, trans. R. Watkins (Columbia: University of South Carolina Press, 1969).

3. On genealogies, see "Diary of Buonaccorso Pitti" in Gene Brucker, *Two Memoirs of Renaissance Florence* (Prospect Heights, IL: Waveland Press, 1967), 19–22, and Benvenuto Cellini, *Autobiography*, trans. G. Bull (Harmondsworth: Penguin, 1998), 2–5.

4. On dowries and wedding exchanges, see Diane Owen Hughes, "From Brideprice to Dowry in Mediterranean Europe," in *The Marriage Bargain: Women and Dowries in European History*, ed. M. Kaplan (New York: Harrington Park Press, 1985), 13–58; Christiane Klapisch-Zuber, "The Griselda Complex: Dowry and Marriage Gifts in the Quattrocento," in *Women, Family and Ritual in Renaissance Italy* (Chicago: University of Chicago Press, 1985), 213–246; Chojnacki, *Women and Men*.

5. Francesco Barbaro, *On Wifely Duties*, excerpted in *Civilization of the Italian Renaissance*, ed. K. Bartlett (Lexington, MA: D. C. Heath, 1992), 142.

6. Alberti, *The Family in Renaissance Florence*, 208–209.

7. On nuns, see the essays by Daniel Bornstein and Gabriella Zarri in *Gender and Society in Renaissance Italy*, ed. Judith C. Brown and Robert C. Davis (London: Longman, 1998), 173–92, 193–212; Chojnacki, *Women and Men*, 37–42; and the more specialized essays in *Women and Religion in Medieval and Renaissance Italy*, ed. D. Bornstein and R. Rusconi (Chicago: University of Chicago Press, 1996). Trexler, *Public Life*, 188–196, quotes Renaissance accounts of the ritual lives of friars and nuns.

8. On patrons and clients, see Trexler, *Public Life*, 168–172, and Joanne Ferraro, *Family and Public Life in Brescia, 1580–1650* (Cambridge: Cambridge University Press, 1993), 143–148. Cellini, *Autobiography*, 75–83, 98–113, 202–204, and elsewhere illustrates the complicated exchanges between patron and servitor.

9. On friendship, see Trexler, *Public Life*, chap. 4, and Romano, *Patricians and Popolani*, chap. 6.

10. On confraternities, see Ronald Weissman, *Ritual Brotherhood in Renaissance Florence* (New York: Academic Press, 1982); Christopher Black, *Italian Confraternities in the Sixteenth Century* (Cambridge: Cambridge University Press, 1989); Brian Pullan, *Rich and Poor in Renaissance Venice* (Oxford: Blackwell, 1971).

# 5

# Hierarchies

Like inhabitants of any complex environment, Renaissance Italians had a social place that was far from simple. Locus had many aspects—some steady, others labile. Therefore, like people anywhere else, Italians invested heavily in negotiating and declaring their own positions and in decoding, acknowledging, and modifying those of others. In their very theatrical culture, self-presentation was one of life's great enterprises. In everyday life, central to self-presentation was precedence: where did one stand on the ladder of prestige? Proclaiming, defining, and contesting the social hierarchy was a main concern of most institutions, groups, and persons and, all in all, a chief activity of the Italian world.

Renaissance Italians were not alone in their interest in who comes first; most societies have their pecking orders and habits of deference. We recognize the same appetite in our own public world, with its sports championships, awards ceremonies, hit parades, best-seller lists, grant competitions, and well-publicized fat salaries. Nevertheless, profound ideological differences distinguish our world from the Renaissance. Almost all the great modern political revolutions—the English of 1642, the American of 1776, the French of 1789, and those that followed—have exalted an ideal of equality. The very premise of working democracy—one vote per head—posits that each elector is as good as the next. This modern premise, on second glance, is a transparent polite fiction, for clearly some voters are more intelligent, better informed, more responsible than others. Nevertheless, despite some doctrines to the contrary, there is today a deeply seated general egalitarian disposition; even if disparately talented, we all deserve an equal voice and an equal chance. To early modern Europeans, such a notion would have seemed grotesque and unnatural.

Renaissance Italians took inequality for granted. To them, it was self-evident, on all sorts of grounds, that the world was arrayed in hierarchies. There were deep cosmic and holy reasons that some people were better or stronger than others; inequality was an expression of the ordered nature of the universe. In their eyes, hierarchy had deep political, legal, and ethical implications; it brought both privileges and responsibilities.

## CULTURAL ROOTS

This vision of the universe traced back to Greek philosophy, especially to Plato and his many followers. In Christianized form, its influence pervaded most medieval and Renaissance thought. Religion and philosophy agreed that God had built an ordered world. The cosmos, composed of four elements, ascended from lowly, heavy earth, through ever nobler spheres of water and air, to the exalted realm of fire, dwelling place of the stars. The metals ascended from base lead to noble gold. The order of beasts climbed from worms and slugs to lions and eagles. Among body fluids, hot blood lorded it over chilly phlegm and the two biles (yellow and black). (See Chapter 14.) In the moral realm, the virtues had their order and, of course, in the general scheme of things, "man" (and woman, subsumed under "homo") was suspended midway between the beasts and the angels, who lodged under God. This hierarchic vision of the world, so foreign to modern habits of analysis, shaped almost every aspect of the high culture of the Renaissance, from poetry and painting to architecture and medicine. It spilled over quite naturally into political theory and helped justify the major institutions inherited from the Middle Ages—lordship, kingship, the Latin church, all of which stressed authority and subordination.

All these theories of an ordered, hierarchic world flourished in medieval Europe as religious, social, and political ideals. They offered a model not only for what was, but especially for what ought to be. They thus served a precious function in a world that in reality was often very far from orderly. Order and hierarchy were also precious in the Italian city-states, where factions and warring quarrels could torment a town. The cities of the North and Center had passed through a democratic phase in which a body of active citizens had shared in governance. Although most cities before the Renaissance fell under the control of lords and princes, in others democratic practices and principles survived. In either case, regimes wrapped themselves in images of order as a bulwark of princely authority or citizen cohesion, against subversion and party strife. Our cultural ancestors, coping with political chaos, sought good order in hierarchy, while we, luxuriating in a more orderly but in fact profoundly unequal world, aspire instead to realize our imperfectly attainable egalitarian ideals. The whole Renaissance hierarchy of privileges had an aura; it was itself prestigious, natural, right, and holy, and thus far less often questioned or challenged than are today's rankings.

Not only did the Renaissance inherit hierarchic visions; it also accentuated them. Everywhere in Italy between 1400 and 1600, a process of aristocratization sharpened social distinctions, amplifying their expression and hampering access to the top. The vestiges of democratic ideals faded, and increasingly the expression of hierarchy occupied the intellectual and artistic energies of Italians. At the same time, the Catholic church, in response to the Protestant Reformation, reaffirmed its holiness, prestige, and power. Protestants, translating Bible and liturgy from Latin into common speech and demoting the clergy by denying their sacramental powers, had raised up instead the congregation of all the faithful. In response, the Catholic church, most comprehensively through the major reforming council held at Trent (1545–63), reaffirmed the sacrality, charisma, and authority of priests and prelates.

There is another difference between Renaissance and modern attitudes toward inequality; the earlier age was much readier to accept and trumpet inherited privileges and places. Status was ascribed rather than achieved, as sociology would say. Our age, by contrast, emphasizes achievement and looks askance at unearned prerogatives. It is true that men and women in the Renaissance could sometimes ascend the ladders of power, wealth, and prestige by their own merits, but birth and inheritance often counted for much more, and personal efforts usually availed far less, than in our more mobile modern world.

Although the notion of hierarchy was pervasive, it was quite impossible to place all Renaissance Italians on a single ladder of prestige, good for all times and places. Rather, the sense that deference was called for, or that one was among equals, much depended on circumstances, for social place had many components. Glory's calculus was never exact. How did a middle-aged lawyer with a doctorate treat the teenaged son of a minor baron? How did the trusted nurse of a patrician family deal with the farmer who brought chickens to the kitchen? Such ambiguities, in a society devoted to precedence, required alertness to signals and mastery of a rich lore about proper social relations. Much of life therefore was given over to fine adjustments of hierarchic relationships.

Sociology offers a handy formula: three factors—power, wealth, and prestige—determine status. At a closer glance, none of these three was simple in the Renaissance, not even wealth, which came in gloriously many varieties. Possessions not only had cash value; they also often worked as social signs with hierarchic implications. Power and prestige

Mounted hunters of high station and their underling on foot.
[Tempesta]

too had many shapes and shades. The determinants of hierarchic place
were many and came by various routes. Some, like sex, age, and ances-
try, were givens, beyond controlling; others, such as public office or social skill, one could strive for. These latter permitted agency. Let us
survey some of these chief measures of status, all of which bore in subtle
ways on everyday life.

## BIOLOGICAL FACTORS

**Gender**     Maleness and femaleness, traits inborn and fixed, were crucial
to status. Although class was even stronger, gender was a powerful discriminant. Males were destined to rule and to lord it
over females. Men had formal authority, electoral franchise, and full legal
capacity to bear witness, to guarantee, to contract. Females did have legal
rights, but everywhere they were lesser. In church and state, males ruled
and manned all offices. Female power was also real but more often

informal: social, familial, emotional. Women, as agents, made their presence felt by deflecting persons, and sometimes, through them, institutions over which, as females, they lacked statutory authority. In social dealings, women, though outranking class inferiors, were expected to defer to males of their own social class. It is true that courtiers at their games and lovers paying court played at putting ladies on a pedestal; nevertheless, everyone recognized the transparent artificiality of such an inversion of the proper order of the world.

A second determinant of precedence over which Italians had no control was age. Unlike gender, age was conferred not by birth  **Age** but by the luck of survival. Our present era, with its vertiginous pace of change, puts rigid age to pasture and privileges the flexibility of youth. Earlier times, slower in their evolution, more readily turned to their elders for wisdom. Another difference is that we live with a stupendous glut of information, transmitted and stored on paper, film, tape, and electronic circuitry. The Renaissance, when the printing press was new and information scarce and often private, kept far more of its knowledge in oral lore and memories. To treasure older people made pragmatic sense; they were the walking encyclopedias. Furthermore, their scarcity, the result of heavy, often early mortality, enhanced their value. Patterns of ownership and property transmission bolstered the wealth and power, and hence the prestige, of the old, for it was only on inheriting that the next generation laid hands on much property. Where most wealth was inherited, those who made the wills necessarily commanded the attention and respect of their potential beneficiaries. True, some forces tilted against the elderly. Women on their own, usually widows, were often poor; they struggled. In both sexes, geriatric infirmity often caused hardship. And those old men who married young brides had to endure teasing and snide doubts as to the new wife's contentment and fidelity; the restless pretty wife of an aging, flaccid husband was a favorite theme of plays and short stories (see Chapter 12). Also, the few men who doddered on well past their prime confronted popular beliefs lampooning senile folly. Nevertheless, custom often extended to them as well the polite respect that one accorded venerable age.

Although years heaped up in continuous progression, other forms of maturation had their sudden leaps. Rites of passage marked major changes of state and status. Of these, foremost for its effects on social rank and weight was marriage. The clergy, of course, were here a necessary exception; they, however, in priestly ordination and monastic vesture, had their own rites of passage, course of maturation, and ladder of prestige. For other men, marriage meant a kind of emancipation and headship of a house. Women, in marrying, gained domestic clout but only changed masters; for them, what completed the move to adulthood was motherhood, which proved their worth and inducted them into the circle of adult women, their peers and public.

## SOCIAL RANK

**Family**
Especially for the upper classes, by far the paramount determinant of rank was family. Families cohered, owned property,
waged politics, and advanced the welfare of their members;
they also had reputations, which they proclaimed, cultivated, and defended. Everyone could name the better and the best. In many cities,
family membership increasingly conferred the right to election to high
public office. Venice had had such a rule since 1323, when it closed admission to its ruling councils. Such arrangements, still rare in 1400, by
1600 had spread to many cities. Increasingly, elites turned inward for
sociability, working alliances, and marriages. As this aristocratization
spread, the same closure infected the professions. Thus, in many cities,
genealogy rather than merit governed entry into the ruling "colleges" of
notaries, lawyers, or physicians. The hierarchy of families and that of
professions increasingly aligned. Even village elites often had a sense of
caste. The working classes and the poor, however, whose families lacked
material and political resources, looked elsewhere in assigning local
rank. There personal attributes usually weighed more.

**Title**
Closely allied with the hierarchy of families was that of noble
titles. Italians revered the labels that traced back to old feudal
powers of jurisdiction and military command. Emperor (*impera-
tore*) came first, then (in descending order) king (*re*), prince (*principe*),
grand duke (*granduca*), duke (*duca*, or in Venice *doge*), count (*conte*), mar-
quis (*marchese*), down to knight (*cavagliere*). Many knights belonged to
one of the military orders, such as the Knights of Saint John in Malta,
that specialized in anti-Muslim piracy, or the less often bellicose Order
of Santo Stefano of late sixteenth-century Tuscany. There was only one
emperor, the so-called Holy Roman, who actually was the elected ruler
of Germany. His prestige was immense. In Italy, there was only one king,
in Naples, until the 1490s, and then there were none. From then on,
foreign royalty took precedence over all native Italian nobles. Tuscany
had a grand duke, by papal grant, from 1569 on. Dukes were fairly common; some of them were independent rulers, others not. Some of these
noble titles were centuries old, and others recent confections bestowed
by grateful rulers as rewards for political or financial support, or even
sold by penurious monarchs for ready cash. Latter-day titles lacked the
prestige of older ones, no matter how venal these once had been. Nevertheless, a new duke could lord it over a *marchese* of great antiquity, for
title denoted rank, not reputation. Family and title were closely linked
because all such honorific labels, like the powers and privileges that went
with them, passed down the male line by inheritance. Usually they went
to the first-born male, for they did not easily divide, though a father with
several titles might spread them among his sons. An heiress, lacking

brothers, could carry a title with her and pass it on to her descendants. Wives, as consorts, carried female analogues to their husband's titles (for example, *duchessa, contessa*) and commensurate prestige.

Alongside formal titles, Italians reveled in a rich vocabulary for distinguishing grades in the social hierarchy. A man of the titled class was a *gentilhuomo* and a woman a *gentildonna*. As in English, these were descriptive terms, not titles. The meaning was imprecise; anyone who lived nobly, titled or not, could share the glow. One could also call such persons a *signore* and a *signora*; these terms could be also used as independent nouns or as titles attached to Christian names. Note both usages in the expression, "The *signore* is not at home. Shall I call *Signora* Antonia to speak with you instead?" Villagers, speaking to one another, would simply call their masters *i signori* (the lords) or *i padroni* (the masters). In Italy today, modern values have democratized these terms of address, as they have *sir* and *madam* in the English-speaking world. In the Renaissance, however, all these words of feudal origin still denoted real prestige. Indeed, God was addressed as "Signore," as in the English "Lord." In Venice, where titles of nobility were not in use, one called the patricians *clarissimi* or *magnifici*. The Italian middling ranks lacked generic terms but had titles of address. Below *signore* came *messer*, a title in the fifteenth century restricted to lawyers and notaries but in the sixteenth extended to other prosperous urban men. The upper and lower boundaries of *messer* were fluid. The same holds true for the feminine *madonna*, a term less grandiose than *signora*. *Madonna* had a huge range; it attached easily to the mother of God, to nobles' wives and daughters, to those of burghers, and even to the wives of prosperous artisans and to courtesans. Among males, independent artisans, masters of a shop, were called *maestro*. A few professions carried special titles: *dottore* for a holder of a university degree; *colonello* and *capitano* for commanders of troops; *monsignore* for high clergymen, *padre* or *don* for priests, *fra* for friars, *suor* for nuns. The poor lacked titles of address. On the other hand, there was a wealth of terms for underlings. Some expressions sneered, such as *persona vile*. Others, like *poveruomo* (poor-man), both a descriptor and a term of address, resonated with Christian charity: "Oh, poor-man, are you ill?"

As the Renaissance went on, Italian speech increasingly swarmed with other titles signaling prestige. These became pompous substitutes for simple *you*. Medieval Italian, like most other European languages, had two forms of *you*: a singular *tu* reserved for intimates, children, and inferiors, and a respectful plural, *voi*. French still conserves this usage. The late Renaissance replaced this simple binary pattern with an ever more nuanced set of circumlocutions: your lordship, your eminence, your beatitude, your excellency. With these titles, the verb switched to the impersonal third singular: "Does your lordship grant me license to depart?" Giovanni Della Casa in his book of manners, *Galateo*, grumbled in 1555 that a stuffy sycophancy was creeping into speech. Nevertheless, he grudgingly counseled his readers to follow fashion, but moderately:

Let us remember, therefore, that formalities—as I said at the beginning—are not necessary by nature. In fact, one could do without them as our nation did until not so very long ago. But someone else's ills have made us ill with this and many other infirmities. For this reason, once we have obeyed custom and used such permissible lies, anything more is superfluous; however it is impermissible and forbidden to go further than custom allows, because formalities then become an unpleasant and boring thing for men of noble spirit who do not indulge in such games and pretenses.[1]

In his campaign to keep courtesies plain, Della Casa was to lose; the new titles flourished and often endured into the early twentieth century. Their ghost lives on in modern Italian grammar, where the formal *you* (*Lei*) is still, literally, a very awkward *she*, standing in for pompous premodern nouns.

**Office**   Another source of rank, closely allied with social station, was eligibility for public office. In cities, towns, and villages, there was a political class, from which, by nomination, election, and lottery, one picked those who served. Since terms of office were generally short, many had a chance to take their turn. Guilds, professional colleges, confraternities, and learned academies often chose their leaders by these means. Corporations and ruling circles also had internal hierarchies. Eligibility marked social standing, but often it came in degrees; only some could stand for the higher offices. Thus, older men usually ran things. Wealth, reputation, and, not rarely, family might also count. Sometimes only membership in one elite body granted admission to the ballot in another. Thus, the pinnacles of society readily became an interlocking directorate of the privileged.

The clergy too had an acute sense of precedence tied to office. While many preferments came by appointment rather than election, the ambitious politicked hard for posts. Not only were there hierarchies of titles to consider, but also great variations in the wealth and power that came with each specific office. Better to be bishop of a rich see than archbishop of a poor one. Sometimes a high prelate might trade a better title for a better income, though, in general, before the reforms decreed by the mid-sixteenth-century Council of Trent, the aim was to snap up plural benefices by the handful. A man, in such a case, was addressed by his best title and esteemed for the whole collection.

Public office itself was a powerful status marker. Italians strove for election not only for pay and power, but also for glory. Both state and church reveled in splendid pomp. In many cities, each post had its magnificent robes of office. Office-holders, both lay and clerical, paraded on the many solemn occasions on which a polity deployed its majesty for the glory of God and the awe of citizens and visitors.

Great occasions, like the summer feast of Corpus Christi, put all a town's elites on show. All the worthies marched in a great procession, with psalms, crosses, banners, and monstrances for the holy wafer. Elite women watched from windows and doorways, while the lower orders thronged the streets to see the passing show. Men marched in groups— the friars with their brethren, the confraternities of laity, the magistrates, the guilds. Within each group, the best went first. Thus, the whole parade was an ambulatory image of the local hierarchy. The order of a festive march was no joking matter. A newsletter of 1555 reported a typical incident, at the great procession of the *Possesso*, the installation of a new pope as bishop of Rome:

Last Monday the pope went to San Giovanni Laterano accompanied by all the court, and the soldiers, and the Roman people in arms, to take possession of his bishopric according to the ancient ceremonies. A bit of a brawl broke out between Papirio Capizucchi, who was in command of a part of the paid soldiers, and the districts of Ponte and Trastevere, about precedence. Things got really rough, and Papirio was wounded with a pike wound in one thigh, and about 15 or 20 others on one and the other side were hurt, and there would have been a blood-letting if the cavalry had not gotten in between them, and Cardinal Carafa came running at the uproar, dressed in crimson, with his cardinal's hat in his hand, and he got in between them and, with his authority and bearing, he made everything settle down.[2]

The Renaissance was keen on competition. Agonism—the zest for contest—obsessed groups and individuals. Collec- **Agonism** tively, solidarities strove mightily for prestige and prece- dence. The reputation of any group rubbed off on its members. Thus, one could bask in the glory of one's patron, one's friends, one's corpo- ration, district, or town. When guilds or districts brawled for a place in a procession or egged on their champion horse and rider in an urban race, the rough-housing and cheers expressed the sentiment that, "as stands my group, so stand I." Glory was contagious. Collective agonism and individual pugnacity reflected and amplified each other, and both engaged status. In a static social order, agency hustled for a slightly better perch.

## PERSONAL ATTRIBUTES THAT GAVE STATUS

Personal attributes of many sorts had bearing on where one stood on hierarchies of prestige. Among their peers, Renaissance Italians were of- ten fiercely competitive for standing; a great deal of energy went into

seeking minor adjustments in public esteem. Agonism therefore was individual as well as collective. One aimed for glory and applause, or for
deference and awe. This was a zone where agency had elbow room.
While no one could escape gender, age or class of birth, there was room,
through education and discretion, to amass and cash in on what social
scientists call "cultural and intellectual capital." By this useful concept,
they mean all those many forms of knowledge that give an edge, because
useful, prestigious, or both. The very Renaissance itself, a glorious bloom
in so many arts, was itself a spectacular investment, individual and collective, in cultural capital. Competition for standing, though not its only
source, was crucial to its verve and ingenuity.

To enhance their standing, Italians fashioned social selves. Their possessions, both intangible and tangible, both skills and solid goods, made
statements to the world. To this end they cultivated mind and body and
wrapped their social selves in buildings, furnishings, clothing, animals,
and servants. All such things were signs, inviting decoding, appraisal,
comment, and response.

One key form of cultural capital was political pull. There was far more
to power than plain formal office. Much prestige went to men and
women who could make things happen. Real influence was a subtle
thing, an amalgam of alliances with patrons and clients, friendships,
credits on others' debts and obligations, secrets and special knowledge,
rights, privileges, access to force, and reputation for steady nerves and
discretion, not to mention personal wealth and prestige. In the face of
many rules and even more ways to break them, men and women invested endless energy in negotiation. Those who could deliver goods and
services earned cooperation and compliance and tokens of esteem, verbal
or delectably tangible.

Social arts also mattered. Like modern high school students, Renaissance Italians had an acute sense that social life took a lot of skill. They
were great admirers of *savoir faire*. A well-timed word, a subtle pause, a
well-calibrated taunt, a fitting gift, and many other apt gestures reflected well on the doer. And, of course, there were utterly endless ways
of fouling up. All social interchange, on every level, received acute attention and endless appraisal. For the elite, the Renaissance wrote books
on how to do it right. Clothing, posture, movement, speech, taste: all
were subjects. The most subtle and most famous of these, Castiglione's
*Courtier*, became an instant and enduring classic. He set his conduct book
at court, where competition for position was most intense. Castiglione
summarized the essential trait of the polished courtier, which he called
*sprezzatura*. The term, meaning strictly "putting a low price to it," is
usually translated as "nonchalance." It meant making the hard look easy.
*Sprezzatura* was an artificial naturalness. In a sense, it was ancestral
"cool."

Moral qualities also affected standing. A coward, a cheat, a liar, a drunkard paid a steep price in the eyes of all, while a person of firm probity and moral or physical courage gained. These vices and virtues would not pry a person loose from his or her social class; a virtuous commoner still had to treat an immoral noble with tokens of respect. However much the commoner might feel morally superior, the rules forbade saying so. This state of affairs often irked those who lacked formal rank and stirred up a certain amount of fruitless literary debate by learned underlings about the proper precedence of nobility of soul and nobility of title. Soul, of course, was doomed to win the bookish argument to no practical effect whatever. Morality was a zone of agency; choice clearly operated, but there was constraint as well, for to do good was costly; it often burdened the doer. Renaissance Italians thus read virtue as proof of wealth and cultural capital.

Intellectual gifts were a font of prestige. Italians of many classes prized cleverness, esoteric knowledge, pragmatic wisdom, and practical know-how. The upper classes competed with their minds. The word *virtù* meant not only moral virtue but also skill. This sense lives on in both English and Italian in the Renaissance term *virtuoso*; it still applies to artists and other adroit performers. The Renaissance valued cleverness of many sorts. It appreciated witticisms and epigrams, good stories, clever jokes. Humanism, the literary cult of ancient literature so central to high culture, also aimed for show; it pursued a pure style and polished, adroit quotations from prestigious ancient authors to glorify both the writer and his audience. The visual arts, with their rich, clever allusions to ancient models, likewise strove for prestige through learning. Not all intellectual life looked backward to the classics. Italians also cultivated skills of observation. Ambassadors, for instance, aspired to advance their careers by canny observation, writing brilliant reports on the place where they were posted. Merchants observing markets sent perceptive letters. Heads of household, especially Florentines, wrote down maxims and comments on the world, to pass on to their descendants as domestic intellectual capital crucial to the lineage's success. Admiration for mental skills was not the elite's alone; before the audience of their profession, artisans vied to prove their skill. Painters, sculptors, and architects did the same for a larger public, and the best among them achieved real fame for genius. We moderns take the cult of stardom as natural; in the Renaissance it was a novelty.

One intellectual gift was good taste. As today, elite groups competed by connoisseurship—the prestigious knowledge of pleasing things. Our cultural snobberies thus have a venerable history. Although there were **Taste and Connoisseurship** some medieval precedents in the cult of chivalry, the Renaissance saw a flowering of forms of knowledge and taste that, by defining elite groups and making entry harder, served as instruments of hierarchic competition. All the arts, including dance and music, invited refined appreciation. One might amass antique statues and illustrated gems; it paid to know one's Mars from Hercules. All such knowledge augmented intellectual capital. Taste mattered much, too, in clothing, wine, cookery, and pretty women. Extensive knowledge of horses and horsemanship, of hunting, of arms and forms of fighting, of famous courtesans all conferred prestige. Increasingly, for the upper classes, formal education imparted prestigious knowledge and social graces. School instructed in polished writing on Roman models; specialized academies taught the elite to ride, fence, and dance.

**Prestigious Consumption**
People also chased prestige by acquiring things.[3] The more and better, the better. As in all else, virtuoso style mattered. Things rare, precious, clever, exotic, old, novel, grandiose, or amazingly tiny all drew admiration. A house or, better, an imposing palace with Romanizing cornice and a handsome portal made a statement to the world. Inside, furnishings were often sparse, but wall hangings of gilded Morocco leather or tapestry were prized, sometimes even more than paintings on the wall and ceilings. Antique busts and friezes on the walls gave patina. Fine horses, a good coach, a handsome sedan chair were items of display. It helped to have servants running along at one's stirrups or before the carriage to hustle pedestrians out of the way. Rich houses were settings for display; feasts especially were times for conspicuous consumption. In the fifteenth century, great families sometimes set their banquets in their street-side porticos, so the whole town could gawk and marvel. Clothing too gave off social signals; Italians had a keen eye for details of dress. As with everything, there was a hierarchy of materials, topped with gems, furs, and silk. The best pieces were intricately cut and crafted.

Because conspicuous consumption was so clear a signal, social competition spurred extravagance. There was no top to more. Consequently, in many cities, government, eager to curb excessive outlay, passed "sumptuary" laws, designed to rein it in.[4] Fur trim and cloth of gold, fancy buttons, great wide sleeves, and countless other costly trimmings were put under solemn rules, limiting or banning use. A frequent argument in all-male councils was that extravagance was the fault of wives, who drove their husbands to ruin by trying to keep up with the neighbors. Could not such money be better spent on the defense of the republic or the advancement of trade? And, churchmen added, reproving women, extravagant dress fostered vain pride, avarice, and lust. In some places, such rules also had an anti-aristocratic slant. Italians often ducked or bought off these rules; the temptation to compete through dress was too strong. The authorities' misogyny was badly placed, for in general men happily paraded themselves, and their wives, to impress

Troops of servants tended the great, here the cardinals in conclave. [Scappi]

and win. Despite the laws, both sexes seldom hesitated to embellish themselves.

Another target of the sumptuary laws were social gatherings, times of fancy dress and ostentatious consumption by which a family expressed its rank. Cities capped the size and cost of wedding parties and funerals. Marriage and death were major rites of passage. Accordingly, they called for public events at which a prosperous house could display its wealth and its alliances by hospitality, largesse, and pomp. Both to curb expenditure and keep the social hierarchy well aligned, cities enacted rules about who could spend how much and then, as usual, sold exemptions.

Another determinant of status was language.[5] The peninsula was a great tapestry of dialects and accents. The great cities and courts set a regional ideal, and scorned village patois. Castiglione's *Courtier* recounts a delicious practical joke, a virtuoso prank in which a nobleman convinces several court ladies that a well-dressed peasant who speaks in an almost impenetrable and to their ears execrable dialect from the countryside near Bergamo is in fact a noble so clever that he can ape rustic speech. The gullible ladies, completely fooled, extol the peasant's genius for speaking the only way he can. The story illustrates perfectly *sprezzatura*— strenuous effort (here only an illusion) on the part of the elite to appear

**Language: Speech and Writing**

altogether natural. It also points out linguistic snobbery. There was more to elite speech than an urban dialect. Precise enunciation, a rich vocabulary, pleasing rhythm, playfulness, metaphoric complexity, and literary allusions all gave prestige. Even better, one could salt one's speech with university Latin or even Greek or quote from the rich store of Italian poetry.

With the aristocratization of the later Renaissance, language became ever more salient a device for marking hierarchy and setting barriers to social ascent. One mark of status was the mastery of *cortesia*, the words and gestures of good manners. As preached by Castiglione and Della Casa, courtesy was a modulation of responses, so calibrated as to give not offense but pleasure. Well-chosen words and actions masked true feelings where necessary, smoothing social relations in the competitive world of princely courts. With time, the courtly model of polite restraint spread across the elites and slowly seeped down into the middle classes.

Like speech, writing brimmed with status markers for the literate. Perhaps half the men and four-fifths of the women were illiterate. The boundaries of literacy itself were blurry; many who could write managed only crude block letters that lurched or sprawled across the paper. Others, struggling with an unfamiliar medium, mangled diction. Schools and tutors taught distinct hands, some of them refined. A handsomely written page, good prose in well-formed letters, proclaimed its author's good schooling and high social position to all who saw it (see Chapter 8).

Erudition too granted prestige—not only academic studies, but all sorts of other learning. Various social institutions not only promoted but exalted knowledge. The Renaissance gave birth to a swarm of academies—clubs of cultured men who discussed philosophy, literature, language, or natural science. There was glory in belonging and further glory in shining. Although women of the upper classes could take no part in public competition for intellectual reputation, a good head and a ready tongue, if not too biting, did their standing good. Only the courtesans, however, could break the rule that kept wealthy women domestic. Among them, intellectual gifts brought prestige and male admiration.

**The Human Body**   The human body itself was an instrument for expressing social hierarchy. Health was a visible marker, for hard work and bad diet were the lot of the poor. Any sign of menial labor, such as callused hands and feet, singled a body out as lower class. Pallor lent a woman prestige, for a tanned skin betrayed lowly outdoor labor. A woman of high class could afford the luxury of an indoor life. Upper-class men, often darker thanks to their sports and soldiering, were often charmed by the whiter skin of a "fairer" sex. The fifteenth-century writer Agnolo Firenzuola opined on the subject of female beauty: "The cheeks must be fair [*candido*]. Fair is a color that, besides being white, also has a certain luster, as ivory does;

Posture and clothing express status, as a beggar woman accosts a rich man. [Bertarelli: Forfanti]

while white is that which does not glow, such as snow. If the cheeks, then, in order to be called beautiful, need to be fair, and the bosom needs only to be white."[6]

In other ways as well, the body displayed class. Elite males cultivated agility in fencing and horsemanship. Athletic skill gave them easy elastic bearing. Upper-class women did no sports but danced and aspired to elegance in carriage.

Renaissance elites were schooled not only in bodily skills but also in physical inhibition.[7] Men and women alike learned a restraint, much like their bridled language, that contrasted sharply with the exuberant physicality of the less privileged majority. Decorum required a measured walk, graceful posture, and restrained gestures. Courtesy manuals inveighed against gestural language—that eloquent use of hands, elbows, shoulders, indeed the whole body as a supplement to speech. To this day, less bourgeois Italians have a rich gesticular repertoire; paintings, stories, and trial testimony prove the same was true five hundred years ago. The elite learned as well other forms of bodily self-denial; the sixteenth century spread the notion that many acts that call attention to the body and its functions should be banished from sight and mind. In many ways, we moderns are heirs to this Renaissance campaign to veil and civilize the flesh. There is no better proof of this than the reactions of today's readers to Della Casa's *Galateo*. Almost invariably, they find many of the author's earnest strictures hilariously absurd, for nobody would do such disgusting things. In fact, when Della Casa wrote, "It is not proper for a well-mannered gentleman to prepare to relieve his physical needs in the presence of others," or when he inveighed against sneezing in people's faces, or admonished servants not to handle their private parts while waiting on the dinner table, he meant to be taken seriously. By our standards, premodern Italy was neither squeamish nor inhibited. Yet the Renaissance saw a gradual spread of fastidious distaste for body functions. This began with the elites and after 1600 infiltrated the middle ranks in Italy and elsewhere.

Renaissance Italians used a codified body language to express social hierarchy. There were inegalitarian gestures of respect: raising the hat, lowering the gaze, bowing, kissing hands. To express radical inequality, inferiors knelt. Supplicants, imploring grace and mercy, fell on their knees or even on their faces, clasping the powerful by the knees or ankles. This desperate gesture of subordination recognized a superior's political and social status, and often his or her moral authority. All such moves had their modulations of duration and intensity. An inferior, for instance, encountering a superior, should doff the hat first. If the superior too removed his hat, the inferior should wait until his better replaced it before replacing his. In Venice, where by civic constitution all members of the elite theoretically were equals, in the official absence of hierarchy, etiquette posed problems. Moryson remarked that two gentlemen meeting in the street would raise their hats and hold them high, passing one another with caps aloft, and take great care not to look back, so that neither could say the other had been the first to cease paying his respects.[8] Often, however, the expression of inequality was inevitable; only one man at a time could pass through a narrow doorway. Thus, portals could provoke elaborate protestations of courtesy, each offering another first place. The same held true of walking. In narrow Venetian streets, the superior walked next to the wall. In broad streets, when three walked abreast, the middle had precedence, followed by the right, and then the left.[9]

## ALL THINGS IN PLAY TOGETHER

The little ceremonies of daily life brimmed with expressions of social ranking. To understand their workings, imagine for a moment that you had to pay a call on a wealthy Roman gentleman.[10] Let us give you handsome clothing and, if you are a *signora*, a fine carriage, or, if you are her husband, a pretty Spanish riding horse with handsome tack. In either case, your footmen with staff in hand escort you through the crowded streets. When you arrive at your host's *palazzo* and ride through the elegant Renaissance doorway into his arcaded courtyard, they help you to the ground. Your host's servants, with slight bows and lowered voices, ask your name and go off to announce your arrival. He, as a mark of respect, comes to greet you at the head of the handsome stairway that leads to the *piano nobile*, the elegant second floor. He salutes you with courteous words, embraces you (if you are male), and then, as a mark of respect, leads you through a chain of ever more private rooms into the intimacy of his study. At the end of your visit, he escorts you back to the very place at which he first had greeted you. For a lesser personage, he would have come less far out and retreated less far in. Had you been his better, he would have greeted and saluted at the foot of the stairs, or even at the portal, or better yet, have escorted you from and to your lodgings. Yours is a simple visit, not a meal, where the complex business of who sits where and who eats first would have brought yet further complexities. All this seems extraordinarily fussy and complicated to us moderns, but, to you, a sixteenth-century Roman, these matters are second nature.

The many rules did not lock Italians in; rather, they gave them all sorts of avenues for nuanced self-expression. Hierarchy, although a social system, left room for agency. In the face of many rules and even more ways to break them, men and women invested endless energy in jockeying for position.

## NOTES

1. Giovanni Della Casa, *Galateo*, trans. K. Eisenbichler and K. Bartlett (Toronto: Centre for Reformation and Renaissance Studies, 1986), 28–29.

2. Biblioteca Apostolica Vaticana, Urb. Lat. 1038, 98r.

3. On conspicuous consumption, see Lisa Jardine, *Worldly Goods: A New History of the Renaissance* (New York: Doubleday, 1996); Richard Goldthwaite, *The Building of Renaissance Florence* (Baltimore: Johns Hopkins University Press, 1980), 77–90, and *Wealth and the Demand for Art in Italy, 1300–1600* (Baltimore: Johns Hopkins University Press, 1993).

4. On sumptuary legislation, see Diane Hughes, "Sumptuary Law and Social Relations in Renaissance Italy," in *Disputes and Settlements: Law and Human Relations in the West*, ed. J. Bossy (Cambridge: Cambridge University Press, 1983), 69–99.

5. On the evolution of Italian, see Peter Burke, "Languages and Anti-Languages in Early Modern Italy," in *The Historical Anthropology of Early Modern Italy* (Cambridge: Cambridge University Press, 1987).

6. Agnolo Firenzuola, *On the Beauty of Women*, trans. K. Eisenblichler and J. Murray (Philadelphia: University of Pennsylvania Press, 1992), 15.

7. On the evolution of the posture of inhibition, see Edward Muir, *Ritual in Early Modern Europe* (Cambridge: Cambridge University Press, 1997), 81–146.

8. Fynes Moryson, *Shakespeare's Europe: A Survey of the Condition of Europe at the End of the 16th Century, Being Unpublished Chapters of Fynes Moryson's Itinerary (1617)*, 2d ed. (New York: Benjamin Blom, 1903; reprint 1967), 417.

9. Thomas Coryate, *Coryat's Crudities*, v. 1 (Glasgow: James MacLehose and Sons, 1905), 462.

10. On palace courtesies, see Patricia Waddy, *Seventeenth-Century Roman Palaces: Use and Art of the Plan* (Cambridge, MA: MIT Press, 1990), 3–13.

# 6

# Moralities: Honor and Religion

The hierarchies and solidarities of Italian society lived in complex symbiosis with its moral values. There, as in any place and time, institutions fostered values that in their turn propped up institutions, in ways so tightly woven that we can hardly say which shaped the other more. Also, as in many cultures, ethical codes were multiple and not always mutually consistent. So how did Renaissance Italians, given their complex and often contradictory values, choose a course of action?

Conflicting moral codes give elbow room to agency. The capacity to choose even while constrained, agency thrives on contradictions, for moral values do not dictate choice, but only help draw boundaries to the set of choices one may make. They set a price and a reward to every option, making some courses cheap, others expensive or quite prohibitive. The complexity that tangles our analysis actually simplifies everyday life, for multiple codes and conflicting moral strictures can liberate. Often one must choose between two goods, or two evils. This fact, though it burdens the choosing, gives us humans leeway, or agency, that no servile computer ever enjoys. Moral dissonance sparks discussion and eases bargaining, two activities central to Renaissance Italian life.

A caution is in order as we survey Renaissance ethics. Moderns looking at the past sometimes mistake moral rules for inviolable commands, as consistent, as logical, and as peremptory as a computer program. They query, for instance, the sensuality of some Renaissance popes or Christian cruelty to Jews and Muslims. "How could they do such a thing? It was against their values!" They expect past peoples to be far more consistent in precepts and conduct than we ever are. Premodern Italians held deeply the values that guided their choices. Yet their behavior corresponded to these rules in as mixed and nuanced a way as does our own conduct when it heeds our moral strictures.

In premodern Italy, two elaborate, very sweeping moral systems contradicted one another on almost every point: a code of honor and Christian virtue. So contrary were they that, at first glance, one might expect Renaissance Italians to have spent their days baffled and torn. Honor urged vengeance, pride, display, and partisan loyalties, all deplored by religion. Religion, meanwhile, preached peace, mercy, and humility and a universalizing social ethic, at odds with honor's deep particularism. Yet Italians absorbed these contradictions readily, for reasons that we shall explore. Alongside these first two ethics were other, less sweeping, but still potent moral codes, anchored in the law and in the customs of family and of group solidarity. These complicated the picture yet further.

Of the two competing chief Renaissance codes, the Christian ethic had the far sharper, more coherent formulation, and perhaps a prior claim to attention and adherence, backed as it was by the potent institutions of the church, a rich intellectual tradition of theological speculation, and God himself, who to enforce good behavior held souls hostage. Yet it was honor that often shaped everyday morality. Not formally encoded or written down and open to wiry adaptation from case to case, honor was learned, practiced, and enforced in the endless routine or extraordinary exchanges of daily life. Therefore, we start our discussion there and then use this largely tacit secular code as a foil for the more explicit religious morality inscribed in treatises, preached from pulpits, and taught in the confessional.

## HONOR

Rather than a formal code of behavior, honor was a set of practices and a logic.[1] Renaissance Italian habits had much in common with a larger cultural complex known as Mediterranean honor that anthropologists have argued about at length. While this pattern has many variants and no clear boundaries in time and space, these concepts help us grab hold of an elusive but central structure of premodern Italian mentality. Its characteristic elements included prickly male pride, violent revenge, suspicion of outsiders, a sharp distinction between males and females, and fierce male responsibility for female chastity. At its core, honor was a social quality, the distillation of reputation. As such, it was external to the self. It existed in the thoughts of casual onlookers who appraised you, as well as in the judgments of the perduring circle of family and friends who monitored your doings. So potent was this bearing of witness that often others' judgment must have seemed to constitute one's very self. In this way, honor acquired also an inward aspect. Knowing that you had acted so that others approved underlay an inner self-esteem. While praise left a glow of satisfaction, probably more acute was the sting of public scorn. This inner anguish that we call "shame," the Italians called *vergogna*. This term had a triple meaning—at once a state of mind, a painful social purgatory, and a capacity of soul. The first is acute embarrassment, the second passing or permanent disgrace. The third merits further examination. In Italian eyes, a person whose soul was "without shame" (*senza vergogna*) would not flinch in the face of public reproof and therefore behaved outrageously. Such people either did not know the rules or simply chose to flout them; they lacked honor.

As a quality of soul, honor, Italians thought, inhered in persons, as a kind of moral potential. "He is a man of honor." Here, the male pronoun fits, for female honor differed. Honor, in this sense, was virtue—any virtue. Nevertheless, certain good qualities more pertained. Paramount was fidelity to word. A person of honor would tell the truth. His reports about the past and present were faithful; his promises about the future held good. The same attitudes applied here as in the torture chamber; truth telling was a luxury, indulged only by those who could afford its costs. A person of honor, the logic went, would keep promises, however expensive, and give true reports, however painful or embarrassing. A weakling would twist the truth. Thus, honesty signaled prosperity and strength. A second virtue, also closely tied to wealth and power, was generosity. This took two forms: largesse and magnanimity. Largesse was open-handedness. One gave gifts, and offered food and hospitality. Magnanimity, as the Latin roots (*magna* and *anima*) reveal, was greatness of soul. The magnanimous person, usually male, forgave enemies and generously forbore vexation. The last chief virtue was courage. All these qualities, fundamentally male, descended from the ethics of the medieval warrior class. Women too might derive honor from their possession, yet the essence of female honor lay elsewhere.

For women especially, and often for children and dependent young men as well, honor, as virtue, often **Female Honor** hinged less on what one did than on what one refrained from. Self-restraint garnered praise. This self-checking looked like a kind of voluntary shame, a self-imposed sensitivity to the judgment of others. Its serene effect reversed that of *vergogna*, the involuntary shame imposed by disapproval. Italians called this good shame *pudore*, just what the "im-pudent" lacked. In women and subordinate males, the marks of good-shame were a quiet bearing, modestly downcast eyes, and a self-conscious, virtuous blush.

Although voluntary shame was important to female honor, the truly crucial quality, closely related to it, was chastity. In a sense, chastity was a passive virtue, quite unlike the active virtues of generosity and forti-

Women of Messina: piety and honor.
[Bertelli]

tude so central for males. At first glance, chastity was what one did not
do—that is, anything the least bit sexual outside marriage or in public.
But hitched to *pudore*, chastity was also active, in that an honorable
woman was expected to express her self-control in countless words and
gestures. She was, for instance, to cast down her eyes, rein in her movements, bridle her tongue, curb her laughter, hide her chest and limbs,
and shun suggestive talk. Especially in the upper classes, where this issue
was most felt, every social exchange made a woman calibrate assertion
and self-checking.

Female and male honor intersected in the collective reputation of the
house and family. Nothing so distilled the honor of males as their capacity to keep their women chaste. The task fell first to fathers and husbands. Brothers and other kinsmen might also shoulder it. By general
agreement, a strong man, because he could drive seducers off, could
guard a house's chastity. Thus, a daughter's seduction or a wife's adultery
brought unspeakable shame, for both acts proved a man's weakness. By
the code, a man of honor should marry off virgin daughters. Nevertheless, if, to his misfortune and hers, a nubile girl lost her virginity, there
were remedies. If the father could take steps, he need not languish in lifelong infamy nor was the daughter doomed to prostitution. Though it
might cost a larger dowry, a husband often could be found. A compromised woman without a dowry was in a rougher fix. In some cities, she
might spend some time mending her honor in a monastery-like house of
reform before being married off on charity or placed in service. Either destination respectably absolved the father of his responsibility and placed
the girl under suitable discipline. Everyone assumed that a woman with
no male keeper, given weak female will and strong female appetite, easily
succumbed to seduction, bringing calamity on self and family.

When a woman did do wrong and brought disaster home, according to honor's notions, her protector could make the damage good. He had several options, which depended on the facts at hand. The harshest solution was to kill both lovers. Fathers sometimes did this drastic deed; it is hard to say how often. When such murders do surface in the records of the courts, the family's grief and its enduring sense of vindication, the community's grim yet sorrowful condonement of the slaughter, and the law's leniency all are patent. Murder aside, the adultery of a wife was a calamity not easily resolved. Nevertheless, honor notwithstanding, Italy was not littered with the corpses of unchaste women. Men often found ways of compromising with what might seem the iron laws of a retributive ethic. The neatest solution, if an unmarried daughter erred, was to force a marriage on her seducer. Second best, but still passable, was to compel the guilty man, in expiation, to cough up a generous dowry, making good the lost virginity, to help the young woman wed another despite her depreciated purity.

---

### AN HONOR KILLING IN THE FAMILY

Here is a story from 1555, from the Sabine mountains east of Rome, told by Nuntio di Polisena, of Rocca Sinibalda. The teller, accused before a court, plays down his part. One day, he informs the judge, he was working in the fields when his brother arrived with an urgent summons to Uncle Barnabeo's house, in nearby Montelione. Why? asked Nuntio, but the brother would not say. Arriving at his uncle's house, Nuntio found that all his kin were there, crying. What is wrong? It is your cousin, Bernardina. She is pregnant, and she was a virgin! Nuntio too burst into tears. Who did it? The village judge! But don't worry; we have his house surrounded, and the priest is negotiating for us to secure a dowry. All afternoon and evening they parleyed, but to no avail. The next morning, the feckless judge decided to make a run for it and, from his window, jumped down Montelione's walls. Dashing for freedom across the fields, he failed to reckon on Barnabeo's lurking kinsmen. They cut him down. At once, word came to the father: the judge is dead! Aware that with the seducer had died the promise of a dowry and of familial honor redeemed, the father took his daughter by the elbow and, under the eyes of the whole village, led her across the field to her lover's corpse. There, as all watched, as if she were his heifer, he slit her throat.[2]

In the eyes of honor, the logic of the story is crystalline. The better recompense was cash. Barring that, one took one's due in lovers' blood.

---

Shamelessness, though costly, was not without utility.[3] In some an involuntary flaw of character, in others shamelessness was a chosen role. The trait attached to those who took on supposed traits of the opposite gender: males who were shifty and cowardly, females who were forward,

**Shame and Shamelessness**

loud, or violent could be called *senza vergogna* (without shame). There was also another term, *sfacciato*, meaning, literally, "lacking face." The face was the body's chief seat of honor; a person without a face lacked good shame. That is why Carnival, a time for impudence, indulged in wearing masks. From *sfacciato* derived a noun, *sfacciatezza*, best translated as "nerve." The Renaissance was fascinated by *sfacciatezza*, the defiance of honor's rules. It was a behavior, not a trait of soul. Nevertheless, the reputation for *sfacciatezza* stuck to certain kinds of persons; here roles mattered. Among males, certain underlings qualified, and many comic actors, beggars, executioners, butchers, gypsies, and thieves. Among females, by definition, prostitutes were shameless; their trade licensed impudence, and they often bore their reputation out. Sometimes, the *sfacciata* role fell to female servants, who in both literature and fact could play the amorous go-between for their mistresses. In a confining world, shamelessness offered advantages. Those with little reputation to lose enjoyed liberties that made them useful to persons more constrained by honor. The *sfacciatezza* of the go-between allowed her a freedom of movement in the city denied to her lady. It also permitted her to hear seductive insinuations that a suitor would hesitate to blurt straight to the ears of a respectable wife. Subterfuge and guile, the stock in trade of the go-between, sat ill with honor. Therefore, lovers bent on intrigue could find shameless underlings very handy, as could plotters who needed an assassin's hand.

**Space, Movement, Bodies, and Honor**
Honor attached to freedom of movement. Since men's honor was very closely bound to autonomy, any act that trammeled them could be taken as an affront. To deny a man access or to challenge his progress in the street if he felt he had the right to advance could provoke a fight.

To bind a man prisoner was an affront so vile that it polluted not only the captive but his captors. The police were especially scorned because their profession made them tie men up.[4] (See Chapter 7.)

At the same time, honor also attached to the power to block others from entering honor-laden spaces of one's own. To invade a man's dwelling or lands affronted his honor. A house should contain its women and keep their virtue and their bodies intact; a male lover therefore pierced several enclosures at once. Notionally, all members of a family, even its guests, were under the protection of the head of household, so that any injury to them, on his property, invaded the enclosure that should shelter them. The same held for his crops and livestock. Enemies bent on shaming often therefore struck at dwellings. They devised conspicuous ways of scorning houses in the eyes of neighbors and passers-by. The repertoire was rich. Under the cover of darkness, one could sing bawdy songs under the windows. Or one could attack the walls, doors, and windows, smearing them with ink or excrement. Assailants sometimes kicked doors or wrenched them off their hinges. They threw stones, breaking panes and blinds, or unhinged shutters. Another ploy was to attach derogatory symbols to the door: an obscenely insulting poem, a sketch of a man with a cuckold's horns or little animal horns (symbols of his wife's infidelity). A drastic step was to torch the door. All these shaming gestures were familiar and easily legible. Their victims rushed to scrub away or repair the offending marks. Allies helped; a friendly neighbor might rise at dawn to collect the taunting horns before those on the street could see them.[5]

The body itself also fell prey to assaults on honor. There was a corporeal geography of honor; the head and face were noble, as were the hands and chest. The belly was a transition zone, while the private parts, by their very nature, embodied and engendered shame. Assailants might bare their victims' nether regions or spank them. The head was a favorite target for attack. One might throw one's enemy's hat to the ground or drag him or her by the hair. Far graver was injury to the flesh. A permanent scar, a *sfregio*, was a terrible blow, for it marred the face one presented to the world. So did a lopped-off ear or nose. It is clear from court records that such assaults were too common to all be brawling accidents; assailants chose their targets expressively.

The agonism so typical of social life provoked many contests for honor, for honor was often best won at the expense of others. One could steal it. To Italian minds, it was rare—a limited good. That is, like land and wealth **Agonism and Honor** in an economy that grew slowly if at all, it seemed a conspicuously finite resource, best gained by depriving others. The scarcities of land and goods were concrete and necessary, that of honor, however, followed no iron laws of supply and demand. Clearly, there could be only one first place in line, one high table at the banquet, one ruler, and one general of the troops, but other honors—a prince's favor, knighthood, a city's praise, a university degree—could multiply. Supply was elastic, economists would say. But all such things had to remain rare or risk debasement.

Struggles for scarce honor involved individuals and groups alike, for both it and shame were contagious. One caught them from the company one kept. Collectivities—cities, trades, professions, neighborhoods, patrons, and above all families—had a notional shared honor that they imparted to their members. The glory, or the disgrace, of the whole in some sense touched the parts. This fact inspired proud display, manly swagger, and much legal and political jostling over what might seem minor adjustments to seating at table or a line of march. There was group dishonor in yielding place, especially if pressed. Many tumultuous and often bloody conflicts of daily life stemmed from struggles not over tangibles but over reputation. In this, what held true for groups held too for persons.

A challenge put honor into question; it put it up for stealing. To refuse the contest was shameful; one lost at once. But to take up the challenge was to stake one's reputation. All sorts of exchanges followed such a logic. Since a man's honor resided in the integrity of his reputation, house, property, body, and womenfolk, all sorts of slights, incursions, assaults, and amorous innuendo could be read as challenges to honor. The interpretation of such moments was elastic; if witnesses agreed that there had been affront, a man had to counterattack or lose standing.

Many honor contests, while deeply earnest, also had a streak of play. Like games, they had formal or tacit rules, sometimes fixed in advance, sometimes improvised on the run. Renaissance Italian conflicts could follow elaborate codes, as when two antagonists settled a quarrel by duel. The sixteenth century evolved a complex dueling etiquette. Printed treatises laid out the rituals. The initial insult, the reply ("You lie"), the cast-down glove, the appointment, the seconds, the choice of weapons, and the fight itself had as little spontaneity as a game of chess and, indeed, almost as many openings for subtle elaboration. Most conflicts were rougher than duels in contour, but they shared an almost ritual shape: friction, challenge, confrontation, decision.

---

## A WORKPLACE CONTEST FOR HONOR

The boastful autobiography of the goldsmith Cellini offers countless examples of contests for honor, which in his tall tales he always wins. (See Chapter 2.) His colorful stories are surely often false in their particulars, but like most good fibs remain true to large cultural patterns. There is often truth in lies! The handsome yarn that follows illustrates many traits of agonistic competition. Employed in the workshop of a young silversmith called Lucagnolo, Cellini claims by charm, good looks, and skill to have won from a rich, lovely Roman lady a commission to reset a jewel. As he tells the story:

> While I was working on this project, that skilled fellow, Lucagnolo . . . took it badly, saying again and again that I would have much more profit, and more honor if I worked on big silver vases, as I had started out to do. I answered that I could make big silver vases any time I wanted to, but that the things I was doing now didn't turn up every day, and that in what I was doing now there was no less honor than in big silver vases, but a lot more profit. Agnolo scoffed at me, saying, "You'll see, Benvenuto, because, while you finish working on your job, I will hurry to be done with this vase, which I started when you began with the jewel, hoping that it will be clear how much profit I get from my vase, and what you get for your jewel." I answered him that I was glad to have a match with a man as able as he, for in the end of the work we would see which one of us was

deluding himself. So both of us, with a slightly scornful smile, bent our heads proudly, eager to finish the job. So that, at the end of ten days, both of us had finished his piece very cleanly and cleverly.[6]

This story follows the typical rhythm of a contest for honor. It begins with mutual boasts. Lucagnolo sets the formal challenge and lays out the terms for the game; the two are to finish at the same time and match earnings. Within Cellini's story, there is a second contest when he delivers the jewel to the beautiful lady, and she challenges him to name his price; he replies with a counterchallenge to her generosity by protesting that her satisfaction is pay enough, and leaves. Cellini, if we can believe him, then returns empty handed, to find Lucagnolo clutching his payment. Invited to finish the contest, Cellini begs off until the following day. In the morning, a messenger brings him a not unexpected packet of coins, the lady's reply to his counterchallenge to her:

To Lucagnolo, it seemed a thousand years till he could match his packet with mine. As soon as we were in the shop, in the presence of twelve workmen and other neighbors who came crowding in to see the end of the contest, Lucagnolo took his packet and, laughing scornfully and crying out three or four times, "Ooh, Ooh!," he noisily poured his coins out on the counter. There were twenty five scudi worth, in [silver] *giulio* coins. He thought I had four or five scudi in cash. Suffocated by his racket, and by the stares and laughter of the people standing around, I peeked in my packet and, seeing that it was all gold, I cast down my eyes and, from one side of the counter, in total silence with two hands raised my packet up way up high, and poured the money out as if from a mill hopper. My money was half again as much as his, so that all the eyes that had been fixed scornfully on me suddenly switched to him. They said, "Lucagnolo, this money of Benvenuto, because it is gold, and because it is half again as much, makes a much prettier show than yours." I was sure that, for envy and for the affront he suffered, Lucagnolo would surely have died on the spot.[7]

In this story, the workmen and neighbors play witnesses and jury. Without their judgment, the whole exchange would have lacked both meaning and a clear resolution. Applause was only half the watchers' job; they also had to show their scorn. Their eyes were avid to see not only triumph but also humiliation for, far more than we, Renaissance Italians enjoyed derision. In honor contests more generally, onlookers sometimes judged both contestants to have emerged with honor intact, but often, as here, a clear winner walked off with reputation's prize.

---

One mark of male strength was the capacity to tell the truth. Honor and honesty vouched for one another. Accordingly, the directest way to challenge a man was to call him a liar. The insult: "Cheating coward!" The riposte: "You are lying through your throat!" At that, out came the daggers. So routine were such exchanges that, as in Shakespeare's England, one called this usual challenge "giving the lie." The formal duel, a

**Truth Telling and Honor**

sixteenth-century refinement on the age-old brawl, almost always preserved this step.

Other challenges were just as likely as "giving the lie" to provoke a
violent response. Shakespeare caught one Italian folkway in *Romeo and
Juliet*: "Do you bite your thumb at me sir?" In fact, any finger would do.

## A VIOLENT FAMILY FIGHT

The following quite typical exchange was reassembled from several testimonies
in a trial of 1557.[8] Unusual here is only that the quarrelers, Roman gentlemen,
are brothers. Ascanio, the elder of the two, is the black sheep of the family; a
notorious cheat at cards, he has a reputation for shamelessness. (See Chapter 16
for examples.) In the courtyard, he has been pleading with two of the younger
brothers for a share of the legacy of their teenaged sister, who died some six
hours earlier. One by one, he has called the two youngest down from an *al fresco*
supper. Pompeo, a third brother and the leader of the group, comes down the
stairs, dressed for dinner in his doublet. He is unarmed, without even his dagger.

> Pompeo:   Ascanio, what is this? What is this you are saying? What is all
>           this shouting about? Your sister's will was well made. There's
>           no need to get you dragged into this! You know that already.
>
> Ascanio:  What do you think I am?
>
> Pompeo:   You know well enough what I think of you. You mean nothing
>           to me. Go on, get a move on! Get out of here! You have no
>           business being here. I think you are . . . I think you are a mortal
>           enemy!
>
> Ascanio:  There are other things than this that I should spend my time on
>           with you!

Ascanio bites his finger at Pompeo. Pompeo at once spins around and thrusts
his bottom in Ascanio's direction, roaring:

> Pompeo:   I want you to stick all the nose you've got up my ass.

Ascanio reaches for the dagger at his right hip and lunges toward Pompeo.

> Ascanio:  You have assassinated me.

A dinner guest leaps at Ascanio, clasping him to prevent an attack on Pompeo.
Pompeo rushes at Giuliano, Ascanio's servant, who is standing by the courtyard
wellhead, grabs the youngster's sword, draws it, and dashes toward Ascanio.
Several bystanders converge to seize Pompeo. In their hands, he trips and falls;
Giuliano's sword goes flying. At once, one of the servants picks it up and hustles
it out of range. The air rings with profanities. Pompeo recovers his balance,
breaks away, scampers up the steps into the garden, and returns brandishing his
own sword. Soon the household servants rush in with battle-axes. There ensues
a melee that, miraculously, produces only a small cut to Pompeo's thumb before
soldiers in the street first join in to defend the underdog and then calm the brawl.

Hierarchy was tightly linked to honor; high status both conferred it and set boundaries to its contests. At the same time, honor pervaded the whole social order. Underlings, even peasants, thieves, and prostitutes, possessed a strong sense of it, but only among their peers. In their struggles for face and standing, they could not aspire to filch honor from their social betters. Nor could their superiors take honor from them. Rather, contests for honor involved near-equals. A gentleman could afford to shrug off an insult by an inferior; indeed, to take it to heart was to stoop and risk derision. Or he could avenge it by some scornful act that inflicted pain and shame without engaging his own honor. This was what Hamlet meant by "the proud man's contumely." Certainly one would never challenge an underling; that would have looked bizarre. Honor usually came into agonistic play among peers, be they lords or stable hands, where real adjustments to prestige could happen. Thus, as a social practice, honor, both expressed and supported Renaissance hierarchy; as an ethic, it was conservative. It also reinforced countless solidarities, for, by its combative ethos, it attached men and women to their groups.

Honor's social utility, oddly, was tied to its vulnerability. A good name was an inexhaustible social asset; one could cash it in repeatedly without its losing worth. Reputation gave leverage. Curiously, honor was also a liability of sorts, for it was easily lost at the hands of others. This notorious fragility of honor was the source of, among other things, prickliness, thin-skinned sensitivity, boastful swagger, and the tussle for position. Because easily damaged, honor functioned as a kind of collateral, placed like a pawn in the hands of one's peers. Renaissance Italy, where the machinery of government was often flimsy, needed noninstitutional ways of enforcing agreements and verifying claims. Honor, as liability, made one reliable. One pledged it: "Upon my honor, I will do it!" "Upon my honor, I speak the truth!" Honor thus could be a sort of hostage.

The logic of this use of honor shows clearly in the torture chamber. Italian courts tortured to gather evidence. But torments seldom befell solid citizens. Rather, the magistrates singled out for pain those "vile persons" who, as poor, weak, and ill famed, lacked honor. The court believed such persons lacked a motive to speak the truth; they had so low a reputation that lying could not hurt it. Lacking the social jeopardy of honor, the judge believed, they needed a different jeopardy: to pain of limb. This the court was well equipped to supply. Prisoners, hoping to parry the magistrates' urge to string them up, paraded a third kind of jeopardy that they insisted kept them honest. Their souls, they protested, were in jeopardy with God. "Your lordship, if I do not speak the truth, may God never let me into Heaven!" In bargaining, before torturers and other overweening tormentors, Christianity was the usual refuge of the weak. This jailhouse bargaining was only one of the countless uses of religion, a second vast cultural system with a cultural logic of great complexity.

## RELIGION AS A MORAL CODE

In its social conservatism and its respect for power and privilege, the honor ethic diverged from Christian morality, which had a subversive streak that often undercut both lay values and many institutions that governed Italian life. This tension between sacred ethics and everyday life was ancient and was and is in many ways peculiar to Christianity. In Italy, where faith encountered life's needs and pleasures, struggle often ensued. Religion urged against warfare and internecine strife—peace; against satisfying desire—chastity; against feeding hunger—periodic fasting; against a Sunday spent at wine and gaming in the tavern or at rounds of mallet ball—sober church attendance; against the strategies of lineage—fat bequests to churches, respect for monastic vocations, and no divorcing a barren wife. The confrontation led to compromises and nuanced adaptations on both sides. Moreover, faith was only partially subversive, for it relied on and sanctified the very institutions—family and state—that it also hedged and chided.

Honor had no church; in this respect, Christianity, differed hugely. Behind everyday Catholic morality stood a vast, complex, sophisticated, immensely wealthy institution of great prestige. The church not only embodied a morality but propagated and enforced it in pulpit, confessional, school, and court of law. Honor versus piety: no contest! Or so one might think, but honor not only thrived but even often hogged center stage. All Italians except the Jews adhered to the faith, but many lent only half a heart to Christian ethics. Therefore, put aside the enduring delusions of many dreary films about supposedly embattled individualism and fanatical, oppressive monks, that the medieval church was a bit like God: omniscient, omnipotent, ubiquitous, all but eternal, and relentlessly meddlesome. Such modern fantasies, which often project onto Catholicism a mixture of the KGB and high school assistant principal, profoundly misconstrue a complex institution. The church, for all that it had a government in Rome, a chain of command, and, for the times, efficient lines of communication, remained a polycentric institution. There was ample room for local initiative, and its many members often walked different paths, worked at cross-purposes, or quarreled. Only after the Council of Trent (1545–63) did the center tighten its hold on the whole. The modern Roman church therefore owes much of its present structure to its response to the Protestant challenge. And not even Trent brought unanimity.

The separation of sacred and profane, and of church and world, though central to the Christian vision, could never be complete. Students

Flagellant beats his back in penance for his sins and others'.
[Bertelli]

often write as if the church stood outside society's tent, barking orders through the flaps. Nothing was ever so simple. Christianity was itself of two minds about the virtues of being in or out; the monastic impulse had always hankered after separation, but social activism plunged deep in. And "church" itself, in its original Greek (*ekklesia*), meant "gathering" and hence community, not of clergy alone but of all the faithful; the notion was inclusive, not separatist. Furthermore, Christian institutions had political and economic functions that embroiled them in practical affairs. Also, while the clergy were indeed legally a separate order, they did not have sole control of Christian organizations. There was much lay initiative—on committees overseeing parish property, in confraternities, pilgrimages, and festivals to mark holy days. And Renaissance Italian clergymen, to the annoyance of assorted church reformers, were notoriously quick, as they politicked for good appointments, to remember their alliances with their families and friends. Thus, much of the debate about religious reform, in the sixteenth century as in the Middle Ages, turned on the issue of how hard one should or could campaign to separate the church from the entanglements and pleasures of the world.

By what medium did the church inculcate values that bore on everyday life? The routes were many. Before Trent, the Roman church as a whole did not put a teaching mission first. Priests as a rule did not preach; they provided sacraments, watched over their churches, and, as peacemakers, brokered social relationships. Only after Trent's reform of the parish clergy did they turn to instructing the laity. Until then, they did confess their flocks, but seldom more than once a year, at Easter. Nor did monks preach; their job was collective prayer, good liturgy, hospitality, and sometimes care for the sick, pilgrims, and the poor. But preaching there was, and it was enormously influential. The task fell to the friars, Franciscans and Dominicans above all, who from the thirteenth century on routinely toured the cities and towns of Italy. To the laity, preachers taught doctrine, but especially morality and devotional practice. In an age where information was scarce, the friars combined the roles of entertainers, broadcasters, inspirers, prophets, and scolds. When gifted, they succeeded hugely; a good preacher could draw thousands and hold them for four hours at a stretch. A truly charismatic one, like Bernardino of Siena or Savonarola, was a political force to reckon with.[9] Such men could evangelize a city, bringing about, for a while, dramatic changes in public and private behavior. But preaching was not the church's only conduit for ethics; there were several others. Uplifting books inspired and nagged the better educated. Especially after Trent, schools for the poor taught catechism alongside the ABCs. Confraternities, under lay control but usually linked to priests, practiced devotions, did good works, and paraded solemnly on holidays. Christian art, some of it narrative and much of it didactic, ornamented houses, street-corner shrines, and countless churches and chapels. Italians recognized their familiar saints, posing with their standard emblems, and picked out readily the famous incidents from the lives of Jesus and of Mary and other familiar sacred stories. Alongside all these channels belonging to or sponsored by the church were others purely social; that is, in ways at once self-evident and very hard to document, Italians imbibed Christian values from one another. Moral examples, precepts, chidings, stories, proverbs, turns of speech, movements of the hands, the head, the body could all impart a religious ethic that, like honor, was deeply embedded in the practices of everyday life.

**The Spirit of Christian Morality**     Although theologians laid out morality as a skein of interlocking rules, Italians, when they invoked or followed Christian values, probably more heeded a rhetoric and mood than principles. They all knew the life of Jesus, as their age understood it. For them, to be Christian was to imitate the savior, or, like a musical string, to resonate in sympathy with his example. Jesus, who was God in human form, had suffered at the hands of others, had forgiven them, and, by his sacrifice, had saved all humankind. To be Christian therefore entailed renunciation, pain, and mercy. But the premodern Christ was not all sweetness. He had a sterner streak less often seen in modern Christianity, for he was also the formidable judge at the end of time, as Michelangelo and so many others painted him. So to be Christian also meant not only to suffer judgment but to judge. The imitation of Christ could never be complete, for, unlike him, men and women, fallen creatures full of sin, were subject to divine wrath. Hell and damnation were real; the Last Judgment warned Italians to take sin to heart.

Christ was not the only model. Unlike her sometimes awesome son, his mother, Mary, though not without anger, was a softer being. Italians often turned to her for help and solace, convinced that she had Christ's ear and much pull on earth; she was a wide path to providence. Mary's grief and purity ennobled all suffering, for she herself knew pain; her tears and swoon at the crucifixion appeared in hundreds of fifteenth-century paintings. Alongside the holy family were the saints, both male and female, many of them martyrs, who also had suffered; altarpieces often showed them with their proper instruments: the toothed wheel, the rack, the grill, the pincers, the thicket of arrows, the pot of oil, the anchor, the fire, the sword. So depicted, they never flinched or raged, but rather bore calm witness to steadfast faith. Like Mary, they modeled courage, endurance, and belief in grace. Other saints showed the way with acts of profound charity, extraordinary service to the church, or mystical union with God. Despite the universalistic values of Christianity, saints were particularists; they had their special places and their traditional protégés: Saint Ivo championed lawyers, Saint Luke painters, Saint Nicholas sailors and Bari, Saint George Genoa. Also, like modern physicians, they were specialists. Saint Margaret protected childbirth, Saint Lucy eyes, Saint Christopher travelers, Saint Sebastian and Saint Roch plague patients, and so on.

Renaissance Italian Christian morality was keen on proper observance. Islam, one sometimes says, is less an orthodoxy—a set of doctrines—than an orthopraxis—a code of right conduct. Although Latin Christianity had its orthodoxy, in daily life practice loomed large. The elaborate Christian calendar set out special times for penance, prayer, and celebration. Certain days and seasons demanded fasting or meat-free diets. Italians heeded these dates. Then, penitential thoughts, sobriety, and sexual abstinence were also recommended (see Chapter 10). Italians respected not only such sacred times but also sacred persons, places, objects, writings, and words; those who profaned them felt pressure from their peers and from the law; all this was part of practice. Not that Italians spent all their lives in a posture of pious reverence. In jokes and stories, they teased the clergy, and many men and some women blasphemed liberally. Oaths could be colorful: "by the breasts of the Virgin!" But, as with us, most profanity, routine and automatic, lost its literal sense. Neither gamblers' and soldiers' blasphemy nor scurrilous tales about amorous friars betokened revulsion or deep rebellion against religion. All Catholic Italians thought of themselves as loyal to the church they might flout or tease.

## TENSIONS BETWEEN RELIGION AND HONOR

There were tensions between Christian ethics and honor.[10] In all its moral teachings, Christianity was universalistic; it posited the brotherhood of all believers and urged equal love for all. Honor, by contrast, was sharply particularistic; it lauded what favored kin, allies, and dependents. We can lay out, one by one, the prized values of the honor complex to see how they might have looked to the eyes of a preacher. Take pride. Honor valued pride and fostered it. A man or woman of high position, gifts, graces, or accomplishments was supposed to show such things off, albeit without silversmith Lucagnolo's swaggering braggadocio. Christianity, with an eye to Jesus, extolled humility. Christian forgiveness also chided honor's wrath; we have seen how readily the tussle for honor bred and lauded rage and violent retribution. "If you shove me, I shove you back, and harder. Seduce my daughter and I slit your throat!" Honor might still forgive; it could evince magnanimity, but only if mildness betokened strength, not cowardice. To a preacher, revenge showed pride and wrath; the life and words of Jesus argued for mercy and peace. And what of wealth, another font of honor? Gorgeous luxuries gave honor. But Jesus, the preacher would recall, had loved the poor; poverty, since late antiquity, had been the ideal of monks and then of friars. Nevertheless, when it came to giving wealth away, the two codes converged, for both expected generosity. While honor's largesse and splendid hospitality vouched for greatness and honored the giver, religion urged giving lovingly in the name of charity.

When it came to chastity, honor and Christianity were closer to agreement, but their reasons diverged. Christianity, from late antiquity, had distrusted sex. This attitude was not especially biblical; it had tangled roots in late antique philosophy, ascetic movements, and monastic practices. Sexual pleasure came to epitomize vanity—the emptiness of the good things of this world—and to seem an impediment on the path to the greater good of the world beyond. It also came to stand for all the many ways in which the imperfect body weighed down the perfectible soul and mired it in worldly things. But the Christian message was mixed. To marry was the lesser path but still holy, and there sex was not only tolerated but, if chastely done, even good. But it had to be inside wedlock. Adultery violated the sacred bonds of marriage; the unmarried, when they coupled, fornicated. In these matters, honor half agreed, but with an eye instead to male control of a lineage's women. Hence, for honor, a wife's adultery was catastrophic, as was the seduction of a sister or a daughter; such things cried out for vengeance. But what the church called mere fornication—the traffic of men, married or single, with slaves, servants, prostitutes, and other women of low status—was for honor a fact of life almost devoid of moral impact. In general, a man of rank could seduce or violate the women of his inferiors without much fear of the law or her male protectors.[11] The law was often sluggish here, and male underlings could not challenge him. Here, again, religion was universalistic; all wrong sex was wrong, while honor, as usual, took note of who was who.

In other zones, religion and lay honor generally agreed. Honesty, fidelity, kindness, forbearance, courage, and steadiness all sat well with both. Nevertheless, so deep were the differences between the two moral codes that Italians had to step adroitly to accommodate both. As usual, where codes diverged, agency gained: "Why did you not strike the rascal dead?" "Am I not a Christian!" Depending on the play of circumstances, either religious values or honor could be called up to explain an act or refusal to act. Still, the coexistence was uneasy.

In general, Christianity took the hard edge off Italian life. It could protect families and communities from the drastic actions that honor so readily justified. The preachers' ideals of peace and mercy could stay a hand before it struck. It did not always work. Giacobo di Tito, a peasant of Montebono, north of Rome, in 1566 found his daughter Daria in the middle of the night, chatting in her shift upstairs in her lodger's room.[12] He rushed downstairs, grabbed his dagger, returned and, after a wild tumble down the steps, killed the man and then caught up with the fleeing girl. Desperate, she threw herself at her father's feet and, under her family's eyes, clasped his legs in Christian supplication, sobbing and begging pardon. All in vain. Had the cries availed her, Giacobo's case would not have come to court, but at least the gesture was there for other daughters we never hear of, their stories untold because they saved themselves, and their fathers, by evoking *misericordia*. Religion also counteracted hierarchy and reminded Italians that they had obligations outside their alliances.

Not only did religion mitigate the everyday; it also opposed it. Thus Christianity could offer utopian moments of withdrawal or social transformation. Italians could flee to religion to escape the tensions of civic life, as they did at gatherings of their penitential confraternities. Or, when a preacher galvanized their town, they could turn against much that honor prized, making private peace, forgiving enemies, stoking bonfires of "vanities"—playing cards, dice, fine clothes, amorous paintings of Mars and Venus—and purging the city of all the usual vices. Such reforms never lasted, but they had a cathartic effect that helped balance the demands and impulses of discordant codes of action. A similar oscillation was built into the rhythm of the seasons; rowdy Carnival and repentant Lent fed off one another. (See Chapters 10 and 16.)

## OTHER MORAL CODES

Tempting as it is to reduce Renaissance Italian life to a restless dialogue between two ill-matched moralities, in truth the picture was more complex. There were other ethics on the scene as well, subcodes more limited in scope and weight but still influential. One of the most pervasive was the law. Renaissance Italy had a rich legal tradition, with intellectual roots in ancient Roman codes, church law, old Germanic legislation, and feudal practices. In towns and country alike, Italians were inured to dealing with the courts and to running to notaries, scribes, secretaries, chancellors, and other officials. All such men purveyed legal language and ideas. The law offered notions of equity, impartiality, due recompense, respect for form, proper consent and consultation, verification, fair arbitration, conditional and unconditional assent or agreement; its terminology infiltrated the speech of every social class. In general, like religion, the law bolstered the notion of a public interest. In this idea, it countered honor's moral particularism, advancing the principle of a more abstract, impartial fairness, guaranteed by due process. Besides the law, there were also other rhetorics, closely tied to family, professions, and other solidarities and to neighborhood. These discourses had much to do with roles: the love of parents, the loving obedience of sons and daughters and the loyalty of servants, the solidarity of colleagues, and the mutual help and discretion of neighbors, who, despite their vigilant surveillance of good local order, should never stick their noses in other people's business. This last double injunction was flatly contradictory. It reminds us once more that no moral code, large or small, is ever internally consistent. Whatever unity any set of values possessed was thematic, more rhetoric than logic. A precious larger lesson for historians, often overlooked, is that, however much past values illuminate some bygone time, they never fully explain its actions.

## NOTES

1. On honor and Mediterranean values, see David Gilmore, ed., *Honor and Shame and the Unity of the Mediterranean* (Washington, D.C.: American Anthropological Association, 1987).

2. Archivio di Stato di Roma (ASR), Governatore, Tribunale Criminale, Processi sixteenth century, b. 34, 44r.

3. On shamelessness, see Thomas Cohen and Elizabeth Cohen, *Words and Deeds in Renaissance Rome* (Toronto: University of Toronto Press, 1993), 185–187, and Julian Pitt-Rivers, "Honor and Social Status," in *Honor and Shame: The Values of Mediterranean Society*, ed. J. G. Peristiany (Chicago: University of Chicago Press, 1966), 19–78, esp. 40–43.

4. On the special shame of being bound, see Steven C. Hughes, "Fear and Loathing in Bologna and Rome: The Papal Police in Perspective," *Journal of Social History* 21 (1987–88), 97–116.

5. On Renaissance Italian honor and insults, see Peter Burke, "Insult and Blasphemy in Early Modern Italy," in *Historical Anthropology of Early Modern Italy* (Cambridge: Cambridge University Press, 1987), 95–109, and Elizabeth S. Cohen, "Honor and Gender in the Streets of Early Modern Rome," *Journal of Interdisciplinary History* 22:4 (1992), 597–625.

6. Benvenuto Cellini, *Vita*, ed. G. D. Bonino (Turin: Einaudi, 1982), 40 (our translation). For the published translation, see Cellini, *Autobiography*, trans. G. Bull (Harmondsworth: Penguin, 1998), 29.

7. Cellini, *Vita*, 42 (our translation). The English translation, Cellini, *Autobiography*, 31, has a few errors.

8. ASR, Governatore, Tribunale Criminale: Processi sixteenth century, b. 31,

case 1, 43–47v, 145r; Processi sixteenth century, b. 33, case 15, 1r; Costituti 52, 221v (all documents 1557). This story is an amalgam of four accounts.

9. On preaching and its audience, see Cynthia Polecritti, *Preaching Peace in Renaissance Italy* (Washington, DC: Catholic University of America Press, 2000).

10. On tensions between honor and religion, see Ronald Weissman, *Ritual Brotherhood in Renaissance Florence* (New York: Academic Press, 1982), esp. 43–105.

11. On the sexual double standard, see Guido Ruggiero, *The Boundaries of Eros: Sex Crime and Sexuality in Renaissance Venice* (New York: Oxford University Press, 1985), esp. 16–44.

12. ASR, Governatore, Tribunale Criminale, Processi sixteenth century, b. 116, case 3 (1566).

# 7

# Keeping Order

Renaissance Italians approached their problems of insecurity and disorder in several ways. Their solidarities, hierarchies, and moralities of honor and religion all helped ward off chaos. Now we turn to the mechanics of social discipline. Alongside institutions—the church, governments, and police—much enforcement fell to less formal groups and practices. To highlight their importance in a society whose state, though expanding rapidly, had yet to achieve full modern competence, we look first at these pervasive and fluid habits of coercion.

## SOCIAL CONTROL

Social control is the shaping of individual and collective behavior by promoting cooperation, enforcing conformity, and squelching deeds deemed harmful. In Italy as elsewhere, some of this task fell to governing bodies—officialdom, courts, and police of both state and church—and some was at the hands of informal groups, that is, of society itself. By setting models, praising, blaming, and dealing out rewards and punishments, Italian government and society shaped behavior. In this process, both official laws and social codes of conduct counted. If statutes and moral rules were tyrants, social control would be a simple matter; people would just obey. But ethical codes have never ruled the world. Rather, simply by being there, they prove that people sometimes flouted them. The same holds true for laws; states seldom ban what subjects never do (we have, for example, no laws against parking elephants at school).

Social control does use laws and morality, but the connections are always subtle and complex. Furthermore, Renaissance Italian social control was different from ours today. Governments weighed less than now; they were smaller, less organized, and less informed. Their paltry powers of coercion barely overawed private violence. Consequently, social control fell less than today to states, towns, and officers and more to society itself, which used "self-help" to police its members. Coined by social science, this term denotes the regulation and persuasion by which informal bodies solve problems and maintain social discipline without calling in the state. While self-help embraces peaceful coercion and surveillance, it often involves private violence to deter or punish offenses. This chapter surveys Italy's mechanisms, both formal and informal, for shaping behavior. We begin with social and economic processes and then pass to regimes: governments and the church.

**The Political and the Social Intertwined** Our distinction between institutional and social processes is tricky, for the line between state and society blurs. Social groups always have their internal politics, and any polity inevitably is also social. True everywhere, this statement holds well indeed for premodern Italy. There, wherever power lay, politics intruded, even in institutions so intimate as the family. And friendship and clientage ran rife in every governing body. For instance, in Rome, the chief prosecutor received melons from his constable and gambled evenings with his notary; every polity had its social side.

Unlike Renaissance Italy, modern democracies extol the impersonal polity. We think that our civil servants, when at work, should put their friends and rivals out of mind. We prefer our institutions, public and private, to treat people as equal, at least in chance to rise and in claims to consideration. Pay, promotion, tasks, and services should all be blind to who one is, to who one's kinfolk are, and to all gifts, favors, and quarrels. When organizations fall short of this ideal, we tar them with favoritism or corruption. The institutions of Renaissance Italy were very different. They were rife with social life; alliances were everywhere. The gravitational tug of kinship, friendship, and clientage often outpulled the common good. The state was a pig trough at which one fed, as was the church; the powerful therefore strove to lodge their favorites' hooves for cozy swilling. Public bodies were therefore full of friends and friends of friends, and shot through with social loyalties and conflicts. Italians did laud impartial government and professional conduct, but these ideals were locked in combat with the ingrained cronyism of life.

Several Italian routines aimed to drive social impulses out of political institutions. One was swift rotation of offices.[1] The longer a man stayed in place, the more he would be ensnared by affection, gratitude, and obligation, so high officers often had to move on within a year or two. A second measure was to employ outsiders as judges, as if in a kin-centered world only a stranger could do justice. A third was electoral lottery. The Venetians, in choosing their doge, raised this device to a high art: men selected by lot elected committees, which ran new lotteries for nominating committees, on and on, five cycles in all.[2] Chance and remoteness of outcome hobbled backstage machination. Less elaborate systems often faltered; the influential Medici in fifteenth-century Florence saw to it that, despite lotteries, their friends still packed the urban councils. In general, by the sixteenth century, small circles of elites often scratched one another's electoral backs.[3] Yet another device for impartiality in offices was formal review of an official's conduct at his end of term. Scrutiny's risks were real: high officers were often prosecuted; many were punished and disgraced, though not a few bounced back. The charges were the usual ones: negligence, graft, cronyism, and ruthlessness. Furthermore, all governance was subject to legal standards; there was spasmodic zeal for orderly records and reporting; the very presence of much paperwork exposed officialdom to judicial oversight. Nevertheless, the whole campaign to squeeze the social out of government never triumphed.[4]

At the same time, things political also percolated through social life. Italy's solidarities were often semi-institutions. Factions, guilds, confraternities, and colleges of officials gathered not only for fellow feeling and mutual help, but also to do good works, to lobby, and to politic. Many such bodies had their statutes, tribunals, rotating councils, and elections. Wherever there were committees, laws, and policies, the political intruded. But politics went further, penetrating nonstatutory groups as well: clienteles, *brigate*, bands of cronies, neighborhoods, and, above all, the family, the central institution, where stakes were often high. There, though the control of resources fortified the household head, all members, male and female, down even to the servants, who knew secrets, might make their influence felt. (See Chapter 4.)

Political activity often worked as social control. Renaissance politics was noneconomic exchange, a barter where material goods, services, power, prestige, position, information, and backing were all commodities. One might give good for good: "Assign me the job, and I will slip you secrets." "Kill a man for me, and I will put you in the cavalry." But power could also harm. Consequently, one might extort: "Do it or I disinherit you!" Extortion could be veiled; heirs, for instance, could act on tacit knowledge that a legacy hinged on their compliance. No society lacks such politics. What distinguished Italy was lively agonism, precise calculations, and alertness to the stakes.

**Bargaining Tactics**

The politics of daily life involved much bargaining. Italians lived in a state of perpetual negotiation. Their bargains varied in rhetoric and form. A historian of Florence has posited two contrasting modes of dealing: "contract" and "sacrifice."[5] Deals of either sort could buttress social control. Contract was tit-for-tat agreement. Sacrifice refused contract's sharp reciprocity: it took the generous pose: "I am yours!" "It is yours!" Honor and religion both exalted sacrifice and scorned the niggardly contractual commercial spirit. So, at first glance, sacrifice might seem bargaining's negation. With hand on heart or Bible, one affirmed one's gratitude, generosity, and love. A second glance reveals that sacrifice, real and feigned, did not ban trading but extended it by other means. Sacrifice was slower and less precise in its claims than was contract, but it did cash in. A vengeful lord reminded a servitor that he had always "eaten the bread of the house" before asking him to kill a man.[6] To be fair, some sacrifice did ask nothing, at least here on earth, and some expressed deep-felt charity or mercifulness.

**Economic Exchanges**

Social control also passed through the economy. Commerce, in theory, is the nonsocial, nonpolitical exchange of money, goods, and services. You want my chicken; I want your cash. Done! Neither the personal nor the political enters. But Renaissance Italian commerce belied this picture; at the end of trading, one was seldom quite "done." Rather, the commercial, the personal, and the political tangled. Transactions ramified. Cash was short, so one often paid in credits. Debt was ubiquitous. Italians rich and poor were enmeshed in webs of money owed. A buyer seldom put all the cash on the barrelhead; rather, one proffered credits on third parties and promises of future delivery. Buying and selling thus often created and canceled myriad debts and obligations. One often raised cash by private mortgages, not by banker's loan. Therefore, for funds, one often turned to allies. Moreover, purchases themselves were often not simple, finite exchanges of good for good; they also stoked a continuing relationship. Webs of economic alliance thus hedged Italians' public actions.[7] (See Chapter 15.)

Noncommercial debts also cemented alliances and shaped behavior. Renaissance Italians were great borrowers and lenders, of clothing, food, tools, weapons, seeds. They borrowed from equals and unequals. Needy peasants, for instance, turned to their landlords. Such borrowing was in part an economic activity, a response to scarcity, where allies helped tide one over. Indeed, willing lenders provided a communal safety net. But credit had a political aspect too. In an insecure world, Italians wrapped one another in coils of obligation, for debt engendered trust—edgy trust, however, for debtors might default. Many a quarrel arose over debts neglected or denied. Nevertheless, indebtedness bloomed; Italians embraced it to cement social ties.

Borrowing was not the only source of debt. Any act that awakened reciprocity bound a person. Here, it was not economic and legal obligation that staked a claim, but gratitude and social propriety. For example, gift giving, as anthropologists note, almost always creates bonds.

**Borrowing, Lending, and Social Control**

Until the recipient responds, in measure if not in kind, a hovering sense of asymmetry binds the giver and the taker. Our own world's attitudes to dinner invitations and Christmas cards confirm this fact. Gift giving, a universal custom, varies in scope and habits. Renaissance Italians, stoking alliances, were avid practitioners. Rites of passage—marriages and births especially—called gifts forth, as did all sorts of social ties.[8] Clients plied their lawyers with hams and wine; villagers feted magistrates come to hear their case; suitors showered girls with pears, slippers, necklaces, and even books. Commoners cemented fellowship with jugs of wine or supper at the osteria. Gentlemen, for friendship, sent presents. Montaigne in Italy received wine and precious early figs by the horse-load, marzipan, quince jam, lemons, and oranges.[9] Princes regaled one another with trains of horses in cloth of gold and bejeweled tack, or giraffes or elephants at which their subjects gaped. Humanists exchanged rare manuscripts, and naturalists traded in cuttings or stuffed exotic beasts.

Because institutions were often weak, trust was hard, for public enforcement of obligations often faltered. Therefore, Renaissance Italians used all sorts of exchanges, both economic and social, to bind one another and to bolster trust.

**Pledges and Hostages**

Thus, they often put themselves in hock. There were two standard moves: to hand over valuables as pledges, hostages to an obligation, or to bind oneself to surrender them if in default. In the first case, one became an actual creditor, in the latter, a potential debtor. Both the state and social practice exploited both devices. For magistrates, one posted sureties; in society, one put one's name at risk. The two sides of social control, by state and community, neatly converged when friends promised big sums to assure a court one would not flee before one's trial. From then on, the friends to save their goods would police one's good behavior. Putting goods at risk was very common. For instance, small loans often came from pawnshops. Chronically short of cash, Italians often pledged their goods. Townsmen pawned their arms and clothing; peasants hocked their vineyards, woods, and pastures. In social exchanges, analogously, Italians made hostage their honor: one said, "Upon my honor, I speak the truth." (See Chapter 6 for this move in court.) Honor was not the only guarantee. Other ploys could cement the slippery loyalties of, for instance, a band of thieves. Malefactors spilled their secrets and, on a joint operation, incurred mutual guilt and risk; in both cases, they gave one another the gift of trust, for each could turn the others in: "I am in your hands, so you can rely on me." As for thieves,

so for all; in social life, one of the best routes to trust, where trust was
precarious, was a sense of your partner's vulnerability in your regard.[10]

**Social Exchanges**
**That Aided**
**Social Control**

Much social discipline is subtler than either power
politics or the market. In any society, the company we
keep molds our choices. Countless small things, like a
blush, a smile, an averted eye, a tear, a choking of the
voice, a kind or harsh word, help attune our dress,
posture, movement, or vocal timbre. Usually we are barely conscious of
this process, though sometimes embarrassment makes us blushingly
aware of it. In Italy, as anywhere, such forces mattered hugely; still,
historians seldom detect them, for, ephemeral and subtle, they left few
material traces.

One powerful form of social control was gossip. The records of police
courts overflowed with it. Renaissance folk lived in dense social worlds;
cities were small and neighborhoods tight. Newcomers did not long stay
strangers. Street and piazza were arenas for social interaction, and, at
their balconies and windows, the women especially witnessed what went
on below. They not only watched; they were also quick to comment,
both to one another and to the people in the street. Their remarks surface
often in the records of the courts: "In the whole neighborhood he has a
bad reputation." In general, the women were the local voice and conscience; males had a wider range.

Neighborhood was more than just an arena of gossip and social pressure. It also protected its denizens. Faces at the windows and doorways
kept a watchful eye on playing children and passers-by and a cautious
lookout for fishy strangers and breakers of the peace. When a noisy fight
broke out, residents came running to their doors and sills. They might
later testify to court or neighbors as to fault and consequences. Witness-
ing was a potent social control. One who felt wronged in public could
bellow, "Everybody bear witness to what he just did." The very presence
of onlookers often checked violence. Sometimes neighbors also intervened to break up a fight. At a wounding or a malicious fire, they came
running to the rescue.

The pervasive quarreling, though disorderly, also worked as a social
control. In the country, hostilities often began with work owed, boundaries moved, or one man's pigs in another's garden. In town, the first
cause might be a straying pet, a children's spat, slops and garbage, or a
disputed place to hang laundry. Very often, women carried out such
hostilities. They used not just words, but fists and nails, clogs and broomsticks. Their fight might draw in male servants and even senior men.
These petty battles could escalate from shouted insults to blows and
vandalism. Often, before things had gone too far, neighbors brokered a
settlement. When local efforts faltered, the state might step in, on its own
or summoned, to impose or guarantee a peace, under pain of fines. Such

squabbling was the most vocal expression of the complex pressures that shaped neighborhood behavior.

Where government was weak, self-help flourished. Strong bonds of solidarity made for chains of reciprocal mayhem as **Self-Help** kinsmen, friends, and clients took up weapons to avenge an injury. When others joined in, one spoke of a *vendetta*, a feud. Some classes—nobles, soldiers, peasants—were more prone to feuding, as were remoter zones less controlled by urban governments. A serious feud could last for years or decades and draw in wide networks of allies.

Vengeance and feud were less chaotic than they seem. Like petty quarreling, feuding helped enforce order and social control.[11] The likelihood of feud inhibited; one hesitated to hurl insults, cheat, steal, wound, or rape, fearing incalculable repercussions for oneself and all one's allies. The specter of reprisal could urge peace feelers and deter retaliation. Yet Renaissance Italy, like any other feuding society, strove to contain violence, for feuds troubled communities. Italians therefore evolved rites of mediation and settlement. The passage from enmity to amity was ticklish; go-betweens stepped in when warring parties could not bear talking eye to eye. Here, churchmen did good service. By their station, they were exempt from violent honor culture, and their values preached reconciliation. When at last enemies patched up their quarrel, they celebrated a formal ceremony, sharing wine and cake, embracing and kissing on the mouth, and often shedding cathartic tears. Yet such pacifications might fail.

In Europe, self-help gradually yielded to public policing and justice. In parallel, health, education, and welfare all migrated from the private to the public sphere. Between 1400 and 1600, Italy evolved. States and cities extended their spheres of competence, and, in many zones, self-help did indeed recede, so that, if not by 1600, at least by 1700, life had grown less sanguinary. This evolution was both gradual and easily set back. For instance, in many zones, the end of the 1500s, a time of hunger, saw a form of self-help—a wave of brigandage that challenged the rural authority of princes. Geography influenced self-help's rate of recession; some zones, such as Venice and much of Tuscany, were swifter to supplant it. In general, cities had solider government than the countryside; the remoter the district, the shorter was the arm of the law.

Nevertheless, do not imagine two opposing spheres, one public, the other private, struggling to hog social control. Rather, everywhere there was fluid symbiosis. Although public authorities might try to banish private violence, they also harnessed it to extend their reach. Bounties on outlaws' heads are a case in point. Meanwhile, ordinary Italians appropriated courts and officialdom for private quarrels. The neighbor's call to witness did just this. Many a judicial action masked a private campaign for leverage or revenge.

## THE ROLE OF GOVERNMENT

The authorities also worked on their own to mold society. Keen to control behavior, they legislated, policed, and prosecuted. Success was mixed; often their hopes outreached the grasp and competence of their forces of coercion. Nevertheless, governments did make a difference, and, with time, their impact grew.

Governance itself was complex. Italians had a baffling kaleidoscope of official bodies. Jurisdictions overlapped, and courts and constabularies vied for authority and precedence. To start with, major towns, unless sovereign, had lords or governors. Almost always, there were also local councils of leading citizens. Guilds of professionals, merchants, and artisans often wielded regulatory rights. Furthermore, diverse officials for health, roads, markets, and the grain trade deployed quasi-judicial powers. Bishops' courts judged morality, marriage cases, and ecclesiastical rights. All of these bodies produced a welter of laws and judgments that bore on social control. Although villages were somewhat simpler places, there too the centers of control were many. There was often a resident judge-administrator—either the feudal lord's or the state's. State magistrates might come through on circuit or for special cases, in the name of higher authority. Lords often had as well an estate agent to squeeze their tenants and, in the fort, a castellan with a small garrison. At the same time, villages often had their statutes and elected councils, with perhaps a secretary or chancellor with divided loyalties to community and lord. The village priest was half insider, half servant of higher authorities. Thus, nowhere in Italy was there a dearth of governance. What was often lacking, rather, was coherence and effectiveness.

**Laws** Italians had a welter of legislation. There was no overarching code but rather a vast mass of ancient Roman compilations, learned medieval commentaries, and case law. Judges heeded this body of *ius commune* (common law). On top of this were local statutes. These rambling collections of coherent legislation and occasional decrees set procedures of governance and established rules about many things, from inheritance rights to commerce, garbage, and stray beasts in street and garden. Statutes were conservative; they brimmed with archaic bans on things no longer done and rehashed ancient rules, for they evolved slowly. Meanwhile, governing bodies legislated fast, spewing out decrees on lanterns after curfew, the width of sleeves, distinguishing clothing for Jews and prostitutes, the duty of hue and cry, gambling, swearing, and how to keep the holy days. Legislation waxed and waned with the ups and downs of regulatory zeal. New decrees were posted in "the usual places"—on the doors of major churches, by government buildings, in the marketplace, on the city gates—and read aloud by official criers on foot or horseback, often to the blare of trumpets. By the sixteenth century, they often appeared in print, under the bold wood-block insignia of their official authors.

In this vast swarm of legislation, certain thematic concerns stand out. One was health; decrees sought to free the town of garbage and dung, confine and cure the sick, and quarantine travelers from suspect places. A second charge was the good order of public space: zoning issues like the lay of buildings and the freedom of the public way from private encroachment, and also the upkeep and operation of public facilities like walls and gates, markets, and fountains. A third issue was public safety. Legislation not only curbed violent acts and insulting gestures, but also regulated the carrying of arms and strived to ban the occasions for fighting. Rules about circulation after dark had this goal, as did the campaign against gambling, a famous brawl spawner. A fourth concern was warding off offense to God. The masters of Venice, keen to fend off divine ire, instituted a special magistracy against blasphemy. Likewise, rules to ensure respect for holy times and to shield churches from ribaldry courted providence. Social regulation also sought to control beggars and the idle poor, who might be banished or, toward 1600, confined to a zone or a workhouse, supposedly for their own benefit. Sexual conduct, too, attracted the governors' eyes. Although Italian cities seldom outlawed prostitutes, they often regulated them; in Rome, by 1600, such women could neither wear the gentlewoman's veil, nor ride in coaches, nor eat in wine shops, nor entertain armed men at home. They were also banned from dwelling in many districts. Homoerotic conduct in some places fell under the jurisdiction of special morals courts, as did other breaches of the sexual rules.

Almost always, in Renaissance Italy, wherever there was a law, exceptions abounded. Many regulations aimed as much at raising money as at squelching behavior; again and again, the authorities sold exemption licenses. Thus, although massive, Italian legislation had uncertain reach, for wealth, power, and privilege knocked enforcement full of holes. Not all exceptions to the law were sold; police jurisdiction had other vacuums. Churches were sanctuaries; he who ran inside ducked arrest. Embassies, and their precincts too, had extraterritoriality. Police who made an arrest in their shadow risked indignant drubbing by the ambassador's servants. Nobles in city and countryside sheltered protégés in their palaces; not rarely, the authorities hesitated to take a magnate on. Many rural outlaws therefore huddled under the protection of the great.

To enforce its will, government needed a constabulary.[12] Larger cities had several competing troops, each under its **Police and** captain. The countryside made do with small local detach- **Courts** ments, plus squadrons out on missions from the city. Nowhere were the police reliable. Recruited from the poorest classes, they had no prestige, little discipline, and a healthy appetite for loot. People

Venetian courtesan: her life and dress were
curtailed by law. [Bertelli]

loathed them; *cop* and *cop's woman* were sharp insults. The police
roughed up prisoners and grabbed their belongings. They seemed especially vile because they bound their captives. (See Chapter 6.) Often
they broke into houses without a warrant, snooping for stolen goods and
breaches of the sexual code. In general, they bullied the weak and cow-
ered before the strong. Paid for each successful arrest, they had a greedy
zeal that blackened their repute.

Allied to the cops were the informers. They were tarred as "spies"; the
word was an insult commonly hurled at snoops. Authorities in bigger
cities like Rome and Venice made energetic use of them. Some were on
retainer. Others cashed in in other ways; in Rome in 1555, two shady
Spaniards convinced the chief constable to let them run an illegal gambling house at the Campo de' Fiori market in hopes, they said, of picking
up military secrets from Spanish soldiers. After a few months, the authorities, concluding that their constable and his spies were really just
raking in the house's take, arrested the police chief and fired his agents.[13]
Not all spies, real or bogus, were steady employees. Lacking a detective
force, Italian authorities relied on informants. Accordingly, very often,
they promised snitches their cut of penalties. Here, the campaign for
social control subverted trust and solidarity. States used similar devices
against rural brigands, dangling pardons in front of bandits who ratted
on their comrades.

Central to governmental control of society were the courts. Tribunals
came in many kinds; some were criminal, others civil, ecclesiastical, or
administrative in scope; not rarely, one magistrate combined several
functions. Courts had their judges, scribes, turnkeys, and torturers, and

Under the same courtesan's dress, forbidden male garb (page flap up). [Bertelli]

in their orbit hovered a swarm of prosecutors and advocates. In general, they were sticklers for procedure; they loved paper, keeping complicated records, often in Latin. To uneducated Italians, courts seemed imposing, with their obscure formulas in a learned tongue, their rituals, robes of office, harsh methods, and heavy punishments. Yet far more than most of us today, Italians knew the insides of courtrooms from rich firsthand experience, for they often took part in proceedings, as plaintiffs, witnesses, guarantors, suspects, or victims of a civil suit. Their testimonies show that they usually understood the rules and rituals and knew how to use them.

Of all state organs, the criminal courts tried hardest to control society. There the rules tilted sharply against the suspect. Examined in a closed room, with neither friends nor counsel, nor public observers, unaware of the charges, accusers, and evidence, the accused was on his guard. The magistrates questioned him cagily, first circling around the issue, looking for clues and inconsistencies, and only gradually tipping their hand as they closed in on the suspected crime. When stories clashed, they could at their discretion call in another witness for a face-to-face confrontation. By theories of proof, a conviction required strong evidence from at least two credible witnesses or confession. Often, lacking good witnesses and detectives to seek them out, the judges tortured.[14] They usually targeted suspects of low estate. They also sometimes tortured witnesses and even the victims of a crime.

There were several methods of torture. Commonest was the rope; the court's men stripped the suspect to the waist, tied his hands behind his back, put a rope to his wrists, and hoisted him. If he did not confess, they might give the cord a jerk, a *strappado*. Other devices in the repertoire varied in severity. On the milder end were sundry instruments to squeeze feet or fingers, sometimes applied to women. More dire were long sessions spent standing in painful postures or fire to the feet, an ordeal so hideous some jurists condemned it. Whatever the torment, all the while the notary wrote down each piteous moan and imprecation; his transcripts prove that the procedures hurt a lot.

Do not confuse this investigative judicial torture with the cruel punishments meted out after sentencing. The investigating magistrates were often harsh but seldom ghoulish. Torture had to follow rules. It should not maim. Suspects with broken or damaged limbs were not to be hoisted up, nor women who were pregnant or menstruating. Furthermore, if torture lasted too long or came too often, the defense lawyer might plead abuse to invalidate the case. For the judges, torture was a means to an otherwise elusive end. Without it, a stubborn or wily criminal could stall forever. Even with it, a strong suspect sometimes toughed it out and escaped condemnation. The court understood the risk that the innocent might confess to flee pain. As a precaution, it always insisted that all who confessed under duress return the next day to ratify what they had said. Those who retracted often faced another session on the rope; this ominous fact, however, aroused little judicial skepticism about post-torture ratifications.

Most malefactors escaped the hands of justice. Inefficient police and holes in jurisdiction lamed the courts. To make things worse, authority's reach was short, for territories were small and borders near. A miscreant's allies often warned of impending arrest. Suspects fled *en masse*. Extradition seldom worked. Repeatedly courts tried *in absentia*, issuing dire sentences to be carried out if ever they caught the fugitive. In the meantime, they outlawed him and seized his goods.

**Executions and Other Punishments**
If one had the bad luck to be caught, hard times often loomed. Not only were courtroom rules stacked against the accused, so too was sentencing. Condemnation was likely and the penalty often harsh. Weak states with inefficient organs of repression used the few they caught to set a horrible example for the many who got away, for justice was meant to teach a lesson. Punishment therefore not rarely employed public spectacle.[15] For lesser crimes, the state used public shame, putting malefactors in the stocks, often to ringing bells and with explanatory placards. Those who had spoken ill of state or church might have their tongues in bridles. Other middling offenses earned a public whipping through the streets or *strappado* hoists on a high pole in the market or at

the gate. For graver misdeeds, sometimes the authorities adorned the body of the condemned with a lasting shameful testimony to their power and judgment; they cut off the nose or tongue, an ear, hand, or foot, or gouged out an eye or two. When they put a person to death, they lacked modern bashfulness. An execution was a major drama for both state and church; they put on a spectacle that drew a crowd.

Several kinds of social control converged on a public execution; many were the actors and the themes. The authorities used the occasion to demonstrate their implacable majesty and to awe their subjects into compliance with the laws. Executions therefore had their solemn, vengeful side; to inflict both pain and shame before their victim died, they might attack his body with knives or incandescent pincers. After death, to drive home the lesson, for major crimes they might quarter, otherwise dismember, or burn the corpse, and then expose it to the air, to crows, to the awed gaze of passers-by and the agony of kinfolk anxious for decent burial. The means of death itself were many; they varied with both crime and jurisdiction. In general, it was nobler to be beheaded like the saints than to hang like Judas. Swords and devices like stationary guillotines were normal. But hanging was the rule for commoners; gallows, empty or with crow-picked carcasses, were a familiar admonitory sight. There was special infamy in hanging upside down, as there was in burning, a fate reserved for heretics and desecrators, most of whom, kindly, one killed first. Assorted other methods—strangling, shooting, cudgeling, drowning, tossing from the battlements—need not detain us here, for they were rarer.

Meanwhile, alongside this grim, vindictive, rather Old Testament *mise-en-scène*, very often there was a second drama with Gospel coloration. Its themes were reconciliation, grace, and salvation. Many cities had confraternities of lay "comforters," whose mission was to visit the condemned on their last night to prepare their souls for death. This task also fell to clergy, some of them specialists in this apostolate. In the eyes of these helpers, despair was the great adversary. They had to convince the condemned that, if only he (rarely she) repented, the body's loss would buy the soul's redemption. It was not easy work. Despite the famous proverb, a looming execution did not readily concentrate the mind. But unremitting prayer, consoling talk, and the contemplation of holy images might keep mind and heart from straying. Not rarely, as the authorities dragged their victim through the streets, visiting the sites of crimes, and hauled him to the "place of justice," the comforters marched along in hooded penitential garb, some holding painted tablets of holy scenes before his eyes. They might even join him on the ladder to the noose. For the onlookers, the struggle for the soul of the criminal was a high drama to which they were more than spectators, for their own prayers counted. They could fall to their knees for his soul's sake, and, if he expressed contrition and begged his victim's kin for grace, they cried tears of compassion and joy. Dying the good death, the criminal reenacted holy martyrdom, and the blessings of the crowd helped reconcile all parties, closing accounts and salving grudges. The defiant convict who struggled and cursed or protested his conviction clearly went straight to hell. That too made a satisfying moral spectacle.

Such executions were special events, part of life, but hardly daily. In general, courts preferred cash to blood. Most murderers, if convicted, suffered only confiscation and banishment. Many other crimes too were fined. Unlike us, Renaissance Italians eschewed prisons; they were expensive and unproductive. Jail was mostly for holding debtors and persons awaiting trial, not for punishment. The galleys were far more useful; a few years spent rowing, chained to a naval bench, was a common sixteenth-century penalty. Jail itself, for Italians of lower station, was a frequent experience. A villager could spend a few weeks in the castle tower while raising money to pay a fine; poor townsmen might be locked up as suspects or even as important witnesses. Until testifying, one might be kept in isolation. Jail cost money; inmates paid their own keep, and the rich bought what comforts they could. Men of power, locked up for reasons of state, might purchase good quarters while awaiting a happier turn of Fortune's wheel. Like all other cogs in the machine of justice, jails were lubricated by lucre.

Banishment was a common punishment. It was cheap and, given all the borders, easily done. States shoved malefactors across frontiers or dispatched bloody-handed noblemen to Hungary to fight the Turks; villages just pushed men out of town. In the latter case, exiled peasants often hovered just down the road or behind the woods, so that wives could scurry out with bread and cheese and newly mended shirts. But even short-range banishment was disruptive; when a man could not work his lands, his family suffered. Without much income, the banished man (*bandito*) often fell back on banditry; our English word shows the old linkage between banishment and brigandage. Thus, as a device for social control, banishment often only exacerbated things, putting rural lives and goods at risk.

Alongside Old Testament severity, Italian authorities also practiced New Testament mercy. To bestow grace combined the magnanimity of honor with the mercy of a Christian. It also might on occasion evince political acumen. Rulers pardoned. They invited back their exiles, restored confiscated estates, and commuted death sentences, in the nick of time or posthumously. Their God-like arbitrariness in dispensing grace increased their stature; like the Divinity, they garnered prayerful supplication and fervent gratitude. This habit of clemency put yet more snarls into justice's very tangled skein. However dire the wages of crime, punishment remained capricious.

## THE CHURCH AND SOCIAL CONTROL

Alongside the state, the church too worked to control society. Down to the Council of Trent (1545–63), the campaign was polycentric and tentative; thereafter, it was more coordinated and assertive. The Council exalted and energized the bishops. From then on, episcopal campaigns to impose Christian morals often had real effect. A second movement, older than Trent but fostered by it, centered on new religious orders, the Jesuits and others. These congregations differed from most of their predecessors in their social activism, which aimed to transform lay conduct and belief. The Jesuits, for instance, ran internal missions in remote districts to instill orthodox beliefs and practices. They and others also set up schools where morality suffused the curriculum. While the Jesuits staffed ambitious colleges offering classics to the elites, the Scolopians opened modest schools to teach the poor to read. Counter-Reformation orders urged frequent confession in place of the old annual Easter pattern; as the habit spread, parish priests gained moral influence.

Two other Catholic Reformation devices addressed social control. The Index of Prohibited Books (1555) worked the less directly, as it oversaw what one wrote and read, not how one behaved. Nevertheless, its campaign for intellectual and moral propriety in print affected judgment and action. The Italian Inquisitions (1542) were a blunter instrument, a set of tribunals in charge of right belief and behavior. Inquisitions have had a bad press, to a degree deservedly. At times they meted out drastic punishments for irregular ideas and, where converts from Judaism fell back on the old faith, they were pitiless. The Italian Inquisitions, however, were often milder than their Spanish counterpart.[16] Their victims, if willing to recant, usually escaped with reprimands or light penalties, plus warnings to desist. A fair bit of Italian inquisitorial activity dealt not with cult and doctrine, but with morality. There, the tribunal, even by Italian standards, was careful and firm but fairly moderate.

## CONCLUSION

In the late 1930s, Norbert Elias, a fine scholar and a Jew, fled Hitler's Reich. As his world sank into unspeakable barbarity, he wrote a book that proclaimed the opposite: to the effect that European history has seen a continual "civilizing process," a victory of genteel self-restraint.[17] Though ironically ill suited to its moment of publication, his argument has been hugely influential for the interpretation of Italian history. Elias saw the Renaissance and the Catholic Reformation as great steps toward self-control. The boisterous violence of the Middle Ages subsided; brawling feuds shrank to polite duels with punctilious etiquette. Some dueling faded to snubs and pamphlet wars. Medieval slobbering and swilling gave way to table manners, and zestful gesticulation yielded to genteel poise. Bathroom matters and everything sexual went private. Shared beds, shared goblets, and shared food on a common plate all disappeared, forks triumphed over fingers, and lapdogs vanished from the tabletop. And, increasingly, restraint replaced expansiveness. There is much general truth here, especially for elites. Together, states and church did extend their controls, taming society. Elias's transformation lives with us still.

## NOTES

·1. On the rotation of officers, see David S. Chambers and Trevor Dean, *Clean Hands and Rough Justice: An Investigating Magistrate in Renaissance Italy* (Ann Arbor: University of Michigan Press, 1997).

2. On Venetian electoral machinery, see Frederick Lane, *Venice, a Maritime Republic* (Baltimore: Johns Hopkins University Press, 1973), 110.

3. On Florentine electoral machinery, see John Najemy, *Corporatism and Consensus in Florentine Electoral Politics, 1280–1400* (Chapel Hill: University of North Carolina Press, 1982).

4. On corruption as a mode of governance, see Jean-Claude Waquet, *Corruption: Ethics and Power in Florence, 1600–1770*, trans. L. McCall (University Park: Penn State University Press, 1992).

5. On the notions of contract and sacrifice, see Richard Trexler, *Public Life in Renaissance Florence* (New York: Academic Press, 1980).

6. Thomas Cohen and Elizabeth Cohen, *Words and Deeds in Renaissance Rome* (Toronto: University of Toronto Press, 1993), 35.

7. On the place of debt in cementing social solidarity, see Renata Ago, *Economia barocca: mercato e istituzioni nella Roma del Seicento* (Rome: Donizelli, 1998).

8. On the anthropology of Renaissance gift giving, see Christiane Klapisch-Zuber, "The Griselda Complex," in *Women, Family and Ritual in Renaissance Italy* (Chicago: University of Chicago Press, 1985).

9. Michel de Montaigne, "Travel Journal," in *Complete Works*, trans. D. Frame (Stanford: Stanford University Press, 1958), 1001–1002, 1005.

10. On thieves and trust, see Thomas V. Cohen, "Three Forms of Jeopardy: Honor, Pain, and Truth-telling in a Sixteenth-Century Italian Courtroom," *Sixteenth Century Journal* 24:4 (1998), 975–998.

11. On feuding as a social system, see Edward Muir, *Mad Blood Stirring: Vendetta and Factions in Friuli during the Renaissance* (Baltimore: Johns Hopkins University Press, 1993), 67–76.

12. On the police, see Steven Hughes, "Fear and Loathing in Rome and Bologna: The Royal Police in Perspective," *Journal of Social History* 21 (Fall 1987), 97–116.

13. Archivio di Stato di Roma, Governatore, Tribunale Criminale, Processi sixteenth century, b. 36, 262r–65r (1557).

14. On judicial torture, see Edward Peters, *Torture* (Oxford: Blackwell, 1985), and John H. Langbein, *Torture and the Law of Proof: Europe and England in the Ancien Regime* (Chicago: University of Chicago Press, 1976).

15. On executions, see Samuel Edgerton, *Pictures and Punishment: Art and Criminal Prosecution During the Florentine Renaissance* (Ithaca, NY: Cornell University Press, 1985).

16. On the Italian Inquisition, see John Tedeschi, *The Prosecution of Heresy: Collected Studies on the Inquisition in Early Modern Italy* (Binghamton: Medieval and Renaissance Studies and Texts, 1991).

17. Norbert Elias, *The Civilizing Process: The Development of Manners: Changes in the Code of Conduct and Feeling in Early Modern Times*, trans. E. Jephcott (New York: Urizen Books, 1978).

# 8

# Media, Literacy, and Schooling

Communications is a vast topic. Everything a civilization does sends intentional or inadvertent signals: clothing broadcasts social station; buildings signal their owners' wealth and power; a smooth highway proclaims a regime's competence; clothing and body language reflect age, class, and sex. These facts are true almost everywhere. What then sets off the Italian Renaissance? First of all, by our standards, is its hypersensitivity to signs and symbols of prestige. Second is a double revolution in communications: printing and naturalism in the arts. New media and new messages, central to the Renaissance of the elite, changed the daily life of all classes. This chapter looks at both these novelties and evolving patterns of speaking, reading, teaching, spreading news, and informing the public.

Although all the body's senses receive communications, the eye and ear have primacy, for only they combine wide bandwidth with reception of signals from afar. The other Renaissance senses also conveyed messages. Touch could feel a nurse's or a lover's gentle hand, or the torturer's cruel ministrations; taste could distinguish a prestigious wine or the lean fare of Lent; smell could revel in sweet incense at high mass. These three senses also invite their scholarly commentaries; yet historical research is hard, for no archive or museum can preserve the vanished stimuli. What we still do have is matter for the eye and ear that Italians stored away: ink on paper or parchment—designs, words, and musical notation; paint on wood, paper, plaster, or canvas; carved stone, stucco, and wood; and decorated bronze, silver, cloth, pottery, and other materials. The sounds and rhythms of speech and music and the gestures of body language themselves are gone. We do possess many relics of what Italians saw and some signs of what they heard; it takes clever historical sleuthing to track down the nature of communication.

## TWO REVOLUTIONS IN COMMUNICATIONS

Renaissance Italy saw two revolutions in communications. The first, in printing, had its origins elsewhere in Europe, but Italians embraced it quickly and fruitfully. The second, in the visual arts, emerged in the peninsula itself and with time colonized much of the rest of the world.

**Printing**   The Renaissance's most radical change was printing. To be more precise, the core innovation was not printing itself, for woodblocks with words and pictures for stamping cloth, leather, or paper were decades older; the novelties were movable type and the printing press. This German invention of the 1440s swiftly spread to Italy; the first press, at the Subiaco monastery in 1465, soon spawned imitators all over the peninsula. As often, one new thing brought many others in its train. Handwritten books had been rare and expensive; at the top of the manuscript market, prestigious tomes of calfskin parchment, beautifully decorated by fine artists, were treasured by princes and rich churches. Less elegant, and less costly, were the practical volumes of professionals, often works on law or theology. Usually devoid of art and color, these books were dense blocks of text in angular gothic script, flanked by commentaries and comments on the commentaries packed densely on the wide margins. With the printing revolution, the hand-made treasures, each unique, slowly gave way to mass production, but not without a fight. The rich continued to buy well-printed volumes where artists had custom-painted coats of arms and ornaments in blank spaces left for decoration. Meanwhile, the works of reference for students and professionals not only fell in price; they also became standardized, for the old individuality of hand-made books gave way. Zeal to publish an authoritative edition stimulated humanist scholarship; men of learning attached themselves to printing houses and, sifting through the conflicting manuscripts, labored to recover the original ancient texts. There were subtle feedback loops; better books produced cannier readers, who hungered after yet more books by publishers, who, with their expanding sales, hired ever more bibliophile scholars. Thus, print stimulated both itself and the republic of letters.

No sooner did commerce get its hands on the printed word than marketing set in: printers vied for customers. As often, consumers benefited as competition improved the product. By the early 1500s, educated Italians could buy readily portable editions of the classics, published in Venice by Aldo Manuzio. Their clear Aldine typeface, named for its inventor, is with us still, living on by that name in many word processors. Most modern print descends from it. The Aldine letters were round and a little slanted, on what scholars then believed, erroneously, to be an ancient Roman model, and the page, with its ample white space between words and lines, was easy on the eyes. The cramped scribal gothic page faded from use. Capitalism also, as it often does, spewed forth heaps of shoddy goods; presses churned out cheap editions, poorly printed, badly edited, on flimsy paper, many of them full of dubious information: booklets, broadsheets, ancestral junk mail. It was this low-end product that found its way into the daily lives of the nonelite. For the first time, many persons handled books. Print robbed the written word of some of its aloof mystique. Capitalist production also concentrated expertise; for the information industry of the sixteenth century, Venice was Silicon Valley. The city's privileged position between Italy and Central Europe, its eastern trade connections, and its polyglot population all fostered big presses, printing serious tomes on, for instance, law and medicine, for peninsular and international markets. The concentration of producers attracted expert workers and fostered a local culture where information mattered. Venice also became the center for nascent journalism.

Illustration, a second aspect of printing, was also influential. Printed image-making soon became a high art, with an ample low end. Prints often embellished books, as decorations or as enhancements to the text. They lent themselves well to scientific illustration and to maps and city views. But the great bulk was devotional. Some blocks were by artists of genius; many others, by lesser talents, helped propagate the fine designs they reproduced or imitated. Yet much of the output, like many illustrations in this book, was technically crude; fairly simple line drawings illustrated all sorts of books, informing readers or, very often, simply offering images of what they already knew. Costumes, games, tools, labors, portraits, famous events all were depicted. Woodcuts enlivened the cheap publications that purveyed news of marvels: floods, earthquakes, monstrous births, and victories over the Infidel.[1]

As books multiplied, libraries grew. When, in 1450, Pope Nicholas V founded what soon became the great Vatican Library, he owned only twelve hundred volumes, all handwritten. By 1600, Italy had libraries with many thousands, most of them printed. The early Renaissance library, like its medieval ancestors in universities and monasteries, usually displayed its precious volumes, chained to lecterns. The reading room, in shape and feel, had much in common with the pillared monastic dining hall, with books set out one by one on lecterns. By the end of the sixteenth century, as books multiplied, bookshelves appeared, often wonders of elegant carpentry so high that a catwalk or even two spanned the higher shelves. The soaring hall often took on palatial grandeur. Many of these beautiful Renaissance libraries are still in business. Some were open to the public; at the Angelica in Rome (1614), by statute, no one was barred. Today, as one ascends the marble stairs, one still encounters a plaque, on the left, reminding readers in a Latin they all once could read that anyone who stole or hurt a book would suffer the pope's thundering anathema. The language of the admonition reminds us that although open to all, libraries took for granted high literacy in all users.[2]

**Visual Arts**  Between 1400 and 1600, Italian art had its own revolution, one that transformed its power to communicate. In this transformation, painting, sculpture, and the various decorative arts acquired ever more refined powers of depiction. They acquired a naturalism that mixed realistic close observation with the depiction of ideas and ideals. The new science of linear perspective and a growing mastery of light and shading gave the graphic arts remarkable three-dimensionality. These technical advances enriched art's capacity to inform and enhanced its emotional force. Renaissance arts carried meaning on many levels: describing, evoking, symbolizing, glorifying, and just plain pleasing the eye and ear. Almost always, there was far more to them than prettiness; works of every size and kind were packed with messages about things sacred and secular, collective and individual. Renaissance people did not see art isolated in museums. Rather, they lived with it all around them—in churches, on the street, in their homes. Usually they understood many of its messages. On the other hand, the growing elitism of Renaissance culture divided both art and its public in unmedieval fashion; some aristocratic art took on esoteric meanings meant for the delectation of elite insiders who enjoyed being in the know.

All the Italian art we see today in art museums is wildly out of place, for the Renaissance had no museums. It did have the great private collections of classical antiques and new productions. Proud owners showed these to their guests; only toward the end of the sixteenth century did the Medici, in a rare gesture, open theirs to the Florentine public. The museum art we see now has shed many of its original messages, for it almost always has been shorn of its original context of other images; paintings sometimes have even lost their wooden frames. Over the centuries, complacent owners, zealous revolutionaries, thieving armies, and unscrupulous auctioneers have dismembered complex altarpieces, scattering their panels across the continents. Portraits and pagan figures once belonged in palaces, and sacred paintings, statues, and furnishings usually stood in churches. Such works communicated to the viewer not in isolation but in concert with their surroundings.

To recapture the everyday experience of Renaissance works, we must remember how one beheld them: *in situ*. The sites were several. Inventories prove that even Italians of fairly modest means could have a holy picture at home. They were not rare; most must have been simple images. The more expensive artists worked on commission and under close instruction, painting, sculpting, building, and decorating for religious houses, guilds, princes, or private families.[3] In the course of daily life, some such art was easy to see, especially in churches—for instance, the great high altars at the end of the main aisle. Chapels were harder; often a high grill restricted access. What one did see, one saw dimly, by candle glow or the thin daylight that filtered through high windows. Dazzling museum spotlights and the coin-box illumination in today's Italian churches, where a 500 lire piece buys two bright minutes, falsify the Renaissance experience of art.

An altarpiece told its viewer a complex story, linking together the bones or other relics in the altar, the holy figures with their familiar tales and emblems, and the donors, whose heraldic symbols appeared profusely in details of the architecture. A family chapel often was also a lineage burial place; it could be crammed with images—portrait busts or supine figures—of the dead, fancy sarcophagi, and flattering Latin inscriptions with their dates and dignities. The chapel glorified at once the patron saint and those who, by the handsome decorations, paid him, and themselves, homage.[4] Churches were densely packed, inside and out, with symbolic messages, many of them readily legible without the help of words: who built the church, who staffed it, who patronized it, who was buried in it, what holy personages it worshiped, what relics it contained, what past Christian events it commemorated, what cosmic truths it evoked. Many Italians were lively spectators who commented on the work their best artists did in churches; onlookers appreciated technique but also felt the religious meanings.

Ceremonies of church and state also brought art out into the streets and *piazze*. Both religion and politics loved a parade. Great events—a victory, a marriage, the installation of a pope—spawned gorgeous ephemera: grand pavilions, platforms, and triumphal arches of wood, plaster, and papier-maché, draped with paintings and bedecked with statues.[5] These temporary structures marked stages along a line of march, settings for a pause to hear a speech or hymn, or to watch a winged youngster in angel dress descend by cable, warbling celestial greetings. The best painters, sculptors, architects, composers, and poets might collaborate in these complex productions, of which we have tattered records, for they were made to be destroyed. Indeed, sometimes, to public glee, for a grand finale, fireworks packed inside blew them spectacularly to bits. The whole festive program had propagandistic messages, some clear to all and some obscure to the uninformed. Floats and tableaux with statues and living performers charmed the eye. Assorted allegorical figures, semi-clad or sumptuously garbed—of tranquility, harmony, industry, peace, the happy concord of the elements, and the submissive loyalty of conquered towns—regaled the honored visitors, the ducal

Carnival: the trade in perfumed eggs. [Tempesta]

bride, or the visiting emperor with their gestures, speeches, and songs. The populace too had its role: to marvel and to applaud. Late Renaissance and baroque art excelled at these orchestrated pomps. Printing presses preserved their memory, sometimes with elegantly illustrated, expensive books, but more often with humble pamphlets that detailed their marvels without the aid of pictures.

**Controlling the Impact of the Printing Press**  Just as they were aware of the persuasive power of the arts, states and churches also quickly learned of the capacities of print and soon took steps to rein it in. Consequently, the technological revolution in communications was less democratic in its effects than one might expect. It might seem that the falling price of the written word should have encouraged literacy and undermined the power and prestige of groups that hitherto had hogged useful knowledge to themselves. In fact, however, the same two centuries that ushered print in also saw an ever sharper distinction between high culture and low and ever more closure of elites. Between these trends, the links were far from simple. Printing encouraged a move toward public knowledge and away from the arcane trade secrets that still typified the craftsman's world. That fact may have persuaded groups who, in the classic way of professions, had enriched practitioners by keeping their numbers down, to find some other barrier than studies. So, in many cities, especially after 1500, physicians, lawyers, notaries, and other groups closed ranks, admitting only members' sons. Political and social elites, ever more given in those same years to rules of closure, must have helped set the model for exclusionary statutes.

When it came to religion, the horrible example of Protestantism, as Catholics saw it, persuaded authorities to drive a wedge between high and low culture. In much of northern Europe, Protestants abandoned the Latin Bible and Latin liturgy. The rebel churches encouraged the laity to read, understand, and discuss; religious turmoil stirred up a storm of books and pamphlets. In the absence of a central theological authority, the swirl of controversy soon gave rise to proliferating sects and churches, beginning the unfinished history of Protestant fragmentation. Aghast at the spectacle of a doctrinal confusion that, in their eyes, menaced immortal souls, Catholic reformers at the Council of Trent resolved to squelch all translations of Scripture and to damp speculation and home-grown spirituality. All doctrinal writings, all church legislation, all higher instruction would remain in Latin, a language accessible only to clergy, the professions, and those rare others who could afford a long, arduous education. Furthermore, according to the decrees of Trent, even the educated needed a bishop's permission before they could read sacred Scripture.

For the masses, the Catholic Reformation did produce works in Italian. These often aimed to teach catechism or moral conduct. They might have woodcuts illustrating points of doctrine. Some, intended for the use in charitable schools, showed vignettes of sins that squeamish modern school boards might want to censor. Such books tended to be long on memorizing and short on theology; their tone was moral, not speculative, for what the faithful needed was faith, reverence, and virtue, not high theology.[6]

The church of the Catholic Reformation, well aware of the dangers of the press, strove to control what came out in print. Books both high and low, both Latin and vernacular, and even handwritten news sheets passed before censors. Busy scholars reviewed texts, imposed revisions, and granted or stayed publication. Works printed earlier, or in other countries, could end up on the Index of Prohibited Books. Thus, the educated too came under intellectual tutelage. This Catholic censorship was not unique; Protestants also banned books, but nowhere was their effort so coherent and sustained.

In Rome, where the censorship was especially strong, the only place one could criticize the church and state in writing was on the pedestals of several "talking statues." These were battered antiques scattered around the town, to which one crept at night and hastily affixed satirical remarks, often in dialect and verse. Romans copied these on the sly and passed them around the town. The most famous of these statues, still active today, a stumpy relic fondly called "Pasquino," gave his name in several languages to "pasquinade," an anonymous topical satire.

## THE AUTHORITIES COMMUNICATE

Not only did the authorities censor the messages of others; they also broadcast their own. Renaissance Italians heard from church and state by many routes. Regulations, laws, news of many sorts, and invitations to join in public rituals all needed media adapted to a world less than half literate. Often a platform balcony, the *ringhiera*, served for speeches and announcements. Also, regimes posted notices or hired criers to read them aloud. Wall posters alerted travelers to bandits. Cannon fire and bells rung in special rhythms could call to arms or salute a princely birth or marriage. Regimes might use public art to insult their enemies; they could paint them hanging by the feet or even depict their palaces of government, shamefully inverted. At strategic points, governments also chiseled their heraldry, a proud memento of authority and strength.

The mighty also carved stately verbal messages into public masonry, for the Renaissance revived the ancient Roman custom of monumental inscription. The Middle Ages had for its rare inscriptions used a barely legible, tightly packed gothic hand borrowed from the written page. The Renaissance returned to the bold capital letters of antiquity, angular like our printed capitals, their descendants, writ very large. Regimes, churches, and great families chiseled big self-congratulatory messages over doorways, on window frames, on plinths and plaques. These almost always were in Latin; they were meant to impress, on the model of the many inscriptions of the Caesars still visible on ruins.[7] Sometimes even those who commissioned these carved messages had trouble reading them. In 1556, a papal judge asked a prisoner, the Roman baron Giuliano Cesarini, to explain an intricate inscription over a gate to one of his towns, where he compared himself punningly to Caesar and slighted the popes' authority. The defensive baron, who did know Latin, retorted plausibly enough, "I never paid any heed to those verses and I don't know what they mean." They were just his secretary's concoction.[8] (For

Military drummer sends signals. [Bertelli]

Cesarini's life, see Chapter 2.) Still, even without much Latin, literate Italians could often pick out the name of the patron, whose coat of arms, not rarely, was also on display.

## THE SCOPE OF LITERACY

Irregular patterns of literacy very much complicated the business of communication. The presence of two written languages, one with many dialects, gave Italy many kinds of literacy and semiliteracy, each with its social geography. Latin itself had a double nature. In the millennium since the fall of Rome, the language had not died at all; like any living tongue, it had evolved to suit new uses. The Renaissance still used this practical Latin, which offered a rich, specialized vocabulary, for the technicalities of the law and intellectual arguments. It remained the language of learned treatises, much legislation, and legal record keeping. Notaries, lawyers, high churchmen, university professors, and many officials wrote this workaday Latin fluently and often spoke it readily. Debaters at university and advocates before a judge could wrangle in it. At the same time, there was an elevated Latin, used for writing letters, poetry, fine sermons, histories, and philosophical dialogues. The intellectual movement we call humanism had, from the beginnings of the Renaissance, rebelled against the working Latin of the universities and courts in the name of the elegant language of the classic authors of ancient Rome. It was this refined literary Latin that the elite's schools taught; the language had its practical uses, for a polished letter, a witty epigram, a handsome sermon, a refined funeral oration both gratified recipients and advanced the author. Polished Latin and a handsome humanist hand were refinements very useful in both state and church careers. It is not clear how much Italians could actually converse in this literary Latin; at stricter boarding schools, pupils were supposed to use it. At some, student spies ferreted out backsliders. Certainly, when one tried to speak, one had to adapt a very ancient tongue to new circumstances.

Italian and spoken Latin leached into one another. Borrowing was all the easier because their close kinship gave them a fairly similar grammar and a vast common vocabulary. The technical Latin of intellectual life and law was full of non-Latin terms transposed from the Italian, words for implements, articles of clothing, foods, and feudal tenures unknown to Cicero or Virgil. Meanwhile, spoken Italian, in educated mouths, was full of technical expressions from the Latin (*et cetera*, etc.), just as English today is full of foreign words. Nobles and merchants, if well schooled, might use them; men of the pen did so abundantly, but women, artisans, and peasants seldom.

With its fixed grammar and spelling, Latin was more standardized than Italian, with its dozens of dialects and countless local variants. Some regional versions—Venetian, Lombard, Tuscan, and, to a lesser degree, Roman and Neapolitan—had written literary traditions in which there was a slowly evolving consensus about usage. In the absence of a hegemonic center of power, there was no agreed national language.[9] To make themselves understood by strangers, Italians used the compromise, *cortegiano*, spoken in princely courts. (See Chapter 1.) When a tribunal's notary took down peasant testimony, for ease of use he transformed it into something more like *cortegiano*. In the sixteenth century, this written Italian very gradually took on more and more Tuscan coloration.

Many Italians who knew little or no Latin were literate in some version of Italian. Just how many is hard to say; in general, few peasants and women could read or write, but many males in towns were fair readers, though fewer wrote. Good estimates from late sixteenth-century Venice suggest that one boy in three and one girl in eight at some point went to school. Rates would have been similar in other cities, lower in smaller places. In general, solid merchants wrote handily; further down the social scale there was a vast zone of artisanal semiliteracy. Unlike quirky English, Italian is phonetically simple; with the alphabet and a little patience one could sound out prose and even write sentences. Conventions for spelling were loose and variants tolerated. Without formal training, however, polished penmanship and composition were much harder. Those self-taught or skimpily instructed often wrote with an unsteady hand and a crude sense of where words stopped; their sprawled, uncertain block lettering betrays a valiant struggle to master an unfamiliar medium.[10] By the sixteenth century, unschooled handwriting sometimes reflected the new letter forms featured on its model, the printed page.

Because literacy was so partial, the boundary zone, for both reading and writing, was a busy place of collaboration and compromise. Often two persons sought the help of third parties. In Italy, such collaboration took many forms: professional letter writers for the illiterate; books of epistolary samples for those who wished to send a fitting letter; notarial routines of reading legal papers back "in a loud and intelligible voice" to assure that those unable to read grasped what they signed; criers to proclaim decrees; the customs of reading aloud to oneself, even when alone, and of reading aloud to groups. An eighteenth-century painting shows what must long have been a common sight: four girls making lace, gathered in their chairs around a fifth who entertains them from a book on their matronly supervisor's lap.[11]

Love intrigue illustrates well the social complexities that might arise as less literate women conspired with their paramours. For instance, in 1572 a Roman mistress, though she herself could write sloppily, imprudently used her well-schooled twelve-year-old younger brother to pen and sign a compromising letter to her beloved about his plot on her behalf to poison his inconvenient wife.[12] Another unfaithful spouse, the wife of a notary, had in 1559 to take seductive letters from the man next door to her sisters, nuns who could read. The gold coins folded inside made the message plain enough, but, for the sweet words themselves, her hungry ears needed help. Another lover, a teenaged boy who in 1602 had seduced the girl next door, used both written words and drawings to communicate his heart's desire. His mother, having discovered the intrigue, had banned him from the bedroom in which, like Pyramus with Thisbe, the boy had whispered to his beloved through a chink. Disconsolate, the young man penned a letter in several literary and emotional registers. He began with an elegant address, "Most worthy signorina . . ." in fine school hand and with poetic platitudes about how she was the heart of his life. He then descended into plaintive moans about his interfering mother and sank at the bottom into bawdy doggerel. He then decorated the margin with sexual organs, the owners' names attached. This bizarrely mixed screed he folded, addressed handsomely, and tossed into the next-door basement window. The girl, when she picked it up, knew at once from the art one theme, but could not read the words. Her curiosity led to grief; despite the starkly incriminating pictures, she took the letter for decoding to a brass smith down the street. The neighbor impounded the missive and called in her parents. Letter and lover ended up in court, while the poor girl, a witness for his prosecution, suffered her parents' ire. The document is fascinating for its mixed nature; it plays in many registers, some far more literate than others. The girl, to receive the message, needed collaborators who bestrode the gap between written and oral cultures.[13]

The boundary between the written and the oral was permeable; cultural messages passed both ways. They usually had to make part of the trip by mouth and ear, not by paper. For instance, in 1574, peasants in the hilltop village of Aspra (now Casperia) at a notary's instigation put on a raucous carnival play that contained among other blasphemies a lovelorn holy hermit who in frustration threw his rosary to the ground. Anonymous denunciations landed the amateur thespians in their bishop's court, where they had to recite their parts—the devil, the necromancer, the nymph-besotted hermit, the amorous shepherd, the wily servant—for the judge. Illiterate, most of the actors had learned their lines by hearing them read from a published text. The written play itself aped, as slapstick, a high literary tradition, with nymphs and stilted amorous shepherds of classical pedigree, Renaissance imitations of ancient Greek idealizations of real herdsmen. These literary figures Aspra's real peasants then portrayed, translating them back into Italo-Hellenic countrymen for a mixed audience of villagers, local clergy, and officials. Here, with the help of the printing press and a literate intermediary, the Renaissance revival of ancient literary art found its way, transformed, to the hinterland.[14]

To give another example of cultural seepage: in 1570 Vespasiano Santi, an archivist in Rome, was set up with teenaged Innocentia by his conniving old wet nurse, now a servant in her house. As the girl was an eager reader, Vespasiano paid court to her with a book in praise of virgins, alongside his more usual suitor's gifts of food and clothing. But, from what Innocentia told the court at Vespasiano's trial for defloration and abandonment, what really tugged at her emotions was that he read her love poetry by, he claimed, the famous Ariosto. He also wrote his own. This she tucked into her heart. Touchingly, to the judges she recited from memory one of his offerings; it was flat, conventional stuff, Renaissance "Moon in June," promising fidelity. This was a case of cultural diffusion: by several channels, the refined poet's name and fame and a shadow of his art stole Innocentia's innocence. The end of the trial suggests a happy ending; hooked legally by his poem—because it swore eternal devotion—Vespasiano cracked in court, made peace with the tight-fisted father, confessed, professed his love, gave up the claim to a fatter dowry that, really, had landed him in jail, and married the girl.[15]

It cost Italy much effort to inculcate what literacy it had.
**Schooling**    Formal education took a smaller bite overall than with us, for schooling was far from universal and lasted fewer years. Nevertheless, elite males studied long, and many others had at least some exposure. Teachers were many, in cities, villages, and the houses of the rich. Unlike teachers today, most of whom serve schools with staffs of dozens, most Renaissance instructors worked either on their own or in small groups. Some were private tutors to the rich, sometimes living in. Many others were petty entrepreneurs, teaching from home twenty to forty pupils. Like artisans, they might keep a few assistants around the domestic shop to take extra classes or drill the students. Many such teachers were clerics. After 1550, the new religious orders set up bigger

schools more like the ones we know, where different teachers taught different grades. As with us, their students, when promoted, rose to a higher class and a new instructor.

Renaissance Italy had two educational streams matching its two languages. Latin schools taught skills desired by the governing classes; Italian schools taught skills for commerce. Some persons, like Machiavelli, studied some of both. The curriculum of the Latin schools cultivated the eloquence of classical Rome; pupils concentrated on a few famous authors, in general the very same still taught in Latin classes today: Caesar, Cicero, Ovid, Virgil. Cicero was especially useful, not only a masterful orator, but also the author of several works on rhetoric and of a mass of personal letters. Since most educated Italians were far likelier to use their Latin for official correspondence than for public speaking, Cicero's epistolary legacy was a precious model. Teachers drilled their students in the variety of sentence forms and made them write imaginary letters. This instruction taught imitation, not originality or discovery; it aimed to produce able readers, good speakers, fluent writers who adapted tone to task at hand. Therefore, pupils kept notebooks in which they culled model sentences from the accepted works, in hopes of imitation. At the same time, this schooling paraded Roman models of the moral public life.

The Italian-language schools taught a different set of skills. They trained students in reading their mother tongue. The texts were very often Christian: moral maxims, the lively stories of saints, the pious *Imitation of Christ*. The material was medieval, easily accessible, colorful, and full of practical morality. Schools also used chivalrous romances, tales of knights, damsels, giants, and battles still vastly popular in the Renaissance. Alongside reading and writing, these schools taught a kind of mathematics called *abbaco*. The Florentines had separate *abbaco* schools for youngsters in their early teens. Other cities often taught math and language in tandem. *Abbaco* was the mathematics of commerce; it dealt with weights and measures, currency exchange, interest on investments, the estimation of volumes, and the calculation of costs. Textbooks set problems not very different from those we see in high school algebra textbooks; nevertheless, students did not use algebraic notation to solve them. Rather, to solve for the unknown answer, the preferred method was to find ratios among the terms. As with our algebra, the goal was nimble problem solving. Like us, Italians learned to recognize new problems as variants of a familiar model they could solve. Sometimes, with *abbaco*, there was also training in accounting.

Of the two kinds, only the Latin school led to university, also taught in Latin. The Italian school, furnishing too little Latin to support further study, led to trade. It is a mark of a deep division in culture that the Latin schools taught no practical mathematics; what little they offered was tied to ancient Greek philosophy. The rise of the humanist Latin school coincided with the aristocratization of Italy; the processes that drove a wedge between merchants on the one hand and the governing classes on the other were reflected in the division of schooling into two zones, both pragmatic but very different.

Many students never went beyond lower school. This bottom level might feed both streams. Children started with their hornbooks, wooden boards holding a page printed with a model alphabet to trace and copy. Sometimes a transparent sheet of horn protected the paper underneath (whence the name). These single pages always started with the cross, followed by the alphabet. They might be in both gothic and Renaissance lettering. After Z, they often laid out all the syllables that made up Italian words; Italian and Latin are both easily phonetic; the whole-word approach sometimes used for quirky English was not needed. The hornbook might also have a Latin Lord's Prayer. Beginners then went on to a primer, a little book of twenty or so pages, with more Latin prayers to learn by heart and simple readings in Italian. In the sixteenth century, charitable Sunday catechism schools taught the ABCs by this system, alongside Christian doctrine.

**Documentation**    Whether or not they could read them, Renaissance Italians took documents very seriously. Written records had great legal weight. Well before the Renaissance, there grew up a complex set of standards for validating them. The custodians of legal paper were the notaries, whose job it was to prepare them and to keep a reference copy in their own orderly registers. These men were the bottom rung of the lettered ladder. Dozens worked in any big city, and others resided or circulated in most small towns and many villages. In drafting documents, notaries observed standard forms: a will, a record of sale, an inventory, a marriage contract, a rent, a loan, a hiring, a peace between enemies each had its habitual order and standard phrases. One began by setting out the date, those persons present, and those absent but represented by their agents, and then rolled through the essentials of the transaction, usually in Latin. The prose, like our modern legal language, was lumbered with redundancies—"to possess, to have, and to hold"—lest there be any doubt, and crammed with stock formulas, many of them concerning liabilities for not observing the terms. At the bottom, the notary recorded the place and the names of witnesses and often put his own elaborate sign. The elite notarized often. A strongbox in the master's bedroom or study held key papers. The rich often patronized a favorite notary, who might also serve as a family adviser. Artisans also used notaries, but far less often, to save on fees. Many of their contracts were unwritten—still binding but harder to prove in court.

Other kinds of systematic records abounded. Governments had an officer, called a chancellor, whose disciplined minute taking was akin to notarial work. It too had its rough copy, its good copy, its requirement for proper storage. Administrative bookkeeping was a separate tradition, closer to mercantile practice. All sorts of public and private offices were required to keep orderly accounts. Landlords, for instance, expected the agents of their rural estates to keep careful records of all income and outlays; tribunals required a log of fines and fees collected; churches kept note of tithes; the city grain office had its registers of bushels bought and sold. Italians, pioneer paper-pushers, were adroit keepers, and occasional fakers, of such records.

Renaissance Italians had many reasons to want news from far away. As a society, they owed much of their wealth to their prowess as traders. From the Middle Ages until the end of the Renaissance, Italians dominated long-distance commerce, everywhere from Constantinople, the Black Sea, and Egypt, through the whole Mediterranean, and up to England and the Low Countries. Their agents went even farther. Trading over such distances forced merchants to master communication and record keeping. They had to direct their far-flung partners and agents, and to receive back from them the accounts they needed to balance their double-entry ledgers. All news of crops, prices, currency fluctuations, and politics was germane to trade. Keeping informed was a tricky business, for the mails moved slowly. Spain was a month away, by sea, as were the Netherlands and England, via the Alpine passes. The eastern Mediterranean was harder to reach and slower to report. Galleys made mail quicker; their oarsmen could keep going even in a calm. Even so, it took several months to have a reply from Alexandria. Because secrecy was crucial, merchants often wrote in code, using a cipher their agents carried with them. They kept careful copies of their correspondence and mustered all their accounts to keep a complex business in clear view.

**Correspondence and Journalism: News from Far Away**

As they developed the machinery of diplomacy, the Italian states took to posting permanent ambassadors to reside in foreign capitals. These officials, as part of their assignment, sent back a stream of letters abrim with astute political observations. These too, for safety's sake, often lapsed into veiled language, code names, and numerical ciphers. Rulers and councils of state, like the merchants, possessed a view of the world at once panoramic and sharply detailed. By a curious evolution, the politicians' private collecting of information gave rise as well to a proto-journalism, a parallel system of information gathering, on retainer. The *avvisi* writers scrounged for rumors, both foreign and domestic. These they penned once a week and sent with the regular couriers as letters to the prince who paid their keep. These bulletins were not secret; they were copied and distributed widely.

Alongside written journalism was an oral mode with a wider audience. Storytellers called *cantastorie* (story singers) or *cantimbanchi* (singers on the stage) made their living by entertaining in the streets. Sometimes they regaled the crowd with old favorites, but their stock in trade included news: as today, a good flood or earthquake caught the public ear. Less mercenary were the prophets of doom, who garnished earnest prognostications with news of recent portents and disasters, odd rainbows, strange swarms of red butterflies, two-headed calves, and ghostly armies clashing in the sky.

## PREACHING

Sermons were another meeting place between written and oral culture. The great preachers were highly educated men, capable of long Latin disquisitions to learned gatherings. But, to reach the common folk, they spoke Italian. They did not read their sermons, which went on for hours, but composed on the spot; the preacher had a sense of route and destination, but, like a good jazz musician, played off his own performance and his audience's response. A good preacher possessed a hoard of proverbs and lively stories, cribbed from anthologies and life, with which to catch the ear and mind. Though his central message had deep roots in written culture, his artistry was oral. At the moment of delivery, however, written culture sometimes retrieved these oral performances; stenographers in the audience took notes. They seldom caught everything. An exception proves the rule: when a notary in Florence recorded the entire speeches of the charismatic Franciscan Savonarola, "the very least word and act being inscribed exactly, without a single iota wanting," citizens called the feat "superhuman" and a miracle.[16] More normal were abstracts, like the best lecture notes, that caught some of the sense and feel of the original. These then circulated among the literate, who sometimes read them aloud to others.

---

### A SERMON FOR THE COMMON PEOPLE

Here is an excerpt from a sermon by Bernardino of Siena, as recorded by a member of his audience. As often, the saint takes an amusing story to make a higher point:

> I once fell prey to the wish to live like an angel. Not like a man, I tell you. I got the notion to live on water, and on greens, and I got it into my head to go live in the woods. I began to say to myself, "What will you do in the woods? What will you eat?" And I answered, talking to myself just like that, "It'll be just fine. Doing it the way the Holy Fathers did. I will eat greens when I am hungry, and when I am thirsty, I'll drink water." And

so that was my plan, to live on the model of God, and I planned to buy a Bible to read, and a pilgrim's vest to wear. I bought the Bible, and off I went to buy a chamois skin, to keep water from coming in the sides and getting the Bible wet. And, with my plan in mind, I went looking for a place to coop myself up. I thought I would go check out the Massa district, and when I was in the Boccheggiano valley, I went looking first at one hilltop and then at another, first in this forest, then in that, and I went along, saying to myself, "Oh, this will be the good place to live! Oh, this one will be even better!" In brief, never turning back, I went back to Siena and began to try out the life that I intended to keep. So I went to a place outside the gate on the Fallonica road and I began to gather me a salad of cresses and other wild greens. And I had neither bread, nor salt, nor oil. And I said, "Let's start, for this first time, to wash it and scrape it clean, and the next time we will scrape it without any other washing, and when we are more used to it, we will do it without cleaning it, and finally we will do it without even picking it." And, calling on the blessed name of Jesus, I started with a mouthful of cress, and, sticking it in my mouth, began to chew it. Chew! Chew! It wouldn't go down. I couldn't swallow it at all; I said, "Enough of that! Let's start by drinking a spot of water." Heavens! The water didn't go down; the cress was still in my mouth. In the end, I drank a lot of gulps of water with one mouthful of cress, and I couldn't get it down. You know what I want to say? With one mouthful of cress I washed away every temptation, and do I ever know that that was temptation! What came after [my becoming a Franciscan] was election [religious choice], not temptation. Oh, how you have to weigh it in the balance before you follow your will, for often many bad things arise, even if they seem good![1]

---

## MEMORY

All Renaissance media—script, image, speech, and pageantry—served individual and collective memory. Religion, lordship, civic identity, family pride, and legal and commercial imperatives all fostered records of the past. The Renaissance evolved in this area; far more than the Middle Ages, it wrote history. There were two distinct practices: retrieving the past to inform the present and recording the present to instruct the future. Historical writing had been a literary genre in ancient Greece and Rome. Educated Italians began, self-consciously, to imitate that model, composing histories of their cities and even, boldly, of Italy itself. They also began to invent tools of scholarship to comment on the laws and customs of the ancient world. Such study very gradually helped build a sense of historical difference, of the cultural pastness of the past, a sense quite foreign to medieval thought, though we now take it for granted. The rise of historical thought probably inspired some of the family chronicles, meant not for publication but for domestic consumption. Marcello

Alberini, a Roman nobleman who wrote just for family, for instance, set his own life, marked by the horrors of the Sack of 1527, in the context of the struggle between his class and the papal court to determine who ruled Rome. Other kinds of family history, however, lacked Alberini's sense of historical evolution. In the sixteenth century, noble families hired genealogists to trace their remotest ancestors, as if the reach were easy; with luck, effort, and self-delusion, one might thread one's way back to a Roman emperor or even a veteran of the Sack of Troy. There was another variety of domestic history writing. The hundreds of family record books (*ricordanze*) concentrated on domestic events and personal doings. Often such records smacked of ledger keeping: enter each wife and her dowry and the birth of each child; debit each of the many deaths. At the same time, the authors often took note of family memories, noted the doings of the extended kin, and laid down lessons in life useful to their posterity, for these writings aimed to instruct one's heirs. A closely related genre was the diary, strictly speaking a day-by-day record of events, though some works we call diaries in fact scooped several weeks into an entry. The merchants' habit of recording outgoing mail may have been one inspiration for the form. Most diaries were relatively impersonal; they focused on public events: wars, politics, portents, and natural calamities. Although they might note the writer's occasional amazement, distress, or indignation, they have none of the self-absorbed introspection of the modern diary.

Not all social memory leaned on script. Families, towns, churches, and states had oral and figurative means of keeping the past alive. Legends, songs, festivals, pageants, treasured relics, and decorated monuments all served to preserve, and to transform, the record of the past. Moreover, religion, by stressing prayers for the sake of one's own dead, fostered a sense of community with those no longer living.

## CONCLUSION

Renaissance Italians were alert to communications of all sorts. In schools and elsewhere, they taught the many subtle skills that made nuanced speech and writing possible. They used their many media—verbal and visual—to transmit practical information, to pass judgment, to express and adjust hierarchy, to exercise social control, and to foster a sense of continuity with bygone days. The new techniques of print and art lent themselves to these complex social tasks.

## NOTES

1. On the reports of marvels and disasters, see Laurie Nussdorfer, "Print and Pageantry in Baroque Rome," *Sixteenth Century Journal* 29 (1998), 439–464.

2. On the evolution of the Italian library, see Nikolaus Pevsner, *The History of Building Types* (Princeton: Princeton University Press, 1976), 91–97, and Armando Petrucci, *Writers and Readers in Medieval Italy*, trans. C. Radding (New Haven: Yale University Press, 1995), 203–235.

3. On how a patron instructed a painter, see Michael Baxandall, *Painting and Experience in Fifteenth-Century Italy* (Oxford: Oxford University Press, 1972), 3–27.

4. On family chapels, see Francis William Kent, *Household and Lineage in Renaissance Florence* (Princeton: Princeton University Press, 1977), 100–117.

5. On pageantry, see Roy Strong, *Splendour at Court: Renaissance Spectacle and Illusion* (London: Weidenfield and Nicolson, 1973).

6. On Counter-Reformation pious books, see Paul Grendler, *Schooling in Renaissance Italy: Literacy and Learning, 1300–1600* (Baltimore: Johns Hopkins University Press, 1989), 359–362.

7. On the history of public inscriptions, see Armando Petrucci, *Public Lettering*, trans. L. Lappin (Chicago: University of Chicago Press, 1993).

8. Archivio di Stato di Roma (ASR), Governatore, Tribunale Criminale, Processi sixteenth century, b. 29, case 7, 10r (1557).

9. On the evolution of a national Italian language, see Peter Burke, "Languages and Anti-Languages," in *Historical Anthropology of Early Modern Italy* (Cambridge: Cambridge University Press, 1987), 79–94, and Peter Burke, *The Art of Conversation* (Oxford: Polity Press, 1993).

10. For photographs of sixteenth- and seventeenth-century popular handwriting, see Armando Petrucci, *Scrittura e popolo nella Roma barocca, 1585–1721* (Rome: Edizioni Quasar, 1982), 78–79, 102, 109, 124–125.

11. Reproduced in Francesco Porzio, *Da Caravaggio a Ceruti* (Milan: Skira, 1998), 235.

12. ASR, Governatore, Tribunale Criminale, Processi sixteenth century, b 180, case 7 (1582).

13. Elizabeth S. Cohen, "Between Oral and Literate Culture: The Social Meaning of an Illustrated Love Letter," in *Culture and Identity in Early Modern Europe (1500–1800): Essays in Honor of Natalie Zemon Davis*, ed. B. Diefendorf and C. Hesse (Ann Arbor: University of Michigan Press, 1993), 181–201.

14. Thomas Cohen and Elizabeth Cohen, *Words and Deeds in Renaissance Rome* (Toronto: University of Toronto Press, 1993). 234–277.

15. ASR, Governatore, Tribunale Criminale, Processi sixteenth century, b. 137, case 5 (1570).

16. Luca Landucci, *A Florentine Diary*, trans. A. Jervis (London: J. M. Dent and Sons, 1927), 130 (entry for February 24, 1497).

17. From Marco Masuelli, ed., *Letterature, religiosi, e società del medioevo* (Turin: Paravia, 1975) (our translation).

# 9

# Spaces

Renaissance Italy, like any civilization, had its own habits of spatial perception and spatial thought. The spaces that the Renaissance inherited or created, urban and rural, public and private, both shaped and reflected Italian modes of seeing. The Italian ambiance thus had its very distinctive look, the fruit of a culture different from our own. Nevertheless, in some ways, the Renaissance is the intellectual progenitor of our own spatial sense, for thanks to its inventions we readily conceive of space abstractly and geometrically. For us, miles and kilometers are mathematical measures, laid across emptiness like giant rulers aligned with compass points. Our travels, by air or along smooth highways, eat up distance with monotonous regularity; we readily calculate arrival times from speed. Our maps are precisely scaled miniatures of real spaces, and our cities and farm plots, especially in lands colonized by Europeans, are often grids laid out by eighteenth- and nineteenth-century surveyors who cavalierly imposed abstract Cartesian geometry on what was, for them if not for the dispossessed aboriginals, blank terrain. The rulered map became the mother, not the child, of landscapes.

But what was the Renaissance contribution to this geometric view of space? There were several aspects to it, all interlinked. The painters' invention of linear perspective was a mathematical operation; the first practitioners often set their saints on a tiled floor, the two-dimensional equivalent of a ruler receding correctly toward the vanishing point. One of perspective's first theoreticians, Leon Battista Alberti, a genius famous for his many talents—author, architect, mathematician, proto-scientist—

The geometry of gardens. [Tempesta]

also pioneered the surveyor's science of angles and baselines for the
exact mapping of cities.[1] At first, little came of this innovation of the
1430s, but, seventy years later, Leonardo da Vinci, using a similar system,
drafted exact urban maps for the ambitious military plans of Cesare Bor-
gia, Pope Alexander's ruthless son.[2] In the late sixteenth century, precise
cartography of cities and the countryside developed swiftly, using both
surveying and the methods of late medieval marine charts based on compass bearings. At the same time, a passion for geometry swept architecture; the ubiquitous Alberti was an early pioneer. From the late fifteenth
century, the same delight in measurement and line inspired a new kind
of urban planning that imposed rational geometry on cities. At the end
of the Renaissance, Galileo brought to both his physics and his astron-
omy a profoundly geometrical conception of body, space, and motion.

Meanwhile, the invention of the siege cannon gave geometry another
boost. By the middle of the fifteenth century, military engineers began
to use the new surveyor's tools to site and sight their guns. In reply to
this new military threat, from the beginning of the sixteenth century, an
Italian invention, the star-shaped fortress with its bastion walls, parried

the challenge of artillery. This military novelty soon swept Europe and its expanding empires. The new fortifications were a geometer's delight; a few degrees more angle here, a few less there for better line of fire, a steeper wall to storm, a deeper ditch to cross might make all the difference between victory and surrender.[3]

Despite these intellectual innovations, everyday life usually experienced space in older, less metric ways. To most Italians, distance was effort; our modern, everyday geometric vision befits a world where travel's frictions are much lower than in Renaissance Italy. How far to the market? Two hundred steps! Two stone throws! A crossbow shot! Or, later, an arquebus shot! The mile (*miglio*) was still, as in ancient Rome, as its name implies (*mille* means thousand) a thousand paces. Often Italians thought of travel in hours and days rather than in abstract distances. Area, likewise, was often labor, or yield. Peasants sometimes measured their woods and vineyards in "labors" (*opere*) or their fields in "days of work" (*giornate*). Grain land might come in yields: "cups" or "bushels" (*rubbie*); a villager could say, oddly, that he had ten "bushels" of land that yielded annually eight bushels of grain. Acreage and yield clearly were linked by a slightly elastic bond.

## RURAL SPACE

So varied was Italian geography that in the Renaissance, as now, there was no typical landscape. Rather, the natural setting combined with local traditions, and economic and social conditions to set the uses and the look and feel of rural space.[4] (See Chapter 1.) Mountains, hill country, and plains had very different appearances. Suburban land, dense with walled gardens, was unlike the open plow land farther out from town. The wealthy, crowded North was unlike the sparsely populated, often poorer South. The geography of land tenure also counted; solid sharecropper farms in the Center contrasted with great southern estates with huddled, shabby housing for their hired laborers.

The mountain landscape was seldom far away. Italians not only saw it; many of them also used it, taking wood and charcoal, and edible chestnuts from the woods, and driving pigs for acorns, and goats and sheep for pasture. In the Renaissance, millions of sheep converged on the high Appennines in summer, wreaking ecodevastation, but earning rulers a good income from the transit rights they paid. A sixteenth-century traveler remarked that, so many were the shepherds' tents and fires in the high Abruzzi, they looked at night like an invading army.[5] The mountains were therefore laced with paths and trails. Renaissance Italians had none of our romantic love of mountainscape; they saw it as rough country, full of rough men and real dangers, but also useful.

On the other hand, Italians loved the hills. They preferred their nature softened by a human touch. The hill country near Venice, Padua, Florence, Siena, Rome, Naples, and Palermo was like a giant garden; around each village extended a widening zone of walled or hedged plots, given over to carefully planted rows of fruit trees strung with grapevines, and to olives, hemp, cane, melons, and garden vegetables. Where the land was steep, walls and terraces of earth or stone prevented erosion and offered cultivation a level surface of shored-up soil. The Renaissance saw a great spate of terrace building; the spectacularly perpendicular lemon groves of the Amalfi coast, for instance, often date from then. The garden zone was often full of farmsteads, with their many outbuildings and constructions: stables, granaries, hay sheds, tall dovecotes, threshing floors, cisterns. In hill country, beyond the gardens was an emptier outer zone of grain and common pasture. There, walls were fewer and property rights less absolute. In these hills, one saw a good deal of geometry—not the precise mathematics of the surveyor but the pragmatic, responsive geometry of agriculture. Terrace walls conformed to contour lines of hills, and fields and trees aligned themselves in orderly ways that pleased both painters and agronomists. The hills also delighted the wealthy villa owners, who, especially after 1500, built themselves commodious country refuges from politics and summer heat. There they installed ornamental gardens, geometrical feasts for all the senses, where the sudden vista of a statue at the end of a tunnel of tall cypresses, or a cool mock-grotto full of dripping mosses, or a hemicycle of antique statues and tinkling fountains might delight and impress a guest or lift the owner's weary spirits.[6] By design, such gardens were complex spaces, full of subtle modulation and contrast.

The plains varied greatly. Lombardy, well watered and full of wealthy cities that invested in the land, increasingly showed the hand of ambitious intervention. Too much water required careful ditching, with canals to carry runoff. These ran ruler straight, and the lines of mulberry trees or poplars, often strung with grapes, that lined their banks, laid out the precise geometry of the big fields. Well-watered meadows supported livestock good for meat and cheese. Other zones, however, off the beaten track, were still swamp, heath, or woods. Another plain, the Terra di Lavoro behind Naples, was full of gardens to feed Italy's biggest city. The plains near Rome and stretching northward into coastal Tuscany were very different. There, in the Renaissance, tillage declined, and sheep and goats took over. Depopulation permitted swamps that fostered malaria and drove off yet more occupants. Travelers to Rome often remarked on the desolation of the lonely landscape—green in spring and full of sheep, but yellow and deserted in malarial summer. In dry Apulia, Italy's Southeast, great estates grew wheat and fed sheep in winter; towns were few and poor.

Whether mountain, hills, or plain, the Italian landscape was emptier, wilder, and more wooded than today. Modern Italy is 21 percent forest, much of it mountainous; in 1500, woods covered some 50 percent of the peninsula, and they were more varied, more robust, and far fuller of wildlife. In the sixteenth century, there still were bears in the Casentino, near Florence, storks and beaver in the marshes near Ferrara, and pelicans aplenty along the Tuscan coast.[7] Wolves abounded in many zones, and there were big game enough to keep noble hunters happy. In 1515, on a single expedition, Pope Leo X and his party bagged fifty deer and twenty boar not far from Rome. Some of the most extensive forests of the Venetian Alps, Tuscany, and Calabria sheltered under the protection of states keen to preserve them for beams for cathedrals, palaces, and ship timbers, and for turpentine for naval caulking. Yet, in the sixteenth century, rising population and lax administration in many zones encouraged illegal clearances, overzealous cutting, and heavy foraging and grazing, all activities that eroded the forest. As deforestation and marsh drainage evicted wildlife, the hunt declined.

Although there was no single village architecture, some general rules did hold. Villages often were tightly packed    **Housing** places. In many zones they had girdling walls with gates that shut at night. In hill country and the mountains, they often perched for safety, high above armies and mosquitoes. There might be a fort, or a palace of their lord, or both; often these were solid, plain structures, with here and there a heraldic emblem on the wall. Almost always there was a square, perhaps beside the church or by the hall where the council sat. Village streets were almost always narrow; some were no more than paths or stairs, one laden donkey wide. Arches and overhanging houses might make streets dark and fairly cool in summer. In the seventeenth century, when painters first depicted country life, they habitually showed villages as shabby, ramshackle places, with cracked plaster, missing bricks, broken furnishings, and humble trim. Some of this slipshod image may have been artistic convention, but there was probably much truth in it, both then and earlier.[8]

In many parts of Italy, especially in the South, outside the villages, there were few structures. The immediate outskirts of cities and towns might have shacks in the vineyards of modest urbanites, and imposing villas of the rich. Farther out, there would be inns along the major roads and mills along streams. Other zones had isolated farmhouses; these were common in the North and Center, Sardinia, eastern Sicily and other regions. In Lombardy, these were often solid buildings around courtyards, housing several families who worked a big estate, somewhat defensible against raiding parties. In the lowland outside Rome, big houses called *casali* sheltered the administration of estates, while the dozens of poor migrant laborers spent their work season heaped in awful shacks. In the grain lands of Apulia and central Sicily, laborers hired themselves out from big villages of mean houses to work the vast *latifondi*, often leaving wives behind to tend their modest garden plots. Some buildings in the country were not for agriculture; in coastal zones, isolated towers, *torri saraceni*, offered quick refuge should a Moorish ("Saracen") slaving raid come through and relayed along the coast smoke signals of the enemy's approach.

**Place Names**    One very sharp difference between the Italian landscape and that of the English-speaking New World is the density of the names it bore. Centuries of use draped a thick quilt of nomenclature over fields, ditches, springs, fountains, woods, shrines, lanes, paths, and other features. Some of these names commemorated persons or events; many others took note of the use and features of the land. Inhabitants of one mountain village in central Italy worked Toadstool Plain, Field of Flowers, Long Clearing, the Cutting, Stick-Stockade, Little Tower, Dark Valley, Greenish Valley, Valley of the Chain-Link, the Swamp, Ditch Hill, Pigeon Hill, Charcoal-burner's Place, the Fig Tree, the Little Live Oak, Little-pole Chestnut, Little Roses, the [sacred] Image, Big Crow, Blind Ditch, Little-market Bridge, Cat Hill, Long Hill, Mountain Hill, Marble Spring, Swamp Spring, Cold Spring, Sun Mountain, Well Woods and many, many other places, some of them as intelligible as these and others, in the usual way of names, now mysterious. Such local names bore rich associations that outsiders would not know. They helped give each village its own lore and anchored collective memory of gifts, dowries, sales, confiscations, quarrels, crimes, fines paid, crops, costly improvements, damages suffered, bandit raids, floods, lightning strikes, and holy visions.[9]

## URBAN SPACE

As spaces, Italian cities were very different from the modern ones we know. They had very distinct boundaries: high walls, often with impressive towers, and imposing gateways with great doors that shut at night. The confining fortifications made them densely settled, for the imperatives of defense ruled out urban sprawl. The older quarters were often a jumble of closely set buildings, some with jutting upper stories. Arching buttresses and elevated passageways vaulted the street, so that little sky showed. Footing was cobblestones or mud. The streets, narrow and irregular, bent and twisted; a walker seldom saw very far ahead. The city looked and, with its livestock, sounded and smelled like a village, though with bigger buildings. The older parts of Viterbo today still have this jumbled quality. In the Muslim Mediterranean, cities built even denser mazes, barely penetrable neighborhoods of tiny alleys, almost sealed off from one another. Italian cities were more permeable; labyrinthine Amalfi, a very Levantine-looking place, was an exception. But to outsiders their medieval quarters were not very legible. Major streets were easier to follow; linking gates and major squares, they cut through the mazes without too many turns. Then the Renaissance, with its nascent passion for rational geometry, imposed a new urban planning.[10] The authorities wanted a transparent city, with long vistas lined with elegant facades. Reason, not tradition or utility, would lay out the town. Geometry testified to princely power. Princes and popes set out on ambitious campaigns to widen squares and cut broad avenues through medieval tangles to impose clean grids on districts. One favorite device was to set a focal monument at the far end of an urban vista; in Rome, sixteenth-century popes re-erected old Egyptian obelisks, stone needles once brought as booty by the Caesars. The pontiff Christianized them a little, perching sacred emblems of bronze at the apex and inscribing pious boasts on the base. Several major streets, arrow straight, would converge on such a monument. This fashion for straight lines and long prospects would have a very long history in Europe and its colonies. Washington, D.C., with its convergent avenues, for instance, is very much an heir to it, as are most grid cities.

Streets often had a very intimate feel. Even the main ones were seldom wide. In much of the Italian North, vaulted arcades ran along the sides, at ground level, holding up the upper stories, protecting commerce and strollers from rain or sun, and, at night, sometimes hiding assailants behind the pillars. Fear of nocturnal ambush, hopes of easing traffic, and new Renaissance taste in palace architecture caused some regimes to knock these convenient shelters down, but in many towns they survive today. Streets were busy places, as full of social life as they were of transport; commerce spilled out of the houses into the roadway as merchants folded their shutters up and outward to make a sloping overhang against the sun and rain, and heaped their wares on jutting benches. In many cities, even palaces had ground-floor commerce and, often, lodgings for the merchants behind the shops or on a mezzanine just upstairs. This source of extra income did not diminish the prestige of these grand buildings.

Amid the palaces and houses, Renaissance streets, despite efforts to clean them, were also often messy. Herds and flocks, mule trains, oxen pulling wagons, horses harnessed or saddled all dropped their droppings. Pigs rooted underfoot. Householders, against the rules, left slops and heaps of steaming stable sweepings. Markets spread rotting detritus. Smelly water sat in ditches. When unpaved, roads alternated between mire and summer dust. Renaissance grandeur often rose amid squalor.

Among the city's houses were other structures. There were churches big and small, arcaded market halls, and solid seats of government. In the mid-fifteenth century, there appeared a new kind of house, so grand as to be called a palace.[11] Other countries would copy this imposing domestic structure, an Italian Renaissance innovation. In the rest of Europe, the medieval elite, being rural, had invested little in urban real estate.

The Renaissance skyline was very unlike ours. Many towns still had their medieval towers. These tall fingers of fortification had been common in twelfth-century Italy; noble families had built them for prestige and for prowess in civil war, sometimes linking several with high galleries to fortify an entire city block.[12] In their struggle to impose internal peace, urban regimes often knocked such towers to the ground or lopped them back to a legislated height, but many of these austere, almost windowless pillars still punctuated the cityscape, vying with the bell towers of the churches and the municipality. As the Renaissance progressed, more and more palaces sported peaceable rooftop pavilions called *belvederes* (the name means "good view"). There, the elite took the evening breeze and enjoyed the prospect of the town below. Furthermore, although the great age of dome building came after 1600, a few early cupolas bellied upward among the angular towers.

The city's grander structures were very solid. Walls could be six feet thick or more, all stone. Lesser buildings were flimsy and often small; they are less likely to have survived. A substantial house or church, with its thick walls and few windows, resisted summer's heat; as now, Italians often passed from the dazzling midday sun to the dim cool of interiors. Winter, sadly, offered no corresponding indoor warmth.

The piazza was a crucial feature of urban life, a place for ceremony, games, commerce, and busy socializing. The bustling urban piazza, enclosed, paved, and uncluttered by structures, is common in Europe (and rare in the New World, where the few squares are mostly given over to greenery and lonesome statuary, if not to a noxious swirl of traffic). These Italian spaces varied in shape, size, and function. Cities often had three major ones—for the market, for the major church, and for the seat of government—each with its characteristic functions. Sometimes one square did several jobs, and sometimes there were multiple markets and sacred sites. There were also lesser local squares. In Venice, for instance, the *campo* (field) in the center of each of the many little islands remained open, functioning as the communal public space for neighbors who lived within a circle of canals. Many other cities also had small squares, the focus of a quarter. They were places where one felt safer, among one's own.

As Italians walked or rode through cities, they felt the continual modulation of their space. There was visual and kinesthetic drama in the passage from tight to open and from open back to tight. Few sights are more splendid than a great square, when you debouche from a narrow, crowded alley. And it stirs the soul to enter a handsome courtyard or a

soaring church. Density, variety, and spatial complexity are always en-
livening, for they keep the senses on their toes.

Although Italians were fiercely loyal to their cities, they
often felt just as devoted to neighborhood.[13] Various urban      **Divisions of**
tracts invited local allegiance. Most cities had quarters or         **the Town**
other major divisions, often responsible for defending an
assigned segment of the city wall; these might also serve as electoral
districts. They possessed their insignia, their places of march in processions, their patron saints, and, often, their well-defined points of entry.
They sometimes fielded teams in civic races and other games, or put on
floats for carnival festivities. Some cities, Pisa and Venice, for instance,
divided in two, the halves of town waging great mock battles on bridges
on the boundary line; the heady partisanship spilled over into endemic
skirmishing and taunts. (See Chapter 16.) Other divisions were less formal. In many cities, strong families colonized certain zones, buying and
building houses and, in earlier centuries, towers along a street or around
a square. Their dependents and allies crowded around them; often such
elite families chose spouses and business partners from nearby streets.
These local loyalties could ramify, to cover much of the city. In Rome,
for instance, in the fifteenth century, the Orsini barons, papal partisans,
and their allies dominated the approaches to the Tiber bridge to the
Vatican, while some ten blocks to the east camped their ancient enemies,
the imperialist Colonna and their clients. In the middle dwelled noble
families who tried to steer a neutral course amid occasional street warfare. When a city was full of violence, men watched their step when off
their turf. One goal of pacification was to make the whole town safe for
all.

Alongside the political divisions of the city were economic ones. There
were often richer and poorer parts. In some cities, the elite built their
houses close together, not rarely around the square of government.
Poorer districts often lay along the walls, far from the seat of power.
Nevertheless, there was less segregation by wealth than in most modern
cities; elite families' suspicion of one another, their renting out shops in
their palaces, their desire for a large clientele of underlings, and their
housing many servants all kept them from withdrawing to an enclave
all their own. Economic segregation sometimes had to do with trades;
certain professions and crafts would settle all in one place. Several forces
concentrated trades. It might be zoning regulations, as against smelly
tanneries and butcher shops, or a local resource, such as plentiful water
for dyers and millers, or ports and roads for taverns and prostitutes, or
the convenience of having colleagues near at hand, as with bankers. (See
Chapter 15.) Another kind of segregation was social. A nationality might
cluster around favorite taverns or the church it sponsored. Jews, even

Sporting sword-
fight on a
Venetian district
boundary.
[Bertelli]

before sixteenth-century legislation forced them into ghettos, usually
lived together for safety and easy access to their synagogue.

All these divisions produced a complex local geography. Often the
names of streets and squares reflected city life: families, trades, activities.
As in the countryside, in towns nomenclature was dense with meaning.
There were no street numbers and, for most of the period, no street maps.
People navigated in nonmetric ways. They described events as taking
place near one or another palace or church, or down by a tree just ten
steps past a familiar shop, and assumed that their hearer also knew well
the texture and layout of the town.

              One other great division of the city involved the sacred.
**Sacred Spaces**    For Renaissance Catholicism, sacredness was far from
              smoothly spread. Although God was by definition every-
where, special holiness adhered to sacred persons, times, words, gestures, and, what is germane here, to objects and places. Holy images of
the Madonna and the saints, relics (precious bones, hair, dried milk and
blood, bits of cloth, and other remnants), and the sacred wafer of the
consecrated host all concentrated God's grace and power. Accordingly,

they demanded reverence and protection. Much such holiness inhered in churches or chapels. Many cities had a patron saint, the chief protector and focus of civic religion, who usually resided in the cathedral. Meanwhile, the Virgin, babe in lap, smiled down from many street corners or sat in a little roadside shrine, where citizens paid their respects with small gifts and burning candles. These madonnas were legion; Venice had more than four hundred of them.[14] They discouraged blasphemy, protected the poor, advanced peace, and warded off disease. Sometimes, in thanks for miraculous help, the faithful nailed beside these icons ex-voto plaques recording the grace received. Some cities put up special monuments in thanksgiving for deliverance, especially from the plague. Thus, although a city's special sacred places and most powerful images lay in churches, under custody of clergy, there was also local sacrality all over town, helping out and admonishing citizens to respect the holy and keep the peace.

The spatial features of Italian cities almost always owed a great deal to the ancient world. Venice is the great exception, for only in the confusion at the empire's fall did mainlanders take refuge on its offshore islands. **Evolution of City Structure** Otherwise, almost always, there is a Roman core or, as in Naples, Siracusa and other southern places, an ancient Greek colony. The shrunken cities of the early Middle Ages cannibalized the ancient buildings for their masonry, colonized and fortified them, or recycled them as churches. Often, later buildings perched on ancient foundations. Thus, thanks to cellars, in many cities the street pattern of the ancient Roman city still survives today. Aerial photographs, a good map, or the view from the cathedral's roof will still show the characteristic tidy grid of square blocks, aligned neatly with the compass points. This is true of downtown Florence, of Piacenza, of Verona (except where the river has bitten off two corners), and of many other places. Naples still has the un-Roman long parallel streets and oblong blocks of its Greek ancestor. In the late empire and the earlier Middle Ages, towns threw up protective walls, usually a tight perimeter, around the Roman core. After 1100, as they prospered and grew, they put up a second defensive ring and then, in the thirteenth or fourteenth century, to accommodate still more growth, built an ambitious third circuit. The geography of these outer zones usually had none of the Romans' prim geometry. The new walls captured radial roads heading for other towns from the original gates; these trade roads determined both the shape of neighborhoods, many of which had begun as extramural suburbs, and the location of the gates in each later perimeter. Sometimes the lesser streets and alleys of the expanding town had once been lanes between old fields. Many cities, anticipating yet more growth, had thrown out a wide circuit of fortifications not long before the Black Death of 1347, and then, under the impact of recurrent waves of pestilence, had shriveled. As a consequence, even in the sixteenth century, many cities still had fields and gardens inside the fourteenth-century ring.

Many cities had a citadel.[15] The term *cittadella* means "little city"— with reason, for this great fortress was often a world apart. Usually it housed the troops of a lord, foreign or domestic, who held the town against its will. The citadel was girt with stronger walls than the rest of town, a tougher nut to crack. Customarily it sat on the edge, as an anchor to the circuit of walls. On its townward side lay a zone empty of houses, a free field of fire, so that, were the town to fall to an enemy or rise up against the regime, defenders could lay down a withering barrage.

## GENDER AND SPACE

Gender sometimes shapes the use of space.[16] Women claim some places, at certain times, as their own; men dominate other locations, where women usually feel out of place. In the Mediterranean region, these gendered differences, though most marked in Muslim countries, are felt in many Christian zones. In general, domestic space, especially the kitchen, is female, while public places—the street, the square, and the inn—are male. But the well and the collective wash tubs (or river bank), though out in the open, are places frequented largely by the women, and the market often has its female sellers. Certainly these general patterns held for Renaissance Italy. That is why so often in paintings of great processions, resolutely male, the windows are full of female faces; the sill was their habitual boundary. In general, the higher the woman's status, the less freely she moved about, and, when she sallied forth, the more she needed chaperons. In Venice, elite women seldom left the narrow boundaries of their parishes. Village women, on the other hand, roamed widely, picking fruits and olives, fetching water, carrying washing, running errands; they were too useful to coop up at home. Similarly, for need and pleasure, lower-status urban women moved about streets alone.

## HOUSES AND PALACES AS SPACES

Houses varied hugely in structure, shape, and size. Since every region had its own architecture, general remarks are hard. Some distinctions made a great difference: urban versus rural, rich versus poor, new versus old. Urban houses were often suited to trade, rural ones to farming. The former often had shops, workshops, storage rooms, and an open front for streetside commerce, while the latter often housed livestock and stored tools and supplies. In some zones, country houses were solid and spacious, in others often mean and squalid. Urban houses, protected by the city walls, less often built safeguards against attack than did isolated farmsteads. As for wealth, the houses of the very rich in the Renaissance were proper palaces, with a sumptuous architecture that made dramatic use of space to delight and to impress. Those of the well-to-do shared some of the same features, especially the desire for convenience and comfort. The urban poor, meanwhile, very often, dwelled in a room or two alongside other households, or shared a bed in a room, in a building neither grand nor solid nor agreeable. Older buildings in the Renaissance, and they were many, still had medieval lineaments: military trim, tight windows randomly placed, bits of structure jutting up or out. Newer ones took on the traits of a rapidly evolving architecture that prized grandeur, symmetry, light, and comfort.

Whether grand or humble, Renaissance buildings had some common spatial traits. An important one was the courtyard. Almost all palaces had at least one great central space and often several minor ones. One entered through an imposing central door, passing down a vaulted corridor, and entered a shapely central yard, paved and lined on all or most sides by columns and porticoes. The palace courtyard was a ceremonial space, embellished with works of art and, usually, with the emblems of the patrons. Simpler houses had humbler central spaces. They were utilitarian expanses, convenient and fairly secure. There might be a well and doors to storerooms; sometimes tradesmen arrived with donkeys to unload gear. Children could play there under watchful eyes, safe from street traffic, and men and women of the several households in the building could meet and gossip. A second common spatial configuration was the loggia, an arcaded porch or balcony. In the Mediterranean, a covered place to take the air sheltered from sun or rain made excellent sense. The colonnaded walks around courtyards fitted this architectural pattern, as did the covered walks of many cities. Some loggias were on the public street; palaces offered them magnanimously to passers-by or used them to hold showy dinners under the envious public gaze. As the Renaissance progressed, this last custom fell from favor; a move toward privacy, and toward class segregation, encouraged indoor loggias, facing the back garden. More modest houses also might have such upstairs galleries. From an upstairs loggia, women might hang washing, observe the men's activities, or flirt from a discreet distance.

Whether grand or modest, houses used the ground floor less for living than for work and storage. Often, to ward off trouble, the downstairs windows had great iron grills. Above this utilitarian level, there might be a modest mezzanine that housed the proprietors of the shops below. Next higher, in a palace, came the *piano nobile*, the "noble floor." It was there that a wealthy resident received honored guests, entertained, and lived; higher floors housed lesser members of the household. Simpler houses were no grander on one floor than on another.

Wealthy kitchen, with piped water. [Tempesta]

Indoors, though palaces invented several intermediate types to create variety, all houses had two basic rooms: the *sala* and the *camera*. The *sala*, the bigger of the two, accommodated the more public gatherings, while the more common *camera* almost always served for sleeping. Nevertheless, our customary division of "living room" and "bedroom," the former public, the latter private, does not altogether fit the Renaissance. In Italy, the distinction was far less sharp. Often people slept in the *sala*; moreover, not rarely, they entertained guests and did business on or by the bed, in the *camera*. The *sala*, being big, was the room most likely to have a fireplace. In simpler homes lacking a kitchen, people often cooked there, and in dwellings of all sizes, they ate there.

The urban palace made assertive use of space. On the outside, the palace was not only big but symmetrical, harmonious, and almost always ornamented with motifs from ancient architecture. It put a bold face to the street; owners sometimes bought up nearby houses, knocking them down to make a square out front, the better to overawe the neighborhood. The truly powerful might even succeed in gutting several blocks, to lay a perpendicular street that terminated impressively at their front door, making it the focal point of a linear perspective. Although the ideal palace had the kind of internal symmetry that delighted architects, in fact, many real palaces were an internal jumble behind a deceptively regular facade. For palaces and houses often grew haphazardly, swallowing older dwellings and reusing their spaces and their internal bearing walls. As families grew, they annexed neighbors or built upward. And, when brothers split an inherited building, they might partition it. Because walls were often thick and sturdy, a wealthy family's city house might rise five or six stories. The Davanzati house in Florence, a wonderfully preserved fourteenth-century complex built in the pre-palace era and now a museum, grew so tall that the tight central courtyard, with its wooden stairs and many hanging runways, feels like an ample light well. The aesthetic and psychological effect is curious; from the bottom, the whole household seems to loom overhead, while a high perch feels like a domestic overlook. It is an architecture of almost cloistered intimacy. Renaissance cities had many such relics of medieval architecture, now almost all of them vanished.

The urban palace differentiated internal domestic space. It had more shadings than the modest house. On the inside, it interposed between the very public *sala* and the master's bedroom a suite of rooms: perhaps a *saletta* for more intimate meals, and an *anticamera* (antechamber). Behind the bedroom were spaces even more private, including, very often, a *studio* for books, important papers, and art treasures. There were no corridors; in general, guests passed from room to room, penetrating the deeper into private space the more the host wished to pay them honor or take them into confidence. The whole series of the master's rooms came in the Renaissance to be called an *appartamento*. Normally the lord's wife had one too, similar in layout. These big buildings also featured many specialized rooms for household activities.

## CONCLUSION

Renaissance Italians had spatial experiences of many kinds, most of them quite distinct from ours. Their landscapes, villages, towns, and houses had characteristic shapes. Italian habits of perceiving them, as their arts inform us, were part of their larger civilization and culture.

## NOTES

1. On Alberti as geometer and cartographer, see Joan Gadol, *Leon Battista Alberti: Universal Man of the Early Renaissance* (Chicago: University of Chicago Press, 1969).

2. For a reproduction of Leonardo da Vinci's map of Imola, see Martin Kemp and Jane Roberts, *Leonardo da Vinci* (New Haven and London: Yale University Press with South Bank Centre), 176.

3. On the new military architecture, see John R. Hale, *Renaissance War Studies* (London: Hambledon Press, 1983); Simon Pepper and Nicholas Adams, *Firearms and Fortifications* (Chicago: University of Chicago Press, 1986), 3–31; Bert S. Hall, *Weapons and Warfare in Renaissance Europe* (Baltimore: Johns Hopkins University Press, 1997), 158–164.

4. On the nature of the Italian landscape, see Emilio Sereni, *History of the Italian Agricultural Landscape*, trans. R. Burr Litchfield (Princeton: Princeton University Press, 1997). For bibliographic orientation and discussion of some Italian topics, see also Peregrine Horden and Nicholas Purcell, *The Corrupting Sea: A Study in Mediterranean History* (Oxford: Blackwell, 2000).

5. For the shepherds' fires, see Rinaldo Comba, "Le origini medioevali dell'assetto insediativo moderno nelle campagne," in *Storia d'Italia: Annali 8*, ed. C. De Seta (Turin: Einaudi, 1985), 392.

6. On villas, see David R. Coffin, *The Villa in the Life of Renaissance Rome* (Princeton: Princeton University Press, 1979).

7. On the ecological history of Italy, most writings are in Italian. For wildlife, see Fulco Pratesi, "Gli ambienti naturali e l'equilibrio ecologico," in *Storia d'Italia: Annali 8*, 53–109, and the other articles in the same volume.

8. Francesco Porzio, *Da Caravaggio a Ceruti* (Milan: Skira, 1998), an exhibition catalogue, offers images of early modern urban and rural poor and of their material surroundings.

9. All of these names and memories come from Rocca Sinibalda, near Rieti: Archivio di Stato di Roma (ASR) Governatore, Tribunale Criminale, Processi sixteenth century, b. 25 (1556); Processi sixteenth century, b. 34 (1557); Processi sixteenth century, b. 35 (1557).

10. On urbanism, see Nicholas Adams and Laurie Nussdorfer, "The Italian City, 1400–1600," in *The Renaissance from Brunelleschi to Michelangelo: The Representation of Architecture*, ed. H. A. Millon and V. Lampagnani (New York: Rizzoli, 1994), 205–230.

11. On the design and use of palaces, see Richard Goldthwaite, *The Building of Renaissance Florence: An Economic and Social History* (Baltimore: Johns Hopkins University Press, 1980), 13–16, 88–90, 102–112, and Gene Brucker, *Florence: The Golden Age, 1138–1737* (Berkeley: University of California Press, 1998), 29, 32–33, 57, 60–61.

12. For towers and a diagram of a tower complex, see Brucker, *Florence*, 38–39.

13. For local loyalties of many sorts, see Laurie Nussdorfer, "The Politics of Space in Early Modern Rome," *Memoirs of the American Academy in Rome 42* (1999), 161–186.

14. Edward Muir, "The Madonna on the Street Corner," in *Religion and Culture in the Renaissance and Reformation*, ed. S. Ozment (Kirksville, MO: Sixteenth Century Essays and Studies, 1989), 28, n. 12.

15. On a great citadel, with good diagrams and photographs, see Hale, "The Fortezza da Basso," in *Renaissance War Studies*, 31–62.

16. On gender and space, see Robert Davis, "The Geography of Gender in the Renaissance," in Judith Brown and Robert Davis, eds., *Gender and Society in Renaissance Italy* (New York: Longman, 1998), 19–38.

# 10

# Time

Time is a frame of understanding so deeply embedded in a culture's consciousness that it is often hard even to see it is there. Time nevertheless is a concept with specificity and history. To examine what it meant in the past, we need to articulate briefly some of our modern assumptions in order to recognize difference. Thus, with a watch on nearly every wrist that counts not just hours and minutes, but days and months and seconds and tenths of seconds, twenty-first-century people can know at any waking moment exactly what time it is. Furthermore, we expect others to know and work with the same time, measured with the same precision. It is possible to make appointments and expect people to gather at a particular moment, or at least know exactly how late they are. We can read a TV guide days in advance and count on seeing a program broadcast from hundreds of miles away begin and end at an exact minute. Furthermore, we can calculate the time anywhere on the globe, knowing it to be in a fixed relation to our own. We rely on this capacity to measure time precisely and consistently to run complex, global organizations and to pursue maximum efficiency so that no time is "wasted." This modern understanding of time forms a basis for defining and regulating behavior so that vast numbers of people can cohabit in ever shrinking spaces.

Renaissance people shared some of our modern notions about time but not others. With them we have in common the basic structure of the calendar and the units of temporal counting—minutes, hours, days, months, years—for these have their origins in various parts of the ancient world. The day-to-day use of that heritage, however, has evolved between the fifteenth century and the twenty-first. Overall, for most Renaissance people, sharp temporal precision seldom mattered very much. Some technology existed for measuring time and announcing it to the public, but its capacity was limited and its availability even scanter. People therefore often lacked a very exact notion of what time it was, nor did their way of life need one. Rather they lived with a set of general points of reference—dawn, dusk, the midday meal, in cities the communal and ecclesiastical bells—and with a sense of sequence. So, when they narrated events, they would say not, "It must have been a few minutes after ten, because I'd just watched the news," but rather, "I'd been with my friend, Ambrogio, and then I had supper, and then I wandered around for a while, and then it happened." When they did speak of units of time, they usually chose broad or approximate terms and often hedged those, as in, "It was circa the fourth hour of the night." Their handling of days and weeks had a similar vagueness: "I met her on the street a week ago last Tuesday, if I remember rightly" or "I got to know him before Lent just past." When obliged, people had concepts and terms to be more specific, but for the most part sequential and more general expressions of time were the practice.[1]

Renaissance time also differed from the modern in being not consistent and universal—the same for everyone—but rather particular to places and persons. First, every city and village had its own time linked to the rising and setting of the sun in that spot. Also, the pattern for counting and announcing that time was shaped by variable local custom. The communal bells sounded with a timing, frequency, and pattern that was distinctive to them. This could become a marker of collective identity, so that by ringing its own time a town asserted itself, even to rivals within earshot across the valley. Second, the cultural packaging of time also depended on ways of life. Peasants and merchants and monks each used the components of the time system differently. At work, some groups followed the earth's own temporal rhythms, while others needed more precise, artificial time patterns, created and enforced by human authorities.

Renaissance Italians understood time in three interconnecting forms: natural, sacred, and administrative. The first was cyclic, the second both linear and cyclic, and the third just linear. Nature's time derived from the movements in the heavens of the stars and the planets, and, especially, of the sun and the moon. Solar time governed the day, with its paired periods of light and darkness, and the year, as the earth counted the sun's orbits around the sphere of stars. Lunar time marked the months and, less sharply, the weeks with the four phases of waxing and waning. The rotation of the seasons from winter to spring to summer to autumn and back also was the work of the physical universe. As for sacred time, God lived in eternity, but instituted on earth a system that marked linear time's advance toward its end, the ultimate redemption that would follow the Apocalypse. In the meantime, Christians arranged their lives cyclically according to daily rhythms of prayers, annual rotations of religious holidays, and the celebration, under papal auspices, of jubilees every twenty-five years. The state's version, though a less powerful shaper of Renaissance experience than the other forms of time, was yet a growing force. Made of dates and documents, this system recorded the linear progression of history. Experientially, people of the past lived at once in all three patterns of time. Now, beginning with the smallest units and proceeding upward through the scale, we will look in more detail at the many ways that concepts of time shaped the lives of fifteenth- and sixteenth-century folk.

## MINUTES AND HOURS

Minutes were invented by the ancient Babylonians, but Renaissance Italians made scant use of their ingenuity. Although scientists, in their abstract, theoretical discussions, wrote of minutes and other similarly tiny units, these had no place in daily life. To measure short lapses of time, sandglasses were available, but we do not know when mechanical clocks could do so. Since the Middle Ages, such timepieces had been telling hours, but through the fifteenth century we have no solid evidence of one that kept count of passing minutes. In any case, there were not many of them around, and people evidently felt no lack. When referring to brief stretches of time, they spoke of fractions of hours, halves or, less often, quarters. The smaller the fraction, the less commonly it appeared, since for most purposes close precision was not needed. When someone did want to designate a short interval, the usual phrasing drew on religious vocabulary, calling up the duration of common prayers: the Paternoster, the Ave Maria, and the Miserere. In examples that nicely illustrate the crossovers among the parallel times of nature, God and state, these measures from the sacred realm were used to describe natural phenomena and the workings of the judiciary. In 1456, a Florentine wrote from Naples of experiencing an earthquake "that lasted the duration it would take to say a Miserere quite slowly and more specifically one and a half times." The correspondent picked this wording to make what he intended as a quite precise empirical observation. With a similar commitment to exactitude, notaries for the criminal courts of sixteenth-century Rome and elsewhere also used the Miserere to record the carefully timed application of torture to witnesses.

The Renaissance found the hour, unlike the minute, a convenient unit for talking about time; they did want to distinguish among parts of the day or night. The term, however, had many senses, dependent on the circumstances of its use. Though the word had a long history, the meaning of *hour* evolved significantly during the Renaissance, as older uses of the concept faded in response to new technology. To have a general notion of a segment of time was not to give it a specific length. That required the capacity to measure, to translate the passage of time into other physical terms corresponding to regular, consistent, and countable motions. Traditionally, the movements of celestial bodies, observed directly in the sky or represented by shadows on a sundial, or mechanical actions like sand's falling in a glass supplied the gauges. With the later Middle Ages, the pendulum tripping the works of a clock added a new device with a potential for continuity and precision beyond that of earlier techniques. Only with this machinery did it become possible to assign an exact and predictable duration to the hour. Furthermore, to make the hour a component of time-telling effective for many daily purposes, one had not only to know the time but also to broadcast the information. As Italians entered the Renaissance, they were learning not only to count hours more accurately but also to communicate that standard of time to larger groups.

Through monasticism, the ancient Romans had bequeathed to late medieval Europe a system for dividing daylight. The Romans and then the monks numbered twelve hours of presumptively equal length, stressing groupings of three. Thus, Prime (first), Terce (third), Sext (sixth), and None (ninth) hours marked the significant segments. Several of these divisions corresponded to readily estimated heights of the sun in the sky. By this scheme, the First Hour followed sunrise, the Sixth Hour came at midday, and the Twelfth Hour belonged to sunset. Between these reasonably fixed points, distinguishing one hour from the next was hard for several reasons. First, the duration of light shifted with the seasons, so that an hour, conceived as one-twelfth of the day, stretched or shrank. Second, the sun itself was an often unreliable gauge. How many degrees of angle actually corresponded to an hour? And what to do when the sun, and also the horizon, were, as often, out of sight? With practice and the right conditions—in good weather, at sea or elsewhere with an unimpeded view of the sky—a fair estimate of the hour should have been quite easy. Yet in many circumstances—at night, with cloudy skies—time telling was guesswork. While a sundial, properly positioned and read, could help give greater accuracy, such devices mostly belonged to institutions or the elite. At best, knowing the hour was a matter for specialists. It was seldom a possibility, or a need, for most medieval people.

Monks were those who most deliberately preserved the old system of Roman hours. Their lives had a sharper temporal ordering than those of most contemporaries. Central to their rule was a daily seven-part cycle of prayers, known as "hours" and named, in part, Prime, Terce, Sext, and None. Around these hours, the rest of the monks' unusually regulated schedule was set. Yet the monastic "hour" was in fact conceptual and not technical. It denoted neither a measured length of time nor a particular moment in the sun's passage. Rather, it was a step in a sequence, marked by a bell that called the brothers to prayer. Over the centuries, monasteries continued to observe the same rotation of "hours," but their actual timing in the day shifted to fit the seasons and institutional convenience. Thus, although tradition associated the Sixth Hour with midday, houses varied in singing Sext; some chanted just before the sun reached its height, while others did so as much as an hour and a half earlier. By such a process, the None—the Ninth Hour—drifted from the middle of the afternoon toward the middle of the day and gave us our word *noon*.

During the Middle Ages, urban governments began to borrow the monastic system of sounded hours for secular uses. Thus, the church bells became the markers not only for sacred time but also for administrative time. The patterns of ringing became more elaborate as they were put to ever more uses. For market people and shoppers, the bells regulated times of opening and closing. For workers, they defined the beginnings and endings of work, including breaks and meals. For officials of city government, they called court sessions and council meetings. One historian has figured that in the fourteenth century, over each twenty-four hours, the four bells of San Marco in Venice rang in distinctive combinations at twelve specific, irregularly spaced intervals. Six of those signals involved long tolling of either a quarter or a half an hour, for total clangor of two to three hours per day. Added to these were calls to mass, ringings for special events and celebrations, and tollings for deaths, not to mention the bells from all the other churches in the city. This proliferation of bongs and clanks threatened cacophony and confusion.

A remedy came in a novel instrument: the public mechanical clock. This device first spread through northern and central Italy from the mid-fourteenth century. As an emblem of civic pride, ambitious communes installed one in the tower of the city hall. But the clock was also functional, for it both counted out time regularly and, soon, with the incorporation of a second mechanism, struck the hours clearly and efficiently. The complicated codes of the church bells were no longer needed. They continued to sound for worship, but much less for other purposes. In the fifteenth century, a simplified round consisting of the Angelus (or Ave Maria) bell at dusk and at dawn marked the ends of the day. In 1456, Pope Calixtus III mandated that a third bell, at midday, signal a similar brief prayer, to ward off the Turkish threat.

During the Renaissance, clocks encouraged a shift toward greater use of the measured hour. It was inserted into the model of the day as made up of twenty-four units or of two sets of twelve—one for the darkness and the other for the light. Both forms persisted in parallel use. For Italy, the count started with sundown, followed by the first hour of the night, and so on. At the equinox, dawn would come at the twelfth hour and midday at the eighteenth or, in the double-twelve version, at the first hour of the day and the sixth. Clocks represented a significant investment, for both the initial installation and the regular maintenance they required. They needed, for example, frequent adjustments to keep up with the lengthening and shortening of daylight. Despite these costs, civic authorities and economic leaders saw to the multiplication of clocks to promote tighter discipline. Large workplaces, such as the shipbuilding works of the Venetian Arsenal or palace construction sites in Florence, regulated labor with their own clocks. Consequently, it became normal to expect city dwellers to know if not the minute, at least the hour and to comply with ordinances cast in that term. Similarly, military leaders issued ultimatums demanding response by a specific hour. Still, only a few people had means of precise timekeeping at home or even nearby in their neighborhood or village.

In sum, Renaissance people, urbanites more than country folk, learned to live with the measured hour. Public clocks made the time both regular and knowable. Authorities used the discipline of hours in their campaigns for order and productivity. Nevertheless, both the meaning of the hour and the obligations attached to it remained much less precise than for the twenty-first century. For many purposes, time remained highly negotiable.

## DAYS, WEEKS, AND MONTHS

The Renaissance day could be long. Although people worked and moved about mostly during the hours of light, which drew out in summer, it was also common to extend the day at both ends. Many rose before dawn to prepare for work or to attend early mass. Some stayed up into the dark hours, to socialize, to patrol their fields, to steal or make raids. The day had a loose rhythm, but its organization was fluid. The pope's mandated midday bell highlighted a customary division of daylight into two roughly equal segments, referred to as *mattina* (morning) and *sera* (evening). Meals came at the end of each of these periods, but people did not eat at set times. Convenience and the demands of particular activities governed the moment. Breakfast was never mentioned, but *pranzo* (dinner) was a serious meal eaten sometime in the middle of the day. *Cena* (supper) typically came soon after dark.

While Italians of this era distinguished ordinary days from holidays, their week did not divide into five workdays followed by a weekend. Differences among days of the week came largely from religion. Wednesdays and Fridays were especially penitential, and the morally scrupulous

September. with zodiac and grape harvest. [Bertarelli: Missale]

might abstain from some foods and from sex; weddings were less often scheduled on these days. Sunday was for church, although in cities, where there were many occasions for worship, the faithful might well attend services other days of the week too. Before, after, or instead of church, Sunday was also time for sociability. Moral reformers repeatedly had to denounce the taverns and ball games that competed with God for men's Sunday attention. Yet if Sunday was owed to God and was sometimes given to play, it was not a day of universal rest. The French visitor Montaigne noted that many Italians worked on Sunday; court testimony bears him out. Even some government officials regularly held meetings and conducted business then. For time out for worship and recreation, the annual Christian cycle of holidays set the schedule more strongly than the weekly rotation of days.

Renaissance Italians continued to use the Roman calendar that combined solar and lunar elements to give seven-day weeks—roughly four weeks per month and twelve months in the year. Consecutive numbering of days in the month, however, for the most part had replaced the cumbersome ancient Roman counting from the Kalends (first day) and Ides (thirteenth or fifteenth day, depending on the month). Days of the week and months bore Italian versions of names mostly familiar to us. The annual rotation of the months was a favorite theme in art, depicted in mosaics on the floors of churches, in tapestries, and in illuminations in prayer books. These images linked the month, the signs of the zodiac, and the human activities characteristic of that season. Italian versions of this series often shared in broader European artistic and economic habits; they showed, for instance, pruning in February, planting in March, the grape harvest in September, and pig slaughtering in November or December.[2]

The astrological signs often in these pictorial calendars suggests the survival of stellar timekeeping. While Christian conceptions of time dominated, astrologers, most of them intellectuals and many of them patron-

December: with zodiac and butchered pig. [Bertarelli: Missale]

ized by rulers, deployed the language of the stars to predict auspicious or threatening events or to explain current events and the more distant past. Military campaigns and weddings were often scheduled for fortunate days. Sermons and popular texts also used this astral rhetoric to prophesy floods, earthquakes, and other catastrophes and to warn of God's wrath. People's reactions were mixed; such prognostications could sow fear across a city, but could also be met with laughter, especially with hindsight, when their dire claims failed.[3]

In a domain far more certain than astrology, the traditional calendar also provided a precise way to express dates, which became increasingly important to administrative time. Within the ever expanding compass of written culture—legal contracts, government orders, parish records, letters, diaries—dates were noted carefully, because they had consequences. In communes it was important to keep track of officials' terms, which might rotate as often as three or six months. Debts came due on specific dates, and interest payments and other penalties were linked to them. Birth dates governed eligibility for government office, and times of death sometimes affected distributions of property. In addition, date sequence was one of the main devices for filing and retracing the ever expanding volume of notarial documents.

At the same time, assorted vagaries up and down the peninsula vexed dating practices. For example, in different places the year began on different dates. While New Year's fell in Rome on January 1, it came in Venice on March 1 and in Florence on March 25, the day of the Annunciation. Consequently, if two contracts were written the same day, one in Rome and the other in Florence, the first would bear the date January 26, 1491, and the second January 26, 1490. Furthermore, because of fifteen centuries of a little too much Leap Year, the movements of the sun and the nominal dates had parted company. By the sixteenth century, the equinox fell around the eleventh of March instead of the twenty-first. To haul things back into line, Pope Gregory XIII in 1582 decreed calendrical reform and suppressed ten days. His improved "Gregorian" calendar is the one we use today.

## YEARS

The year measured fundamental cycles in both natural and sacred time. The regular annual rotations of agricultural tasks and religious celebrations were complexly intertwined. The two rounds of activities did not always match neatly. Natural time flowed in seasons marked by changes in the weather that had a pattern but varied in timing from year to year. The church calendar, on the other hand, was a crammed roster of feasts, some of which always fell on specific dates fixed in the solar schedule of months and days and others that shifted against them every year with the movements of the moon. The interwoven sequences thus gave people a familiar set of temporal expectations, but asked them to keep adjusting the details. The occasional reorderings of what felt normal sometimes bred anxiety. On the rare occasion, in 1383, when the lunar holiday Easter occurred before the fixed date of the Annunciation (March 25), the Florentine notary Naddo da Montecatini urged his readers to beware "that great novelties ought to be in the world from which God in his piety guard us."[4] Altogether, the combined natural and religious annual cycles strongly shaped Renaissance Italians' experience of time.

Mediterranean patterns of temperature and rainfall governed the agricultural rhythm and the movement of workers up and down the landscape. The winter, chilly and punctuated by rains, or by snow in the mountains, was a fairly quiet season for people on the land. It was a time to mend gear and practice home industry, to migrate to the lowlands for work, or just to rest. Then came spring, temperate and well watered, keeping peasants busy pruning vines and orchards, plowing and planting summer crops, and lambing. After lambing, shepherds moved their flocks from lowland winter pastures into the hills and began to make cheese. As summer arrived, bringing Mediterranean heat and dryness, farmers harvested winter grain and made hay. In the fall, as the temperature moderated, came another round of harvesting and processing, including of grapes and olives. Before the heavy rains of late autumn, peasants planted the winter grain crop and shepherds brought their flocks back down from the high country. The great diversity of Italian landscape and crops led to many variations in the timing and weight of these moments, but some pattern of this sort gave temporal form to most Renaissance lives. Important social and religious events fitted in among these yearly agricultural cycles.

The Christian calendar was an intricate roster of liturgical seasons. Only the clergy followed all the many lesser details, but major religious holidays punctuated the year for all Renaissance Italians and gave them reference points in time. The calendar not only recognized a crowded pantheon of saints, but also reenacted over the year's course the redeeming history of Jesus and his resurrection and, secondarily, the story of his mother. The religious year included two major sequences of observances, Christmas and Easter, each preceded by a long penitential preparation. Ascension Day, commemorating Christ's rising into heaven, occurred forty days after Easter. Also, from the thirteenth century there developed a very popular, often elaborate celebration dedicated to the Corpus Christi, the body of Christ made visible as the eucharistic host; this feast, linked to the movable cycle of Easter, followed Pentecost, in June. Interspersed through the year with these Christ-focused occasions were three important holidays honoring the Virgin Mary: February 2 marked her Purification after the birth of Jesus, March 25 recalled the angel's Annunciation of Mary's pregnancy, and August 15 celebrated her posthumous bodily Assumption into heaven.

Though distinctly lesser than Easter, Christmas, celebrating the birth of Jesus, was a principal religious feast. Based on the solar calendar of fixed dates, its cycle began with Advent, which lasted from December 1 until Christmas Eve. During this period for special penitence the devout could fast, abstain from sex, and listen to sermons. At its end, on the night of December 24, the vigil of the Nativity, people customarily went to church. Services were also held on Christmas Day; according to the traveler Montaigne, in Rome, the pope, assisted by several cardinals, performed an unusually grand mass at St. Peter's basilica. January 6, Epiphany, celebrating the biblical three kings with their rich presents for the infant Jesus, occasioned both pageantry and jollity. From the late fourteenth century, Florence enjoyed especially elaborate observances; a Company of the Magi staged mounted processions and enacted the tale of the kings' visit to Herod. St. Francis of Assisi is said to have first arranged a crib with a doll to represent the holy infant; such a dramatization is recorded in a Florentine friars' church in 1498. In imitation of the generosity of the magi, the Christmas season also brought forth gift giving and hospitality, though on a scale much more modest than in the early twenty-first century. Lords distributed coins to their dependents, and offerings of food circulated.

Easter, a movable feast in March or April linked to the moon, anchored the longest and most important celebratory cycle of the year. It began soon after the twelve days of Christmas—in Venice, even overlapping them—with Carnival, a season of license that figured vividly in the popular temporal imagination. Echoing the ancient Roman year-end Saturnalia, Carnival was a time for parties, masquerades, theatrical performances, parades, athletic contests, street dances, jokes, egg throwing, flirtation, general high jinx, and bloody mayhem. Several weeks of festivities accelerated toward a culminating series of "fat" days. On *Giovedi*

Carnival
musicians play
lutes and dance.
[Bertelli]

*Grasso* (Fat Thursday) Venetians crowded together to watch a bloody
ritual during which a bull and twelve pigs were formally condemned to
death, then chased around the piazza in front of the doge's palace and
decapitated; the meat was then butchered and shared among the presiding dignitaries.[5] Such rich foods were then penitentially renounced on
the next Wednesday, the day of ashes, as Lent began. This period of
renunciation and penance that prepared for Easter was known in Italian
as the Forty Days, *Quadragesima.* Like Carnival, Lent was a temporal
interval that Renaissance people linked to special behavior, a stark inversion of what had gone on before. While in Carnival people played
and took moral chances, in Lent they tried harder than usual to live by
the Christian rules, fasting, praying, hearing sermons, abstaining from
meat and play, and shunning sex. Testimony in court alluded to Carnival
as indeed a time for greater sexual indulgence, and seasonal declines in
births suggest some restraint during Advent and Lent.[6]

The week leading up to Easter itself was marked by processions and
dramatic reenactments of the religious events. This was the peak of the
religious year. Palm Sunday commemorated Jesus's arrival in Jerusalem.
On Holy Thursday, the pope, nobles, and their ladies imitated Christ's
charity and humility by a ceremonial washing of the feet of the poor.
Good Friday recalled Jesus's crucifixion. Churchmen ritually enacted the
burial of his body, and passion plays often retold the story before gath-

ered crowds. On this bitter and sorrowful day, emotions ran high and
sometimes broke out in violence. Troops of flagellant confraternities
so harshly beat their bodies that, through the sixteenth century, bishops, especially in the south of Italy, repeatedly banned their self-
mortifications. The Passion dramatized in the Colosseum in Rome moved
its audience to attack the city's Jews and in 1539 was therefore abolished.
On Sunday, Easter liturgies celebrated the resurrection, light and joy
contrasting with the dark pain of the days just past. During the Renaissance, when most Christians practiced seldom the sacraments of confession and communion, Easter was the season for making at least the
required annual connection with their church and their savior. By the
late sixteenth century, priests had to prepare for the holiday by compiling a census of their parishioners, who could then be checked off when
they made their communion.

The holidays dedicated to the Virgin Mary and to a number of saints
were celebrated in many cities with similar religious pageantry and festivity. These occasions often blended general Christian significance with
special local meanings. Military victories or miraculous apparitions that
saved a town from catastrophe or plague were often linked with specific
days in the religious calendar, and on those days Mary or the protector
saint would be venerated and their aid remembered. While some principal saints' days were honored throughout the peninsula and in the
church as a whole, many celebrations belonged to particular communities or groups. Villages, guilds, and families all had their favorite holy
patrons, whose feasts loomed large in the celebrants' yearly calendar.
Thus, the feasts of St. John the Baptist in Florence (June 24), of St. Mark
in Venice (April 25, June 25), and of St. Nicholas in Bari (December 6)
were both religious holidays and major occasions to assert civic identity
and pride. While most such patriotic observances were linked to saints'
days, some were not, like May Day in Florence, when the whole city,
even the women, danced in the streets.

For Renaissance Italians, the experience of the natural and the sacred
year intermingled. The prehistoric inclination to mark the sun's annual
cycle was grafted onto the Christian holidays, with Christmas absorbing
the winter solstice, Easter occurring near the spring equinox, and St. John
the Baptist's day falling near midsummer. Similarly, fertility ceremonies
to favor economic productivity clustered in the season of the Ascension,
in late spring. Then, in many places, processions went out into the fields,
where the crops were blessed. Analogously, in Venice, a bishop blessed
the Adriatic while the doge, representing the city, ritually married the
sea, the source of wealth.[7] Saints' days marked key moments in the agricultural regime. For the shepherds and wool merchants in Apulia, the
two great transitions of the year—when the animals left the lowlands
for summer pastures in the mountains and when they descended—were

linked to Saint Michael feasts (May 8 and September 29). The warrior archangel, believed to have appeared in the region at Mount Gargano in the fifth century, was a powerful local patron saint. In the pivotal season of early May, devotees made pilgrimages to his seaside mountain shrine, as they did to a lowland sanctuary that harbored the Virgin of the Sacred Wood of the Incoronata. The spring movements of the herds and these religious observances also coincided with big wool fairs at Foggia, when merchants bought and sold the year's fleeces and paid the government for winter pasturage. Late in September, around the second feast of San Michele, people expected the flocks' return.[8]

## HISTORY AND THE END OF TIME

While the cycles of days and years dominated Renaissance Italians' experience of time, they also sometimes saw themselves as belonging in history, which followed a linear course. The Christian vision of biblical time set the model. Looking backward, most people saw their era as beginning with the birth of Jesus, although some southerners followed the Byzantine practice of counting the years from Creation. Looking forward, all anticipated worldly history's ending in an apocalypse that would usher in the Second Coming of Christ and the Last Judgment. No one knew when these last things would come, but, even without an imminent millennium on the calendar, prophets and their listeners believed the end might not be far off. On a less cosmic and godly plane, people also had some understanding of a human past, but for most it was not ordered into neat and numbered units. Some intellectuals kept chronicles that recorded significant events year by year. Other Renaissance scholars and statesmen even composed histories that began to assign meanings, logical connections, and a narrative line to the raw sequences of happenings. For many ordinary men and women, however, the past may have looked rather like a clutter of isolated notable moments. These often were hardships, like floods, famines, and violence, but heroic feats and victories, some enshrined in the roster of civic festivals, also counted. As memory or as heirloom, things from the past that cast glory were treasured. Even nonelite families might preserve their honorable history as genealogy. Yet, more than a few generations back, these accounts were likely more jumbled myth and fantasy than accurate record. (See Chapter 8.) Major events in living memory could serve as temporal markers. Someone might identify a lesser happening by relating it to a greater one, as before or after the big fire or at the time the soldiers left for the war. Speaking of the more distant past, however, Italians seldom evoked periods or sequences, let alone precise years or centuries; commoners had nothing of the present textbook habit of chopping history into tidy periods like "Middle Ages" or, indeed,

"Renaissance." While eschatological time, with its distinct beginning and end, followed a linear progression from Creation to Last Judgment, in most minds the rest of human history had no such clarity.

## NOTES

1. General sources for this chapter are, on time keeping, Gerhard Dohrn-Van Rossum, *History of the Hour: Clocks and Modern Temporal Orders*, trans. T. Dunlap (Chicago: University of Chicago Press, 1996), and, on calendars and ritual, Edward Muir, *Ritual in Early Modern Europe* (Cambridge: Cambridge University Press, 1997), 55–80. On Florentine notions of time and, especially, the ritual calendar, Richard Trexler, *Public Life in Renaissance Florence* (New York: Academic Press, 1980), 73–83, 215–278, 333–336.

2. A large Renaissance example of the monthly calendar of labors is the Trivulzio tapestry series in the Castello Sforzesco in Milan.

3. On mocking prophets and astrologers, see Ottavia Niccoli, *Prophecy and People in Renaissance Italy*, trans. L. Cochrane (Princeton: Princeton University Press, 1990), 152–166.

4. Trexler, *Public Life*, 81.

5. On carnival, see Edward Muir, *Civic Ritual in Renaissance Venice* (Princeton: Princeton University Press, 1981), 156–181.

6. James Grubb, *Provincial Families of the Renaissance* (Baltimore: Johns Hopkins University Press, 1996), 35.

7. On marriage to the sea, see Muir, *Civic Ritual in Renaissance Venice,* 119–134.

8. John Marino, *Pastoral Economics in the Kingdom of Naples* (Baltimore: Johns Hopkins University Press, 1988), 40–44.

# 11

# Life Cycles: From Birth Through Adolescence

## LIFE STAGES AND LIFE EXPECTANCY

Renaissance Europeans, using ideas rooted in their ancient and medieval pasts, imagined human life as a series of stages. The "ages of man," as this tradition was known, appeared, for example, in illustrations in early printed books that showed the life span divided into three or seven or more phases. Although the number of steps varied, this imagery always saw human existence as a predictable curve of waxing and waning capacities. The simplest models distinguished only youth, maturity, and old age; the longer sequences broke the ascending and descending slopes into several parts. Some writers ascribed conventional ages, typically in rough multiples of seven years, to the different stages. To give an Italian example, the fifteenth-century Florentine Matteo Palmieri, in a treatise on the good conduct of civic life, used a well-known version in six stages. While the markers between his "ages" highlighted the acquisition and later loss of abilities, the breaks only partially fit the habit of counting in sevens. First, following birth, came infancy, which, etymologically, means "without speech." Of course, babies learned to talk long before the age of seven, where the numerical conventions fixed the end of the primary phase. Childhood, the second step, continued until the young-ster achieved, supposedly around age fourteen, "discretion," that is, the capacity to make decisions, to tell good from bad. Next, adolescence extended from the mid-teens to the mid-twenties, to age twenty-eight if one was multiplying sevens. Only in the next "age," virility, did a man attain his full powers, which he could expect to enjoy for a full four sevens, until age fifty-six. Thereafter, decline set in, though gradually, first old age until seventy years and then a collapse into final decrepitude. In describing this vision of the life cycle, we, like Renaissance writers, have spoken only of men. A women's pattern was seldom represented; when it was, standard practice, as in other spheres of thought, showed females as mere mirrors of males.[1]

This tradition of imagining the life cycle did not reckon with the realities. Average life expectancy fell sharply in the decades after the Black Death. At some points it was below twenty years, though after 1450 it again crept back up to forty. Stillbirths and infant deaths were rife; they brought the statistics down. Even those who survived the early cullings did not expect to live long past thirty-five. Consequently, Renaissance Italy had a young population. When parents were struck down by high mortality, their children likely trod the stages of life sooner than the theorists said. Nevertheless, some people did reach ripe ages of seventy, eighty, or more. A sizable cohort of the elderly lived long enough to track the tidy symmetrical rise and fall of the "ages of man" imagery.[2]

Although the intellectuals' neat schemes about how life's cycle ought to run failed in face of the harsh works of the Grim Reaper, Renaissance Italians still expected life to follow an evolution with a pattern. There were some signposts along the way. For all Christians, several of the seven sacraments provided important rites of passage that marked life stages. Baptism signaled birth and extreme unction death. Between them, marriage was another turning point most experienced, although the church's role in it became very central only as the period went on. Other moments of lesser resonance, some ritualized and many others not, punctuated the process of growing up. For some men, by birth or choice there were entry ceremonies such as the ordaining of priests, the dubbing of knights, or the receiving of masters into guilds. But even where formal recognition of such transitions was lacking, we can trace the general shape of a sequence of life stages for men and women.

**Ideas about Childhood**      Looking at growing up in the Renaissance, we must remember that we perforce peer through a distorting lens. As usual, most of our evidence comes from the elite, and from the Florentine elite in particular. For the bulk of the population in other places and, especially, other classes, we must build from inference. In this process of filling in the many blank spaces, modern preconceptions concerning an emotionally charged topic like children easily get projected onto the past. Also, many of the sources are prescriptive; treatises and guides written by various privileged authorities told parents, teachers, and medical practitioners how to deal with the young. The historian's challenge is to interpret all this advice and admonition. Do we assume that these expert words represent generally accepted wisdom and therefore reflect what many people actually did? Or do we believe that the instructions are intended to correct faulty care-giving, and that therefore common practice was often the opposite of what was said? How do we interpret the frequent contradictions among the experts? With too few other documents to test our views, depending on the approach we choose, we can draw mutually inconsistent conclusions about how this society treated its children.

Historians of childhood have in recent years debated whether, due to their society's ideas and behavior, premodern European youngsters suffered. A pioneer in the field, Philippe Ariès, argued that before the seventeenth century children were treated simply as small adults, for they had no special identity or place. For some scholars this presumed conceptual vacuum, when combined with other fragmentary evidence, conjured up a past of widespread neglect and abuse. Other studies highlighted parental attitudes and practices that, because they violated twentieth-century dogma, were presumed to have done much harm. This rather bleak picture has been countered by more optimistic approaches that attend to parental expressions of concern, love, delight, and grief. And further work has shown that children were in fact not then understood as just like adults. The most truthful view would see Renaissance childhood as a mix of difficult and happy experiences but would eschew hasty general judgments. The fates of premodern children and the challenges facing their caretakers were different from today's. History shapes both the capacities and resources available for child care and the feelings and intentions of those who do it. Nevertheless, in the past, as now, there were both many stresses and lots of good efforts. And the results, then as now, varied. Here we survey the practices and circumstances that shaped the lives of Renaissance youngsters in struggle and in pleasure.[3]

## COMING INTO THE WORLD

The arrival of a new baby was both welcomed and feared. Birth was a moment when the differences between Renaissance Italian and modern North American expectations appear very clearly. In **Birth** the past, there was little control over whether, when, or how many. Children were the natural consequence of marriage and the fulfillment of the biblical injunction to multiply. They were also the family's future, often the foundation of its continuing economic and social well-being; to the poor, they were also more mouths to feed. Parents greeted new children with acceptance and often warmth and praise to God. At the same time, birth was a focus of anxiety and stress. The delivery was dangerous for both mother and baby, and death always lurked nearby. Unlike modern parents, Renaissance ones could never count on a happy outcome.

While families embraced the arrival of both boys and girls, males were especially welcome. High-ranking couples marked the arrival of first-born sons with special parties. A ruling dynasty, when an heir was born, funded rejoicing throughout its domain. The fragile infant embodied the future of the lineage name and the promise of its economic and political security. Daughters, especially one or two whose marriages would build useful alliances, were a boon, but also a worry and a burden. Their chastity risked the family honor, and their dowries threatened to deplete its fortune. While one Florentine father professed equal pleasure with girls and boys, another sent joking condolences to his friend on the birth of a daughter. Responding to the desire for sons, advisers on family life offered various suggestions of how to conceive a boy. For example, masculinity was associated by humor theory with warmth. Since the right side of the body was warmer, organizing sex crossways, so that seed from the right testicle lodged on the right side of the womb, helped. So too might warming herbal treatments or the mother's consumption of malmsey wine. One writer recommended intercourse in a virile setting, perfumed with musk and bedecked with paintings of valorous men.

Typically Italians entered the world in the family home. One or several women attended the delivering mother, including, if possible, an experienced midwife. She knew a repertoire of physical maneuvers to steer the baby along its course and, in dire necessity, to try to extract it by force; to ease the labor, she might also deploy herbal teas, potions, and salves of her own making. Yet her skills were limited, and she offered neither the relative security nor the intense intrusiveness of later obstetrical practices. Healthy newborns underwent the exertions natural to the process, but escaped such prophylactic medical interventions as eyedrops or, for boys, circumcision. Difficult deliveries often damaged babies, as well as mothers, and many were disabled or died. Once born, the baby was washed, wrapped tightly, and placed in the bed with the mother or in a cradle.[4]

**Baptism**

Baptism was the ceremonial acknowledgment of the new arrival through which he or she acquired a social identity and a Christian soul. Normally the baby was carried by the midwife and accompanied by a few friends and neighbors to the church or baptistery. There was enacted what anthropologists call a rite of passage, in which a person moves from one life stage into another through a ceremonial sequence of steps: first, a separation from the past, then an intermediary limbo, and finally an incorporation into a new social state. Thus, baptism began in front of the building, where a priest first exorcised the child to banish the spirits of evil into which, as a descendant of Adam, it had been born. Then the assemblage moved with the newcomer, now without sin but still without identity, into the sacred space. Immersed in or sprinkled with water at the baptismal font, the baby received a name and acceptance into the Christian community, a membership necessary for salvation and heaven. Because the child's soul was at stake, baptism had best occur promptly, within a day or two of the birth. If it looked as though the newborn might not survive that long, the church authorized that fathers or, more often, midwives perform an emergency form of baptism at the bedside. Indeed, they were even to christen a protruding arm or leg when it was feared that the baby could not be delivered alive.

Godparents, not parents, were central participants in a baptism. Although the father could attend, the mother could not. Not only was she likely still recovering physically from the birth, but also it had rendered her unclean; by custom she was not supposed to enter a sacred precinct until a churching ceremony, some forty days afterward, had purified her once again. As godparents, each baby had at least one man and one woman from outside the family who undertook to steer their charge into a righteous life. They received the child from the hands of the priest, and their embrace represented incorporation into the larger community. Godparents could well serve their ceremonial offspring as patrons in worldly life as well. Parents might choose them with a careful eye to reinforcing connections useful not only to the child but to the whole family. For the same reason, ambitious families sometimes gave their children several sponsors at the font. Such prestigious godparents were expected to bestow honorific gifts as well. A rich Florentine merchant wrote that two large cakes, boxes of spiced cookies, and handfuls of candles and small torches were customary godparental contributions to the party that followed the rite. In many cases, however, not only among modest folk, but also not infrequently among the affluent, godparents would include ordinary Christians, usually neighbors or friends. Inviting a social inferior, even a pauper, to serve not only bolstered local alliances; it also reenacted the humility and charity that Jesus himself had modeled for his followers.[5]

Along with a collective identity as a Christian and a member of a particular social community, baptism gave the baby an individual identity marked by a name. We hear elite fathers speak of choosing what to call their progeny, but mothers must some- **Naming** times also have helped pick. Certainly, when, as not infrequently, the father was elsewhere at the time of birth, the mother or even, in some circumstances, the midwife or the priest might give the name. Most children carried only a single tag, but some received two. Some double-barreled ones became customary pairs, like Giovanni Battista or Pietropaolo. But ease of use tended to discourage long names. Parents who gave two names at baptism would declare one for everyday use. The same needs encouraged contracted nicknames as well. Giovanni Battista typically became something like Titta, Tommaso shortened to Maso, and Elizabetta to Betta. Another playful naming practice that sought to distinguish particular people often took these contractions and lengthened them again with further endings. Thus, two early Renaissance painters were known as Masolino—little Tom—and Masaccio—bad Tom, and girls called Betta might become Bettuccia—cute, little Betty. Baptismal names were just the first step in a process that gave a child a social identity.

The name a baby received at baptism might have come from several sources. The repertoire of likely names varied from place to place. Regional heroes, rulers, and saints supplied possibilities, as did particular family traditions. Infants were named after ancestors, but especially after recently dead relatives, including siblings; fathers then spoke of "remaking" a member of the lineage. Unusual names often came from such local sources. Another colorful though uncommon sort of tag invoked blessings or good fortune: the goldsmith Cellini's name, Benvenuto, meant "welcome." Naming practices also followed larger policy or fashion. By the fifteenth century, the number of commonly given names had contracted sharply. In Tuscany, for example, nearly half the male population bore one of only some fifteen or so names. Most honored prominent saints, including Antonio, Francesco, Giovanni, and Bartolomeo. Similarly, many women bore female versions of these same names, but the favorite was Caterina, after the Sienese mystic. Birth close to feast day of the saint might govern the choice, or a parent's special devotion, or even a vow made in hopes of a safe arrival. But other kinds of names continued to circulate as well. Strikingly, despite the resurgent humanist interest in the Roman and Greek classics, fancy appellations rooted in antiquity graced only a few Florentines in this century. Perhaps with time they grew more popular, as they were in the city of Rome in the mid-sixteenth century, where, for instance, Pompeo, Marco Antonio, or Cesare and, among women, Lucrezia, Faustina, or Camilla proliferated.

Registering name and precise birth date only gradually became common practice during the Renaissance. Earlier, during the Middle Ages, personal names had been various and fluid, and a man during his life might have been known by several. By the fifteenth century, however, pressure from both church and government sought to stabilize names, so that people could be identified and held responsible. Here we see the beginnings of modern institutional ambitions to document and control. The earliest personal records were private, however, kept by the same literate merchants on whose diaries historians have been so dependent. Eventually the church provided a more public record. Beginning in the fifteenth century, though only systematically from the mid-sixteenth, parish priests began to maintain lists of the baptisms, marriages, and deaths over which they presided. From that time, for the larger population, official identities marked by name and birth date became possible. Most people, however, had little use for these. They knew their names and did not celebrate their birthdays. (If anything, they observed the day of their patron saint.) Only the government seemed to care exactly how old they were.[6]

---

## BRINGING CHILDREN INTO THE WORLD: AN EXAMPLE

The "diary" of successful merchant Gregorio Dati, introduced in Chapter 2, illustrates many attitudes and experiences around birth and naming. Dati was an old hand at procreation, fathering, all told, twenty-six children. Bandecca, his first "beloved wife," died childless after two years of marriage of a nine-month illness brought on, he believed, by a miscarriage. The merchant's first child, borne him the next year in Spain by his Tartar slave, was a son, whom he had brought to Italy and raised under his eye. By his second wife, he had eight progeny. The first daughter he called Bandecca in memory of his deceased spouse, a naming custom observed by others as well. The next born, his first legitimate son, Dati named after his own father. Alas, in the boy's second year,

> Our Lord God pleased to take to himself the fruits which He had lent us, and he took . . . our most beloved, Stagio, our darling and blessed first born. He died of the plague on the morning of Friday, 30 July 1400, in Florence without my seeing him for I was in the country. . . . May God bless him and grant that he pray for us.

A year later, God "lent" Gregorio another son, and he again called the baby Stagio, adding as a hopeful second name Benedetto, meaning "blessed." But shortly "Divine Providence was pleased to take him back and for this too may he be praised and thanked." Of his last child by this wife, Dati recorded:

> On 5 July 1402, before the hour of terce, Betta gave birth to our eighth child. We had him baptized straight after terce in the love of God. His godparents were Nardo and blind Margherita, and we called him Piero Antonio because of Betta's special devotion to S. Antonio. God bless him and grant that he become a good man.

Note the very precise dating, the prompt christening, the mother's contribution to the name, and the disabled godmother. Early in August, however, this baby too died, and his mother followed in October.

Dati remarried quickly a twenty-one-year-old widow, Ginevra, with whom he had eleven children. The first, a son, he named after his brother who had recently died. The second child was premature, but survived to be baptized "at once in the church"—with a boy's name, because at first they had not recognized that the child was female. The third child, "a fine full-term baby girl," he named Elizabetta to honor, as before, his previous wife. The sixth child was a boy he called Girolamo "from devotion to Saint Jerome since it was yesterday [his feast day] that her [Ginevra's] pains began." For similar reasons the seventh was named Giacomo Filippo after the two holy apostles on whose feast day he had arrived, but, said his father, the baby was to be known as Filippo; later Gregorio called him by the contraction Pippo, when reporting his death at age four. The eighth was a girl born "after a painful and almost fatal labor" and named in memory of her recently departed paternal grandmother. In 1420, Ginevra died "after lengthy suffering" in childbed with what would have been her twelfth. At that time, Dati totaled up his offspring at twenty—ten boys and ten girls—of whom he reported only five were then living. Within a year, Gregorio, himself aged fifty-eight, married for the fourth and last time a somewhat older widow of thirty. She gave him nonetheless six more children, of whom at least three died young.[7]

## INFANCY

Renaissance Italian portrayals of infancy reflected the same ambivalence that birth evoked. On the one hand, there is the delighted love for young children that shines out of so many of the religious paintings of the period. Increasingly naturalistic portraits of the infant Jesus, tenderly held and gazed on by a Madonna and sometimes handed toys by a boyish playmate, the young John the Baptist, hung in hundreds of churches and sat on altars in dozens of private chapels. Artists attuned to the market filled acres of background on panels, canvases, and walls with countless chubby putti and round-cheeked child-angels. All these reflected a warm and hopeful appreciation of idealized youngsters. On the other hand, as with Dati, there was the unrelenting loss of children, especially to disease. Half or more of the children born died before reaching maturity—about half of those in the first year of life. Modern historians trying to imagine the impact of such losses on parents have suggested that resignation or even indifference must have been common. The most bearable way to cope psychologically, these scholars have argued, would be not to invest in infants until one knew that they would survive, at least for a while. The undercounting of babies in censuses that demographers have uncovered would fit such an attitude. So too has been interpreted the rhetoric of "God gives and God takes away" that Dati used in the examples. Alternatively, these words may represent an effort to find religious consolation in grief; tone is always hard to reconstruct from formal documents. Certainly numerous anecdotes show fathers and mothers emotionally engaged with youngsters: tending their needs, worrying over their illnesses, happily watching them play. Taken together, the various sources from Renaissance Italy show us a society that cared about its children and in trying to bring them to adulthood struggled against many obstacles.

Infants belonged in the domain of women. Women nonetheless bore a heavy load of diverse responsibilities. Mothering was just one, and not necessarily the most crucial for the family's well-being. Although their particular tasks varied between city and country, and up and down the social scale, few mothers had the luxury to devote lots of time to direct care of their babies. Consequently, infants and older children had to share maternal attention not only with siblings but with other people and activities. Frequently their care fell in some or substantial part into the hands of other women—grandmothers, older sisters, or servants.

The customs and techniques of handling the very young passed by word and example from woman to woman and from one generation to the next. During the Renaissance, however, male experts also began to pronounce on pregnancy, infant care, and raising families. Though sermons might be in Italian, much of this literature was in Latin. Even when, from the late fifteenth century, the spread of printing brought these texts into wider circulation, only educated men—and a very few women—could read them. The one guide in the vernacular, by Michele de Savonarola and explicitly addressed to the women of Ferrara, remained in manuscript, probably known to only a handful of its intended audience. These books thus were a long way from what women actually did, but they do hint at what their learned contemporaries thought they ought to be doing.

The central and most worrisome part of infant care was feeding.[8] All babies, with a few unfortunate exceptions, were fed at the breast. The experts expressed grave distrust of other sources of nutrition, and with reason. Animal milk, even where available, was unsafe; other liquids, such as almond water, or more solid foods, such as boiled wheat porridge, did not provide what the new baby needed and often troubled its digestion. Such food, people thought, might even addle the child's mind. A mid-fourteenth-century author, Pietro da Certaldo, cautioned against giving "the baby the milk of a goat or sheep or ass or some other animal because the child, boy or girl, nourished on animal milk doesn't have perfect wits like one fed on women's milk, but always looks stupid and vacant and not right in the head."[9]

**Mother's Milk**

While the doctors warned against overfeeding infants, the much commoner problem was lack of breast milk. Because many women's supply failed for one reason or another, emergencies cropped up in which an alternative had to be found quickly. An informal sharing among nursing women was the best solution; one would offer her breast to another's baby, hoping that someone would do the same for her another time. At other times, when no woman with milk could or would step in, infants were no doubt offered risky substitutes. Many died, but not all. The biographer Giorgio Vasari wrote of one artist who, as a two-month-old, after the plague killed his mother, was suckled by a goat.

Procuring "good" milk also posed a challenge. Male authorities urged mothers, for moral as well as medical reasons, to nurse their own children. To the mind of these educated men, milk was a powerful and resonant fluid, concocted of the woman's blood and, like it, bearing the imprint of her body and soul. Therefore, milk carried to the infant not only physical benefits but also psychological ones. The character and social attributes of the nurse passed along to the nursling. And what traits better suited babies than the heritage of their parents? Nevertheless, mothers sometimes found breast-feeding hard. Besides weakness and strains on their health caused by pregnancy and delivery, there was an array of specific impediments for which physicians laid out remedies in their books. For example, one 1577 text showed a woman using a breast pump, a bulb with a long tube probably made of glass, to suck off painful excess milk. For others the difficulty was producing enough. Some mothers could not nurse; others for social and economic reasons chose not to. Among the well-born, maternal feeding was not usual practice. The reasons, according to indignant moral commentators, were parental selfishness: women's vanity about their looks and their husbands' dislike of the long abstinence imposed by the customary taboo on sex while nursing. Forgoing the contraceptive effects of lactation also led to many pregnancies and big families that fortified prestigious lineages. But not only the wealthy withheld mother's milk from their babies. Especially in the city, middling sorts frequently imitated the patricians in this practice, as did even some artisans, who perhaps held their wives' other work too valuable to sacrifice. Babies whose mothers could not or would not feed them came into the arms of paid wetnurses. But would their milk be "good" enough?

**Wetnursing** The difficulties of finding and keeping a suitable wetnurse, or *balia*, preoccupied parents and the medical experts who sought to advise them. While in general women handled infants' needs, the selection and payment of wetnurses was one responsibility in which fathers took part. Wetnurses were typically lower-status women who needed income. Their socially superior employers harbored chronic doubts about the physical health and moral character of these women on whose milk their infants would depend for their lives and even their personalities. The guides for parents offered detailed counsel on how to pick a good wetnurse. Savonarola recommended a woman in her thirties, sturdy of body but not fat, with skin unblemished and milk a good white, not pale and watery. If she had last given birth to a boy, her milk would be warmer and purer. She should be good tempered, not melancholic. If not a widow, she had to have a husband willing to sacrifice his marital rights, to enhance the family income. Pregnancy meant the end of good milk. Evidently finding such a paragon was not easy. Savonarola joked that chances were about as good as of seeing a white crow. And timing complicated matters. The *balia* had to have milk; that is, she had to have recently given birth or been nursing a child. Yet a commercial wetnurse promised exclusive access to her client. That meant either that her own baby had just died or been weaned, or that she had gotten free of it in some dubious fashion, abandoning it as a foundling or giving it to another, presumably inferior woman to feed. With a keen eye to fraud, fathers feared that the nurse they hired might try secretly to divide the milk between two. Thus, even with a wetnurse, it was hard to ensure that a steady supply of good milk would flow when and where it was needed.

Although the wetnurse was hired for her milk, she took responsibility for the infant's full care. Typically she became, more or less completely, a surrogate mother. Children sometimes developed an enduring affection for their "milk mothers," who retained a connection with the family through many years. More common, perhaps, was the experience of interrupted relationships. Displaced by a nurse's illness or pregnancy, a child often suckled from a series of different women. Where circumstances—money and space—permitted, a live-in *balia* was preferred. Mothers could then enjoy their children's company and oversee their good care. In particular, the wetnurse's own regime of nutrition, sleep, and behavior could be monitored; to prevent harm to the baby and expense to her employer, she was to eat and drink moderately, avoiding foods too salty or full of garlic, onions, and heavy wines. Securing such a resident wetnurse was not easy or cheap. A domestic slave was one solution, or a lone woman whom misfortune had left on her own. Otherwise it was necessary to negotiate the nurse's absence from her own family, at additional cost. Providing a scarce resource on favored terms, the live-in *balia* enjoyed a relatively privileged position. Most often, in large, wealthy households, she worked as a well-paid servant, but occasionally, especially in much smaller ones, she also became a kind of mother's companion. If the *balia* could not dwell in the house, better she lived nearby. Florentine women living in the city were known to send their own babies away to distant nurses in order to supply their milk to the local market at premium prices.

For many parents, in fact, to use a wetnurse meant sending the child away to live in her home, usually in the country. Thus, only a few hours or days after birth, a city-born infant departed from its natal family and spent many months—even one, two, or more years—in a modest rural household. The distance caused stress. While some parents may have given little day-to-day thought to their absent offspring, others clearly worried, seeking reports on their health and arranging visits. Concern and forethought also sometimes appeared in rich families' record books, which sometimes cataloged elaborate layettes sent along to provide for the infants' needs. In one case, the provisions included "a branch of coral with a silver ring," likely intended to serve as both toy and amulet. Many children died in their wetnurses' care. Condemned as ignorant, slovenly, and greedy, these surrogates often got blamed for the loss. Grieving parents charged them with neglect and cutting corners. But infants died everywhere in premodern Europe. It is hard to say whether spending the first years in the country as a nurse's paying guest was necessarily rougher than in the more contagious city, in the hands of servants at one's parents' house.

Experts recommended that infants take their nutrition from the breast, but not indefinitely. In most views, weaning best occurred for girls at eighteen months and for boys at two years. Actual ages were probably very variable, dependent on unpredictable events like those that shunted infants from nurse to nurse. At some point it became easier to nourish them entirely with other food. Probably they had already sampled various foods deemed suitable for infants. Boiled wheat porridge, likely first fed through a hollowed horn, was a good beginning. Sops of bread dipped in broth, oil, or watered wine also served. Childcare manuals discouraged fruits because they were hard to digest. Yet other adult food, if prechewed by the mother or nurse, could be gradually introduced. Once able to eat such adapted forms of regular food, infants at the wet-nurse's could go home if their families were ready to receive them. For those youngsters, the change in diet led to a dramatic shift of life. For some it might be the first time they knew their parents and siblings.

**Swaddling**  Besides nursing and the web of arrangements around it, the defining feature of earliest life was swaddling. Fresh delivered from the mother, the newborn's body was washed and dressed in loose garments and diapers. Then the baby's limbs were carefully straightened, and strips of fabric were wound around from toe to head, often leaving only the face exposed. Experts claimed that swaddling kept the baby warm and secure from drafts and discouraged any movement that might invite danger. The wrapping was supposed to be done carefully to prevent too much pressure on fragile organs. Savonarola warned against left-handed women who would swaddle badly. Thus bound, the infant lay in a cradle that could be moved from place to place, but probably stayed mostly near the mother or nurse. Fittingly, doctors expected infants to sleep a lot.

A good regime of care also called for unbound times for hygiene, stimulation, and exercise. Diaper cloths were to be changed several times a day, and experts recommended frequent baths. It was good to wash babies more often than adults washed themselves. Besides cleanliness and comfort, bathing provided an occasion for the child to move and stretch, free of tight swaddling. Caregivers could seize these moments to cuddle and play with the little ones. The friar Giovanni Dominici, who rather austerely advised a widow against petting, embracing, or kissing her son after age three, obviously expected these intimacies to occur with an infant. These sessions of interaction were probably also important for learning to speak, although our sources say next to nothing about this essential early skill. While we may guess that women, busy, often ha-

Child in walker, as women spin and sew. [Bertarelli: Lucrezia]

rassed, and not seldom poor, did not easily fulfill all the injunctions of male pundits, we should also not assume that, by the standards of the time, babies were routinely mistreated or neglected. How long the swaddling stayed on we do not know: a week, a month, several months? Perhaps it was prolonged in the cold season. Certainly by the middle of the second year, children were expected to be moving around and playing with other youngsters. Learning to walk seems to have taken place amid the characteristic Renaissance mix of parental delight and fear. A number of protective devices were available to reduce the risks: harnesses, wooden-frame walkers that in the sixteenth century acquired wheels, and in Rome light helmets made of cotton and silk strips wrapped in a cross shape over the crown of the head.

A number of infants grew up in foundling homes. This form of charitable institution multiplied during the Renais-   **Foundlings** sance to help cope with the evolving problem of unwanted and abandoned children. From the mid-fifteenth century in Florence, Bologna, and other northern cities, specialized hospitals opened to combat a perceived spread of infanticide, especially by neglect. Funded by communes and charitable religious companies, these houses accepted infants whom their parents would not or could not keep. Foundlings generally came from illegal unions, involving slaves or priests, or from pregnant servant girls unable to secure a husband. In times of crisis, the very poor as well handed across youngsters for whom, for the time being at least, they could not provide. These latter sometimes left letters with the children, telling of pitiful hopes to reclaim them in better times. In Florence, notably more girls than boys ended up in the house of the Innocenti; the statistics suggest a greater willingness to sacrifice daughters. Although called hospitals, these homes offered little medical care. Rather, they provided for their charges according to the conventional regimen for children by age. Once received, infants stayed only briefly; as soon as possible they went to wetnurses in the country. Mortality was very high. After weaning, survivors returned to the city, where the hospital trained them to take jobs and support themselves as soon as possible.[10]

## CHILDHOOD

Children, having left the breast and capable of speech and independent movement, entered a new phase of life. Their parents were responsible for beginning to teach them the values, attitudes, and skills that would enable them to function as adults. Some of this knowledge, such as fundamental religious and lay moralities, was nearly universal. Many other lessons were specific to the particular social niches to which gender and rank destined each child. When, as often happened in a world of such high mortality, father, mother, or both could not play their roles, others might step in, more or less willingly, more or less capably. Older sisters, aunts, grandparents, servants, workers in the family business, tutors, masters, or others replaced or supplemented parental efforts. In farm families or among Florentine patricians, where widowers were wont to remarry rapidly, a stepmother was another common possibility. As in infancy, so in childhood, caregivers and adult models might well rotate with time. Youngsters needed to be able to compete for attention. Where necessary, this reliance on multiple adults occurred more readily because most social environments did not segregate age groups. While, by convention, males and females did not always share spaces, the old and the young generally could. With some exceptions, Renaissance children did not pass long hours in rooms or terrains dedicated just to them and their activities. Again, this mixing did not mean they were thought to be "miniature adults." Children had their own capacities and inclinations, but they mostly practiced them in companies and spaces that also served adult affairs.[11]

Until the age of six or seven, children remained largely in the turf of women. Fathers sometimes showed great interest in their offspring, but in early childhood it generally took the form of visits with them in domestic spaces. For instance, Alessandro Pallanterio, a Roman lawyer and high bureaucrat, and in some ways a thoroughly wicked man, kept the child of his horribly abused young mistress, the daughter of a lute maker, in the artisan's house across the street. To his own family's distress, the lawyer in the evenings would often slip across the way, to enjoy the singing and dancing of his four-year-old bastard son.[12] About the age of six, as children became ready to take their first steps toward future adult roles, fathers began to participate more directly. They assumed responsibility for the education of sons, overseeing training where they did not themselves teach. For girls of this same age, in Florence, fathers started paying into an account with the civic dowry fund, the Monte delle Doti, so that ten years later the daughter would be able to marry. As these paternal activities suggest, at this stage gender differentiation intensified. Earlier, although parental expectations for girls and boys were clearly distinct, their care and experiences had a lot in common. They wore similar clothes and played similar games. But at six or seven years, gender differences began to sharpen.

Before the age of six, children had few obligations. While some began early to acquire special skills—Pallanterio's four-year-old son's singing and dancing, Giovanni de' Medici's spelling at the same age—these seem to have been done in a spirit of play more than of earnest preparation for the future. Nevertheless, these and other initiations led toward a more serious phase of learning about to commence in the domains of religion, work, and, for some, intellectual skills.

Religion was the fundamental knowledge shared, though in many forms, by all Renaissance Christians of whatever social rank. So pervasive was it that youngsters must have begun to acquire religious culture as soon as they became conscious of anything outside themselves. To their ears came prayers muttered over them, invocations of the deity in moments of excitement or fear, and cautionary and inspirational tales told by mothers or nurses. For the eyes, there were printed images tacked to homely walls and street-corner madonnas honored with votive candles. In wealthy houses, colorful holy paintings featuring youngsters like themselves may have struck a special chord. For the spiritually precocious, these early encounters resonated strongly. According to their biographies, future saints as children often played house in caves as hermits, acted out holy rituals, or made vows of virginity.

These impressionistic lessons set the stage for more formal religious education and observance for children between six and twelve years. In fifteenth-century Florence, confraternities especially for boys gave them a setting in which to learn and enact their religious duties. Aimed originally at boys of twelve to fifteen years, they came to admit ones as young as eight or even six. Meeting regularly on Sundays, these clubs sought to give constructive shape to youths' leisure time, leavening the dose of religion and organizational life with ball games and virtuous play. Catechism classes, multiplying across Italy especially during the sixteenth century, offered preparation for first communion to children between six and twelve years old. These lessons aimed to teach basic Christian belief and practice to those of modest means. In Bologna these schools reached more than half the boys. Girls, for whom such public activities were thought less suitable, seldom had a chance to participate. Yet, in one specific context, this same age frame did shape young females' religious life. The daughters of affluent Florentines destined—by family strategy or by personal vocation—for the convent typically moved in at age six or seven, took the veil as novices sometime between ages nine to eleven, and made their final vows at age twelve or thirteen.

For many children, introduction to work occurred between ages six and twelve. In city and country, in homes and workshops and on farms, youngsters learned the elementary practices of adult work. Girls observed the mixed tasks of housekeeping—including preparing foods, sweeping, fetching water, washing and drying clothes, feeding and minding small animals—and began to perform the simpler ones. Boys too gradually acquired basic skills, while their orbit of activity expanded beyond the domestic compass to streets and hillsides where they ran errands and watched over grazing animals. For some number of boys and a few girls, education in reading, writing, and arithmetic might also begin in these years. While scions of the elite were sometimes tutored at home, a variety of schools trained city children. (See Chapter 8.)

Economic stress and demographic accident could make for a difficult childhood. At worst, some youngsters found themselves without sustenance and adult care. Alone or with peers, these children had to cope on their own: wandering, begging, and thieving were often their lot. While forced to prey on others, they were very vulnerable to exploitation themselves. Other children, though not wholly abandoned, lived where there was not enough to go around. Therefore, besides helping out in their own families, youngsters sometimes were sent into service in other people's houses. Such work was very common among males and females in their teens; often, however, when boys and girls of even six or eight or ten years became servants, their families had defaulted in some way. Parents and guardians benefited from not having to support the children and sometimes even sold their labor for a fee. The youngsters, usually not paid regular wages, received shelter and food and, if fortunate, the promise of money or goods at the end to help set them up as adults. Thus, Anna da Cattaro, an orphan from the Venetian hospital of Santi Zanipolo, went to serve from the age of nine until seventeen as a "little housekeeper" to a goldsmith. In parallel fashion, adoptions or less formal arrangements saw poor relatives or other children move as de facto servants into rich households that could afford to keep them. But less fragile families could also adopt service, even at an early age, as a means to training and connections for their offspring. A resident from Egypt who placed his ten-year-old son in the service of a Venetian nobleman may well have had such assets in mind. Most parents who could choose waited until their children were somewhat older before setting them on this educational path.

## ENTERING ADOLESCENCE

Somewhere in the years between age twelve and fifteen, childhood merged into adolescence, with neither a sharp break nor a major rite of passage. In becoming adolescent, older children gradually took on a range of new physical, sexual, moral, and intellectual capacities that translated into greater social and legal responsibilities. According to the thinking of Renaissance Italians, younger children, while possessed of sufficient reason for primary learning, were still innocent. They lacked the judgment to discern good and evil in the world around them. Adolescents, in contrast, were acquiring that discretion and thus, incrementally, became liable for the consequences of their actions. The law, for its needs, translated these steps into ages. Historians can use these as markers, but should not read them as corresponding to sudden changes of life or behavior. Through a rather drawn-out process, adolescents became increasingly like adults. Yet as a category they remained distinct.[13]

Even before adolescents reached their full physical growth and strength, they probably passed puberty. Both the capacity to procreate and the desire for sex among those not deemed, as a rule, socially ready for marriage required regulation. The differences between males and females became even sharper, and the need for close control over their relations acute indeed.

Sexual maturity marked a major change for girls. For them, the acquisition of adult physical capacities led not to an expansion of their social range but to risk and restriction. From the heritage of the ancient Romans, twelve was the official age of female puberty, and so it remained in the fourteenth century. In the fifteenth century, experts, perhaps observing girls of their era more closely, tended to expect the onset of menstruation later, at age thirteen or fourteen. The church nonetheless retained its traditional twelve as the minimal canonical age for a girl to marry. (For practice, see Chapter 12.)

**Female Teenagers**

The notion that women as young as twelve could legally consent to marriage meant at the same time that they could consent to sex. Their sexual potential, coupled with general recognition of women as creatures of desire and poor self-control, made it credible that even a young adolescent who lost her virginity or got pregnant might have done so willingly. In a law court, an adolescent girl was no longer presumed innocent; she had to convince the judges she was not complicit. The specter of illicit sex alarmed a young female's keepers; protecting her from abusers, other seducers and her own weakness required keeping her as far from trouble as possible. Guardians, be they fathers, mothers, brothers, masters, or mistresses, were supposed to restrict her public movements and supervise her contacts with men. The application of these principles varied with social status. The elite could afford to seclude its nubile daughters, but working families had no such luxury. The story writer Bandello conjured a tragic tale of a poor girl who was raped because she had to work alone in the fields to help support her family; afterward, all she could do to save their honor was drown herself in the river. Though the story was perhaps fiction, the dangers were real, as were the consequent restraints on young women's freedom. Yet we should not exaggerate their degree. Adolescent girls were not routinely locked up and shut away.

**Male Teenagers**   Adolescent boys' experience was rather different from that of their female agemates. The males' growing capacities, though potentially destructive, did not invite the same collective anxiety and clamping down as did those of females. Boys grew physically bigger, capable of heavier work but also of greater violence. They also achieved sexual maturity, although its arrival was not sharply defined or much remarked. Boys, sometimes as young as ten, engaged in sexual encounters for which courts might assign a measure of legal responsibility. Not until age fourteen, however, or, in some places, eighteen were they deemed fully accountable under the law. While at this age church law allowed males to marry, they seldom did so until at least into their twenties. Unlike females, to whose sexual maturity society responded by trying to wall it in, males, the authorities felt, should be offered some means of satisfaction. In general, the city fathers favored providing prostitutes, suitably labeled and contained in discrete districts. Prostitution, said the theologian Saint Thomas Aquinas, served the public good as did a sewer: it disposed of noxious wastes, so that they did not contaminate respectable society.

Economically and politically, young men continued in a state of incomplete adulthood from their mid-teens to their mid-twenties. Though still in many respects dependent, youths in this period entered the economy. We have already mentioned the many adolescent boys—and girls— who worked during their teens as servants. Under more and less formal arrangements, these were the years for learning trades. Young men destined for careers in the church or professions continued their studies on into university, a few remaining at their books until the age of thirty.

Unwed Venetian girl, her face well hidden. [Bertelli]

Others launched careers by accepting junior posts in the bureaucracies and courts. Florence was, as always, not necessarily typical in detail, but it supplies us with the fullest age-linked ramp of steps to characterize this stage of life. There, fourteen was the official age for beginning formal apprenticeships. Only slightly older began the emancipations by which some fathers formally relinquished their authority over the sons so that they could conduct business legally on their own. While the young man acquired ostensible autonomy, this maneuver was usually part of a strategy intended to benefit the family as a whole by diversifying and managing debt. Although the average age for emancipating sons in the fifteenth century was about twenty years, some merchants typically did so as young as fifteen and sixteen. The practice of emancipation, discouraged in some cities, became less common in Florence itself as the period went on. Adolescents also began to take on civic personality as they became eligible for the head tax—country boys at fourteen and city dwellers at eighteen. They were not, however, qualified to serve the government in elective offices until reaching twenty-five years for some posts, thirty for others, and older still for the highest honors.

In contrast to their restricted sisters, male adolescents, often acting in groups, played roles in the public sphere. In several forms, ritualized behavior by groups of young people, almost exclusively males, served as a kind of collective conscience for society as a whole. The conventional notion of the innocence of the young could be played on for the general benefit. Processions of children and adolescents invoking God and true religion were a familiar sight in Renaissance cities. Occasionally, apparently spontaneous congregations coalesced in times of crisis. In 1483, at Brescia, during a severe drought in the region, and in 1505, at Bologna, after terrible earthquakes, youngsters trooped through streets calling for divine mercy. To the spectators, the hope that God would listen better to these youthful cries made these events notable. In other situations, mendicant preachers drew on the boys' confraternities to organize phalanxes of adolescents, sometimes dressed as angels, who processed around the city to promote moral improvement. The radical Dominican politician Girolamo Savonarola sent boys out into the streets to point out moral lapses and to collect the "vanities"—dice, cards, gaming boards, pagan paintings, and licentious books—to be burned in purifying bonfires in the main square. In this instance, he deployed the image of the innocent to shame their elders out of worldly behavior.

The public image of male youth was not always so orderly and beneficent. Adolescent males, along with those somewhat older males who were still unbound by adult commitments to marriage and work, produced much of the chronic violence of Renaissance Italian society. Wielding fists, sticks, stones, knives, and, with time, guns, young men battled readily for personal honor and for the power of their quarters, factions, or cities. Efforts to reduce violence and teach self-control targeted this age group. The authorities, while they tried to harness the undisciplined vitality of the young, sometimes tolerated in them some forms of ritualized violence. These customs could vent, vicariously, strong emotions that their seniors themselves also felt but did not deem fitting to express.

Ritualized youth violence took several forms. One common custom was to hold competitions and mock battles. In cities across northern and central Italy, from Perugia to Modena to Milan, groups of young men, often representing their sections of town, gathered to fight for victory and prestige. There are some analogies with teen gang wars in our own era. Bridges that marked the boundaries between neighborhoods were a characteristic site. The protocols for combat varied with place and time; observing the ritual order was supposed to moderate the violence. Often youth struggled en masse; sometimes the danger was reduced by the designation of a single champion to fight for each side. Even when the "play" of the battle was obvious, as when warriors waged "mounted" warfare, riding staffs like hobbyhorses, there was great risk of injury and even death. In some places city leaders succeeded quite early in taming these melees into more elegant, less often gory diversions. The "brigades" of Florence, led and subsidized by the gilded scions of the city's elite and bearing names such as "of the Parrot" and "of the Flower," conducted jousts and feats of arms. In the "most serene" republic of Venice, companies of young noblemen garbed in distinctive multicolored hose, likewise sponsored festivities, although usually comedies and parties that lacked the component of warfare. All these events acted out in tamed versions the habitual rivalries that characterized Renaissance political life; they also allowed the young to strut before a large audience, displaying their virile prowess without much bloodshed.

In another, more occasional form of violence, crowds of young males embellished the punishment of political tyrants or despised criminals. When someone particularly heinous had been executed, a mob of adolescents sometimes captured the corpse and heaped further shame on it through desecration. For example, after the hanging of Jacopo Pazzi, the ringleader of the conspiracy that nearly killed Lorenzo de' Medici in 1478, a crowd of boys dug up his body, dragged it around the city and even in front of his own house by the cord at his neck, and then dumped it disparagingly in the river. Chroniclers told similar stories of dismemberment and even cannibalism. At times older men instigated these shaming ceremonies and accompanied the boys committing them, but the young people's participation had special importance. As incomplete adults, they embodied vitality and the future, at the same time that they retained vestiges of irresponsibility and even innocence. The young could go overboard in order to castigate the culprit on behalf of the whole society. When they did, it signified the enormity of the offense. At the same time, extreme or impulsive deeds, which in mature men would disturb, were tolerable in boys. Thus, the ambiguous, fluid nature that Renaissance culture ascribed to adolescence, while troublesome in some ways, could also be put to use. The unsettled shifts from virtue to violence and back again helped express and manage, if not resolve, some of the tensions entrenched in the society.[14]

## CONCLUSION

The young of Renaissance Italy who survived the cull of disease and hardship passed through a sequence of life stages. Although the transitions between them often lacked distinct times or ritual markers, the pathways were widely understood and expected. With passing years came more differences between the genders. For boys, greater physical, social, and intellectual capacity brought greater responsibility and some public roles; for girls, maturation called for greater effort but also for more restraint, imposed both from without, by other people, and from within.

## NOTES

1. On life stages, see Rudolph Bell, *How to Do It: Guides to Good Living for Renaissance Italians* (Chicago: University of Chicago Press, 1999), 177–178, and Elizabeth Sears, *The Ages of Man: Medieval Interpretations of the Life Cycle* (Princeton: Princeton University Press, 1986), 135–137.

2. On life expectancies, see David Herlihy and Christiane Klapisch-Zuber, *Tuscans and Their Families* (New Haven: Yale University Press, 1985), 83–86.

3. On ideas about childhood, see Linda Pollock, *Forgotten Children* (Cambridge: Cambridge University Press, 1983), 2–12, 52–59.

4. On pregnancy and birth, see Bell, *How to Do It*, chap. 3.

5. On baptism and its evolving meanings, see Edward Muir, *Ritual in Early Modern Europe* (Cambridge: Cambridge University Press, 1997), 20–27, and Silvano Cavazza, "Double Death: Resurrection and Baptism in a Seventeenth-Century Rite," in *History from Crime*, ed. E. Muir and G. Ruggiero (Baltimore: Johns Hopkins University Press, 1994), 1–31.

6. On naming, see David Herlihy, "Tuscan Names, 1200–1530," in *Women, Family and Society in Medieval Europe* (Providence, RI: Berghahn Books, 1995), 330–352, and Christiane Klapisch-Zuber, "The Name 'Remade': The Transmission of Given Names in Florence in the Fourteenth and Fifteenth Centuries," in her *Women, Family and Ritual in Renaissance Italy* (Chicago: University of Chicago Press, 1985), 283–309.

7. "Diary of Gregorio Dati," in Gene Brucker, ed., *Two Memoirs of Renaissance Florence* (Prospect Heights, IL: Waveland Press, 1991), 112–117, 126–128, 132, 134–136.

8. On infant feeding and wetnurses, see Bell, *How to Do It*, 124–145, and Valerie Fildes, *Breasts, Bottles and Babies* (Edinburgh: Edinburgh University Press, 1986); for the illustration of the sixteenth-century breast pump, see p. 143.

9. Quoted in James Bruce Ross, "The Middle-Class Child in Urban Italy, Fourteenth to Early Sixteenth Century," in *History of Childhood*, ed. L. DeMause (New York: Psychohistory Press, 1974), 187.

10. On foundlings, see Richard Trexler, "The Foundlings of Florence, 1395–1455," in *Power and Dependence in Renaissance Florence*, v. 1 (Asheville, NC: Pegasus Press, 1998), 7–34, and Philip Gavitt, *Charity and Children in Renaissance Florence: The Ospedale degli Innocenti, 1410–1536* (Ann Arbor: University of Michigan Press, 1990).

11. On childhood and child rearing, see Christiane Klapisch-Zuber, "Childhood in Tuscany at the Beginning of the Fifteenth Century," in *Women, Family and Ritual*, 94–116; Bell, *How to Do It*, 145–174; Ross, "Middle-Class Child," 183–228.

12. Archivo di Stato di Roma, Governatore, Tribunale Criminale, Processi sixteenth century, b. 36.

13. On adolescence and the transition to adulthood, Stanley Chojnacki, "Measuring Adulthood: Adolescence and Gender," in *Women and Men in Renaissance Venice* (Baltimore: Johns Hopkins University Press, 2000), 185–205; Bell, *How to Do It*, chap. 5. On links between the life stages of old and young Florentine men, see David Herlihy, "Age, Property and Career in Medieval Society," in *Women, Family and Society*, 261–278.

14. On the public roles of youth, see Ottavia Niccoli, *Il Seme della violenza. Putti, fanciulli e mammoli nell'Italia tra Cinque e Seicento* (Rome: Laterza, 1995), 41–88.

# 12

# Life Cycles: From Marriage Through Death

Adulthood had many dimensions; one moved into it by increments. Maturity demanded respect, but only for a few did it bring independence. While circumstances and timing varied with social class, for females marriage provided a fairly clear moment of transition. Within the values of her culture, the status of wife, although subordinate to husband, earned a woman recognition and honor. To a wife came the full range of responsibilities that society imposed on females. At the same time, a few women—for example, nuns and dowryless poor—never married, yet still left childhood behind. As for men, marriage also served to mark adulthood. It meant dominance over a wife and children. In other zones of life, adulthood brought new roles, but an autonomy that was often only partial. Economically, much depended on the longevity of a man's father and on the structure of the family enterprise. Although an adult male had the physical abilities and technical skills to earn a living, more senior men often exploited or controlled his labor. In his social and political relations, a grown man had room to maneuver, but only within the bounds of his niche in the hierarchy and of his responsibilities to his peers and dependents. Yet, for all its limitations, adulthood still was the peak—the goal toward which all earlier stages had built. What came afterward was, reputedly, almost all downhill.

## MARRIAGE

Fundamentally, for women, but also significantly for men, marriage was a banner of adulthood. For many Italians, marriage coincided with the passage out from under the power of fathers, who had dominated the hierarchies ruling childhood. Although marriage often just exchanged one obedience for another, it signaled a major break with earlier life. A wedding rearranged one's closest social relationships. Most adult Italians married. Elite families, for honor and thrift, did send some children into celibate careers as priests or nuns; especially for surplus daughters, a convent dowry was far cheaper than a worldly one. Yet even those who took religious vows were sometimes said to marry Christ or the church. Renaissance people had a hard time imagining a mature life without a spouse—divine for a few, but human for the vast majority. It was possible to live singly, and some men and women did, delaying marriage for economic or other reasons until death caught them first. But to most minds it appeared an anomaly, a misfortune, never to have married at all.[1]

Renaissance ideas about so important an institution as marriage were not simple; they came from at least two crucial sources. Religion, for one, construed marriage as a pillar of the earthly order that helped advance salvation. Social traditions, meanwhile, looked to marriage to secure a family's well-being in this world by cultivating alliances with other families and ensuring a line's survival into future generations. Neither approach to marriage shared the modern stress on romantic love and psychological fulfillment.

**Religious Concepts of Marriage**     For the Catholic church of the Renaissance, marriage was a sacrament, the sign of a divine intervention that sanctified its participants. Yet, before the mid-sixteenth century, a man and a woman could—and often did—contract a religiously binding alliance without the presence of a priest. By church law, the core of a marriage was the free consent of the two parties in "words in the present tense." These are reciprocal vows in the form—"I, Caterina, take you, Pietro, to be my husband"—that remain at the crux of the Christian ritual to our day. This exchange of commitments, once sealed by sexual consummation, created an unbreakable bond. Earlier public statements of the intention to marry "in the future tense," witnesses to such vows, and a priestly benediction were all desirable. Still, even without publicity and blessing, a secret marriage was legal and binding. From the medieval church's point of view, the couple and their obligations to one another were the center. The purposes of marriage were to procreate and to aid one another, especially toward salvation. In particular, marriage avoided sin by providing sexual appetite a legitimate outlet. Sex was a marital right; husbands owed it to their wives, not only vice versa. While in the early Renaissance many married without the church's sacrament, these religious ideas nevertheless colored everyone's experience of matrimony. With the reform decrees issued by the Council of Trent in 1563, the church's role grew.

Thereafter, parish priests had to preside over the exchange of vows, as well as to make public the proposed union, three times, in advance.[2]

Regarding matrimony, social traditions had concerns quite different from those of religion. The dominant model, reflecting elite views and practices, saw marriage as linking not merely two individuals but two families. Exchanging economic and political resources and cementing social alliances, it benefited not only the bridal pair but also wider **Social and Economic Concepts of Marriage** networks of kin and associates. Reflecting the concerns of household heads, this way of thinking put group interests ahead of personal comfort. The private feelings of the couple mattered little. While the bride might have strong preferences and certainly a great stake in the outcome, her role was largely passive. She was the principal object in a complex exchange, in which responsibility for her body and honor passed from her father and male kin to her new husband.

In the exchange that was key to marriage, each side gave and received, but the offerings did not balance. On one side, a family gave its daughter, including her sexuality, fertility, and labor power, along with a dowry, to the husband and his family. The dowry, complemented by a trousseau of linens and household wares, was a sizable chunk of assets, usually partly in cash and credits and partly in goods and sometimes real estate, that underpinned the new unit economically. Socially, the dowry also manifested the honor of the bride and her family. Therefore, up and down the social scale, where there were assets, and even where they were lacking, to marry, a girl needed a dowry. Furthermore, where the market for good husbands was competitive, dowries tended to inflate. Lawmakers' efforts failed to curb their rise. Consequently, dowries burdened patrimonies; the daughters' portion sometimes even outstripped the sons' inheritance. On the other side of the marriage bargain, having received the fair boons of woman and dowry, the groom then reciprocated with gifts to the bride. In wealthy families, these often included jewelry, clothing, and adornments for the nuptial chamber, whose cost might be worth a third to half the dowry. Sometimes the completion of the marriage depended on down payment of enough dowry to afford the groom the funds to buy these presents for his bride. Besides these ceremonial donations, which the husband might later repossess, he also committed himself to support his wife during his lifetime and, at his death, to restore the dowry to support her needs. A widow's claim on her often quite substantial dowry in turn threatened to disrupt her marital family's well-being; it often led to drawn-out, tense negotiations.

These imbalanced exchanges and the anxieties they provoked were most dramatic in the upper ranges of Italian society, where ruled the model of marriage as an alliance of large lineages. Lower down the economic ladder, marriages also involved dowries, but the union focused largely on the couple, not on kin. In those classes, marriage still assumed gender hierarchy and male responsibility for female honor, but, because women's labor supported household income, the pair functioned as a fuller partnership. Across society, marriage brought both husband and wife status, greater responsibility, and somewhat more independence than they had enjoyed in their preadult condition.

**Age of Marriage**

The considerations on when to marry differed for women and for men. For females, the precariousness of honor pushed for early marriage, but the search for dowry argued for delay. By these logics, girls from families rich enough to dower them from wealth on hand wed younger than those from poor ones, who had to earn money themselves. Demographic pressures and the heat of the marriage market also affected ages of first marriage. The average varied: between city and country, by social class, and over time. Although young brides were desirable, the fourteen-year-old Juliet of Shakespeare's play was unusual. No one was surprised by a married fifteen- or sixteen-year-old, but, even in Florence, where average ages were among the youngest found, the age was seventeen to eighteen. In smaller towns, in the countryside, and toward 1600, brides were older yet, twenty and above. Everywhere, nearly all women became wives (and sometimes even widows) by the age of twenty-five.

Concerning marriage, men had some other things to think about. For them, given the double standard around sex and honor and the availability of prostitutes and, illicitly, serving girls, the hurry was less. Moreover, the need for a means to support a family urged prudent slowness. In the country, the supply of land and local labor practices determined whether an early wife helped or hindered a man's career. In the city, if an artisan was not yet master of a shop, he needed at least to complete his training and find steady work before marrying. Advice manuals discouraged men from marrying before age twenty-five, and, addressed as they were to elite readers, they sometimes recommended thirty-five or forty years old. But quantitative evidence suggests that most people ignored these pundits. In patterns that invert those of women, country men usually married sooner than city-dwelling Florentines, on average at age twenty-five to twenty-seven instead of thirty-one or thirty-two. As a result, age gaps between brides and grooms were typically five or more years, not the fifteen years common among urban patricians.[3]

**Making a Match**

So how did Renaissance Italians find a mate? While they generally did not practice formal endogamy, that is, marry only inside a defined group, as a rule they chose partners among those who were familiar, with whom they shared social rank, neighborhood, or economic ties. While marrying well was a strategy for rising in the world, most people aimed just to secure their position by marrying someone fairly like themselves, whose economic

Courtship among spring flowers. [Bertarelli: Missale]

interests and honor matched their own. Alongside material assets and social connections, appearance and health counted. Elite girls, shut in their homes much of the time, were looked over when they appeared in church. A desirable spouse also should have at least a compatible temperament. Too quarrelsome a domestic life subverted the goals of marriage. Normally, for cooperation's sake, men sought a docile female. These criteria so narrowed the field of potential mates that finding a suitable choice at the right moment and winning her family's agreement posed a challenge. The bargaining was often a delicate business, and the stakes, in wealth and prestige, were high. Thus, many Renaissance marriages were arranged by third parties.

In theory, church law firmly demanded the free consent of bride and groom, but in practice often, and among the elite always, the match was negotiated and made by others. Making marriages for their offspring was a parental responsibility; for daughters especially, it was a critical part of launching them into adulthood. So weighty was the dowry that giving or receiving one affected the larger family's well-being. Therefore, for heads of households, marriages were a major concern. Property issues thus shaped parental decisions: how many matches, whose, when, to whom, and at what price? During marriage negotiations, through emissaries and directly, the two families dickered over who would give what when. In a competitive and nosy society, this stage cherished secrecy. Men usually conducted the face-to-face negotiations, but women— the mother, even the bride, or veteran female servants—might have their say. Thus, a Florentine patrician had to haggle for a satin dress requested by his daughter, though he himself thought this bid too lavish and it threatened to stir up jealousy in her unwed cousin.

Where parents were absent or needed help, other family members or even nonkin often stepped in to secure a match. Relatives and friends pointed out possible candidates and served as go-betweens. Masters and mistresses might see to marrying off their servant girls respectably.

Rather than resent such match-making as a threat to autonomy and future happiness, many young people likely welcomed their elders' assistance. To assemble a solid partner and a reasonable dowry often took more effort and more resources than just two young people possessed.[4]

The dowry, the largest piece of the property exchange, could call on assets from a network of sources, both male and female. While fathers had a duty to dower their daughters as best they could, this was a burden not easily shouldered alone. Contributing to dowries was a favorite good deed. Mothers, masters and mistresses, senior male relatives, friends and allies would make donations, sometimes as deathbed bequests. Young working women saved their earnings in order to marry. Yet the specter of the dowryless poor girl, teetering on the brink of concubinage or worse, beckoned to the charitable. From the late fifteenth century, special confraternities in many Italian cities devoted themselves to showering hundreds of dowries on vulnerable virgins. For example, an energetic congregation at Santa Maria sopra Minerva in Rome promised a respectable though not lavish sum to poor girls over the age of fourteen, of good and "honest" local parentage; later, "foreigners" too could apply. Annually, on the feast of the Annunciation, the candidates, demurely dressed, paraded through the neighborhood, attracting a crowd; watchers seeking wives passed their choices to the administrators and, after proving suitability and good intentions, received their brides, properly endowed.

The couple's part in making Renaissance marriages ran the gamut, from almost nil to doing it all themselves. For elite families, where the stakes of honor and property were very high, the nuptial pair often had almost no control. A man, if fully mature, especially if his father had died, could make his own choices, but still might leave the initiative in others' experienced hands. Typically, at this elite level, bride and groom first met during the wedding ceremonies. Courtship consisted of negotiations over material matters and ritual gestures extended through "ambassadors." Among those of lower status, some imitated such arrangements as best they could, but others went about it differently.

In both city and country, working men and women sometimes found their own partners. They met on the job, in the street, or at public festivities. While girls of this class had honor that they and their guardians sought to protect, they did not live under steady supervision. Men could pay court to them with conversations at doors and windows or across the rooftops, and with serenades, gifts, and trysts. Hoping to marry, the couple might then seek parental backing and enlist others to help muster the needed funds. Some young people had disapproving parents or mentors, however, or no one at all.

Thus, many couples were on their own. Putting together a dowry entailed long delays. In the meantime, the couple, having promised each other to marry in the future, might embark on a sexual relationship. Before the Council of Trent tightened policy, the combination of agreement and sexual companionship was, in many people's minds, binding, like a marriage. Once the pair had "carnal knowledge" of one another, authorities, public and familial, usually wanted to regularize their alliance. If a pregnant girl claimed convincingly to have received marriage promises, both community pressure and church courts would lean heavily on the reluctant suitor. This strategy did not serve every seduced woman; some men fled. Couples balked by family opposition might exploit the same logic, by having sex in order to extract grudging consent.

The rituals of the wedding itself had three phases. These might bunch together over a few days, but could also stretch   **Weddings** over weeks or months. The solemnities had no single crowning moment; thus, when trouble intervened before all the steps had been completed, there might be disputes over whether the couple were in fact married. The first formality was the signing of the contract. At this all-male assembly in front of the notary, supporters from both parties witnessed the groom and the bride's father put their names to a legal document detailing the agreement. Exchanging handshakes or kisses, the men made public their mutual commitments. Only at another gathering did the bride herself appear. This second stage of the wedding took place at her house. With a small party, the groom came and, before a company of her kin and friends and a notary, exchanged consent with the bride, marking the event by giving her a ring. He also bestowed other gifts that made up the "counter-dowry." The bride's family then sponsored a banquet and festivities for their guests. The ring ceremony initiated the symbolic transfer of the woman out of her natal family and her incorporation into her marital one. This transition was completed only during the third phase of the nuptial rite of passage, with the physical movement of her person and goods to the home of her new husband. In a highly visible procession, the bride, clothed in her finery and accompanied by her trousseau, went to her new residence. There the man's family offered further celebrations and gifts. As part of the display, wealthy families liked to have chests, and even walls, lavishly painted on nuptial themes. The consummation of the marriage, which definitively displayed the bride's honor and placed it in her husband's hands, traditionally occurred that night; guests might make much ado of bedding the new couple. The wedding night and the morning after often featured playful, noisy, and often bawdy revelry. If, however, delay was anticipated in this "translation" of the bride, sexual relations might have begun earlier, at the bride's house, even following the ring ceremony.[5]

**Living Together, Making a Family**

Once all the wedding steps were done, the new couple generally set up on their own. They had to learn to live together and to collaborate in earning a livelihood and running a household. Probably husband and wife had already learned many skills for these tasks, but they might never have been in charge before. They could continue to draw on the more or less welcome advice of family and neighbors. Sometimes, however, in the countryside and among the urban patricians, the newlyweds began their married life as part of a larger, existing household. There, as they adapted to one another, they would have both more assistance and less privacy. (Chapter 4 describes views on the behavior expected of good husbands and wives.)

Producing and raising children was one of the principal functions of marriage. Advice books directed prospective parents to undertake conception soberly, for the natures of the future offspring were at stake. According to a speaker in Leon Battista Alberti's dialogue on the family,

Husbands . . . should be careful not to give themselves to their wives while their mental state is troubled by anger, fear, or some other kind of disturbing emotion. The passions that oppress the spirit slow up and weaken our vital strength. Those passions that inflame and excite the mind disturb and provoke to rebellion the masters whose task it is at that moment to form the human image. Hence it may be found that a father who is ardent and strong and wise has begotten a son who is fearful, weak, and foolish. Sometimes from a moderate and reasonable man springs a mad and bestial youth.[6]

Whether or not couples paid such cautious heed to moods, wives could expect a chain of many pregnancies at average intervals of about two years. Six or seven deliveries were common, and many women had more. In some circumstances, especially after a number of children had survived infancy, some couples may have sought to contain the number of their offspring.[7] The available means were not very effective, and the demographic evidence for a concerted practice of family limitation is not strong. Barrenness, on the other hand, was clearly a hardship, even a curse. Sufferers sought remedies through prayer at special shrines dedicated to the Virgin Mary, Saint Margaret or the archangel Michael at Gargano. If that did not work, the desperate might resort to magic.

Women faced childbirth with fear. While we should not exaggerate the numbers who died of delivery's consequences, we should also not dismiss its costs to women's life, health, and tranquility. Rationally, many picked this occasion to write their wills. Anxiety had its antidote in the female solidarity that supported the new mother. Besides the midwife, other matrons gathered around the laboring woman. And after the delivery, female relatives and friends assembled to celebrate with conversation, jokes, and delicacies. Rich Florentines had birth trays finely painted with classical allusions and lineage emblems to transport gifts of food for these festivities.

Not all marriages were successful, let alone happy. Husbands sometimes drank and beat their wives, not only temperately for "just correction," but excessively. Occasionally women had to flee. Also, not infrequently, men abandoned their wives and children—sometimes deliberately, sometimes through inadvertence. Wives too failed in their duties. They scolded and hit their spouses, and even tried to poison them. They committed adultery. Now and again, a wife not only ran off with another man but took with her the linens and furniture. Though exceptions, such breakdowns provide a valuable corrective to the prescriptive literature's image of marriages as always orderly and disciplined. Both church and lay courts had to adjudicate matters arising from failed marriages. The shared goal was to return the couple to proper, tranquil cohabitation. That could well prove impossible. Many troubled couples probably lapsed into cold war or de facto separations; for ordinary folk there was no official divorce as we now know it. Those few who could handle the time and expense might for serious cause petition the church for a formal "separation from bed and board." Such a decree left the marriage in place but suppressed its obligations; the partners were not free to wed again.[8] Only the very rare annulment, on technical grounds, permitted remarriage.

**Remarriage**

Cruel demography broke up many marriages before old age; the loss of a spouse did not happen at any one time of life. In the absence of divorce, it was high mortality that left many partners newly single. Overall, men were much more likely to remarry than women. For men, taking a new wife and dowry paid. Because the values of the marriage market favored them, widowers often snatched up desirable young brides. Gregorio Dati, who professed convincing respect and affection for his wives, nonetheless was no mournful widower; he remarried three times and promptly. For women, opportunities depended on age and circumstances. A widow who reclaimed her dowry could use it to wed again, to the cost of her children by the first marriage. More experienced and less dependent than when they first married, widows sometimes took a more active role in deciding whether and with whom to make another alliance. Young widows, however—those most likely to attract a profitable second match—could find themselves once again subject to their fathers' strategies. Older widows, as fertility ended, would not easily find another partner. These, with more interest in tranquility and the salvation of their souls, often preferred a divine spouse and entered a convent.[9]

## OLD AGE

Renaissance understandings of old age were full of contradictions. On the one hand, growing old was a loss to dread. Muscular, mental, and reproductive powers all waned; looks faded. The old, at least in literature, were the object of scorn and obloquy. Old women, when cast as spiteful crones, might suffer persecution and even suspicion of witchcraft. At the same time, the old of both sexes could also invite condescending charitable solicitude, perhaps mingled with respect for years. On the other hand, there persisted the classical notion that age brought wisdom and judgment. Fittingly, some of the most powerful leaders were elderly. Thus, for some, age brought poverty and neglect; for others, enduring control of great wealth, prestige, and power. The fortunate old were numerous and vigorous enough to wield substantial influence over their world.

The borders of old age lacked sharp definition. They seemed very much a matter of state of mind. There was nothing resembling modern retirement, sharply defined and enshrined in laws and rites of passage. Some people did retire, withdrawing from public roles or private business, but did so as a personal choice about lifestyle. No set age imposed the change, or even suggested it. Some people spoke as if, having reached thirty-five or forty years, they felt they had reached a turning point and should prepare for death. Others were going strong at sixty and seventy years and beyond. Renaissance bodies suffered so much wear and tear, even while young, that pain and weakness were not much blamed on years. Rather, the experience of old age came with actual decrepitude, whenever it chanced to hit rather than setting in at an expected time. The poor and sickly became "old" early, while the vigorous and successful carried on without much change of life. The condottiere Bartolomeo Colleone led his last battle at age sixty-seven; in the next five years he was still receiving—and declining—offers of further military commissions from the pope and the duke of Burgundy. The popes themselves were usually old; thus, in the sixteenth century, average age at election was sixty-one years, eight months. The doges of Venice were often similarly venerable in years. Artists, too, stayed in harness. Michelangelo was sixty-five when he began the *Last Judgment* in the Sistine Chapel, and he worked on it and other painting and architectural projects for another twenty years. His contemporary, the Venetian artist Titian, was still active when he died at age ninety-nine.[10]

Old age was harder on women than on men. In the fifteenth century those who lived long tended to be men, though in the sixteenth century the life expectancies of older women increased some. Women were much less likely to enjoy a comfortable and potent old age. Old women, although most had theoretical claim on dowries, were in fact very often poor. The opportunities to earn a living were few. Some older women returned to domestic service, although, as they aged, their capacities declined. When they could no longer work, some masters sent them away, but some allowed them to remain as dependents in their households, "for the love of God." Other women were reduced to begging. Past their thirties, women did not readily remarry. Although they sometimes lived with their adult children, they were often forced to live alone or in households cobbled together with other poor women. Another alternative that expanded during the Renaissance were charitable hospitals that gave food and shelter to the aged. Those who could pay their keep sometimes found their way into nunneries.

Although some males suffered similar tribulations, overall old men fared better. They had better chances of hanging on to money and the resources to make it. They rarely lived as solitaries, but, holding onto the economic reins, continued to rule a household of their offspring and servants. Or else they remarried and engendered more children. Fiction and drama were full of stories of weddings between May (the young bride) and December (the doddering husband); the old man could take the fresh female as his prize, but he could not keep her faithful and earned his shame as a cuckold. Although the tales may reflect the envy of the young more than the actual experience of the old, they represent the belief that the old successfully claimed scarce goods for themselves. A similar rationale made such matches a common target for charivaris, insulting noctural serenades.[11] In the political sphere, a parallel resentment evolved as the party of youth complained against elderly men who monopolized more than a due share of power.

## DEATH

Death was on the minds of people at all stages of the life cycle. While death felt more imminent in the later phases of life, it could and did strike at any time. From Christianity came the notion that all of life prepared for death and for passage to another life that followed. In the long run, Christians aspired to salvation and heaven, though the irredeemably wicked faced an eternity of torment in hell. Most Renaissance people, however, expected a stint in purgatory, an intermediate domain in which sinners—that is, more or less everyone except saints—expiated their transgressions before being admitted to paradise. The belief in purgatory sustained links between the living and the dead. In a circuit of supernatural patronage, saints in heaven could intercede with God on behalf of mortals, and living human beings with prayers and masses could boost the souls in purgatory upward. Thus, the quick and the dead, allies still, continued to foster one another. Providing for the future of one's soul in purgatory was one of the features of a "good death."

**The "Good Death"** With death unpredictable and all around, Italians had reason to fear being caught unprepared, their souls unshriven and their families and goods in disarray. Preachers and confessors used this threat to pressure their flocks into good behavior so as to be always ready to face God. You should live well, fearing death. You should die well too. There was a clear picture of what to do with the last hours. The scene at the deathbed was a sacred and a social drama. It became a moment of gathering for family, associates, a notary, and a priest. While some people prepared their wills in advance, many did not. Some used their last breaths to make or remake the arrangements, as the possible beneficiaries hung about grieving and offering solace, but also vying with rivals to protect their interests. The death of a wealthy paterfamilias with many dependents to provide for was a particularly intense occasion. Wills settled worldly matters, often parceling out major assets among the heirs and showering gifts in cash and kind specified at length—clothing, jewelry, weapons, art—on kin, friends, and faithful dependents. Testaments also typically attended to the fate of their makers in the life beyond. Donations to charity and the church to rectify specific sins such as usury were intended to unburden the soul of part of its weight of transgression. In the later Renaissance, dying penitents made fewer such designated bequests, but left more and more funds to religious institutions to pray and say masses for their souls and for those of deceased family members. On their deathbeds, people strove to make their purgatory as short and light as possible. With the future of the testator and his or her kin provided for as best as could be, the dying person then confessed and received the sacrament of extreme unction.[12]

---

## A HERO'S LAST MOMENTS

In 1584, the Italian baron Marcantonio Colonna, the hero of the great naval defeat of the Turks at Lepanto, died in Spain at the age of forty-five after a brief illness. A member of his household sent home a long, detailed report on his care. Clearly, to the anonymous author's approving eye, the nobleman had died a good death: "He asked for extreme unction, . . . saying it should come quickly, and father Luis gave it to him, and gave him many reminders, asking him questions and to everything he answered literally, and with attention, and after that he spoke no more, but remained with his eyes fixed on the most holy cross, and when the Creed had been sung he expired with no travail or movement of any sort." Because the man had been important, the physicians opened the corpse to find the cause of illness.[13]

---

**Funerals** Death set in motion a further series of customs and rituals. As with other rites of passage like marriage, arrangements, from grand to miserable, varied. Here they depended on the wealth and the taste of the deceased and the mourners and also on the circumstances of the death. In times of plague, for instance, funerals were rudimentary and hurried. We will describe the full panoply of observances with the understanding that for many people these went truncated or little adorned.

The first stage was a vigil around the corpse in the family house. Family members and neighbors burned candles and kept watch. Tradition called for women to mourn dramatically, crying out, unbinding their hair, and tearing their skin and clothing. Women also had the practical role of washing the body and dressing it for burial, usually in its best apparel. Sometimes preparing the corpse, as well as transporting it, was the job of specialists such as the *beccamorti* in Florence, but usually this task fell to ordinary women who were available when needed.

After the domestic vigil came the public stages of the funeral: the procession, requiem, and burial. These usually took place on the day after death, although, in the sixteenth century, for the great the final steps might tarry to await a more splendid crowd. Earlier, even for state obsequies, the period for viewing and paying respect to the dead usually lasted not more than a few hours. Techniques for slowing decomposition were ineffective, and only the very holy were allowed to remain unburied for more than a day. One mark of sainthood was the supernatural preservation of the body, which gave off not the stench of the sinner but the sweet "odor of sanctity." Allowing time for this miracle tested or confirmed sainthood and afforded opportunity for veneration.

The public rites focused on honor. They both cared for and celebrated the dead and affirmed the continuity through time of the collectivity, especially the family. Funerals were made for the dead but by the living, who shared in their honor. The procession, in particular, was often marked by great pomp. Troops of clergy to accompany the body, crowds of mourners, family members in rich but somber garb, caparisoned horses, banners and drapery, many candles and torches: all proclaimed the prestige of the deceased, but also of the family or the corporate bodies to which he or she had belonged. The grandest obsequies glorified rulers and others who had nobly served city or community. In the same spirit, rich families would seize a funeral to celebrate their past or trumpet an even greater present. Thus, while lavish rites as a rule marked the deaths of men, a socially aspiring husband or son might also stage a handsome funeral for his wife or mother, milking the pomp to extol his lineage. For ordinary people, death rituals were less grand affairs. Nevertheless, the commoner's desire for a decent funeral, on the part of both the dying and survivors, reflected similar attitudes. Belonging to guilds or, especially, confraternities allowed men and women with fewer assets to enjoy some funeral splendor. A major function of these corporations was as burial societies; they provided mourners, regalia, and sometimes even funds to see their members conveyed to the grave with due honor.[14]

The procession moved from the dead person's house to the church, the usual place of burial. For the important dead, the mourners might trace a longer route to exalt the occasion. Benches set out along the route could seat mourners and gawkers. The typical procession had three sections. First walked the clergy; for a high-status event, since more was better, several religious communities would be invited, at a price, to swell the ranks. In the middle, carried on a bier, came the body, usually wrapped, but without a coffin. At fancy funerals the corpse might sport expensive scarlet or purple fabric. Some persons of rank, however, preferred to go to their tombs in the guise of Christian humility; these requested for their grave clothes the ostentatious poverty of a plain religious habit. In third position followed the mourners, in significant formation, those nearest to the body being family members and other prestigious associates while lesser folk and those with looser ties brought up the rear. In the procession, only men were welcome, for the occasion combined public display and decorum. Women, whose presumed fragile self-control might not avail to stem their grief, should not make a wailing spectacle of themselves in the streets; therefore, they better mourned indoors—at home or in the church at the requiem.

The requiem was a mass offered on behalf of the dead. A priest officiated before the gathered mourners, male and female. A bid for honor might clothe the chief women in expensive veils and mantles, some fur-lined. The requiem, in response to the social rupture caused by death, reincorporated the survivors, male and female, into an intact community. The liturgy might end with a sermon eulogy. In Florence, the preacher, reiterating the theme of collective continuity, praised the family as much as the deceased.

The burial itself attracted less fuss. Unless a will made another request, people were normally buried in their parish—in the church itself or in its yard. When room ran out, external cemeteries were used. Collective tombs, for families or corporations such as confraternities, were common. When testators asked for burial somewhere besides their parish, it was usually in the church of a religious community they admired or with relatives entombed at a different site. The wealthy buried their dead in a family chapel inside a church they patronized. After the observances at the church, family and guests might repair to the house for a mourning banquet.

Through this ritual process, the dead and the living, having both acknowledged their connections, were freed to pursue their now-separate paths. The dead, thus duly helped on their way to their next existence, should not hang around to harass those left behind. Their worldly goods passed to their survivors, who would pray for their souls in purgatory and perhaps attend commemorative masses provided for by the testament. But, affirming the continuing vitality of the surviving community, the living would also carry on with their earthly tasks.

## CONCLUSION

Renaissance Italians understood life as a series of stages, each with its own capacities, concerns, and rituals. For men, full physical and social maturity knew no single moment of arrival, but for most women marriage served as a ritual induction into adulthood. After the prime of life, the later steps for many, though not all, brought loss. Many women and some men found themselves weak and vulnerable. Despite the damage wreaked on the old by illness, hard work, and misfortune, other men continued to work, deal, command, and govern until very ripe ages. Sooner or later, death came to all. Its customs arranged for what the deceased left behind to be distributed for honor and profit. For most, the soul headed for purgatory with the hope of heaven beyond. Of the worldly remains, the bones rested in fitting sites where mourners could pray for and revere their ancestors. Properties passed to family and church to support the living.

## NOTES

1. On marriage in its many aspects, there is much to read in Italian and English. Several of the major studies in English appear in this chapter's notes. A recent anthology includes a general introduction to the issues, *Marriage in Italy, 1300–1650*, ed. T. Dean and K. Lowe (Cambridge: Cambridge University Press, 1998), 1–21. A valuable Italian collection (which may soon be available in English translation) is Michela De Giorgio and Christiane Klapisch-Zuber, eds., *Storia del Matrimonio* (Rome: Laterza, 1996).

2. On concepts of marriage and canon law, see James Brundage, *Law, Sex and Christian Society in Medieval Europe* (Chicago: University of Chicago Press, 1987), especially chaps. 9 and 10.

3. On the age of marriage, see David Herlihy and Christiane Klapisch-Zuber, *Tuscans and Their Families* (New Haven: Yale University Press, 1985), 202–211, and Stanley Chojnacki, "Measuring Adulthood," in *Women and Men in Renaissance Venice* (Baltimore: Johns Hopkins University Press, 2000).

4. On matchmaking and family strategies, see Anthony Molho, *Marriage Alliance in Late Medieval Florence* (Cambridge, MA: Harvard University Press, 1994), and Sandra Cavallo and Simona Cerutti, "Female Honor and the Social Control of Reproduction in Piedmont," in *Sex and Gender in Historical Perspective*, ed. E. Muir and G. Ruggiero (Baltimore: Johns Hopkins University Press, 1990), 73–109.

5. On marriage rituals, see Edward Muir, *Ritual in Early Modern Europe* (Cambridge: Cambridge University Press, 1997), 31–41, and Christiane Klapisch-Zuber, *Women, Family, and Ritual in Renaissance Italy* (Chicago: University of Chicago Press, 1985), chaps. 9, 11.

6. Leon Battista Alberti, *The Family in Renaissance Florence*, trans. R. Watkins (Columbia: University of South Carolina Press, 1969), 120.

7. On contraception, John Riddle, *Contraception and Abortion from the Ancient World to the Renaissance* (Cambridge, MA: Harvard University Press, 1992), and Herlihy and Klapisch-Zuber, *Tuscans and Their Families*, 250–254.

8. On marital relationships and troubled marriages, see Rudolph Bell, *How to Do It* (Chicago: University of Chicago Press, 1999), chap. 6; Joanne Ferraro, "The Power to Decide: Battered Women in Early Modern Venice," *Renaissance Quarterly* 48:3 (1995), 492–512; Lucia Ferrante, "Il Matrimonio disciplinato: processi matrimoniali a Bologna nel Cinquecento" in *Disciplina dell'anima, disciplina del corpo et disciplina della società tra medioevo ed età moderna*, ed. P. Prodi (Bologna: Annali dell' Istituto storico italo-germanico in Trento, 1994), 901–927.

9. On remarriage, see Christiane Klapisch-Zuber, "The 'Cruel Mother': Maternity, Widowhood and Dowry in the Fourteenth and Fifteenth Centuries," in *Women, Family and Ritual*, 117–131.

10. On old age, see Georges Minois, *History of Old Age from Antiquity to the Renaissance*, trans. S. Tenison (Chicago: University of Chicago Press, 1987), chaps. 8 and 9.

11. On charivaris, see Christiane Klapisch-Zuber, "The 'Mattinata' in Medieval Italy," in *Women, Ritual and the Family*, 261–282.

12. On death in premodern Europe, see Muir, *Ritual in Early Modern Europe*, 44–51, and Philippe Ariès, *The Hour of Our Death*, trans. H. Weaver (New York: Knopf, 1980). For a discussion of death in Florentine popular piety, with Renaissance illustrations, see Donald Weinstein, "*The Art of Dying Well* and Popular Piety in the Preaching and Thought of Girolamo Savonarola," in *Life and Death in Fifteenth-Century Florence*, ed. M. Tetel et al. (Durham, NC: Duke University Press, 1989), 88–104.

13. Biblioteca Apostolica Vaticana, Vat. Lat. 7031, 292r-93v.

14. On death rituals, see Sharon Strocchia, *Death and Ritual in Renaissance Florence* (Baltimore: Johns Hopkins University Press, 1992).

# 13

# Houses, Food, and Clothing

## TENDING BODILY NEEDS

Daily life takes its flavor not only from people and their relationships but also from the routine activities that sustain the body—eating, sleeping, and hygiene—and the everyday objects that support them—furniture, storage vessels, wells, hearths, brooms, bedding, cooking pots, and clothing. Renaissance Italians had to meet the basic human needs for food, rest, and shelter under much greater constraints than ours. They lacked our technology and energy resources. Their bodies were routinely assaulted by physical dangers and irritations, ranging from plague to lice, from crippling injuries to smoke-red eyes, that most readers of this book encounter only rarely. Caring for themselves drew heavily on what resources in time and material there were. Some burdens weighed alike on the well-born and the lowly, but degrees of wealth or poverty gave great diversity to material circumstances.

Well-being was linked to social as well as physical circumstances. Not just life and livelihood were at stake, for bodies and their appearances were also prime social and cultural markers. Beauty and good carriage, smooth features and straight limbs, nimbleness, and strength all contributed to honor (see Chapter 5). Clothing and cosmetics highlighted a body's assets or covered up and redesigned its flaws. Norms laid out expectations fitted to status, age, and gender. Given the challenges of the physical and social environment, few could display the peak of health and allure, but daily routines served to keep people as well and healthy looking as possible.[1]

Renaissance Italians, who found honor in health and good appearance, did not flinch from showing or seeing bodies. Though heirs to Christian traditions that feared flesh as a distraction from spiritual things, they enjoyed the display of physical beauty. Though attentive to reputation and wary of affronts to female sexual propriety, they were not prudish. They were indeed often quite matter-of-fact about bodies, and their fluids and excretions. The abhorrence of nudity and visible sexuality we call "Victorian"—our picture mislabels and exaggerates this prudery—hardly infected premodern behavior. In Renaissance Italy, men appeared on various occasions publicly nude or seminude. Book illustrations show agricultural workers with bare legs both stomping grapes in vats and working in the fields. Men swam naked in the Tiber in the center of Rome. The English traveler Thomas Coryate commented with northern surprise at scant or absent clothing. In Padua, he reported, a bankrupt would have his debts remitted if he sat three days at the Palace of Justice with his buttocks exposed.[2] In the currency of shame, this was an expensive choice, but the strictures about nudity did not render it unthinkable. In Piedmont the Englishman saw children scampering in June with their bottoms bare. And women workers nearby, wearing only light smocks, seemed to him scarcely clad. He credited the warm climate for these practices, but local norms about the body were also at work. Overall, gender prescribed for women less bare flesh than for men, but another observer told of seeing through open windows city women with little on, as if the demands of modesty were not sharp. Nor was sex easily shrouded. Couples might seek a modicum of privacy, but since most had to choose between crowded quarters at home or outside corners where others might stumble by, there was little security for intimate encounters. Shame attached to public and improper sexuality, but one encountered or discussed it without squeamishness.

Evidence of exposed bodies also comes from preachers and moralists. The vanity of women and especially—they said—lewd decolletage and even uncovered breasts were a favorite target of sermons. In part these gibes were conventional, assaults on general immorality, but pictures of women's dress lend plausibility to the friars' complaints. Other moralists of a humanist bent advocated not only female modesty but also a more general civility by veiling the body and its functions. In the mid-sixteenth century, Giovanni Della Casa wrote a handbook on the manners of a gentleman. High on his list of prohibitions were bodily displays in public, such as yawning, scratching, cleaning teeth, or even being seen washing hands after excretion, because that reminded the viewers of what the handwasher had just been doing. "And when you have blown your nose," hectored Della Casa, "you should not open your handkerchief to look inside, as if pearls or rubies might have descended from your brain."[3] We moderns, reading this, blush or giggle, for such rules seem mere basic courtesy. But in the Renaissance they appeared as novelties, things to learn if one aspired to fit in among the best. For most people, the body with its shameful parts and its nail parings, phlegm, urine, blood, and milk were familiar and routine. Conventions shaped their handling, but certainly did not banish them from sight, touch, or talk.

Most Renaissance Italians ate, slept, washed, and dressed at home. Nevertheless, these personal activities did not occur in the private and isolated environments familiar to us today. Renaissance bedrooms often had semipublic functions, and bathrooms like ours did not exist. As we have seen in earlier chapters, domestic space was porous in several ways. Rooms served multiple purposes; people came and went—not just family members, but also servants, workers, and guests. In the countryside and even in the cities, animals too might live at close quarters. Many Italians also routinely tended their bodily needs in other settings. Institutions like monasteries and hospitals housed substantial numbers. Others ate and slept in taverns and boarding-houses. Some—migrant workers, shepherds, soldiers, bandits—camped out for months at a time.

Although the wealthy enjoyed greater comfort than the poor, by modern standards all Renaissance houses were quite primitive. Without electricity, artificial illumination required controlled burning. This was dangerous, costly, and dim. With few exceptions, there was no private running water and no piped sewage. Poor heating and ventilation left winter rooms drafty, smoky, and smelly. Against the heat of summer, the only remedy was to preserve the cool of night or winter as long as possible inside dark, thick-walled dwellings; ice was a rare luxury. To succor the body amid these stresses, household goods and possessions were relatively few. Those few were solid, treasured, cared for, and much reused. Much furniture, equipment, and clothing did daily service for years, even for a lifetime, and then passed down to the next generation. Many items showed signs of repeated repair; others remained in use though worn or tattered. Some belongings were inventively adapted to new purposes. People knew their few things intimately and could describe them in great detail; they distinguished carefully between old and new.

As the Renaissance went on, Italians acquired more goods for their bodies and homes, and the wealthy, especially, consumed many more, richer and finer. Fifteenth-century Italians produced astonishing art in many media, some of which embellished private palaces as elites increasingly invested in handsome surroundings as markers of rank. North Italian taste set the style for all of Europe. By the sixteenth century, appetites for domestic elegance supported energetic and artful production of wall painting, ceramics, metalwork, and ornamented furniture. Where beauty had its day, Renaissance domestic furnishings easily rivaled or trounced their modern equivalents. At the same time, even Italians of high status lacked basic physical comforts that most of us now take for granted.

## DOMESTIC SETTINGS

**Walls, Ceilings, and Floors**

As we saw in Chapter 9, domestic spaces could be large or small. Most people lived in only one or a few rooms, but the rich occupied long chains of chambers, built tall and broad. Walls, especially in cities, were made of brick or stone, often faced with plaster. Such construction discouraged fire, even in densely settled neighborhoods. Maintenance was haphazard; the wear and tear of weather, coupled with man-made damage, left a raddled surface, punctuated with chinks. Tales of daily life might well turn on information overheard at a literal hole in the wall or on a letter passed surreptitiously through one. Walls, sometimes as much as several feet thick, could be cut for window seats and for niches and shelves. The affluent embellished their internal walls in many colorful ways. On plaster as fresco, on canvas, or on leather, Italians painted. More routine treatments featured geometric designs or shaded stripes to resemble folds of cloth; the grandest choices were mythological story paintings or images that evoked the family—its achievements, myths, and heraldry. Walls could also be hung with tapestries or gold-framed mirrors or tiered pictures up to the ceiling. Sculptured moldings or stucco work sometimes divided and accented rooms. Fancy ceilings often showed their beams, arrayed with colored designs and carving. Rich Italians beautified their homes for their pleasure and to awe their guests. Ironic proof of this taste comes from a *novella* by Bandello, in which a visitor to a courtesan's lavishly appointed home spits in his servant's face, explaining that, when forced to spit, he has chosen the only ugly thing in sight.[4] In many houses, however, rafters were rough-hewn, and only a cheap religious print might relieve the bareness of walls. Humble packed dirt or wide boards made more floors than the herringbone brick, ceramic tiles, or marble of the rich.[5]

**Openings, Light, and Heat**

The openings in the walls of Italian homes—doors and windows—demanded deft management by the occupants. These were places through which the social and physical environment penetrated. Goods, people, sounds, air, heat, and light came and went. Some of these arrivals were welcome, others not. Both security of honor and property, and comfort, urged control of human and environmental traffic. Warmth was to treasure in some seasons and shun in others. Light was often scarce, but sometimes too bright and hot. The design and use of doors and windows thus had to balance several sometimes contradictory claims.

Doors came large and small. Portals ten and twelve feet high admitted light as well as goods and persons, even some on horseback or in coaches, to the premises of the great. Inside palaces, people moved between grand public rooms through big doors elegantly framed with classical moldings. Doors into more private or modest quarters could be small and narrow—sometimes little more than five feet high and two feet wide. These let scant light in, and then only if left open. Italians, living close together and worried about their property and reputations, preferred to keep street doors closed and, at night, latched and locked. By modern standards, door keys were often big and cumbersome. As police records show, these precautions discouraged, but did not always bar insistent intruders. And they sometimes inconvenienced both residents and visitors. Romans, who typically dwelled in upper stories above workshops, used a handy device that released the door below by pulling an upstairs string.

While windows in the Middle Ages were often few, small, and haphazardly placed, during the Renaissance they grew larger and more regular. They faced onto the courtyards at the center of many buildings and also onto the streets. Flower pots sometimes graced their sills. Watching from windows, residents—especially women—kept track of local goings-on. From the fifteenth century, the rich began to install glass in their windows. Cloudy and cluttered with much leading, the small panes were hard to see through. Instead of glass, translucent blinds made of oiled cloth on frames of wood and wire provided some illumination while checking drafts. Many windows remained unfilled. For privacy, comfort, and protection, people also used indoor or outdoor wooden shutters with assorted panels to adjust the flow of light and air. When natural light was not enough, the fireplace, candles, oil lamps, lanterns, and torches made good the lack, though at some cost and risk. Brackets and hooks high on walls supported burning lights, out of harm's way. But only the wealthy could afford the brilliance of chandeliers. Overall, despite more windows and supplemental light from controlled fire, indoor life was often rather dim.

In some seasons, domestic life lacked not only light but heat. Although the Mediterranean climate was temperate, in winter many parts of the country, especially in the North and in the mountains, were cold and damp. The illuminated manuscript calendars classically illustrate January with an image of people huddled inside by a fire. Such comfort was precious, for heating was poor. A simple household had a single fire for warmth and for cooking. In primitive houses, the fire was in the center of the main room, on the floor or set in a mud hearth or a metal brazier. A small hood might speed cooking by catching the heat. Concentrating the warmth, however, deprived other corners of the poorly insulated space. People hung cloth over openings and along walls to cut drafts.

Smoke found its own way out eventually, through a hole in the ceiling, but wandered the room en route. So, besides all-too-common accidental burnings and scaldings, such heating taxed health as bad ventilation irritated eyes, windpipes, and lungs. For people with means, structural improvements in the form of fireplaces, built against the wall and served by a chimney that carried smoke outside, multiplied rapidly in the fifteenth century. But even for the rich many rooms remained unheated. In chill sections of the house, metal pans filled with heated stones or coals and ceramic containers of hot water to warm beds and hands gave slight comfort.

**Water and the Lack of Plumbing**
Another challenge for Renaissance housekeeping was water. It was sometimes neither clean nor safe to drink, and often was not conveniently located. Some houses had private wells, and by the late fifteenth century a very few well-appointed, innovative palaces, as at Urbino, enjoyed a system of pipes and drains that brought more and less clean water for different uses to several parts of the building. But most people relied on the river or on public wells and fountains. From the late Middle Ages, many Italian cities invested in civic works to bring water to as many neighborhoods as possible. Women fetched water at the public source, stopping a few moments to chat, negotiate, and argue, before carrying it home on their heads in jugs. Because it was heavy, it was easier for some tasks to bring material to the water rather than vice versa. Thus, washing—clothes, but also dishes—often took place in public rather than at home. Laundry was spread out to dry on grassy banks or, in cities, hung on lines strung in loggias or between houses. Tempers sometimes flared around the stresses of doing laundry and getting it home clean. Women squabbled over good hanging space and "accidentally" splattered dirt on the clean linens of neighbors against whom they bore a grudge. For Renaissance housekeepers, water problems made washing a major headache. They spoke also of making beds and sweeping; the always-handy broomstick was a common weapon in women's street fights. Yet these latter jobs inspired neither the effort nor the anxiety that laundry did.

People also used water to wash themselves.[6] How and how often is hard to say. There were commercial bathhouses in towns, spots where men and women—preferably at separate times or locations—went not only to get clean but also probably to socialize, as in *hammams* of the Islamic world. By the sixteenth century, many of these premises had closed, condemned for presumed links with prostitution and venereal disease. We have a few references to bathing in tubs at home and more to washing hair. Scholars have suggested that by 1600 the same motives that shut down the bathhouses were discouraging people from bathing altogether. Washing face and hands remained routine, but a full-body cleansing with water became an uncommon rite, often practiced to mark a major life passage. Personal hygiene for the elite ever more involved applying powders and perfumes to the body rather than washing off sweat and dirt. Smell became increasingly a marker of social status. Without deodorants, however, Giovanni Della Casa's injunction that a gentleman should smell neither foul like a beggar nor sweet like a harlot was difficult to achieve. Nor did teeth cleaning rely on water. Della Casa implies that people customarily did this at meals, rinsing their mouths with wine and then using napkins, fingers, or toothpicks kept on strings around their necks to dislodge anything left behind.[7]

The other modern use of water, for flushing toilets, Renaissance people also did without. The management of excretions posed an eternal problem to architects and housekeepers. The better-off used individual close-stools—chairs with chamber pots inside—while servants and lower-status folk sometimes endured less privacy at many-holed banks of seats suspended over a pit or void, a convivial arrangement with antecedents in the ancient world. Nevertheless, there was a sense of propriety about place, and a sixteenth-century man caught urinating in the street might invite sharp rebukes from nearby residents. In dense communities, latrines were hard to place, for heaped excrement bred stink and illness. Where possible, they could jut out from the backs of buildings, venting directly onto unused terrain. Or they could occupy a courtyard nook as far as possible from public activities. Elites, however, wished not to trudge to inconvenient, smelly corners to relieve themselves. Their close-stools thus typically lodged in bedrooms, from which, in a well-run house, the servants would carry away the refuse whenever necessary. Even better were tiny, separate rooms, close at hand, sometimes excavated in the outer walls and just large enough for a one-seat privy.

To a modern eye, the furniture in even a wealthy Renaissance house would have looked sparse, bulky, and unvaried. Carpenters built solidly and simply in wood. During the fifteenth and especially the sixteenth centuries, the rich more and more purchased fancy, decorated pieces—embellished with carving and inlay and upholstered with tassels, scallops, and fringes. Yet basic types and designs of furniture remained few: beds, tables, seats, and chests. A mix of these, often only a few per chamber, lined walls throughout the house. These pieces were heavy, but one moved them as occasion required.

**Furniture and Household Goods**

The bed was, both symbolically and functionally, at the center of the house. When a newly married couple set up their home, the bed was their principal acquisition. Lucky ones might get an heirloom. Its bedding and sometimes its frame were usual parts of the trousseau. In this bed the next generation would be conceived; there women would later gather to congratulate the new mother and her child. Suitably, the bedroom was often better furnished, decorated, and warmed than other parts of the dwelling. Located as far as possible from the outside world, it was also the strong room; Italian men and women hid not only jewelry, papers, and money in, under, or near the bed, but also their grain, arms, and armor. Paradoxically, beds and bedrooms were also important sites for sociability. Not only women after childbirth, but also men, even officials, sometimes entertained guests and petitioners from their beds. Beds were also shared for sleeping. Assorted family members commonly slept in the same bed, as, sometimes, did mistresses and their servants, or friends, or even strangers thrown together in an inn. Though sex might happen, no one equated shared beds with sex.

Beds varied greatly in size and comfort. Those of sixteenth-century saints Filippo Neri and Giuseppe Calansanzio, preserved at Roman shrines, are fittingly narrow and, in Neri's case, very short. Religious activists, these men put comfort last. Many other beds were wide indeed, ample for several sleepers. The simplest bed frames consisted of planks or rough boxes set on low trestles. At the high end of the spectrum were substantial wooden structures built tall and flanked by low, flat-topped chests, on which guests might sit or servants sleep. In fifteenth-century Florence, where luxury furniture-making flourished, a wealthy consumer might pay a skilled worker's annual wage for a highly decorated bed or chest. From the 1490s, good beds boasted columns at the corners to support hangings. Even before four-poster beds came in, curtains suspended variously from walls and ceilings were an important aid to sleep. Draperies in winter held warmth in and in summer kept bugs out. Also, as elsewhere, rich fabrics were a badge of affluence and glamour. Courtesans liked to sport a "pavilion"—a circular arrangement of hanging drapery spread to the sides of the bed. In daytime, bed curtains were looped into knots to keep them out of the way.

Bedding, along with other linens such as tablecloths, napkins, and towels, made up much of the value of many people's household goods. Mattresses, pillows, and sheets made beds comfortable—the more the better for those who could afford them. In cities poor or transient people could rent mattresses and sheets separately from a space to sleep. Bedding was sometimes even the currency of survival, all the poor could pawn.

Though less central than beds, tables and places to sit counted among the most common kinds of furniture. Like beds, tables ran a gamut from simple, easily dismantled rigs of boards and trestles to broad, heavy edifices of carpentry, of the sort now seen in museums and historic castles. An ordinary household might well have only one table used for meals, but also for work, recreation, and sleep, as needs arose. When people sat—at the table, near the fire, or elsewhere—what few seats there were may have been uncomfortable. Sometimes they sat directly on the ground or floor or cross-legged on flat platforms, as tailors did for work; even patrician women might be painted sitting with only a cushion for support. But there was also furniture. Pictures of peasant houses feature wooden stools and benches. These are depicted in urban and wealthier settings too, but chairs of several sorts also appear. Some were little more than stools with narrow backs; some had seats of woven fiber; others folded for easy portability. For the grand, who bought more ease and prestige, there were armchairs, sometimes upholstered in leather or gold-embroidered velvet.

Chests of various kinds made up the last great sort of furniture for the home. Storage—of food, dishes, clothing, linens, tools, work supplies, weapons, money, books, papers, playthings, and so on—was an essential house function. Accessibility and security were both great concerns. For clothes in frequent use, pegs attached to the wall were handy. Foodstuffs could be kept away from vermin by suspension from ceiling hooks. Barrels gave compact storage to bulky goods. Much of a household's worth, however, lay stowed in chests of many sizes. Some small ones enclosed valuables, while others, for clothing, were large enough to hide a person, as happened, at least in fiction, in several of Boccaccio's salty stories. To secure them, chests were frequently fitted with locks and sometimes strapped with stout metal bands. Into the sixteenth century, most chests stuck to a basic rectangular shape. Elegant inlay decoration or narrative painting from a premier workshop could turn even a wooden box into a luxury item. Fancy chests bore high honor; they served as potent markers of status when transporting the trousseau at a patrician wedding or when given as a gift to a foreign potentate. In the later Renaissance, the forms of the chest elaborated; some, acquiring legs, doors, and drawers, became more like cupboards and wardrobes. The credenza, a sideboard-chest supporting shelves for showing off dishes and silverware, was one popular variant. Even desks, which multiplied in the Renaissance, evolved into storage chests for small books and papers. Beautiful examples of artful Italian chests grace museum collections, but we should remember that most people stored their belongings in rather plain and functional pieces.

Besides these larger pieces of furniture, a Renaissance home also contained a motley of other equipment and goods that served the needs of the occupants. We can track the possessions of different sorts of people in the postmortem inventories recorded by notaries. In addition to serviceable belongings worth passing on to heirs, these catalogs list quantities of worn or broken items that were kept perhaps with an eye to future repair or recycling. People frequently stored tools and materials in their houses, including horse gear and weapons. Women had spindles, embroidery frames, and sewing supplies. For recreation there might be musical instruments and games; some householders kept birds in cages. The literate acquired books, and rich connoisseurs bought art and antiquities. Many homes had religious icons, plain or splendid, most often an image of the Madonna.[8]

## FOOD

**Cooking and Serving**

Among the household goods not yet enumerated were the equipment and dishes for preparing and consuming food. For everyday fare, Renaissance Italians used plates, bowls, trays, and pitchers made of dull metal or simple terracotta. For banquets and for display, the rich liked silver or fancy majolica, a new Italian specialty, admired across Europe. These tin-glazed ceramics featured colorful pictures, often outlined in blue against a light background. Although only the wealthy could afford large pieces, smaller, less elaborate ones bearing, for instance, a person's name were within the means of artisans or monks and nuns.[9] Tableware consisted of usually rather large spoons and knives; forks for individual use were a novelty that spread during the Renaissance from Italy to other parts of Europe, usually moving from the top of society downward.

Eating was commonly a domestic activity, although one often shared with friends as well as family. While eating together was enjoyed, there is little sign of protocol around ordinary mealtimes; those on hand when food was ready ate, and those missing ate when they could. In large palaces, servants and other menials dined in a separate place from the lord and his guests. The introduction of courtly manners for eating came to distinguish high table etiquette. Inns, wine shops, and street vendors fed people who were out of reach of home or had no food there. Not everything consumed at home had been cooked there. Many Italians not only purchased the staples of bread and wine ready to eat, but also often bought cooked meat as take-out.

Not all residences had kitchens, but better houses had a dedicated room for cooking, with the necessary andirons, hooks, spits, and cauldrons, and occasionally even running water. Because cooking produced heat, smoke, smells, and noise, the well-to-do preferred to locate the kitchen at some distance from their living spaces, at the back or in a garret. Some apartments had a separate kitchen elsewhere in the building. Simpler dwellings used a fireplace in the main room or had no facilities at all. Especially in modest arrangements but even in well-equipped ones, cooking was physically demanding. It involved much squatting and kneeling on the floor, bending to lift hot and heavy containers, and taking care to avoid burns and fires. Wood and water had to be fetched. In a large household with many mouths, the cook usually had helpers and was often male. In an ordinary family, cooking was only one of many jobs that the housekeeper—be she mother or servant—had to juggle.

Bags to store flour and spices. [Scappi]

## COOKERY

Following are two of many recipes offered by Platina in his late fifteenth-century guide to health and good eating. In the second, verjuice and must refer to forms of unfermented juice from grapes, the first notably sour.

### *Sicilian Macaroni*

Beat well-sifted white flour with egg white and rose water and plain water. When it is mixed, draw out into thin strips of dough in the manner of straw half a foot long. Hollow them out with a very thin iron rod. When you draw out the iron, you will leave them hollow. When it is dried in the sun, the pasta of this sort will last two or three years, especially if it was under the waning moon of August. If it is cooked in rich broth and poured into serving dishes, it should be sprinkled with fresh, new butter and sweet spices. The dish requires two hours' cooking.

### *Stuffed Eggs*

Make fresh eggs hard by cooking them for a long time. Then, when the shells are removed, cut the eggs through the middle so that the white is not damaged. When the yolks are removed, pound part with raisins and good cheese, some fresh and some aged. Reserve part to color the mixture, and also add a little finely cut parsley, marjoram, and mint. Some put in two or more egg whites with spices. When the whites of eggs have been stuffed with this mixture and closed, fry them over a slow fire in oil. When they have been fried, add a sauce made from the rest of the egg yolks pounded with raisins and moistened with verjuice and must. Put in ginger, cloves, and cinnamon and heat them a little while with the eggs themselves. This has more harm than good in it.[10]

The Renaissance diet lacked many foods central to Italian eating today: tomatoes, corn, potatoes, chili pepper, chocolate, and coffee. Gelato had yet to be invented, though, late in the period, bins for storing snow to chill drinks were the experimental plaything of a few rich men.[11] Pizza was a simple, flat bread, not ubiquitous and never red. Pasta was no staple, but an occasional treat. Most of the missing ingredients were products of the New World, whose culinary gifts first infil-

**Diet**

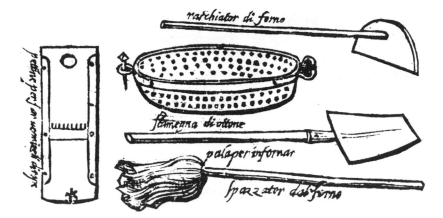

Cooking utensils, including tools for a bread oven. [Scappi]

trated Europe only in the mid-sixteenth century. Then they were only
for occasional or special uses. Tomatoes, for example, served first as medicine and aphrodisiac, then enlivened salads, but routinely sauced spa-
ghetti only in the 1800s. Similarly, maize was cultivated in Veneto from
the 1540s, but corn-based polenta did not feed many North Italian peasants until the eighteenth century. The victory of potatoes came just as
late. The Americas also provided new meats; during the Renaissance, at
aristocratic banquets turkey sometimes stood in for peacock, while cod-
fish caught off Newfoundland, dried and salted as *baccalà*, emerged as a
cheap food for fasts. Some new foods reached Italy from the East rather
than the West. Coffee, for instance, found its way from Arabia via Egypt;
it arrived in Italy, at Venice, only late in the sixteenth century and dif-
fused rapidly from there. Italians probably also owed the Arabs for pasta,
made from particular hard-grained wheat. Pasta was known in the Middle Ages, but during the Renaissance it cost three times more than bread
and usually appeared for special events, not for everyday nutrition. Not
until the seventeenth century, in Naples, and later in other zones, did
pasta become ordinary people's daily fare.[12]

As a rule, Renaissance Italians ate well, in quantity, and in variety and
balance. Famine was a risk, but, between 1400 and 1580, critical shortages
were only occasional and local. In moments of crisis, town governments
stepped in quickly to ensure that food, especially bread, was available
to all at a reasonable price. The waves of epidemic mortality, keeping
demand from pressing hard on land's productive capacity, helped keep
survivors well nourished. Indeed, in this period, Italians were on average
bigger and more robust than they would be during the much more impoverished centuries to follow; even 1900 was less healthy than 1500.
The structure of their diet, however, differed from our twenty-first-

century patterns. Many Renaissance Italians ate, by premodern standards, fair amounts of meat and other animal protein. Still, they depended on carbohydrates, including those in alcohol, for the bulk of calories. Fats, rather than a health hazard, were desirable, for overall intake was low and much of it came from healthful sources like olive oil and fish.

Carbohydrates were central to Renaissance nutrition, growing more so as the population rose. Because land yielded five times as many calories per acre from grain as from meat, it fed more people on bread. And because grain consumed "whole," that is, only partially refined, wasted less nourishment than more polished forms, most bread was brown. Once the grain had been milled into flour, baking bread was heavy work. It took energetic kneading in a wooden trough, often on the ground. In cities and villages, specialized artisans made most bread. Typically it was dense, perhaps lumpy, and wrapped in a thick crust; such loaves kept longer but required serious chewing, even when fresh. Rather than making sandwiches with thick fillings and dressings, ordinary Italians often ate their bread plain, in hunks, perhaps seasoned in peasant fashion with a bit of raw garlic or onion. As a moister alternative, bread might serve as a plate under a helping of meat or cooked vegetable or as a sop dipped in an individual bowl or in a common pot in the middle of the table. For the many people with missing or damaged teeth, such a meal was easier than plain bread. Wheat was the preferred grain for bread, and white bread commanded more prestige and a higher price. In southern Italy and in northern cities, everybody, even the poor, ate wheat bread. Elsewhere, peasants often had to eat loaves made at least partly with lesser grains, cheaper and easier to grow but harder to digest. Depending on the region, these included millet, oats, rye, barley, and spelt. In the high country, another starch that supported some villages for months at a time was flour from chestnuts. In addition to bread, Italians consumed much carbohydrate in the form of boiled grain, as mush (thick), porridge (thinner), or *minestra* (thinnest).

At the high end of the scale, more costly grain foods included rice and pasta. Rice production from the fifteenth century spread rapidly in the Po Valley, but supplied a luxury trade for soups and medicines. Pasta, made from special hard wheat flour, was rolled, cut, and dried on frames. In various parts of Italy, the Renaissance knew it in different shapes and with varying names and preparations: macaroni, ravioli, tortelli, papardelli, lasagne. It was served usually for a special event, or as a Sunday treat in a monastic institution, not with the savory tomato sauces of today, but either plain with meat or fish, or dressed with cheese and "sweet" spices like cinnamon.

In the Renaissance, sugars were a far smaller component of the carbohydrate diet than for many twenty-first-century eaters. Much of the sugar came from wine. Because almost everyone drank wine, straight or watered, as their principal beverage (estimates vary upward from two-thirds of a liter per person per day), it was a big source of calories. Most people drank cheaper local wines, but for the affluent there was also a lively trade in prized vintages such as the sweeter ones from Naples, which traveled well, or whites from Chianti. Besides wine, Italians consumed sugars in sauces for meats, fruit preserves and syrups, and a few pastries such as marzipan and *mostacciolo*, a dense fruit cake. Italians certainly liked sweet tastes, but the ingredients added extra costs to a food budget. Sweet therefore was long associated with the elite palate, while salt—especially because it was used as a preservative—was dominant for ordinary folk. Cane sugar, grown under Venetian monopoly in Cyprus in the fifteenth century and later much more extensively in the New World, replaced honey in most Renaissance recipes. Medical texts recommended sugar as an aid to digestion and sweet alcoholic cordials as promoting health.

While carbohydrates supplied the bulk of Renaissance calories, meat and other animal proteins were reasonably plentiful in the diet. The fifteenth century marked a high point of consumption, after which a rising population needed grain that competed for productive acreage; higher prices reduced meat eating. Around 1600, children in a Roman orphanage were allocated about one-third pound of meat per day, while across town the Jesuits' adolescent male students received twice that amount. The poor who lacked the benefit of charity would likely see meat only rarely. In general, however, more people ate more flesh than in succeeding centuries. Cooks prepared meat for the table by boiling and roasting, sometimes in combination. Long cooking, which helped destroy dangerous microbes, left meat soft, bland, and, if affordable, ready for a sweet or tangy sauce. Nuts, fruits, and "sweet" spices such as cinnamon, cloves, nutmeg, and ginger were welcome components, yielding a flavor akin to our mincemeat for pie, which derives from medieval cookery and originally had meat in it. Saffron, another favorite seasoning, besides adding taste, gave the dish a glamorous golden color that suggested well-being.

The meat consumed varied with the season and the eater's wealth. Except for Lent and fast days, when they ate fish, Italians, especially the well-to-do, ate beef, available all year round. But, for many people, the meat diet depended on cheaper animals, whose availability shifted with the time of year. Pork, killed in early winter and preserved as ham and sausages, was eaten until Lent; lamb, born in spring and symbolically tied to Easter, supplied the months following the holiday. For variety there were chicken and rabbit, as well as game caught by hunters. Aristocratic banquets featured a stunning display of exotic meats, prepared to delight the eye as well as the taste buds: boar, venison, peacock, swan,

Roasting meat on spits in a fireplace.
[Tempesta]

crane, and cormorant. During the Renaissance, the elite increasingly preferred the lighter flesh of fowl and fish to the heavier flavors of big game.
Though linked with fasting, fish was much enjoyed, especially fresh-
water sorts, including eel and lamprey, transported alive in barrels or
baskets. Not only the patricians relished such delicacies. One police chief
in Rome raged jealously at his concubine because of an eel that, he believed, she had received as a gift from a rival lover.[13]

Though seldom abundant in Renaissance life, fats were very important
for a balanced diet and for cooking, as well as for lighting and making
soap. Not only did the cost of fats limit consumption, but so did the
religious calendar of fasts, which restricted meat and lard. "Fat Tuesday," the day before the forty-day Lenten abstinence, reminded celebrants of lean weeks to come. For cooking, much of Italy—the alpine
lake district and the regions south from Tuscany—relied on olive oil.
Good oil was prized; in the fifteenth century, the best was said to come
from Apulia. At that time, Lombardy, in the upper Po Valley, was adopt-
ing the butter that reigned among its transalpine neighbors, while some
of Tuscany used lard and liquefied pork fat. Where olive oil was not
standard, Jews met their dietary rules with goose fat. Eggs and dairy
products, specifically cheese, were another significant source for the Ital-

ian diet. Fresh milk was generally unsafe to drink and did not keep. As cheese, however, it could be processed during the summer, in the mountains, and then, especially in hard and dry forms, saved for eating year long. Cheese was popular; it appeared in many dishes, including pasta. The richer in fat, the pricier the cheese. As today, there were countless kinds; a treatise by a fifteenth-century physician from Turin cataloged a host of varieties.

Europeans from the North regarded Italians' diet as unusual for its copious vegetables and fruits. Renaissance Italians made good use of protein-rich pulses such as beans and chickpeas. They ate cabbage, squashes, artichokes, spinach, and other greens as well as garlic, onions, and leeks. Selection varied with the season. Vegetables were served both stewed and raw; salads—dressed amply with oil, moderately with salt, and lightly with vinegar—were widely popular. Although not costly and eaten by modest folk, such dishes appealed also to the elite. Thus, recipes for condiments redolent of the garlic and onions associated with peasants appeared regularly in cookbooks for the upper-class table. Fruits, including apples, grapes, peaches, pears, and oranges, were more of a treat. Still, custom was sufficient to support, for example, wandering orange vendors in Rome's streets. People gave prized varieties of fruit, like melons or pomegranates, as gifts.

## CLOTHING

Clothing was very important to Renaissance Italians. As in many cultures, clothes not only protected the body from the elements but also marked people's social identities and thus shaped their daily transactions.[14] Frequently issued civic regulations specified what types and styles of apparel should be worn by different social ranks. While these sumptuary laws sought to ensure modesty and social propriety, they were also concerned about costs. Clothes and ornaments for the body were often pricey, and city authorities wanted to discourage wasteful expenditure. Cloth itself, which came in many qualities, weights, fibers, and colors, was often quite valuable. Unworked bolts of fabric appear in wills as significant bequests. Good cloth was substantial and tough, meant to last; like many other material goods, it was used and reused. Nonetheless, aside from shirts and collars, many garments got washed seldom, if ever. Most people owned only a few and wore the same ones all the time. When witnesses in criminal investigations described culprits by their clothing, they could reasonably expect that the identification would hold because most had few other garments. The rich had much larger wardrobes, but even for them, a new cloak or dress was a serious investment. The clothing that a patrician groom bought for his bride might cost a third of the dowry he received from her father.

Because cloth and clothing were so valuable, their manufacture loomed large in the Renaissance economy. Many people made part or all of their living in a large range of crafts that moved material from fiber to yarn to cloth to garments or to draperies, bedding, and table linens. In connection with the trade, various specialized artisans produced the lace, gold thread, embroidery, and buttons sought as ornaments for fancy dress. In the Middle Ages, clothing was made largely of linen and wool; under wool, a linen undergarment was recommended, to prevent chafing. During the Renaissance, for those who could afford it, silk competed with the other fibers. Its lightness and sheen were prized; dyed in brilliant colors—red, purple, saffron, indigo—it could be woven into thick velvets and multicolored damasks. In cities, but also in many country villages, the transformation of cloth into clothing was the business of professionals, generally men, especially for more elaborate garments made of costly fabrics. Women contributed to the production of apparel, combing and spinning, for instance, but their work was typically less structured and worse paid. Many seamstresses took much of their livelihood from mending and alterations, although they may also have fashioned smaller and lighter items. Other women made lace or embroidery for the market.

While most clothing was custom made and intended for a particular wearer, use and reuse meant that fit was often approximate. For something quick and ready-made, people looked for an old-clothes seller, a trade commonly plied by Jews, and made do with what they found. Buyers wanting something new and to a particular design needed more time. They might purchase the fabric and decorations themselves and then seek the services of a tailor to make it up; or they might ask the tailor's advice in choosing and buying the materials. A tailor was, from the origin of the word, a cutter of cloth. He knew the shapes and sizes of pieces for a gown, doublet, or cloak and, if skillful, how to lay them out to maximize comfort and sturdiness with the least waste of fabric. Then he stitched, finished, and fitted the garment in consultation with the customer. A tailor also did good trade in altering existing clothing as it passed from one use or wearer to another. Even so, although some Renaissance styles fitted more closely to the body than their medieval predecessors, the sizes of garments remained irregular. The cut and design of both male and female clothing allowed room for adjustment without resort to the needle. Laces at crucial junctions, instead of seams, made fitting easier.

Among the forms of social place that clothing announced, gender stood out. Regulations forbade each sex to adopt the apparel of the other. Cross-dressing did occur, for both practical and transgressive reasons. While men sometimes donned female garb as a carnival masquerade, it was more often women who got caught in the wrong clothes. Some dressed as males in order to travel more safely and freely, incognito. In popular expectation, however, the most common practitioners were courtesans, who played with the moral ambiguities of their trade to tit-illate their customers. These rare exceptions only stressed the general commitment to difference in male and female appearance. Hair styles, headgear, necklines, and the coverage of the lower body were among the sharpest markers.

Basic male attire was a shirt and tunic with hose. The shirt, a loosely fitted linen garment worn against the skin, was the item of clothing most often changed and washed. Over it, men usually wore some form of tunic or jacket that extended partway down the legs and cinched at the waist or hips. With the belt, length could be adjusted to accommodate the needs of work. Lacking zippers or elastic and using few buttons, Renaissance men kept their close-fitting hose up by tying laces through holes in the upper and lower garments. Early on, these hose consisted of two separate legs not seamed together. This drafty arrangement, while convenient for excretion, depended on the overhanging tunic for mod-esty. As the Renaissance progressed, the two columns of fabric came to be joined at least partway around. Short breeches also filled the gap; in the sixteenth century, for fashion-conscious men, these became quite puffy and might be accessorized with a codpiece at the front. Hose tended to wear through at the knees. So, for warmth and protection, working men sometimes wore extra leggings bound around the lower leg and over the knee. A cloth cape—sometimes trimmed or lined with fur for the wealthy—usually completed the ensemble. Such were the standard components of the male "short" costume. For reasons of age, civic office, or membership in a profession or the clergy, other men wore "long" garb, which replaced or covered the thigh-length tunic with a straight or flowing robe that ended near the ankles. Caps and hats came in a variety of colors and silhouettes: some of cloth fitting snugly to the head or rising to high, even bulbous crowns; others of felt or straw with broad, flat brims. Gracing a prime site of bodily honor (see Chapter 6), headgear served tastes from the soberly functional to the fashionably flamboyant. Footwear ranged from wooden clogs to thin-soled leather shoes.

Although women's clothing distinguished them from men, breeches aside, it had many elements in common with male garb. Under it all went the shirt, for women sometimes cut wider at the neck. Over it went a one-piece dress, with fitted waist, from which fell a long, fairly full skirt. Its folds fell close enough to the body, especially when layered over the tails of a long shirt, to provide warmth and modesty. Italian women wore stockings but only rarely leggings rising to the waist. Nor were they needed before the arrival of the Spanish fashion for bell-shaped hoop skirts that stood out from the body, exposing it to drafts.

For much of the Renaissance, the often square-cut neckline was quite open, allowing the shirt underneath to show. Sleeves often came separately and attached to the armholes of the dress with laces; one relatively cheap way to refresh a wardrobe was to get a new pair. When needing another layer of clothing or for sheer display, women wore a flowing overgown that sometimes trailed on the ground. Urban women shod their feet in slippers sometimes made with colored fabrics; the soles were firm enough, however, that they sometimes served as weapons. To rise above mud and water in the streets, in Venice especially, there were high-heeled shoes or pattens of wood and cork that lifted the wearer even a foot above the ground; these caused women to hobble precariously, and some critics claimed they led to miscarriages. On their heads, atop often elaborate hairstyles, women generally wore veils. Although those in mourning and nuns shrouded the body and sometimes the face with long and somber folds of fabric, Italian ladies are often depicted with light, sheer, backspread veils that more enhanced than hid their looks.

During the Renaissance, fashion came into its own. For the wealthy, clothing became more elaborately shaped and decorated. Courtiers and their rich imitators began to distinguish cuts and ornaments and to define themselves by wearing what was novel and prestigious. Competitors for status sought not only lavishness but style. The cut of sleeves, for example, became a focus. For both men and women, they grew bigger and layered; from some, arms emerged through slits while the rest of the ample sleeve drooped almost to the ground. Others puffed out at the shoulder but fit snugly to the forearm. Eye-catching sleeves, like other items of apparel, might be trimmed in gold thread, embroidered with flowers and leaves, or strewn with pearls. Another decorative fad was slashing: cutting across the fabric to allow the underlayer, in white or a contrasting color, to show through. This fashion much reduced the possibility of reuse and drew criticism as wasteful. Indeed, the pursuit of fashion in general was frequently condemned as expensive, inconvenient, vain, and immoral. Sermons and sumptuary laws, however, never quenched the appetite to spend and flaunt. While many reproaches targeted women, portraits show that men too invested heavily in an impressive, modish look. In these and other fashions, during much of the Renaissance, Italy was Europe's trendsetter. Even the king of France, François I, requested from Isabella d'Este, countess of Mantua, a doll dressed in courtly style as a model to take back for the ladies of Paris. Costume books published from the middle of the sixteenth century show the growing awareness of fashion. With pictures and text, Cesare Vecellio's book, for example, highlighted variations in dress both over time and among regions even within Italy. By then, however, clothing in general was shifting to a more sober tone. With the emerging "Spanish" mode, paralleling Spain's sway in the peninsula, black replaced the old vibrant colors and women's décolletage gave way to high collars and ruffs.

---

## EXAMPLES OF MEN'S AND WOMEN'S DRESS

Cesare Vecellio described the characteristic attire of late-sixteenth-century ladies from Milan.

> Noble Milanese matrons cover their heads with silk in a dark color of their choice, leaving to be seen little except some curls around the forehead and some ruff at the neck. They wear overgowns [*Romane*], in length a quarter-measure above the ground, of figured damask or worked velvet, that are attached with gold buttons down to the belt and from there to the feet they lie open, through which openings are seen a silk soutane extending to the ground, with a band [at the bottom] of figured velvet, or of gold brocade. The overgown [*zimarra*] has open sleeves and the arms are clothed in the sleeves of the soutane.[15]

A Spanish pickpocket, on trial in Rome in 1557, described the dress of a soldier, probably a countryman, he had known in Naples:

> He is a man of some thirty years, tall, a little plump, a round face more brown than not, and rather good looking than not. His beard is brown and long and round, his hair black. He usually wears a red mantle [*tabarro*] in the German fashion, a velvet collar with four long slashes, with five or six gold buttons at the throat and on his chest. And sometimes he wears black hose with cut velvet uppers, and sometimes they are gray, also velvet, and sometimes he wears a red pair, also velvet, and on his head, when he is wearing his red mantle, he wears an embroidered red hat, and when he does not wear his red mantle, he wears a black cape with velvet finishings and a velvet cap.[16]

---

## HAIR AND COSMETICS

A *bella figura* required attention not only to clothing, but to hair and face. Mostly the arts of coiffure and cosmetics belonged to women, but men too took pains with their appearance. Males frequently cut their hair at chin or shoulder length. Many are depicted as clean-shaven, though the fashion for beards came and went during the period. Paintings show both head and facial hair as often curly. For some, curls no doubt came naturally, but Della Casa reproved as effeminate men who crimped their locks with warm irons. Printed recipes for potions "to blacken the hair and beard" suggest men also used dye. Women's hair grew long and was generally worn piled on the head in simple chignons or intricate confections of rolls and braids. At court and for special events, gold chains, gem-studded nets, and other jewelry ornamented

Sun-bleaching hair with a special hat. [Bertelli]

these elaborate coiffures. Women took much trouble to keep their hair fashionably beautiful. They plucked their hairlines well back to achieve the admired smooth, high-domed forehead. Because blond was much prized on women, long hours were devoted to bleaching. According to Coryate, the English visitor, Venetian ladies spent every Saturday afternoon treating their hair with oil and other "drugs." They then spread it over special straw hats with a hole in the center and very broad brims, and sat in the sun to let it dry. Later, they curled the resulting "whitish" locks and wound them into a distinctive two-horned coiffure.[17]

The culture of Italian beauty included cosmetics for the skin. While Della Casa's chastisement implied that some men used makeup, perfecting the appearance of the skin was women's business. The special Venetian hat that used the sun to bleach hair also protected the face from turning brown. During the Renaissance, tanned skin was a sign not of beauty but rather of outdoor toil and low rank. White was the desirable color for a woman's face, hands, and breast. Where nature and precaution did not suffice, women resorted to cosmetics. Preparations drawn from a tradition of herbal wisdom and applied chemistry promised to soften the skin and remove or cover spots and blemishes. Powders or heavy pastes laid a white shell over the face. Other concoctions sought to make the cheeks pink and the eyebrows dark. As with other female vanities, moralists condemned these cosmetics as injurious to soul and body. Associating them with prostitutes, these commentators saw face painting as tempting the flesh and harming the skin. Other men objected because a rigid mask did not in fact entice. Nonetheless, whatever the grounds, the gale of reproach itself suggests that not just prostitutes but also respectable wives used cosmetics. The knowledge of how to make and use them circulated among women, and some made money by making and selling these wares. In 1584 Isabella Cortese (perhaps a pseudonym) marketed a successful book, *Secrets*, in which she offered a host of recipes that people could prepare themselves; mixed among dyestuffs for leather, polishes for metal and semiprecious stones, and cures for impotence and for worms in horses were many varieties of cosmetics, soaps, perfumes, and treatments for the skin and hair.

---

### RECIPES FROM THE *SECRETS* OF ISABELLA CORTESE

#### Face-Water from White Beans

Take peeled white beans and put them in white wine to soften for nine days; then pound them and return them to the wine; and take goat's milk and whole barley and boil it with the milk, until the barley grains are broken; then mix together all those things, and add six fresh egg-whites and mix everything well; and set it to distill. Make the water two weeks before you use it; then it can be used, and washing the face with it, it will do very good job.

#### To Keep Hair Black

Take four or five spoons of quicklime in powder, two pennyworth of lead oxide with gold and two with silver, and put everything in a mortar and grind it with ordinary water; set it to boil as long you would cook a pennyworth of cabbage; remove it from the fire and let it cool until tepid, and then wash your hair with it. After an hour, wash your hair with clean, warm water and no soap, and then wash yourself with ordinary cleaning agent and soap your hair as usual; and do this every week.[18]

---

## CONCLUSION

Renaissance arrangements for homemaking, eating, and clothing met bodily needs and served social and psychological appetites. Both for their own delight and to win the esteem of others, people of high status and wealth invested money and taste in enhancing the elegance of their household, their personal possessions, and themselves. The privileged few, clothed in colorful and ornamented silks, lived in handsome palaces bedecked with beautiful paintings, and banqueted on peacock and eel. But the vast majority of folk, while they might see gorgeous art in churches or ogle nobles as they passed in the street, lived with few and modest belongings. They ate their bread with an onion or a hunk of ham. These goods, however, sustained them, shaped their lives, and commanded close attention. The poor kept a sharp eye to what they and their neighbors owned and used. They struggled to acquire and hang onto what they needed and made patient and inventive use of recycling to provide for themselves. While the rich certainly enjoyed greater physical security and comfort than their less fortunate compatriots, even they faced the inconveniences of domestic life without good heating and ventilation, reliable lighting, or, of course, refrigeration and air-conditioning. The material culture of Renaissance Italy was a dazzling mosaic of contradictions.

## NOTES

1. On attitudes to the body and sexuality, see Sara Matthews Grieco, "The Body, Appearance, and Sexuality" in *A History of Women in the West*, v. 3, *Renaissance and Enlightenment Paradoxes*, ed. N. Z. Davis and A. Farge (Cambridge, MA: Harvard University Press, 1993), 45–84. Useful primary sources include: Giovanni Della Casa, *Galateo*, trans. K. Eisenbichler and K. Bartlett (Toronto: Centre for Reformation and Renaissance Studies, 1986); Agnolo Firenzuola, *On the Beauty of Women*, trans. K. Eisenbichler and J. Murray (Philadelphia: University of Pennsylvania Press, 1992); Jerome Cardan, *The Book of My Life*, trans. J. Stoner (New York: Dover, 1962).

2. Thomas Coryate, *Coryat's Crudities*, v. I (Glasgow: J. MacLehose and Sons, 1905), 280; Fynes Moryson, *Shakespeare's Europe* (New York: Benjamin Blom, 1903), 165, also notes the practice.

3. Della Casa, *Galateo*, 7.

4. Matteo Bandello, *Novelle* (Milan: Armando Curcio Editore, 1978), Day III, story 42.

5. On domestic spaces and furnishings, see Peter Thornton, *The Italian Renaissance Interior* (New York: Abrams, 1991); Charles de La Roncière, "Tuscan Notables on the Eve of the Renaissance," in *A History of Private Life*, v. 2, *Revelations of the Medieval World* (Cambridge, MA: Harvard University Press, 1988), 178–200; Gene Brucker, *Florence: The Golden Age* (Berkeley: University of California Press, 1998), 225–226. Luciano Berti, ed., *Il Museo di Palazzo Davanzati a Firenze* (Electa, [1971]) offers many photographs of furniture and interiors. Renaissance paintings are a major source; calendar images for the winter months and scenes depicting the holy births of Jesus and Mary are especially useful, although none cannot be interpreted literally as photographs of the past.

6. On bathing, see Matthews Grieco, "Body," 47–51.

7. Della Casa, *Galateo*, 54, 57.

8. Domenico Sella, "Peasants as Consumers of Manufactured Goods in Italy around 1600," in *The European Peasant Family and Society*, ed. R. Rudolph (Liverpool: Liverpool University Press, 1995), 154–164.

9. For examples, see Wendy Watson, *Italian Renaissance Maiolica from the William A. Clark Collection* (London: Scala Books, 1986).

10. Platina, *On Right Pleasure and Good Health*, trans. M. Milham (Tempe: Medieval and Renaissance Texts and Studies, 1998), 333, 405.

11. On ice and ices, see Elizabeth David, *Harvest of the Cold Months: The Social History of Ice and Ices* (Harmondsworth: Penguin Books, 1994), 1–17.

12. On diet and food preparation, see Jean-Louis Flandrin and Massimo Montanari, eds., *Food: A Culinary History from Antiquity to the Present* (New York: Columbia University Press, 1999), and Massimo Montanari, *The Culture of Food* (Oxford: Blackwell, 1994). A Renaissance treatise on food and the good life is Platina, *On Right Pleasure and Good Health.*

13. Archivio di Stato di Roma (ASR), Governatore, Tribunale Criminale, Processi 1600–1619, b. 23, 110 (1602).

14. On clothing, for general discussions with some attention to Italy, see Joan Nunn, *Fashion in Costume, 1200–1980* (New York: New Amsterdam Books, 1984), 29–51, and Diane Owen Hughes, "Regulating Women's Fashion," in *A History of Women*, v. 2, *Silences of the Middle Ages*, ed. C. Klapisch-Zuber (Cambridge, MA: Harvard University Press, 1992), 136–158. On Italy, see Cesare Vecellio, *Vecellio's Renaissance Costume Book* (New York: Dover, 1977), 1–66; Stella Mary Newton, *The Dress of the Venetians, 1495–1525* (Aldershot: Scolar Press, 1988); Brucker, *Florence*, 164–165, and throughout the book for illustrations of Florentine dress.

15. Cesare Vecellio, *Habiti antichi e moderni di Diversi parti del Mondo*, quoted in Paola Venturelli, *Vestire et apparire* (Rome: Bulzoni, 1999) 39–40; for an image, see *Vecellio's Renaissance Costume Book*, 50.

16. ASR, Governatore, Tribunale Criminale, Processi sixteenth century, b. 31, case 7, 417v (1557).

17. Coryate, *Crudities*, v. 1, 401.

18. Isabella Cortese, *I Secreti della Signora Isabella Cortese* (Venice: Iacomo Cornetti, 1584; reprint Milan: La Vita Felice, 1995), 80, 140 (our translation).

# 14

# Disease and Healing

Disease was a facet of the natural world that we still face and fight, but it threatened the people of the Renaissance infinitely more than us. The difference between then and now was stark. In the eyes of modern epidemiology, disease is a curious part of nature, for most disease organisms live, as parasites, in intimate contact with their human hosts. They are therefore a part of nature that is more inside us than out in the wild. We are our microbes' ecological niche, to which they have adapted by sly Darwinian tricks. Our modern picture of disease has several elements: contagion, personal and social susceptibility, and efficient medicine.

The Renaissance perception of disease had some elements in common with ours and some that were radically diverse. It is worth pausing to reflect on the raw experience of disease. Although our medicine is far from omnipotent, we trust its powers to shield us from many dangers and, above all, to dull or even banish pain. A fundamental fact: the Renaissance had no aspirin, or other pills, for pain. Headaches and toothaches—and they were common—simply had to be borne. Those with fever burned or shivered, and sweated, and waited for relief. And childbirth hurt a great deal more than it does today. Furthermore, without reliable antiseptic or anesthesia, internal surgery was extremely perilous. A condition like hernia, now cured by a simple operation, had no safe fix; its victims might go years or decades with their intestines, painfully bloated, sheathed in trusses outside their bellies.[1] Italians, like other Europeans, learned to live with pain. They also lacked cures for infection.

Thus, they went in fear of untimely death. They had their remedies, and their hopes in them, but they lacked our luxury of trusting one antibiotic or another to do its job and save us. Hope therefore was shot through with an anxiety we can hardly comprehend.

## MEDICAL THEORIES

The Renaissance conception of patterns of infection was unlike ours. Like us, Italians were aware of isolated illnesses and of epidemics, waves of sickness that swept through houses, towns, and districts. To them, as to us, these were manifestations of the natural world. However, for Christian reasons, they were also part of a larger divine plan—God's providence. Thus, one response to infection was prayer and ceremonies. There were other differences in response as well. Only late in the nineteenth century did medicine discover germs and work out a clear theory of contagion. Renaissance learned medicine, though aware of transmission, still hewed to ancient Greek theories that held that sickness commonly came from imbalances in the body. The four humors (body fluids: blood, phlegm, black and yellow bile) were out of healthy equilibrium. Each humor combined two factors: hot or cold, wet or dry. Thus, if sickness struck, the goal was to restore deficiencies and to remove excess: to warm the cold-wet sufferer and bleed the hot-wet one and so on. To sustain health, one should aim, physicians said, for a temperate life, regulating diet and exercise, cultivating peace of mind, and calibrating the soul. Diseases, then, came from God, from the natural world, from the disorder of human souls and bodies. But they also proceeded by infection, and the vectors were not organisms but miasmas. Vapors. Smells. Malaria, for instance, means just "bad air."

The bad air theory galvanized authorities. Ignorant of germs, they went after smells, and in doing so probably improved the general health. In the sixteenth century, the Grand Duchy of Tuscany had a vigorous body of health inspectors, who collected reports on the air of towns and villages. Their reports of manure piles, garbage-strewn streets, open sewers, and casual latrines remind us that the Renaissance had its smells, as well as colors, sounds, and textures. Where successful, the officials' efforts at hygiene probably curtailed water-borne diseases. They were, however, irrelevant to respiratory ailments and to the deadly sicknesses borne, as we now know, by insects: malaria, typhus, and bubonic plague.[2]

The whole complex of Renaissance theories of infection thus called forth an elaborate program to defend public health. Authorities, with an eye to general welfare, developed a series of measures—some in fact appropriate, and others either irrelevant or even harmful—to hedge the spread of epidemics. Infected travelers could carry serious illnesses from one city to another. Thus, early on, cities learned that they could sometimes prevent an epidemic by excluding suspect travelers. The English word *quarantine* is of Italian origin, tracing back to the common practice of making incoming ships from plague-ridden ports anchor in isolation for forty (*quaranta*) days. The practice was often effective; the wait in fact was long enough to kill off the crew or prove a vessel clean. It was much harder to prevent contagion's spread overland; terrestrial human traffic was both heavier and more diffuse. Nevertheless, since cities were walled, they could close their gates to travelers from infected zones. During epidemics, travelers had to show a certificate to prove they came from uninfested places. Although open to corruption and cheating, these measures did afford some protection.

By the same logic, when highly infectious diseases did strike, one response of the authorities was to isolate the victims. They often sequestered the poorer patients in a hospital. This measure, though it might help the populace as a whole, was often deadly to the sick. Renaissance hospitals, for all their good intentions, lacked efficacious medicines. Crowding and a plethora of diseases in cramped spaces made them fairly deadly. A second recourse, often tried against bubonic plague, was to seal up a house if one resident fell sick, and not unseal it until the dying stopped. Due to the complex epidemiology of plague, this measure did little good and much harm, for houses were actually more contagious than their denizens. Unable to flee, imprisoned family members were thus at much greater risk. The experience of plague had taught Italians that flight was the most prudent remedy. For example, in 1462, Pope Pius II and his court were in Viterbo, celebrating the feast of Corpus Christi with sumptuous processions. Pestilence cut short the festivities. He records in his autobiography:

But what joys of mortals are lasting? All that pleases is too brief. Grief succeeds happiness. Lamentation follows hard on laughter. While the Curia was exulting over such a state of affairs [a festival] and the city was elated with excessive joy, they were stricken with a sudden plague. A wasting poison and fatal pestilence carried off many, both citizens and curials [members of the papal court], so that the terrified cardinals asked that the Curia be moved. The Pope kept a few with him and allowed the rest to go where they pleased to escape the fatal sickness.[3]

The behavior of the papal court here was normal. The rich, with their villas, were better placed to flee the city; though they too succumbed, plague increasingly smote the lower classes.

## INFECTIOUS DISEASES

**Patterns of Morbidity**    Among infections, plague, a spectacular killer, was not alone. Historians find it hard to lay out a statistical balance of its morbid rivals. For one thing, medical terminology was vague; for another, the actual symptoms of some diseases have changed as the microorganisms, and their victims' responses, have evolved. Medical historians thus have a lot of detective work to do. Nevertheless, they can point to some general patterns. As with us, but worse, the winters, when families huddled in damp, close quarters, were the season for respiratory infections, including bronchitis and influenza, at times deadly, and pneumonia, yet more perilous.[4] These diseases especially afflicted the very young and the old. Unlike us, except in poorer countries that today still lack refrigeration and clean water, Italy had sickly summers. Minor stomachaches and serious dysentery were rampant. In infants, easily dehydrated, severe diarrhea could kill swiftly. The hot season therefore took a heavy toll of babies once they consumed foods other than breast milk. Poor, malnourished infants were particularly susceptible.[5] As we shall see shortly, some other diseases also had their seasonal patterns.

Of all other causes of death, bubonic plague far outweighed the others. Fifteenth-century Florentine records dating from six years bracketed by plague blamed perhaps two-thirds of all the city's mortality on the disease.[6] Plague fell most heavily on children and adolescents. Older Florentines, who had survived earlier epidemics, less often succumbed. These statistics are imperfect, given the imprecision of the records. Nevertheless, they give some sense of the extraordinary power of that pestilence and its grip on the collective imagination.

**Three Insect-Borne Infections: Malaria, Typhus, and Plague**    Some of the gravest illnesses had insect vectors. These diseases had geographic and seasonal patterns linked to the life cycle of their carriers. Malaria, for one, was very common. Sufferers could carry the microbe for years and unexpectedly relapse at any season. But since mosquitoes were the hosts, summer was the season for infection. Although they had no notion of the insects' role in the disease's propagation, Italians knew well that in some way it came from swamps—whence their notion of *mal aria*, dank air that spread fever. The great campaigns to drain the swamps had the express goal not only to reclaim land for the plow but also to drive off fever. Commonly, malarial fevers are cyclical, in synchrony with the life cycle of the parasite that infests the blood. In the Renaissance, therefore, countless Italians complained of falling sick with *febbre terziana* or *quartana*, an acute fever that hits every three or every four days. Despite the vagueness of these

Beggar showing off his sores. [Bertarelli: Forfanti]

common terms, most often, malaria must have been the cause. Sometimes fatal, malaria was and is debilitating.

A second insect-borne infestation was typhus. Transmitted by lice, it came in epidemics. Although almost everyone had body lice, the poor were more often stricken, for they had fewer changes of clothing, less money to spend in bathhouses or to pay washerwomen, more reasons for sharing beds and for living at close quarters. Winter weather, when one huddled under infested wraps, fostered epidemics.

The third and by far the deadliest insect-borne pestilence was the bubonic plague. This utterly terrifying disease first returned to Europe in 1347 after eight centuries of reprieve; it afflicted Italy and the rest of Western Europe for more than three hundred years and then, for reasons still hotly debated by historians of medicine, retreated eastward. Plague spread appalling devastation wherever it went. Generally it was an urban disease, sometimes endemic, but more often appearing in massive epidemics. Through much of the Renaissance and down to the 1650s, these would hit a city perhaps once a generation. The epidemiology of bubonic plague is fascinatingly complex, for it involves four organisms: bacilli, fleas, rats, and humans. The course and rhythms of the disease, and the efficacy of remedies, depended on the biology of all four organisms and the material culture of the human hosts. Occasionally plague took a pneumonic form, spreading from human to human. Generally, however, humans caught it from the bite of a rat flea. Although plague bacilli do not make fleas ill, they clog their digestive tracks. Unfortunately for humans, when fleas bite, they also regurgitate, spitting up bacteria. What complicates the picture is that, for a rat flea, a human, as a meal, is no treat. So it was only when there was an epizootic—a great dying off of infected rats—that their hungry fleas would leap, reluctantly, onto unpalatable human prey. Meanwhile, humans had their own fleas in itchy plenty, but our insect species—because they do not regurgitate—are inefficient carriers of plague.

The lessons of all these facts are several. For one, humans were not themselves a major source of contagion. Rather, it was usually sick rats on the move that brought the disease to an uninfected, vulnerable rat population, from which it spread to humans only when most of the local rats took sick and died. That is why ships, often rat infested, were so dangerous and quarantine so useful. This pattern also shows why locking stricken families in houses was a mistake, for it was the house, with its dying rats and ravenous rat fleas, that was dangerous, not the inhabitants, even if already infected. Those who fled town, like Pope Pius and his court, thus took the prudent course. At the same time, some of the other plague remedies, such as burning the clothing of the dead or sitting near hot fires, drove off fleas and probably did some good.

The medical effects of the plague were dramatic. The characteristic mark of the disease were the buboes, great swellings of the lymph nodes of the armpits and groin. Mortality was usually well in excess of 60 percent and death came within a few days. The social effects of a serious epidemic were almost as dramatic. Boccaccio's famous description in his *Decameron* of the 1347 plague depicts the dissolution of human ties. When the disease appeared, he writes, as people fled in terror, many of the bonds that held society together collapsed. Even family, the primary social institution, dissolved, leaving the sick in the hands of mercenary caretakers, men and women of low station who for pay would risk all. The obsequies for the dead suffered the same fate. In normal times, a proper funeral and a requiem were moments of solidarity that served both the grieving survivors and the soul of the deceased. In a raging epidemic, there were corpses everywhere and almost no one left to bury them. Carts, driven by brave, desperate men, might gather up the dead from streets and houses and haul them unceremoniously to a mass grave. In a world where the solidarity of the living and the dead was of the first importance, this disruption of good funerary order appalled everyone.

**Syphilis: A New Disease**  Another disease that especially frightened Renaissance Italians was syphilis. The novelty of the ailment baffled physicians; there was nothing like it in the ancient Greek and Roman doctrines of their textbooks. Some medical commentators looked to the stars; baleful Saturn had been in the house of genital Scorpio. Most, however, soon agreed that sexual contact was a likely cause. Its particularly disgusting symptoms struck terror. The great Veronese physician Fracastoro, whose long poem on the subject gave this ailment its modern name, described it as follows:

In the majority of cases, small ulcers began to appear on the sexual organs [and they were] intractable and did not depart. . . . Next the skin broke out with encrusted pustules . . . and they soon grew little by little till they were the size of

Sick man riding in a wheelbarrow.
[Bertarelli: Forfanti]

the cup of an acorn, which they in fact resembled. . . . Next these ulcerated pustules ate away the skin . . . and they sometimes infected not only the fleshy parts but even the very bones as well. In cases where the malady was firmly established in the upper parts of the body, the patients suffered from pernicious catarrh [respiratory infection] which eroded the palate or the uvula or the pharynx or tonsils. In some cases the lips or eyes were eaten away, or in others the whole of the sexual organs. Moreover, many patients suffered from the great deformity of *gummata* [rubbery lumps] which developed on the members; these were often as large as an egg or a roll of bread. . . . Besides all the above symptoms, as if they were not bad enough, violent pains attacked the muscles. . . . [T]hese pains were persistent, tormented the sufferer chiefly at night, and were the most cruel of all the symptoms.[7]

In Fracastoro's day, almost no one in Italy called this shameful ailment "syphilis." Rather, they called it "the French disease." Much of Europe followed suit; Shakespeare's England called it "the French pox." The French, who abhorred this credit, rather called it "the Neapolitan disease." Both appellations made good sense, for the malady seems first to have appeared, dramatically, as if from nowhere, when a French army in 1495 laid siege to Naples. The French in 1496 retreated up the peninsula, frequenting prostitutes in the usual military way and leaving behind them a trail of pustules, racking pains, and slow death. One proposed remedy was to test the prostitutes and lock the sick ones up. But, since a lively sexual commerce was tolerated and legal, no such thing happened, and with astonishing speed the illness spread through all social classes, infecting commoners, princes, and cardinals. As with many new diseases, syphilis was very contagious and virulent. With time, microbes evolved into milder forms.

Although Renaissance medicine could not overcome the scourge, it proposed some treatments. One was to roast the disease out; poor sufferers would be shut in barrels for several hours, with hot stones piled around them to make them sweat. A common remedy was the application of mercury to the sores, a risky measure giving some relief. Physicians already knew that mercury was severely poisonous, and many urged a light dose. This therapy continued into the twentieth century, when effective antibiotics at last appeared. Another cure was "holy wood" (*lignum vitae*), a resin derived from the guaiacum tree, native to the Caribbean. This gum did in fact ease the pain of the awful pustules; a great transatlantic trade grew up to feed the appetite for relief. The big Roman hospital of San Giacomo of the Incurables in a year could consume almost four tons to treat some 2,000 patients. San Giacomo, still a hospital today, was refounded in 1515, with ample papal blessings, for the poor sufferers of "incurable diseases," mainly cancer and syphilis. One goal was the relief of suffering, another the clearing of the city streets of putrid, pustular beggars. Similar foundations sprang up in many Italian cities. Administered by energetic religious orders, they served at once two urges of the elite: compassion and social discipline.

## TREATING THE POX

Here are the recommendations of the papal physician Gaspar Torella for a psychological and physical regime to ward off or cure the French disease:

As for prevention, the person should avoid anger or melancholy. Who was likely to contract the pox? Those who "make use of salt or sharp or bitter foods or drink . . . who do not take baths as they used to do, who do not change their clothes; who do not take any exercise or massage; who take meals or medicine that brings matter to the skin; who drink sharp and old wines or those sweet and heated too long."

As for treatment, optimistic confidence on the patient's part would help a cure. To remove the "morbific" matter or "peccant" humors (bad fluids), according to standard medical doctrines, he recommended evacuation (bleeding), resolution and dessication (the sweat box, to drive the humors to the surface), and consumption (removing the lesions where the humors had gathered from the skin).

For this last step, to remove the lesions, Torella recommended ointments, liniments, and lotions. From the surgeons, he took recipes for corrosive and abrasive mineral substances designed to clear the skin: mercury, yellow litharge (lead monoxide), sulfur, ceruse (white lead), watered and live calx (residue of various burned minerals), ammonia and verdigris (copper acetate), alum (potassium aluminum sulfate), rock salt, tartar emetic (a poisonous salt of potassium), ink, vitriol (metallic sulfate or sulfuric acid), and aqua fortis (nitric acid). To these minerals and acids, he recommended adding substances of vegetable origin: turpentine, incense, and three gums—mastic (aromatic, from a Mediterranean shrub), myrrh (sweet-smelling, from East Africa and Arabia), and galbanum (stinking, from West Asia).

These recipes, typical of early modern medicine, show several things. For one, such treatments were only for the rich, for the many ingredients were exotic and expensive. For another, the minerals, especially the mercury, but the copper and lead as well, were toxic and the acids painful. As with many other diseases, with syphilis, professional physicians probably did more harm than good.[8]

## DIABOLICAL POSSESSION: A NONINFECTIOUS DISEASE

Lacking a theory of microbial infection, Renaissance Italians were usually less likely to see sickness as an invasion of the body from without than as a disorder of its internal components. There was one great exception to this diagnostic habit, over on the boundaries of what we today would call mental health. Like other early modern Europeans, Italians took demonic possession very seriously. In their eyes, real demons—sometimes one, sometimes a whole rowdy pack—could enter a victim, commandeering thought, speech, and actions. *Spiritati* (spirit possessed) and *indiavolati* (devil possessed) were not rare. Some of these were persons we might diagnose as suffering a serious disorder of the brain. Others almost surely were sane but believed themselves haunted. In either case, the possessed often followed a traditional and recognized routine. They gnashed their teeth, rolled and thrashed, spoke in altered voices, and almost always lashed out at bystanders and at things held sacred. Sometimes the possessed blamed others for their condition; an ill-wisher, using magic powders or other diabolical devices, had infected them. This grave accusation could instigate prosecution for witchcraft. Thus, the possessed sometimes had agency; even unwittingly, a sufferer might fall into an altered state to take revenge. In other cases, experts could inject the notion of diabolical possession into a patient, when an intractable physical illness baffled diagnosis and cure.

To cure possession often required the aid of a professional exorcist, whose job it was, with the aid of prayers and holy water and astute or stubborn arguments, to refute, vanquish, and banish the devils, thereby restoring health. Exorcism, a venerable practice dating from the first years of the Christian faith, was still a lively activity of the Renaissance church. There were other remedies as well; friends and family could take the patient to a miracle-working image, usually a Madonna, to pray for succor. On the flanks of orthodoxy were lay exorcists and sorcerers, willing to try their hands at an unlicensed cure.[9]

---

### A YOUNG BRIDE POSSESSED

Here is a case of bewitchment and exorcism that shows many of the elements of such tangled stories. It takes place in Naples, in 1573–74, and 1580.

The story goes as follows: Laura, the beautiful daughter of a tax collector, lives in a fishermen's quarter. Liso, the captain of a sailing ship, with her father's approval seeks her hand in marriage. But, defying her parents, she instead espouses Giovanni Battista Marsicano. It is a love match. But a few days after the wedding, Laura begins to act possessed, to hate her new husband, calling him a devil, and to yearn instead for Liso. A few days later, her husband also starts to act as though he has the devil in him.

Suspicion falls at once on Dianora, Liso's mother. The district midwife, she is feared as a magic worker and witch; people say she murders newborn babes. The resident devils, speaking through the mouths of the newlyweds, accuse the midwife, her son, Liso, and a third party, a teacher also reputed a sorcerer. The neighbors are persuaded that these things are true. Furthermore, they have heard Liso and his mother say that they want revenge for the failed courtship. One day a stranger, also crazy, comes to Laura, claiming possession by the souls of two murdered men, and blaming Liso's mother.

It is a hard case of multiple possession. A physician gives up the cure. Clerical exorcists fail. A pilgrimage to a famous healing church does no good. The only thing that quiets Laura's soul is hearing that the distant sails she sees from her window belong to the ship of her now beloved Liso.

More possessions follow; Laura's sister falls into possession, as do two cousins, daughters of the groom's brother, and the daughter of a local fisherman. All these, through their devils, accuse Liso, his mother, and the teacher. At this point, the archbishop's court is called in to take depositions.

The bishop hears testimony about Dianora's past career of magic, her using powders, nail parings, hair, and blood to patch up a marriage. Laura's doctor reports she has wanted to jump out the window and asked the devil to take her soul. When the exorcist came in, says the doctor, Laura swore and writhed and asked to be taken to Dianora's house, saying that the tools of magic would be there. The court, skeptical, asks the doctor if Laura might not instead have melancholy, but the physician is sure that this is different. Still, the court does not yet press the case.

Note several lessons. First, the first two victims of possession, the young married couple, could be using their affliction as a weapon against their supposed bewitcher. Second, the accused is often very vulnerable, especially if, like Dianora, she is in fact a practitioner of magical remedies. Strangers flock to give evidence of her guilt. Third, possession itself is contagious, by suggestion, within a family and among neighbors. So, clearly, it is not always the expression of neurosis. Rather, possession can offer an avenue for saying things one otherwise dares not say.[10]

---

## THE VARIETIES OF HEALERS

Like spirit possession, the diseases of the body attracted a variety of practitioners. Most Italians had little traffic with the university-trained physicians. These long-robed, bookish dignitaries did not deign to touch their patients. They peered intently, however, at glass vials of urine, for its color was a key diagnostic tool. The rich consulted these learned doctors, as did the big charitable hospitals, which employed them to tend their inmates. Other Italians generally turned for cures to other professionals, semiprofessionals, and amateurs. Wounds, broken bones, and skin problems were in the purview of the surgeons and barbers. Thus, the usual aftermath of a bloody fight was an urgent message to the surgeon to come clean up the havoc. Apothecaries prepared medicines from a smorgasbord of flowers, roots, gums, minerals, and other exotic materials, stored in labeled jars on their shelves; a guild usually regulated their work, as it did that of the "empirics," narrow specialists low on the ladder of prestige. Other remedies, often with secret ingredients, came from itinerant medicine sellers. In many places, these men too fell under the supervision of the medical inspector's office. Some of these patent remedy merchants were skilled hucksters, akin to the snake oil salesmen of North American legend. Indeed, not rarely, snakes and venom were part of the pitch and stock in trade. The showmen were called *ciarlatani,* a word derived from a verb meaning "to chatter." Our modern *charlatan* evokes the old suspicion that greeted their patter. Another name was *montebanchi,* for to make their sales they mounted a *banco,* a little stage. All these curers and sales folk belonged to the world of medical practice, as supervised by the public health authorities.

## MOUNTEBANKS

The English traveler Thomas Coryate has left a handsome picture of a late sixteenth-century Venetian mountebank at work (we modernize his spelling, but not his vocabulary and grammar):

> ... [W]hile the music plays, the principal Mountebank which is the captain and ring-leader of all the rest, opens his trunk, and sets abroach his wares; after the music hath ceased, he maketh an oration to the audience of half an hour long, or almost an hour. ... [He] maketh an extemporal speech, which he doth eftsoons intermingle with such savory jests (but spiced now and then with singular scurrility) that they minister passing mirth and laughter to the whole company, which may perhaps consist of a thousand people that flock together about one of their stages. ... I have observed marvelous strange matters done by some of these Mountebanks. For I saw one of them hold a viper in his hand, and play with his sting a quarter of an hour together, and yet receive no hurt; though another man should have been presently [right away] stung to death with it. ... Also I have seen a Mountebank hackle [slash] and gash his naked arm with a knife most pitifully to behold, so that the blood hath streamed out in great abundance, and by and by after hath applied a certain oil unto it, wherewith he hath incontinent [right away] both stanched the blood, and so thoroughly healed the wounds and gashes, that when he hath afterward showed us his arm again, we could not possibly perceive the least token of a gash.[11]

Still another sort of lay medical practitioners were men and very often women who prepared folk remedies. These were mostly people of modest means and scant literacy. Their concoctions typically combined

**Folk Healers and Magicians**

Mountebanks on their platform.
[Bertarelli: Forfanti]

herbs and other natural substances, gathered in the fields and woods or cultivated in gardens, and then processed according to recipes passed through oral tradition. A body of venerable but uninstitutionalized knowledge guided these preparations, but their makers—often called *magare*, magic makers—could also improvise, following their own intuitions and experiments. These lay healers were specialists within a larger domain of informal, do-it-yourself health care that likely included much of the female population. One consulted the wise-woman when the usual widely known home remedies did not avail. As an alternative, sixteenth-century printers began to offer literate women published household compendia with specialized recipes for treating many ills. By the later Renaissance, the wise-women faced pressures from several directions. Not only had they to compete with these books and with other more prestigious medical practitioners, but also they became increasingly suspect as purveyors of not only healing cures but also harmful spells.[12]

The difficulties of the wise-women and men arose from the close ties between their preparations of herbal remedies and the practice of magic. Ointments to cool fever and salves to induce or banish love looked quite alike, and the underlying principles understood to do the job were often the same. Though medical in intent, cures might well call on supernatural as well as natural powers. Even the devil might be invoked, as when, for example, the healer deemed the illness to be brought on by a curse that could be countered only by a like force. Thus, sufferers might seek out magic itself to ease their pain or weakness.

Magic, as a shield against illness, was, unlike medicine and religion, an ethically ambiguous force, sometimes benign but often malevolent (or both at once). That which helped one person often hurt another. For example, almost everyone believed that love magic could bring on lovesickness, sometimes called the hammer (*martello*), which enthralled the victim's emotions and weakened her or his body; this served the yearning lover but not necessarily the reluctant beloved. Such charms could also rattle proper gender hierarchy by taming a man, subjecting him to a woman's will. In the hands of a jealous woman, magic could cause impotence in a straying man. Similarly, a resentful competitor or a vengeful neighbor might buy from a sorcerer or witch a spell to cause bodily illness, diabolical possession, or death. Not all magic dealt harm, nor was human health its only domain. People also sought out workers of magic to solve problems of locating water, finding lost objects, or curing animals.[13]

Magical beliefs belonged not just to commoners. Well-born and even educated Italians dabbled in magic, and among men accused of sorcery some were priests. Learned churchmen and magistrates took such matters seriously, because to their eyes, magic was not mere silliness but possibly the work of the devil. The sixteenth-century movements of religious reform mounted increasingly sharp campaigns to suppress superstitious practices and witchcraft. Nonetheless, to bring Satan and his disciples to heel, the Italian authorities often adopted relatively mild tactics. While the Inquisitions prosecuted hundreds of women and men on various charges of illicit magic and witchcraft, unlike in some parts of Europe executions were few.

## CONCLUSION

Against the fearsome powers of disease, Italians of the Renaissance could resort to three general kinds of helpers: churchmen, medical people (physicians, surgeons, barbers, apothecaries and, at the edge, charlatans), and workers of traditional remedies and magic. A comparison is interesting. The first two groups had access to prestige and to elite, Latinate education. As professionals, they were allies who respected one another's spheres of competence. The third group, nonelite and largely cut off from Latin high culture, was scorned and sometimes persecuted by the other two. In the eyes of the elite curers, this third zone shared their professional traits but in debased, perverse forms. For the practitioners of magic, like the doctors and members of the medical profession, used ointments, powders, plasters, and other materials that worked in mysterious ways. These might have their inherent powers, but, often, for magic to make them work, special prayers and spells were helpful or necessary. Thus, calling on supernatural power, the practitioners of magic also trespassed on the clergy's zone of competence, the manipulation of the providential power of God and the saints. They also sometimes trafficked with the devil. Because the boundary between high and popular culture was porous, magic-workers appropriated and modified materials and formulas from their social superiors.

The great variety of helps, secular and sacred, against disease, shows how preoccupied Italians were by the risks of illness. Although this rich multiplicity of curers was in some ways reassuring, it also could be confusing. Moreover, no helpers, from whatever zone, inspired great confidence. The clergy were benevolent, but the powers of fasting, pilgrimage, prayer, and exorcism were never sure, for God's ways were mysterious. The nostrums of the lay healers may sometimes have been as useful as the often-dubious remedies of the physicians. But their general benevolence was in doubt, for when they dealt in magic, these folk could as readily harm with their spells as help with their charms.

Not all illnesses were as drastic as those surveyed here. Like us, Renaissance Italians caught cold and suffered indigestion and other passing ailments. Certainly twinges and sniffles did not catapult them into despair. Nonetheless, when sick, as they often were, they were on their guard in ways that we seldom have to be.

## NOTES

1. On hernia and its treatment, see David Gentilcore, "The Fear of Disease and the Disease of Fear," in *Fear in Early Modern Society*, ed. W. G. Naphy and P. Roberts (Manchester: Manchester University Press, 1997), 192–194.

2. On the Tuscan health inspectors, see Carlo Cipolla, *Miasmas and Disease: Public Health and the Environment in the Pre-Industrial Age* (New Haven: Yale University Press, 1992).

3. Pius II, *Memoirs of a Renaissance Pope: The Commentaries of Pius II: An Abridgment*, trans. F. A. Gragg (New York: Capricorn, 1962), 269.

4. On the seasonality of infections, see Ann G. Carmichael, *Plague and the Poor in Renaissance Florence* (Cambridge: Cambridge University Press, 1986), 9–14.

5. On weaning and the summer deaths of infants, see ibid., 41–49, and David Herlihy and Christiane Klapisch-Zuber, *Tuscans and Their Families* (New Haven: Yale University Press, 1985), 279.

6. Herlihy and Klapisch-Zuber, *Tuscans and Their Families*, 274–275. The years were 1424–30.

7. Quoted in Jon Arrizabalaga, John Henderson, and Roger French, *The Great Pox: The French Disease in Renaissance Europe* (New Haven: Yale University Press, 1997), 205–206.

8. Ibid., 134–144.

9. For a lay exorcist, see Thomas Cohen and Elizabeth Cohen, *Words and Deeds in Renaissance Rome* (Toronto: University of Toronto Press, 1993), 201–241.

10. Giovanni Romeo, *Inquisitori, esorcisti e streghe nell'Italia della Controriforma* (Florence: Sansoni, 1990), 109–111, 127.

11. Coryate, *Coryat's Crudities*, v. 1 (Glasgow: James MacLehose and Sons, 1905), 410–412.

12. On female healers, see Katherine Park, "Medicine and Magic: The Healing Arts," in *Gender and Society in Renaissance Italy*, ed. J. Brown and R. Davis (New York: Longman, 1998), 129–149.

13. On love jealousy, see Guido Ruggiero, *Binding Passions: Tales of Magic, Marriage, and Power at the End of the Renaissance* (New York: Oxford University Press, 1993).

# 15

# Work

To comprehend Renaissance work, we have to put aside some modern assumptions. When we think of work abstractly, what first springs to mind is labor exchanged for income; our model is the market, with its jobs and sales. Not all our labor follows this notion; our housework, schoolwork, and volunteering are unpaid and outside the economy. We therefore tend to overlook them when work comes to mind. For the Renaissance, it helps to conceive of work in the largest sense as all pragmatic effort, whether for money or not, for then, though the economy and hard cash counted, both were less dominant than today. For one thing, cash was rarer and other payments much more common. Because payments blended with gifts and services, the line between economy and society was blurred. For another, Renaissance Italians, though they had to labor hard to sustain themselves, often also worked to noneconomic ends. The domain of social service and ritual work—charity, worship, and celebration—loomed larger than today. Church, state, and community invited and required effort, thought, and emotional investment. Although some of this endeavor fell to professionals, much fell to the populace at large. So, to see Renaissance workers as they saw themselves, we must look beyond jobs and wages.

Work had several functions, all crucial to society's survival and well-being. As everyday experience, work was shaped by both its goals and the means at hand. This chapter first surveys the large social division of labor. It then looks at the cultural meanings of work, their bearing on status and self-worth. Last, it turns to the conditions of production.

This last section of the chapter explores the many effects of work's general domesticity and social entanglement. Though not all workplaces were homes, the domestic model shaped many workers' experiences. The space and time of Renaissance work therefore look unfamiliar. So do work discipline and the gender division of labor. Moreover, small units of production and weaker governance made for close but often unsystematic surveillance. And the worker, not the boss, more often set the schedule. Women, though barred from many jobs, by virtue of their domestic role bore many of production's hidden burdens. The social meanings of work also reflected conditions of production. For us, work and private life are often sharply sundered in space and social setting. Therefore, our work more defines our public face and standing, for our private lives are less in sight. Premodern work bore on status too, but its meaning was often more tightly bundled in familial and communal circumstance. Renaissance experiences of work therefore differed from modern ones in many ways. These often stemmed from production's tight household links.

## THE DIVISION OF LABOR

A useful way to view work is to catalog what needed doing and who did it. The sections that follow survey the work involved in producing and distributing goods, in conveying information, in governance and social control, and in worship and celebration.

**Production**  The biggest job of the Renaissance economy was the production of goods: grain, animals, fibers, cloth, garments, shelter, furnishings, glass, leather, shoes, tools, weapons, and all the other raw and finished items that Italian and foreign customers consumed. The great bulk of the population labored in this zone of work. The pattern of household production, by both peasants and artisans, is described in Chapter 2. Output was mostly small scale and often domestic; large estates and great industrial workshops were rare.

Although expert workers sometimes specialized, the daily and seasonal rounds of labor demanded flexibility and general competence at many tasks. The Renaissance economy had little of the modern industry's extreme division of labor, with its narrowed skills and deadening routines. Country folk, to keep the farm going, juggled varied duties to many beasts and crops. Artisans had a narrower range of output, but most goods took many steps. Some trades did become highly specialized. For example, in cloth manufacture, notoriously subdivided, the stages from unwashed raw fiber to finished fabric passed through many separate shops, each of which did one thing only.[1] More commonly, however, a single roof sheltered a whole production, from start to finish. To go from wood to chair or from cured leather to saddle took many expert steps. Within a shop, some skilled workers might have special tasks, such as the master painter who did the hands and faces, leaving clouds and drapery to the underlings, or the expert stone carver who finished a block rough-hewn by lesser masons. Less skilled subordinates usually moved between a host of chores. Even the master craftsman who specialized in the finest details also had to manage the shop and its workers and sell to customers. Thus, most workers needed competence at diverse tasks.

Because the household was so often the place of work, the tasks of production and reproduction tangled. Social scientists sometimes use *reproduction* to cover far more than bringing a new generation into the world. They stretch the sense to cover as well all those actions that support existing producers and train future ones. Reproduction includes preparing food, fetching water, tending clothing and other possessions, nursing the sick, nurturing and educating youngsters, and the myriad other actions that ensure a household's future. In the Renaissance, without many labor-saving domestic tools, this was slow, hard work, much of it on the backs of women. Production and reproduction intersected in several ways. Economically, the same fields and gardens both fed the tillers and brought them income. Socially, household workers mingled production and nurture. Culturally, the values and attitudes of the home and workplace converged, as at their parents' side youngsters learned a trade. This overlapping distinguished the Renaissance from our world, where home, school, and work are often separate and distinct.

While some distribution fell to merchants, specialists in moving goods, some remained in producers' control. Big merchants dealt in goods that needed expert handling either because they were bulky like grain, or hard to organize like cloth, or of exotic origin like spices. Grain, a politically sensitive major trade, often passed through the hands of landlords, big jobbers, or state granaries, or all three in sequence, before reaching bakers.[2] Cloth when spun, woven, dyed, fulled, stretched, and otherwise treated often belonged to the rich contractors who ran the complex trade. More modest itinerant retailers in the market circuit, country peddlers, and urban street vendors carried specialty goods across the landscape. Meanwhile, small-scale local commerce often remained in the producer's hands. Cultivators went to a weekly market or hawked along the roadside their fruits and vegetables, poultry and eggs, or the birds they snared. Artisans such as tailors, saddlers, furniture makers, coopers, jewelers, and many others combined making with selling. They were their own advertisers and distributors; their shop was both workshop and place of sale.

Women milking sheep and feeding chickens. [Tempesta]

**Distribution and Control of Information**

Work not only produced and distributed goods; it also created, transmitted, and stored information. Only some of this task fell to professionals; in varied ways, most Italians took part. Our own economy, which seems to churn out fewer things and ever more data and illusions, both suggests this topic and alerts us to vast differences between now and then. Renaissance media, by our standards, were slow and unsteady. Storage of knowledge was haphazard, access privileged, transparency rare. Still, information was critical to economic and social life. (See Chapter 8.) There was a modest communications sector. It included clergy, professors, and high professions—lawyers, physicians, notaries. There also were publicists—proto-journalists, printers, publishers and booksellers, and scribes, secretaries, and teachers. All these men dealt in the written word. In the oral sphere were preachers, prophets, storytellers, and balladeers. Many other workers produced and passed economic information. Merchants and bankers, for instance, devoted hours to business correspondence. Artisans and peasants mostly passed useful news by ear and mouth.

In Italy, state, economy, and society were opaque and secrecy was prized; much information was held tight to chest. Therefore, brokering and mediation throve. Brokers, by definition, offer privileged lines of communication. They help clients find contacts who have special knowledge, needs, and powers and then, for the service, charge a toll in cash, gifts, or friendship.[3] Mediators are a little different. They are messengers acceptable to parties who feel uneasy face to face. Renaissance honor made negotiations ticklish; mediation thus lubricated bargaining. When neutrality, tact, and contacts coincided in a single messenger, mediation merged with brokerage. Italy swarmed with go-betweens, arranging marriages, peace pacts, jobs, sales, and loans, and finding allies inside government. The courtier, quintessentially, was a well-placed broker—not a parasite, but a facilitator of good relations between prince and subjects. Think of him as a lobbyist in silks and pearls. He worked, after a fashion, for his rewards.

Another form of work, social control, was more remote from economic exchange than was the movement of information. (See Chapter 7.) The task was widely shared, for the Renaissance state, far smaller and less competent **Social Control as Work** than ours, left much more of social discipline to nonstate bodies: household, peer group, guild, and parish. Thrashing youngsters, at home or school, was work of sorts. So were scolding, praising, and modeling good conduct. Publicizing social rules and laws and enforcing them fell to guild and town and state, to magistrates and their underlings—town criers, police, prison guards, executioners, and soldiers. Governance took time and effort; many adult males spent time at it, some employed as functionaries, others as part-time councilors and committee men. As for soldiers, even war—a stab at interstate control—though it wrecked much and produced nothing, save fickle local security, was work.

Like social control, worship and other rituals were work, but only partly economic. The Renaissance invested heavily in God, Mary, and the saints. Much of this effort **Worship and Ritual Work** fell to professionals in prayers and sacraments: priests, monks, and nuns. Think of them as brokers with celestial contacts. Their service, in Italian eyes, was productive, not of goods but of grace and divine providence. Clergy were endowed, salaried, and paid fees for services rendered; their holy work thus took part in the economy. At the same time, not all effort of worship and celebration fell to clerics. A great sacred festival, with its music, decorations, and throngs of marchers, required much labor, some bought, but much of it gladly donated. The laity devoted sweat, time, and ingenuity to their acts of worship. Such gifts were outside the economy.[4] Meanwhile, the festivities of town and state spurred further efforts. As with us, a holiday required care and energy. But our exhausting Thanksgivings and Christmases are largely private festive labors; Renaissance celebrations were more often public and communal. Another zone of ritual work on the edge of the economy was curing and magical conjuring (see Chapter 14). These two examples, faith and healing, prove how varied work was and how marginal it could be to the economy of cash and trade. All together, Italian rituals demanded far more energy than do ours. The large lesson is that there was far more to labor than just tillage, lathes, and looms.

## WORK AND IDEOLOGY

While Renaissance Italians possessed no general ideology about work, they did have assorted attitudes toward it. Work, as concept, was less central to their culture than to ours. They lacked our modern "work ethic," our compulsion to be working and our prejudice against idleness. They did not share our belief that work validates and defines our lives. Renaissance Italians also lacked our modern rhetoric, now fading, the product of democratic, socialist, and labor movements, that bestows dignity on idealized toil. About work, Italians did, however, have ideas that bespoke their rank and economic status. Some took great pride in craft or profession and propped their self-esteem on the work they did. Others vaunted their superiority over any work at all.

**Words about Work: Effort and Craft**
The laboring classes, when they talked of work, had a rich vocabulary for effort. Since manual labor was often a source of sweat, hunger, thirst, and aching muscles, work—*lavoro* (labor)—could also be called *fatigare* (to get fatigued) or *stentare* (to make an effort). As one man said, "I came [to Rome] to labor and to make an effort hoeing."[5] Peasants groaned and complained: "It was with my efforts [*stenti*] that I wanted to give her a dress [for her dowry]," or "We, by the strength of our arms, pulled all the wood into the castle. It was a great effort [*stento*] and fatigue [*fatiga*]," or "The garden and the hunting park were made with the sweat of everybody in the village."[6]

At the same time, working men could stress their occupation's dignity. In this less plaintive mode, they often called their work an *arte*. This term, meaning "craft," connoted skill and respectability. It applied as readily to the toil of peasants and artisans as to Raphael's painting at the Vatican. As one casual laborer testified with modest pride, "I take my pleasure at [*mi diletto a*] laboring in the vineyards, and leading horses, and other arts [*arti*] of the outdoors."[7] Artisans, in self-description, happily claimed to have an *arte*. Because the term also meant "guild," it glowed with traditions of corporate solidarity and political participation. Nevertheless, notaries, lawyers, and physicians, as men of status, seldom used the term, for they stood above the *arti*. Meanwhile, men below them—beggars, thieves, and assassins—however adroit at shady practices, never dared boast an "art." If soldiers might, the despised cops could not. Nor could women, however skilled. In men's eyes, an *arte* distinguished them from the shiftless, the helpless, and the dispossessed who thronged the cities; it was a badge of worthiness.

For the nobility, work subverted status. So when lords sold the products of their estates or oversaw commercial investments, to them it was not work. Happy to strain and sweat at fencing or the pursuit of deer and boar, nobles sneered at underlings' more fruitful exertions.[8] The proper activity of a **Work and Noble Status** man of rank was to manage lands, urban properties, and interest-bearing investments. Often any real supervision of estates fell in fact to paid agents; the lord, if careful, just kept a sharp eye on his overseers. Governance and military command also befitted aristocratic rank. On the other hand, in North Italian cities, nobles did engage in commerce and in the liberal professions, at least until the sixteenth century. Then, in much of Italy, patricians increasingly deserted trade for landed income. As elsewhere in the European old regime, those below noble rank strove for social elevation by marrying their children into the idle elite, for, however rich the fathers grew, snobbery held new money down. Fresh wealth reeked of work. Merchants and officials who waxed rich, honestly or crookedly, would therefore cleanse male progeny by buying them sinecures, real offices, knighthoods, military commands, and sufficient lands to support a life of prestigious leisure. In the later sixteenth century, the Roman Curia was another ladder of ascent so useful that elite families sometimes destined their first-born for the church, hoping to reap a cardinalate with all its patronage. Prelates, running the church and the Papal State, did indeed work hard, but governance—deemed clean, prestigious employment—still sat well with elite status.

So, to the Renaissance, work looked both good and bad, depending on who was looking. On the one hand, it raised the working commoners above the lazy and the indigent. On the other, it undercut noble status.

## WORK AND WOMEN

Women too devoted much energy and time to work. Like their husbands or brothers, noble women were leisured. Their activities were not work, for effort was unseemly. Yet, while elite women did not govern, fight, or preach, their diligence as managers at home and brokers in neighborhood and at court did foster their families' well-being. Among affluent merchants, matrons played similar roles. While unwelcome in commerce, women did influence the family matrimonial strategies that, through big dowries, shaped enterprise and investment. Women

Women washing clothing in a river.
[Tempesta]

engaged in some limited kinds of business. In medieval Genoa, they invested in trading companies as silent partners, although, in fifteenth-century Florence, Leon Battista Alberti in his dialogue urged against allowing wives even to see the account books. But Florence's intensely patriarchal practices may not have applied elsewhere. While, in Florence, female control of property was subject, if sometimes nominally, to male supervision, in other places women often took active part in contracts concerning their assets. Widows had more autonomy than wives; they sometimes helped administer property on behalf of minor children.

Further down the economic ladder, women of the artisan and peasant class worked hard, combining domestic labor with a range of productive activities. Housekeeping itself imposed an endless string of tasks. Preparing, serving, cleaning away, and conserving food; caring for, teaching, and disciplining children; fetching water; washing and mending; sweeping; and making beds typically fell to wives, daughters, servants, and other household women. Yet women had no monopoly on this domestic work. Men, especially servants and innkeepers, might shoulder some of it. Also, urban housewives might farm out some household labor to paid washerwomen and wetnurses and buy water, bread, and cooked food.

Ordinary women, in both country and city, also took part in production for the market. This work was typically part-time and loose jointed, for women juggled domestic tasks with varieties of labor for the market. Where residence and workplace coincided, wives and daughters of peasants and artisans helped win the family livelihood, as they still do in many places studied by modern anthropologists. Rural women tended livestock and gardens, gathered fruits and olives, helped harvest grain, combed and spun hemp and wool, fetched water, grain, and laundry, ran errands to the mill, staffed lime kilns, and drove or carried loads for construction projects.[9] Townswomen helped run the shop, serving customers, minding stock, and keeping an eye on apprentices and servants.

Much of this informal yet essential effort eludes the documents, so we cannot see well its extent and nature. If not head of household, a woman seldom got credit or a label for her work. But her contributions mattered, and she could take over when her men went away, as they often did. Some women's names do appear in records of crafts and service trades. Some were widows carrying on the family business, while others were wives with occupations of their own. In general, as the Middle Ages became the Renaissance, the ranks of women formally employed shrank, only to swell again at the sixteenth century's end, presumably due to labor market shifts. By 1600, women's paid work was largely in the textile industries. Renaissance women also worked for pay in various less structured occupations, often offering—as boarding-house keepers, midwives, and wetnurses—services linked to domestic work. Even prostitutes sometimes served as part-time semi-wives to many men at once, offering not only sex and companionship but also washing, mending, storage, and hospitality to friends.[10]

## CONDITIONS OF WORK

Renaissance working conditions were more fluid than ours. The difficulty of transmitting or concentrating energy helped keep workplaces small. Employment therefore had a sparse geography that encouraged the movement of workers from place to place and task to task. The lower ranks of the labor force were especially mobile. Because production was fragmented and legislation spasmodic, work's schedules—in the day, the year, and the lifetime—were also supple. Discipline, though pervasive, was neither regular nor rigid.

Renaissance work was much the harder for lack of cheap, plentiful energy. Only in the past two centuries has **The Ecology** our economy used, and heedlessly squandered, much fos- **of Energy** sil fuel, a vast store of ancient sunlight caught by living things and preserved as coal, gas, and petroleum. Lacking this abundant source, the premodern world, for energy, fell back on something far less rich: current sunlight. The sun, through evaporation, raised water that fell on hills as rain and then powered river mills. The sun's heat, lifting warm air, caused wind that propelled ships and windmill sails. Sunlight caught by the leaves of trees became wood that, burning, warmed the house, cooked food, melted glass and metal, and heated water for dyeing, washing, and other uses. Other plants made oils and, with insect help, beeswax for illumination. Muscle power, animal and human, also traced back down the food chain to green plants; it was sunlight too. Since other energy did not transport readily, muscle was crucial for moving things. Mills, restricted to their riverbanks, in the absence of electricity could not transmit energy farther than their machines could reach.

Furthermore, the Renaissance knew no way of transforming fire into useful mechanical motion; there was no steam or internal combustion engine. The only conversion of heat to motion came from gunpowder, superb for hoisting fireworks, bullets, cannon balls, or an enemy bastion into the air, but so brief and violent as to be useless for anything but pyrotechnics or destruction.

Italy was energy poor. Scantily endowed with rivers and forests, it harvested little power from falling water and burning wood. Short of summer grass for grazing beasts of burden, it lacked abundant hoofed muscle to pull and carry. It did use intensively what resources it had. Mills were everywhere, damming minor streams and floating tethered off urban riverbanks. One response to shortage was ingenuity. Italian craftsmen and engineers devised clever windlasses and rigs of block and tackle, screws, gears, bearings, counterweights, and levers that captured and transmitted water power and muscle energy, both animal and human. Such engines could transform and carry energy and force, though only so far as their cables, wheels, and beams could reach. Construction yards and cannon foundries were full of such devices. Leonardo da Vinci's ingenious machines thus grew out of a long tradition of making the most of a scarce resource.[11]

**Work and Time**    Work fit into the Renaissance's sense of time. Our economy uses and reinforces modern concepts: our time is inflexible and precise. In the premodern world, in contrast, several interacting kinds of time produced work rhythms that were predictable but flexible. The new mechanical clocks did help set work's pace, but their use often had to adapt to religious, social, and economic needs. (See Chapter 10.)

Both the natural and the sacred calendars shaped work rhythms. The seasons with their shifting weather and hours of light imposed adjustment. Lamps and candles were no match for cheap, strong sunlight. Work therefore contracted in dim, short winter days. The six-hour December day of the Venetian Arsenal stretched in summer to eleven. And the rural year dictated a whole cycle of activities, both on the land and off it. In slack seasons, agricultural laborers turned their hands to other trades that fluctuated in synchrony with farming. The sacred calendar bore on work less strongly. Though feast days and Sundays in theory canceled secular work, for many, they did no more than slow it, diluting it with devotions and diversions. Some big operations did shut down; between Sundays and holidays, the Arsenal in Venice closed 100 days a year. In the many small shops that made up most of the urban economy, masters often chose just when to work. And chose how long; schedules lacked synchrony. No rush hour!

In the Renaissance, neither clocks nor work habits locked pay to time. We moderns calculate blue-collar wages and professional fees by the

From wheel to crank: reciprocal motion draws wire. [Biringuccio]

hour and white-collar salaries by the day or month. Premodern clocks were too vague and work rhythms too supple. Italians therefore often paid piecework, for a product: a bushel of olives, a saddle repaired, a document copied, an altarpiece completed. They did buy some blocks of time, but in units larger than the hour or day: soldiers received their tardy wages, if ever, by the month. A gentleman might also retain a courtesan by the month, with extra cash for clothes. Masters often hired their servants by the year. Churches, too, gave some clergy annual stipends. In these four cases, the product, personal service, was not easily appraised, for it was irregular in shape and rhythm. Employers therefore exchanged a general payment—a retainer—for a long stint of assorted useful work. Paid by piece or by year, Renaissance workers usually escaped the tyranny of the clock. They also missed the blessings; starting and stopping times were vague and paid vacations unknown.

The life cycle, another kind of time, also bore on work in unmodern ways. (See Chapters 11 and 12.) For us, work is a life stage some forty years long, sandwiched between almost two decades of formal schooling and, for many, several decades of retirement. Although some of us do take part-time jobs while studying, work proper, a life stage, signals young adulthood. The Italian pattern was less neat. Only a few lawyers, physicians, and ambitious clergy stretched studies to age twenty or beyond. Most others, if artisans or merchants, went into apprenticeship in the early to mid-teens. Household servants were often even younger. Country children of both sexes made themselves useful as soon as they could. Those who did study usually mixed a little school with much work. As for retirement, the Renaissance had neither the concept nor the legal and financial underpinnings. High mortality swallowed many before senescence sapped their powers. The lucky few who lasted to the age of decline often just tapered off productive work. On the other hand, there still were some truly old or disabled folk, too weak to support themselves. Many were poor; one gave them alms, housed them in hospitals, or took them in as lodgers "for the love of God"—for charity.

**Work and Space**      Renaissance work had complex spatial arrangements. For many, home was workplace; others traveled far to earn a living. Some workers settled, like barnacles, in a lifelong occupation, while others wandered from place to place and shifted jobs. In towns, some enterprises clustered, like with like, while others scattered.

The home often anchored Renaissance work. The family farm excepted, the modern economy has divorced work from household. Recent innovations in information technology, allowing work to return home, in some ways carry us back to premodern spatial arrangements that mingled labor and residence. Many Renaissance men and women, from peasants and artisans through merchants and officials, up to the rulers, worked where they ate and slept. Princely palaces were big in part to make room for business. There were, of course, exceptions. The executioner, for instance, did not inhabit the gallows, nor the stevedores the docks, nor the pickpocket the crowded street where he found his victims. Nor did a parish priest dwell inside his church. And some small shops had no beds attached. Employees of the rare big establishments—the Venetian Arsenal, the big Florentine cloth workshops, major construction sites—did not work at home. Many of these workers, however, lived near their employment. Long commuting, common between village and fields, was rare in town.

For other Renaissance workers, work required mobility. International merchants, especially early in their careers, often traveled far and long, while some judges and officials had itinerant posts to keep them honest. Sailors, soldiers, mule drivers, coachmen, carters, and herdsmen crossed country as part of their jobs. Other workers, especially the less fortunate, migrated to seek a job. Some such movement strayed a few miles at most. Other migrations were long; both city and countryside were full of workers from far parts of Italy, some stable immigrants, but many others transients who slept in inns, boarding-houses, or makeshift bivouacs in fields, sheds, stables, and ruins.

While the elites of the workforce enjoyed occupational stability, the less fortunate were forever shifting, not only place but also job. A notary, a banker, a shopkeeper, a peasant with ample lands, or a master artisan usually spent a lifetime at one pursuit. Those many with little capital—in learning, cash, land, tools, a shop, or skills—scrambled. In villages, while those with enough acreage sat tight, neighbors with skimpy holdings came and went. Men ducked in and out of tending stables, watching flocks, guarding fields, driving livestock, and harvesting. When local work ran short, the poor ventured farther in anxious search of income. Some returned to work their lands part time; others drifted off for good. In cities, too, those with only general skills and few assets they could not carry bounced from post to post. If jobs grew scarce, they tried another town or went home to their village. For the many poor workers, livelihood meant coping, improvising, and frequent moving.

While in the countryside, almost everybody did the same tasks, city work was much more varied. There, masons, cooks, straw braiders, apothecaries, tavern keepers, landlords, boatmen, and dry goods merchants lived and labored side by side. All, however, kept to the alliances and schedules dictated by their trade. In general, commercial activities more often scattered than clustered: armorers, tailors, notaries settled everywhere, not just on a single street. There were exceptions to this pattern. Facilities like a port or running water might concentrate some trades. Moreover, at times, legislation pushed dirty activities like dyeing, tanning, and butchery into a remote corner. And some forms of commerce, banking especially, worked better when practitioners settled side by side.

While practical conditions allowed workers some autonomy, they often remained under others' authority, for the **The Social** economy reflected the constraints of solidarity and hierar- **Discipline** chy. (See Chapters 4 and 5.) Yet the fragmentation of pro- **of Work** duction usually freed Italians from close scrutiny, that trait of modern industry. Peasant tenants, for example, planted and cultivated some crops according to stipulations in the lease, but set their own daily pace. Teams, on the other hand, had to reckon with their heads, be they construction workers, soldiers, policemen, or harvesters on a big estate. Brigands on a raid took direction from their captain. And servants fell under the watchful eye of masters and mistresses. The large staffs of palaces had a complex internal hierarchy; a groom or chambermaid had to obey high-ranking servitors, who in turn took orders from the house's head. Many master artisans, despite their independence, had to reckon with the collective, fitful scrutiny of the guilds they had to join. Some of these organizations could inspect the worksite, assessing the product, setting limits to prices and wages, and regulating the hiring and treatment of apprentices and the placement of shops; there were fines for breach of rules. Sometimes the state also oversaw a product. Mostly, though, masters followed their own inclinations.[12] Renaissance work was thus often flexible, but seldom at total liberty.

## MONEY AND CREDIT

The same improvisation that marked labor also infected commercial exchange. Despite Italy's invention of banking and bookkeeping, by our

Repairing a bell with the furnace custom fit along the crack. [Biringuccio]

standards its monetary system was ramshackle. It had problems with what economists call liquidity—easy payment and the rapid circulation of money in all its forms. Making change, converting currencies, collecting a payment or wages owed, raising cash for a purchase or capital for an investment: all these things go better when liquidity is high and money moves fast. In this department, Renaissance Italy faced shortages and frictions.

One great obstacle to liquidity was the hideous complexity of the currency. There was no paper money, only coins minted from gold, silver, and copper. Coins took their value from their bullion's mass and purity. Buyers and sellers had to be alert, for their money's weight and worth kept shifting. Also, the three metals fluctuated in their relative values. And governments, to cover debt, sometimes debased their coinage. Counterfeiting made matters worse. Furthermore, there was no single currency; each state minted its own. In addition, Italian and foreign coin circulated side by side. In Venice, Coryate encountered not only local money but French crowns, German ducats, Spanish pistolets, and Hungarian and papal gold.[13] The major cities—Venice, with its ducats, Florence with its florins, Rome with its scudi—set a measure for the others. But the exchange between them was always complicated and inconstant.

Italy had various devices to improve liquidity. To the vagaries of exchange, an antidote was money of account. This was a bookkeeping convenience, never a tangible piece of bullion. Moneys of account were flexible, stable, widely recognized, and largely free from governmental tampering. Best of all, there was no need to scrounge them up among the bankers, for they were virtual money. Therefore they were much used in accounting, administration, and contracts. The usual currency was the lira, meaning pound (*libbra*) of silver. But the lira too varied from city to city. Thus it took arithmetic skill to figure out the equivalents between assorted lire and the varieties of coin. Thus, money of account, while it helped liquidity, did not solve all problems.

Another barrier to liquidity was a general shortage of ready cash in the economy; it caused Italians to turn to credit. Borrowing and debt were everywhere. Big transactions—a dowry, the purchase of lands and houses, of a public office or a ship's cargo—and even modest sales often deferred payment. Italians issued promissory notes and letters of credit. These became a form of currency, for one could pass them to third parties as payment. Some credits drew on bankers, but many more stemmed from private persons. Rather than put money in the bank, wealthy families often bought private bonds. A borrower put up as collateral his houses and estates and issued the bond, promising steady interest and eventual redemption. If he defaulted, unforgiving creditors could swallow the ancestral lands. Big transactions often required rickety scaffolding, rigged out of interlocking private loans. Mortgaging and pawning ran the social scale. Peasants, often drastically indebted to their landlords, hocked their vineyards to pay rents and fines; soldiers pawned their swords and armor to pay for food, wine, and lodgings at the inn. As with the rich, bad luck could bring ruin; bankruptcy was a painful escape from debts. To a degree, Italians used these webs of debt and credit as a device for social solidarity and control (see Chapter 7). Yet the habit also served economic necessity; quick cash was hard to raise, so one played one's network to muster coin and promises.

Because money was scarce, Italians often turned to the *compagnia*, the partnership, to raise capital. Among merchants, artisans, mercenary captains, or rural enterprisers, pooled resources aided operations. Often some partners put up funds, while others saw to the work. Companies—big and small, enduring and brief, sealed by charter and by handshake—were everywhere. For instance, many noble landlords barely cultivated their estates; instead they rented out the grazing and the timber cutting rights to a *compagnia* of grazers who then brought in vast woolly flocks. In such contracts, the sheep owners almost always came in twos and threes. They pooled resources to buy beasts and grass.

Such grazing contracts show not only *compagnia*, but also another trait of a cash-poor economy: the habit of "farming out." It was a form of borrowing, funded with lost revenue. For a timely payment up front, one leased the running of an enterprise to a stand-in who reaped the eventual profits. Thus, landlords who sold off grazing rights settled for less money, sooner, without effort, rather than for more money, later, earned by operating the estate themselves. Cash-hungry states often did the same, farming out their revenue-bearing operations—customs, taxes, mines, forests, and levies on transhumant sheep—to private operators who paid promptly.

One more response to low liquidity and short cash was barter and payment in kind. This device survived in myriad forms. Masters and mistresses paid their servants in shelter, food, and clothing. Towns and states rounded out the stipends of functionaries with hams, melons, barrels of flour, and casks of wine. Cultivators often paid their share-crop or feudal rents and court fines with the products of their fields. And shepherds signed on to run a mixed flock for several years, replete with rented guard dogs rigged with wolf-proof spiked collars and great cheese molds, in exchange for annual lambs and kids, and half the cheeses. Landlords also rented out dairy cattle and beehives, to be paid in calves and honey. With officials, payments in kind easily blurred with gifts and bribes. The same economic melange of fees and gifts surfaced in the sex trade, where men plied their hired consorts with meat pies, roasts, bread, wine, slippers, cloth, and even domestic furnishings. One grateful, if shady, customer even dropped off a heavy bed, nimbly stolen from a cardinal's house.[14] These modes of payment exemplify how versatile were Renaissance financial arrangements. Taken together, all the various devices show Italians' supple adaptation to the quirks and drawbacks of their premodern economy.

## TWO EXAMPLES

**A Rural Vignette**     For a better sense of Renaissance work, let us follow some workers through their day. As usual, court papers supply vignettes. Our first trial shows the texture of rural labor. In the hill town of Fara, Agostino, a serving man recently immigrated from eastern Italy, is murdered well after midnight, in October 1555, as he drives a gray, droop-eared donkey, laden with newly ground flour, homeward from the mill. When last seen, as he drives the beast, he is singing to himself. Shortly after, some villagers hear a shot, and a few even see the flash of powder. Early next morning, several women, having risen early and descended, jug on head, to fetch water at the spring, discover Agostino's corpse, shot and beaten, by the Fountain of the Hawk. Both ass and cargo have vanished.

Suspicion falls on two local boys, Lorenzo and Giacobo Boccardi. The morning of the crime, they were seen carrying a long gun. The local court, arresting the brothers, makes them account for their movements. The lads, it eventually turns out, were innocent. The bloody hands belonged to a notoriously thuggish thief, exiled from a nearby village. But their testimony illustrates the rhythms of rural labor.

The night Agostino dies, around two in the morning, the boys rise from the bed they share with their mother and their brother, and head off to patrol their fields. Normally, for safety on such outings, Lorenzo carries a sword and Giacobo a battle-axe, but, having left these arms in another house, they have borrowed the friar's loaded gun, a powder

Horses threshing grain by trampling. [Bertarelli: Missale]

flask, and one extra bullet. The pair go first to a grove of oaks at Little Fountain Hill to be sure no thieves are in their acorns. All is well. They then go to a vineyard of theirs, at Mangle-wolves Hill, and find that some of the threshers who roam the district, renting out horses for trampling loose the grain, have broken in to loose their beasts to feed. The gun persuades the intruders to surrender a knife; this the boys will deposit at the village court as surety that the threshers will show up to be fined for damages inflicted. Fines for trespass and abuse to crops, fences, walls, and other outworks were the daily meat of rural justice. Having shooed the men and their horses from the vineyard, Lorenzo and Giacobo check their oak grove again, find it secure, and then go over to a house, where they eat a light meal. They then cross to a nearby meadow, where they join two herdsmen, acquaintances down from Ornaro, a village some miles to the east. The herdsmen have lit a predawn fire to warm themselves as they watch their oxen. In the gray early light of a foggy morning, the boys leave the fire and their companions' conversation to make one more tour of inspection, first to their vineyard and then to their oaks, and then head back toward Fara, high on its hilltop. First, however, in an outbuilding of theirs they stow the gun under a pile of hemp. As the youngsters start up the slope, they hear the Ave Maria bell, calling the village to morning prayer. One hour after a foggy sunrise, Giacobo joins his mother, harvesting olives in a family plot. Lorenzo goes not to the fields but to the village school, to recite his lessons, and then, when school is over, joins the others picking olives.[15]

What Renaissance patterns appear in this vignette? One touches on how work slotted into time and the rest of life. The pattern is preindustrial: no clocks, no tyranny of time, no boss, no cleavage of work from the rest of life. The two young guardians slip easily, or groggily, from bed to armed patrol, and from there to snacks and fireside talk. Their work is loosely scheduled and open at the edges. On the other hand, as often in the Renaissance, their work is long, hard, and dangerous. Giacobo and Lorenzo risk injury to guard their lands. They spend a cold October night prowling fields and then, at the break of day, instead of crawling into bed, go to school or set off to pick olives. Peasant life is seldom easy.

Furthermore, Giacobo's and Lorenzo's work is often varied. The family practices a mixed agriculture, typical of small holdings in hill country. The boys, their brother, and their mother must do many things. They have hemp to harvest; they may well also extract the fiber, which their mother would comb and spin for making rope and burlap. They have acorns to gather, for sale or for feed for their own pigs. They have olives to prune, graft, pick, and transport to a press for crushing and boiling, vines to prune, stake, hoe, ditch, manure, weed, and to guard from livestock, birds and thieves, producing grapes to pick, haul, and press. And, probably, like other villagers, they grow grain for which they plow, once or several times. Then they must sow, cut, gather, and haul it to the threshing floor so horses can trample it free of the stalks. Like most peasants, this family are not specialists; the rounds of the agricultural year demand many skills. Each crop exacts knowledge, effort, and time.

A third lesson is interdependency: the boys form part of a family team. One man alone could not easily have cultivated the lands and guarded them from nocturnal intruders. Their farm, like many Renaissance enterprises, requires several sets of hands. Family is well adapted to such enterprises; different members, including women, bring different skills and capacities. But Renaissance family was a notoriously changing unit; demography never stood still. Thus, to fit a household to a workplace, one often needed to import or export labor. Hired men—like the murder victim, Agostino—helped balance the domestic workforce.

**Urban Labor Patterns**   Urban patterns of work, sociability, and use of time had things in common with rural ones. In the city too, work and sociability intermingled, and time and place were flexible. Artisanal conditions, however, were less often harsh. An episode from Rome shows how, on a Sunday, supposedly a day of worship and repose, work and the rest of life interlocked.

Late on a Sunday afternoon in February 1572, a gang of thirty nobles and their servants marshals in Piazza Altieri, in central Rome, spoiling for a fight. Though nothing bad ever happens, the next day, inquisitive, the criminal court calls in thirteen of the piazza's artisans: five shoemakers, three tailors, two saddlers, a carpenter, a box maker, and a fruit seller's helper. With his usual guile, the judge says only, "Tell us what you did yesterday." Listening for clues, he lets the witnesses reveal the rhythms of their lives.

Andrea the saddler, for instance, rises late, about an hour and a half after winter sunrise. His first errand takes him to the nearby Caetani palaces to discuss with the master of the accounts a velvet saddle he is making. He then goes to his guild's church, San Salvatore della Pietra, where he lights a candle to honor Sunday and stays for mass. He returns home, fetches his balls and mallet, and heads to the Colosseum—fifteen minutes away—for a bout of *palla maglia*, robust croquet. He returns home for the midday meal and finds his partner, Giulio, back from church, attaching fringes to horse gear. Giulio informs him that two gentlemen from the Conti palace have stopped by to summon a saddle of theirs. Right away! So Andrea, though hungry, puts the saddle on a horse. The two partners and Niccolo, their agent, go to the Conti, back by the Colosseum. After delivering horse and saddle, the three saddlers eat their midday meal at a nearby inn. Then Andrea and Niccolo take the *palla maglia* gear to the church of San Vitale—another fifteen-minute walk away—and there spend the afternoon at play. Giulio, the partner, returns to the shop, hangs around with the local artisans, and then goes strolling and visiting in the Corso, the main street of Rome. Home before the others, he is back in time to see the menacing crowd of nobles, to pick up gossip about the wounding that has provoked it, and to warn Francesco, a tailor, to stay home in case trouble brews. When Andrea returns, all is calm; he finds Giulio reading and takes him off for supper at an inn.[16]

The Sundays of the other men have many of these same elements: work, worship, play, sociability, and repose. Sunday, not a normal workday, mixes their labor with a lot of church and leisure. Of the eleven artisans who tell full stories, seven nevertheless do spend part of the day at their trades, and an eighth devotes all of Sunday to errands for his kinfolk. On the other hand, only one, an underling, works all day. One man plays all day, one visits and worships, and one spends his holiday at play or worship (we know not how) at the far basilica, Saint Paul Outside-the-Walls. Of those who do work, five are in their shop, four go to wealthy houses to deliver or fashion goods, and one, a fruit seller's shop boy, peddles wares around town. As in the country, work is fairly mobile. As for church, most go, some once, others twice, before and after the midday meal; one goes twice in an afternoon. For this group of working men, there is no local church of choice; while several seek out sermons in the nearby Franciscan church, the Aracoeli, others go all over the city. Their recreations also vary; the men play, gossip, stroll, visit their friends. One dines with his mother. Unlike the saddlers, most take meals at home, though it is unclear how they feed themselves. Are there cooks in the house, or do they bring bought food home? Rome is a city with few women. The narratives are strikingly male; all customers, messengers, friends, gossipers, and partners in work and play are men; the tailor's mother who dined with her son is the only woman to appear. Women figure little in these stories male artisans tell a judge about how they had spent their day.

## CONCLUSION

Renaissance work was larger than the economy, for many aspects of daily life required effort, planning, and a sense of purpose. Work was extremely varied and thoroughly pervasive of daily life. Nevertheless, it did not take existence over. In the absence of a work ethic like ours today, Italians were less likely to define themselves or shape their lives by work alone. As the next chapter shows, they also invested heavily in leisure and active forms of play. Note how blurred was the boundary between work and the whole rest of social life. Productive labor mingled with many things: governance, celebration, worship, leisure, and companionship. The unclarity of work's edges was typical of most Renaissance activities, as was work's flexibility in place and time. Short resources imposed adaptiveness. Thus, though hierarchic, rule conscious, and sometimes harsh, the Renaissance did not pin working people in a single posture or pen them in a narrow band of labors. Rather, it let them adapt and improvise, for rigidity in some places required give in others.

## NOTES

1. For a convenient diagram of wool production, see Gene Brucker, *Florence: The Golden Age* (Berkeley: University of California Press, 1998), 104–105.

2. On the managed grain trade, see Melissa Bullard, "Grain Supply and Urban Unrest in Renaissance Rome: The Crisis of 1533–34," in *Rome in the Renaissance: The City and the Myth*, ed. P. A. Ramsay (Binghamton: Center for Medieval and Early Renaissance Studies, 1982), 279–292.

3. On the anthropology of brokerage, see Jeremy Boissevain, *Friends of Friends: Networks, Manipulators and Coalitions* (New York: Saint Martin's Press, 1974).

4. On ritual work, see Edward Muir, *Civic Ritual in Renaissance Venice* (Princeton: Princeton University Press, 1981). On the social and psychological nature of early modern European ritual, see Edward Muir, *Ritual in Early Modern Europe* (Cambridge: Cambridge University Press, 1997), especially 1–17.

5. Archivo di Stato di Roma (ASR), Governatore, Tribunale Criminale, Costituti 169, 90r (1570).

6. Ibid., Processi sixteenth century, b. 25, 111r, 126r, 190v (1557).

7. Ibid., Costituti 170, 88v (1570).

8. On the many ambiguities of noble status, and the playing out of the aversion to work, see James Grubb, *Provincial Families of the Renaissance* (Baltimore: Johns Hopkins University Press, 1996), 170–184, especially 175–176.

9. Examples come from the central Italian villages of Fara and Rocca Sinibalda: ASR, Governatore, Tribunale Criminale, Processi sixteenth century, b. 25 (1556); Processi sixteenth century, b. 26, case 2 (1555); Processi sixteenth century, b. 35 (1557).

10. On women's work, for a general discussion see Merry Wiesner, *Women and Gender in Early Modern Europe* (Cambridge: Cambridge University Press, 1993), chap. 3; on Italy, see Judith Brown, "A Woman's Place Was in the Home: Women's Work in Renaissance Tuscany," in *Rewriting the Renaissance*, ed. M. Ferguson et al. (Chicago: University of Chicago Press, 1986), 206–224 and Deborah Parker, "Women in the Book Trade in Italy, 1475–1620," *Renaissance Quarterly* 49:3 (1996), 509–541.

11. For photographs of models and designs of Leonardo's own machines, and for their links with earlier devices, see Martin Kemp and Jane Roberts, *Leonardo da Vinci* (New Haven: Yale University Press, 1989), 218–232, 236–241.

12. On guild powers, see Luca Molà, *The Silk Industry of Renaissance Venice* (Baltimore: Johns Hopkins University Press, 2000), 112–120, 300–301, and elsewhere; Richard Goldthwaite, *The Building of Renaissance Florence* (Baltimore: Johns Hopkins University Press, 1980), 242–286.

13. Coryate, *Coryat's Crudities*, v. 1, (Glasgow: James MacLehose and Sons, 1905), 422; Brucker, *Florence*, 70–71.

14. ASR, Governatore, Tribunale Criminale, Investigazioni 80, 86r ff. (1563).

15. ASR, Governatore, Tribunale Criminale, Processi sixteenth century, b. 26, case 2, 634r-58v (1555).

16. For the days of the artisans, ASR, Governatore, Tribunale Criminale, Processi sixteenth century, b. 177, case 2 (1572).

# 16

# Play

Renaissance Italians had a profound sense of play that ran through all of life. In Chapter 15, we saw how the boundaries between work and play blurred. Play, like work, had its varieties of timing; it could choose its spontaneous moment or could honor the traditional festive calendar. It could improvise or follow deep customary tracks. Play included games, sports, contests and even fights, music, dancing, stage plays, ceremonies, parties, excursions, practical jokes, strolls, conversations, and plain idling to watch the passing scene. Despite its myriad forms, Renaissance play had several consistent traits. First, it belonged to leisure: to those occasions when people did things because they wanted to and anticipated pleasure or release—from labor, from discomfort, from constraint, from abstinence and self-control. A second feature was the quest for bodily well-being and sensory or mental stimulation. A third was sociability. Company and shared enjoyment made activities more fun, stirring emotions and lightening the heart. Social play also offered the excitement and piquant delight of rivalry. Gatherings, harmonious or competitive, not only refreshed their members but also eased group tensions and fortified solidarities.

A striking trait of Italian play, highlighted by the historian of popular culture, Peter Burke, was its theatricality. In Italians' taste for drama, playfulness and love of performance converged. They took their leisure, and indeed conducted much of their lives, as if actors on a stage, watched by an audience. As in all cultures, people shaped their words and actions by shuffling and recombining elements from familiar social scripts. Yet Renaissance Italians did so with special gusto, flair, and love of making an impression. People stepped in and out of roles built from a huge repertoire of stories, proverbs, stunts, stock characters, and gestures; they deployed familiar wisecracks, taunts, exclamations, excuses, and consolations. Not only their formal ceremonies, in churches, palaces, and on the piazza, but even many of their everyday exchanges—requests, complaints, challenges, negotiations—had a dramatic streak that caught the eye of travelers. Italians shifted easily from performer to spectator and back. In the realm of play, they took pleasure from both dramatizing themselves and watching others' shows. The watchers, too, by praising, counseling, or heckling the actors, became part of the event.

## BASIC PLEASURES: BODY, SOCIABILITY, AND THE SENSES

For many Italians, everyday play often met the body's needs in congenial company. Men stopped together in the evening for a pitcher of wine; a woman supped on artichokes at her sister's house. Food pleased the palate and filled the belly; drink warmed the blood and left a pleasant alcoholic buzz; rest soothed drained limbs and tired brains. Meanwhile, sociability enlivened and consoled. At home, on the benches in front of shops, at a tavern, people liked to eat and drink with friends and family. Indeed, these shared activities, necessary but comforting, marked a human bond. They reinforced old ties and forged new ones. We have a word for this phenomenon, *commensality*, whose Latin roots mean "sharing a table." Those who do so are *companions*; the word itself once meant "sharers of bread." Commensality suggested friendship and alliance. Magistrates probing a crime therefore often asked, "Do they eat together? Do they drink together?" One witness, struck by the ironic falling out, replied, "The two of them were companions, and that very day [that the one knifed the other over a woman], they had drunk together."[1] Judges also asked if suspects "had slept together." The issue was not sex, but friendly bonds woven by the sociable pleasures of conversation and rest under a shared blanket.

Renaissance Italians also sought to stimulate the senses. Much of leisure went into walking, standing, or sitting and just seeing or hearing pretty things, both natural and contrived. The eye was paramount. It loved a landscape or an urban prospect, a handsome man, woman, or animal, a shimmering gown, a virtuoso painting, a well-laid feast, a harmonious facade, a fine machine, and countless other sights. Playful eyes not only admired but also inquired, marveled, gawked, scowled, and leered, for they enjoyed social as well as natural scenes. They delighted in festive pageants and relished banal dramas, accidents, and prodigies. Second came the ear. It enjoyed birdsong, bells, music, and the splash of fountains—delights that nature or art provided. The ear and mind also reveled in talk in all its forms: storytelling, poetry, wit, news, and gossip. Other senses, although high culture courted them less, had their recreations too. Smell savored flowers, perfumes, and incense. Taste lapped the sweetness of fruit, the tang of garlic, and the zest of pepper, cinnamon, and ginger. Touch skimmed the smooth nap of velvet, the slickness of worn leather, and the softness of human skin.

## TIMES AND PLACES TO PLAY

Play had its special times. Holidays, both local and universal, stood out, as did those special occasions— a peace, a coronation, a princely birth or wedding, a royal cntry —when a town downed tools to celebrate **Times for Leisure and Amusement** (see Chapter 10). There were also seasons. In Venice, mid-August to Christmas was a time for interparish rivalry, in the form of games, festivals, and fights.[2] In much of Italy, the spring, from Easter to Pentecost, was the time for courtship, which invited jousts, parades, and dances.

Carnival, the giddy prelude to lean and sober Lent, was the season *par excellence* for fun and wildness. Carnival was fat, bibulous, and ribald. A hierarchic society with sharp rules about rank, age, gender, and comportment badly needed time out to let loose. Its sport took many forms. One was formal theater; in cities and villages, amateurs and professionals staged plays in palaces and streets. Another form of play, almost theater, was masquerade. Carnival put on masks that, by obscuring the honor-bearing face, unleashed impudence. Protected by disguise, people broke rules, refusing deference, flirting outrageously, and courting violence. Like some other Renaissance play, Carnival had a cruel streak. A gentle form was throwing eggs; from carriages and balconies, from horseback and the street, Italians pelted one another. Some eggs were benign— gilded and charged with perfume; others were putrid. Lacking eggs, one could always fall back on snowballs, turnips, rotten apples, glops of mud, and assorted garbage. A second minor cruelty was satire, in verse, mime, and costume. A third version, more vicious, was the harassment of animals, tormented and killed to amuse the crowd. Venice staged with pomp a slaughter in Saint Mark's square; Rome rolled pigs in carts down hills. A fourth cruelty figured in some races, such as the famous rowdy four in Rome where "naked" Jews (actually clad in turbans, shoes, and drawers), old men, donkeys, and placid mozzarella buffaloes were forced to compete; all these contestants had to run the length of town past jeering, jostling, filth-throwing spectators.[3] Rome had slightly nobler but still raucous races for higher prizes, as did other towns. In many cities, wider, tradition-bred violence broke out in massed fights between neighborhoods. Everywhere, Carnival was a reprieve from order, a season for seductions and for settling accounts with blood. For those who came through unscathed, the experience was cathartic; it fortified them against the austere Lenten piety to come.

**Green Spaces: Countryside, Gardens, and Villas**
    Perhaps because their civilization was urban, Renaissance Italians loved taking leisure amid space, light, good air, and greenery. So they often fled their domestic haunts and workplaces in search of natural settings that soothed and stimulated town-worn senses. Riverbanks were popular for strolling and fishing. Rivers and lakes welcomed swimmers and boaters, and, on the rare occasion when they froze solid, invited games, races, and even an impromptu market.[4] But the sea was not to toy with; beaches were for working fishermen, not for play. Another natural site for recreation were the hot springs scattered across volcanic western Italy. People believed in the curative powers of these mineral waters. Some of these attracted so many patients that a spa life sprang up, with hostelry and social gatherings. Montaigne devoted much of his Italian voyage to long cures for his kidney stones. He soaked at length in hot and tepid pools, drank prodigious quantities of smelly water, and chronicled his belly's every stirring. Between aquatic moments, he attended dances, exchanged gifts and courtesies, and enjoyed the company of well-born seekers after health.[5]

A convenient green space for urban play was a *vigna*.[6] Literally, the term means "vineyard," but the typical *vigna* also sported fruit trees and vegetables and might house rabbits, chickens, or pigeons. Many such small farming plots lay close at hand, on cities' outskirts. Their owners often lived in town, hired a *vignerolo* to work them in exchange for part of the crop, and used them for outings in good weather. Roman court records are full of *vigna* matters—not only squabbles over boundary ditches and fences or over thefts of fruit and water but also troubles arising from play gone awry: raucous parties, seductions, and brawls. A trial in July 1563 shows a police official, Captain Ottavio, riding back at dusk one Sunday from his vineyard to the pleasant sound of a lute and a woman singing. Returning with the captain from his picnic were a band of friends, kinsmen, and servants, some with swords and halberds and others with musical instruments. The party included two clergymen, a prosecutor and his wife, a butcher, the captain's own son and daughter, several serving men and women, and five Jews wearing the yellow hats required of them by law. One of these, elderly, paunchy, bearded, and bent, was Mastro Abraham, strumming his lute as he rode. To avoid nonkosher meat, the Jewish guests, said Abraham, dined at a small table of their own, off bread and cucumber salad. In the growing gloom, as the captain's party descended a steep, narrow road toward town, a pack train, outward bound, forced the women's horses against a looming wall. "The street is plenty large! No need to crowd the ladies," the captain said. Harsh words ricocheted, and soon the captain's servants, taking up another common recreation, hurled stones on top of insults at the departing drivers. Had his men but known that the drivers were the pope's own grooms carrying in their baskets a fragile gift of wine from their master to a great lord, they would have been more discreet, the flustered captain later told the judge.[7] Note how mixed the excursion's company had been; clergy, laity, men, women, Christians, Jews, parents and their offspring, masters and their servants had, on a summer afternoon, enjoyed food and music together amid suburban greenery.

Renaissance Italians not only took pleasure from the working landscape; they also loved to reshape it—as garden and villa—into artful forms. Lacking the modern cult of nature as raw wilderness, they preferred a pleasant, safe, and ordered domain stocked with flora and fauna of their choosing. This appetite and the building projects that it fed had a long pedigree. The ancient Romans had been great builders of villas and gardens. Cicero, among others, had praised such retreats for fostering a civilized life of leisure and contemplation. Later the walled medieval garden and monastic cloister hearkened back to Near Eastern images of paradise (the word, in old Persian, meant "garden"). Renaissance landscape architects and their wealthy patrons, steeped in humanistic admiration of classical ways, transformed the simple medieval close, with its modest geometric plots of herbs and flowers, into a far more ambitious space, traversed by tunneled arbors and well-laid lanes and ornamented by intricately patterned beds, fountains, pools, ancient and modern statuary, and artificial grottoes. Sometimes peacocks pecked and strutted under the orange, lemon, pear, and laurel trees. Grander gardens had wide lanes for running horses and for jousting, and paths for bowling and mallet ball.[8]

The gardens of the rich figured in Renaissance intellectual and cultural life, both sober and playful. Circles of learned men met under the trees to discuss politics, religion, and literature, to declaim poems and orations, or to hear music. These gatherings also punned and joked; participants might take on fancy, mock-serious Latin or Greek names and celebrate a literary hero or debate an outlandish proposition. Many gardens were also open to the public; some posted Latin inscriptions citing ancient Roman customs of inviting strollers to enjoy them. Montaigne reports his uninvited visits to those in Rome and remarks that not only could one enjoy the birds, fish, and art, one could even take a nap.[9]

Some elegant Renaissance gardens were built in or near the city, while others attached to pretty rural mansions called villas. These were a Renaissance development, as the more violent Middle Ages had discouraged country building for sheer pleasure. Like the ancient Romans they admired, urban elites retreated to a villa to relax with rural pastimes—strolling, riding, and hunting—and to delight and awe their guests.

Many Renaissance villas thus grew out of earlier farms or forts, but transformed them with elegant, classicizing pavilions and grounds. While owners did often oversee leisured agriculture, many villas put beauty and entertainment well ahead of function. Fanciful waterworks, a clever marriage of art and engineering, were a favorite showpiece. Many of the famous sixteenth-century fountains of the Cardinal d'Este at Tivoli still spout and spray. In their heyday, these great set-pieces featured a water-driven musical organ and singing birds of bronze that fell silent at the approach of the statue of an owl. There were also practical jokes, hidden nozzles, triggered by trick paving stones, to douse the unsuspecting guest, and oozing benches with tiny pores, to soak unwary bottoms.[10]

**Urban Settings: Homes, Streets, Taverns, and Brothels**

The house or palace was a prime site for play. The basic pleasures of eating, drinking, sleeping, and keeping company often took place at home. Occasionally there would be parties, celebrating Carnival or a wedding. But recreation, especially for women, also reached out from domestic space with the eyes, ears, and voice. Women idled at their windows, watching and commenting on the passing theater of street life. For processions, races, and other spectacles, they dressed up to be seen at their sills; they were part of the show. The doorstep was another woman's place; there are countless tales of conversations in the street and of children playing out front, under female eyes. Another pleasure was just to soak up a view. In the late fifteenth century, the Renaissance invented a high porch or gallery called a *belvedere*: the name means "Nice view!" The most famous belvedere, a long, high passage atop the Vatican, still bears the name and murals by Raphael's workshop. Roofed for shade and lit by ample windows, these elevated perches let one catch the sun or breeze while chatting and feasting the eye.

City streets also were playgrounds. While nonelite women did move about town and gather at fountains and washing places for sociability as well as work, it was more often men who took their ease away from home, in one another's shops, or walking about *a spasso* (for pleasure). Peddlers sold hot chestnuts in season and *ciambelle*, circular cakes, fast food for strollers. Horseback riding was another male recreation in the streets, and from the sixteenth century on, women and mixed company took to coaches.

A favorite spot for sociable recreation was the tavern. It served the lower classes especially, and more men than women. Simple wine shops and slightly grander inns with beds and stables were everywhere, in towns and villages and along the road. At some, strangers mingled, while others served a local clientele. People drank, ate, and took their ease, warming themselves by the fire, telling stories, gambling at dice and cards, singing, dancing, flirting, and sometimes brawling.[11] They also passed news, made deals and, trials prove, plotted crimes. (To find a good hit-man, scout a tavern.) Naturally, preachers eternally flayed the inns, dens of vice and distractions from attending mass. No less naturally, inns flourished. An early sixteenth-century Florentine devotional painting with nine framed scenes—the pious tale of a man who drank, gambled, lost, cursed, stomped off to stone an image of the holy Virgin, was condemned to hang, and died repentant—begins with a fine, if homely, picture of the tavern where the trouble all began.[12] The Inn of the Fig, as portrayed, was a simple affair, a courtyard paved in rough flagstones and with one big table lined with benches. A wall sports a mural of a woman and a big fig tree. The three fateful dice lie on the table; while one player dozes off, another, the winner, raises his hands in exclamation as the loser, a devil at his ear, stalks off raging. To one side is a crude bench with a simple tablecloth, a jug, and two ceramic mugs. To the other is an indoor kitchen open to the courtyard, where a servant ladles food from two wide bowls resting on a cloth-covered table. Devil aside, we see tavern life at its most normal: food, drink, play, sleep, and dudgeon.

Another important place of recreation was the red-light district. Although both honor and religion sternly condemned the prostitute, commerce with her had little stigma. This paradox had complex roots. Medieval theology acknowledged prostitution as a necessary evil that served public hygiene, as did a sewer. For much of the Renaissance, therefore, city fathers allowed districts of toleration. The trade protected the established sexual order, as it distracted men from seducing chaste women. Furthermore, in the eyes of honor, unlike the sexuality of females, that of unmarried males—unless directed toward other men, as Florentine civic authorities, in particular, feared—was no great vice. Prostitutes' customers did no harm because the women had no more shame to lose. Accordingly, young men of every social class readily invited friends and colleagues to join them at the house of their current hired lover. There they ate, drank, diced, played cards, sang, heard visiting musicians, danced, gossiped, joked, and flirted. The more refined courtesans might recite poetry and raise conversation to an art. Although there was much kissing and embracing in front of all, sex itself was usually more private, the paying customer withdrawing with the woman behind a bedroom door or at least into a separate bed. Many men came along just for the company. As at the tavern, in the brothel the mix of drink and gambling, here aggravated by flashes of sexual jealousy, made for frequent brawling and sudden bloodshed. Authorities therefore often strove to disarm and police these hot zones.

### AN EVENING CHEZ ALESSANDRA

In 1557, Francesco, a Roman tailor, was suspected of a theft. To supply him an alibi before the magistrates, Alessandra, a prostitute, described a normal evening in her quarters. The food the men supplied came from an inn.

> If I remember well, it was Thursday evening, around the second hour of the night. [8 P.M.] Francesco came to my house with three companions; one of them was Geronimo, and Paganino the book-seller, and another one I do not know. And they brought supper, though they hadn't said they intended to come have supper with me. Each one of them brought something, but I don't know who paid. They brought bread, wine, and roast and stewed meat. In my house, there was my mother, and her husband, who is called Antonio, and there was me. At that time, my sister, Caterina, was in jail. There were seven of us in all, and after we ate, we kidded around until the fourth hour of the night, and then two of them left, and two stayed, that is Geronimo and Francesco stayed to sleep in my house. . . . And both of them slept in a bed of my sister's, in the bedroom. I slept on a mattress in the same room, near their bed.[13]

Alessandra claimed that she had sexual relations only with Francesco and that Geronimo just spent the night.

## ACTIVITIES

**Music and Dance**  Renaissance people produced and consumed music prodigiously. Many slipped readily between performing and listening. The streets were full of song. Some artisans, if we can believe *novelle*, sang Dante's poetry while working. In Chapter 15, Antonio ambled to his sudden death, singing as he drove his mule. Idlers in the evening sat on steps, picking on the lute-like stringed *chitarra*. Gypsies played in search of coin. Revelers, on a shaming expedition, attacked their victims with a nocturnal serenade of insult songs, strumming and caterwauling below the windows. Groups too had their street music: soldiers marched to drums and trumpets; clergy and devout laity processed to psalms and *laudes*, songs of praise to God. Not only religious liturgy, but secular events—pageants, jousts, and banquets—came with music. For courts, composers developed new polyphonic musical forms, combining multiple voices and instruments in motets and madrigals. Performers, such as Laura Peverara and the women singers at Ferrara, helped shape these innovations (see Chapter 2). Toward 1600, song, dance, and storytelling were yoked to create the first ballets and operas. About the same time, music, prayer, and sacred narrative merged to produce the oratorio. Many Italians studied with music masters to learn to play the clavichord, a proto-harpsichord, and other instruments and to sing sophisticated harmonies to amuse themselves and friends.

One job of music was to animate the dance, a pastime central to Renaissance festivity, fun for both participants and spectators. At court and elsewhere, dance marked special occasions. Weddings, May Day, and Carnival were prime occasions. Jews danced for Purim, their early spring holiday, much like Carnival, full of wine, masks, and mischief. The rather formal dances of the court we know fairly well from paintings, written accounts of celebrations, and manuals by dancing masters. Elite dance both fed off and fed a vital popular tradition, one we can see far less well. At its most flamboyant, court dance produced great allegorical or mythological pageants, splendid with costumes and stage machinery, where the prince inevitably danced Hercules or Zeus, while the squires and maids-in-waiting played mere centaurs, nymphs, and shepherdesses. Other court performances featured couples, who took turns showing off their steps. On less formal occasions, sometimes in the women's quarters, courtiers danced for their own delight.

Renaissance dance, in its rhythms and movements, was unlike modern. On the beat, dancers rose, not fell. They held their upper bodies gracefully upright, keeping their hands mostly low. The lively movement was in the legs, where complicated steps, kicks, hops, and stamps showed style and virtuosity. Improvisation was prized. Men, in their hose and short tunics, had more room—and encouragement—to show off. Images of dancing usually show them kicking merrily, while their female partners, demure in long gowns, lift a hem to reveal not feet, but a fancy undergown. Though encumbered by skirts and proprieties, women dancers were still much admired for skill and elegance. Sometimes a girl soloed with her teacher to entertain the court. Images also often feature women dancing in circles, holding hands. The elite danced to small bands of a drum, pipes, and several shawms (like oboes); peasants often resorted to bagpipes. Tempos varied from the slow *bassa dansa* to the quick *saltarello* and *piva*.

Choreography was richly varied. Group dances shared much with modern country or square dancing, forms descended from Renaissance court dance. For example, couples held one another by the hand, waist, or shoulder; in facing rows or circles, they "reverenced" or honored one another and moved through symmetrical patterns. While many dances enacted courtship, only a few featured close embraces. Some dances were games, and some for men mimed combat. Dancing masters recorded, invented, and published steps, carrying court forms far and wide. Their skills were in great demand, for dance figured in the curriculum of schools for nobles and aspiring bourgeois, for whom good footwork was a social grace. Masters even gave lessons in villages. Commoners, schooled or self-taught, danced for their own pleasure, but sometimes also entertained the public. One Roman Carnival company, led by a stocking maker and including a weaver, a slipper maker, a saddler, and a shoemaker, turns up practicing their *moresca* in a cardinal's garden before performing in the city.[14]

---

## HOW TO BOW

In this dancing lesson, delivered in the characteristic Renaissance form of dialogue, a master (M) instructs a humorously dull disciple (D) on how to bow:

D.  Please tell me whence comes this term, "Reverence"?

M.  This term derives from "to revere," since by humbling your body a bit, drawing back your left foot [and] bending your knees a little, you revere that person toward whom you make a *Reverence*.

D.  With which foot should it be done—with your right foot, or with your left?

M.  Let me say that it should always be done with your left foot.

D.  Why with your left, and not with your right? For you have just told me, Sir, that in doffing your bonnet, you must use your right hand, since it is nobler than your left. Please clarify this point for me.

M.  You should make a *Reverence* with your left foot for the following reasons. First, your right foot provides strength and stability for your body, and since it is its fortress, you should do this movement with your left foot, because it is weaker than your right; now this is the first reason. The second is that you honor that individual who is close to your heart and toward whom you wish to make a *Reverence*, and since your left foot is the limb corresponding to the side wherein your heart lies, you should always make it with your left foot.[15]

---

**Spectacles**     The pleasure of attending music and dance performances belonged to a larger Renaissance love of spectacles. Because big events were expensive, elites staged most of them. Church and secular leaders, corporate bodies, and private persons all put on shows, for themselves and for society at large. Their goals were mixed and multiple: sponsors sought to trumpet their own honor and authority or to cajole and distract a restless populace or to legitimate a policy. Spectators—often taking time off work—flocked to marvel and gawk, to listen and react, to learn and affirm, to find excitement and solace. Even where religion or politics were at stake, the experience partook of play.

Italian Catholicism had dramatic genius. It deployed spectacle to praise God and the saints, make politics, reform morals, raise hopes, and, in the sixteenth century, to secure faith and loyalty in the face of the Protestant challenge. Renaissance churches were full of dazzling art. The liturgy, with its lights, music, incense, and fine vestments, charmed the senses. Sermons, processions, and holy plays drew rapt crowds. There were more intimate dramas too. People would go to watch a public exorcism, the harrowing struggle of a priest to drive reluctant demons from a writhing patient. Be the event grand or modest, Renaissance Italians were no mere idle spectators at religious ceremonies. They came—often as penitents or pilgrims, or even as a preacher's vocal audience—to be moved and touched by grace and to lend their prayers to God's work.

The civic liturgy of states, cities, towns, and even villages had things in common with religion. Though grace was not at stake, excitement, awe, and communal fellow feeling again were goals. Like the church, the state had music, speeches, processions, great gatherings for cheers and tears. A victory, a peace, a prince's wedding, the feast day of a patron saint, a royal entry, or a good execution (see Chapter 7) set in motion the machinery of solemnity. Bells, cannons, bonfires, fireworks, torches, colorful finery and glittering metal on men and beasts, the blare of trumpets, the thump of drums and marching feet, the clatter of massed hooves: all put on a show to shiver the spine and stir the soul.

Private spectacles too might open up to public eyes. In the early Renaissance especially, magnates still held great feasts in street-side loggias, under the gaze of passers-by. As time went on and social distance grew, such events withdrew into palaces and gardens. Withdrawn or not, great banquets caught public notice; the proto-journalist *avvisi* authors often published breathless accounts of heaped-up magnificence. Renaissance banquets were far more than too much food on long tables. The silent precision of the liveried servants, the dexterity of the head carver, the dazzling dishes of gold and silver, the lights, the music, the costumed dances, and the display of the food itself all feasted the eye and ear. There were food tricks: live rabbits, birds, or piglets baked into a pie, while the guests feasted on their late brethren. Fish swimming in aspic. Roast birds refeathered. And edible statues of antique gods, and course on course, in dazzling variety, for hours and hours. Besides banquets, other private ceremonies entertained and moved the public; weddings and funerals brought kin and guests into the streets, in procession, dressed for the occasion.

Unlike us, who curb the violence of our sports—boxing and North American hockey excepted—Renaissance Italians relished violent play. They watched it and massively took zestful part. Their real warfare not rarely had its play- **Competition and Combat** ful side, and much of their play was warlike. The Middle Ages had imparted a tradition of fighting for fun. In many Italian towns of the early Renaissance, teams of young men, marshaled by their captains, would march on the chosen day to the field, square, or bridge appointed for battle. Their adversaries almost always were fellow townsmen, from another parish or quarter, ancestral enemies against whom they sang insulting songs and shouted slogans. Or there might have been a provocatory sally, when a few made a mad armed dash by into hostile ter-

Football match with house-shaped goals and few holds barred.
[Bertelli]

ritory.[16] Then, the notion was to storm in, often mounted, to taunt
adversaries or cow them with a show of force, and then to scoot back
home before the defenders fielded a response. On the big day itself,
fighters came armed with swords and clubs of hardened wood and with
wicker shields and helmets. A clash, with its single combats and grand
melee, could go on for hours. Almost always, there were wounded and,
not rarely, several corpses.

This violence provoked opposition but was only slowly tamed. The
usual preachers preached their usual sermons, and town councils passed
countless futile ordinances. Yet Renaissance sportive brawling throve in
Carnival and burst readily forth whenever neighborhoods or parishes
skirmished for place, as when marshaling a procession. Only very gradually did the mayhem lose its cutting edge. Swords and clubs yielded to
stones and fists, but those remained in plenty. In Venice, against the
general trend, fistfighting throve well into the eighteenth century, much
applauded by the elite, who backed champion pugilists and flocked to
see the bridge-top fist wars from their gondolas, keeping just a little back
to avoid the knots of brawling men who tumbled still grappling into the
canal (see illustration in Chapter 9).

The sons of the Renaissance elite gradually deserted street fighting for
safer, more elegant forms of combat. Patricians increasingly turned to
expensive formal competitions, based on revived rites of chivalry. Drawing on the mythology laid out in medieval romance, they played at a
world of knights in shining armor who undertook military contests to
win honor and the hand of a lady love. Well-born sponsors of ritual

fighting wrapped the whole occasion in fancy rhetoric, writing pompous challenges and evoking allegories of love, youth, fidelity, and other overblown virtues. The elaborate ceremonies and play combats enacted by Renaissance lordlings partook more of nostalgic fantasy than of the robust crudity of real medieval warfare. The tourney, for example, was a set-piece mock battle, with field combat and perhaps a siege or naval fight. The joust pitched riders, lance in arm, one on one, against one another, or ran them at a target, perhaps a dummy or a hanging ring. Lance splitting set riders noisily ramming their weapons against a wall or other barrier. All three sports featured gorgeous costumes and fancy horsemanship. Helmet plumes stood up to six feet tall. Riders wore costly armor, exquisitely wrought and flashing with gems, and rode fine horses mantled in brocaded coats and rigged with jingling bells and sparkling trim. Alongside the splendid fighters were troops of retainers on foot, adorned at their leader's expense in his colors and devices. The whole spectacle had undertones of courtship; the ladies were part of the show. It fell to them to praise riders and accept dedicated prizes. Mounting a tourney was costly. Besides the equipment of the combatants, there were jousting barriers to rig and seats and judges' booths to install. In addition, sponsors paid for the floats and other decorations, a lavish banquet, and, from the fifteenth century on, sometimes a finale with fireworks. While both these spectacles and the neighborhood street battles had their rituals, the expense and the feudal trappings set the former apart. The chivalric nostalgia fit the aristocratic ambitions of elite Renaissance families and prettified the autocracy of regimes. Ironically, the resuscitated medievalism coincided with the rise to supremacy in real warfare of gunnery, grisly nemesis of the mounted knight.

Hunting and fishing that long had supplemented commoners' diet, though akin to work, also had their pleasures. A judge once asked a witness, "Are you and the suspect friends?" He answered, "At times we fished together, and he told me one thing and another."[17] Thus, like commensality, a shared river bank, rod in hand, signaled alliance. Bird catching too was companionable; it was a beloved subject of sixteenth-century and later art, a cloying image of rustic sociability. Italians ate birds of every size and shape. They had ingenious devices for catching them: gooey limed twigs, hidden nets, caged songbirds to call the wild ones down, dummy birds of prey, and insidious baited traps.

**Animals and Leisure: From Blood Sport to Pets**

In the later Middle Ages, lords increasingly shouldered ordinary folk out of hunting, and even fishing. They laid claim to communal woodlands and river rights, selling fishing privileges for money and grabbing for themselves the meatier, more prestigious big game: boar and deer. Princes built great hunting lodges, with stables and kennels, to support

The end of the hunt: a horse laden
with game. [Tempesta]

lavish expeditions for dozens, even hundreds of participants. Nonetheless, by the Renaissance, rising population and shrinking habitat had in many regions reduced the nobles' hunt. Pockets survived in the valley of the Po and the empty landscape near Rome. There, hunting continued as a grand affair, a fancy picnic crossed with butchery. Popes, cardinals, and princes did not chase their victims but camped at a suitable spot. Then they waited while a horde of dogs, mounted huntsmen, and beaters traversed the woodland, barking, shouting, thrashing the underbrush, and applying smoke to drive the wild animals toward cloth enclosures and nets, where the patrons could slaughter them at leisure.

Our notion that animals may have rights or feelings worth respecting never crossed the Renaissance mind. Alongside the hunt were other cruelties. An animal's death struggle was a common entertainment, not only during Carnival but also at other times. There were still bears enough to furnish an occasional bear-baiting. Many cities staged bullfights; Naples had a *corrida*, with cape and sword on the classic Spanish model, but elsewhere the fight was more a crazy melee, as at Pamplona now, but bloodier, as men with swords and spears dodged and thrust among the animals. In 1584, a Roman duke, to show his wealth, staged a three-way fight, pitting a lion against a bull and dogs. To spectators' chagrin, the lion, terrified of the bull, wasted his ferocity on the dogs.[18] To make sense of this, remember that Italians saw death, animal and human, all the time. What amused them here was not agony but the unpredictable

Baiting a bull with an ear-biting dog. [Bertelli]

fight and the ticklish confusion of the boundary between beasts and men locked in struggle.

Cruelty to some animals did not prevent kindness to others. Renaissance Italians, both nobles and commoners, kept pets. Medieval falconry was fading by 1600, but caged songbirds gladdened houses. Some people had favorite horses or hunting dogs or beloved smaller canines. The duke of Mantua had painted into the famous family portrait in the Camera degli Sposi some of his beloved dogs, including a woolly-coated spinoni and a huge red-brown beast snuggled under the ducal throne. In the city, many a quarrel flared over a dog stolen, borrowed overlong, or hurt. Women sometimes fondly nursed puppies, like children, at the breast. Cats were another matter, good for catching mice but usually beneath respect or love. Still, since courtesy books warned against letting them onto the table at meals, they must have prowled the palace.

---

## A PET BIRD AT THE SCENE OF THE CRIME

The following vignette of almost cinematic irony is in the words of a young man in the bird cage trade.[19] Captain Giacomo, the victim of imminent murder, had brought in his cage for repair.

And Captain Giacomo stayed there in the shop. He was standing, leaning on the counter, and dragging back and forth some little bags, and a green bird was pulling its food and drink from him, for it was inside those little bags. And while the bird was pulling the bags with his beak—they were tied by a string—Captain Giacomo was pulling them away, and the bird kept coming back to pull them up. And while Captain Giacomo was standing like that with his back to the street, I saw a man come in through the door of the shop, and without a word, with a broad dagger, or perhaps a Pistoia-knife, he struck Captain Giacomo on the head with the cutting edge.

---

**Games**   Children and adults alike played a multitude of games. They ranged from cards, dice, and chess to more athletic stick-throwing and jumping contests. There was also an array of more or less orderly ball games. There was a form of indoor tennis, with leather, down-filled balls, and a raucous kind of wall-ball, where one struggled to catch the rebound. Renaissance Italians already had a game like modern *bocce*, an outdoor form of bowling. A very popular pastime was *palla maglia* (mallet ball), a robust ancestor of croquet. They also played *pallone*, a rough-and-tumble kind of football with shielded arms in play. These sports were male. Girls were more confined; we see them less in outdoor pictures and know less about their games. They certainly played, but more often in the house, courtyard, and garden than in the street.

---

### A PALLONE MATCH

The English traveler Thomas Coryate described a holiday *pallone* match that entertained both players and hundreds of watchers:

> Every Sunday and holy day in the evening the young men of the city do exercise themselves at a certain play that they call Balloon, which is thus: six or seven young men or thereabout wear certain round things upon their arms made of timber, which are full of sharp pointed knobs cut out of the same matter. In these exercises they put off their doublets, and having put this round instrument upon one of their arms, they toss up and down a great ball . . . ; sometimes they will toss the ball with this instrument, as high as a common church, and about one hundred paces at least from them. About them sit the Clarissimos [gentlemen] of Venice, with many strangers that repair thither to see their game. I have seen at least a thousand or fifteen hundred people there. If you will have a stool, it will cost you a gazette, which is almost a penny.[20]

---

Dice and cards were among the most common games. Playing cards were already on the scene from the 1370s on, but only in the sixteenth century did cheap decks spread. By the seventeenth, they were ubiquitous; ragged card players perched on wagons, walls, or handy lumps of ruin became a painter's emblem of the daily life of commoners. As for the dice games, there were several variants. In one, a player called out

Gambler risking body and soul. [Bertarelli: Gioco]

the total of three dice before the throw. In another, called *zara*, contestants moved colored pieces—squares, circles, stars—on a checkered board, taking turns. If one threw a seven or less, or a fourteen or more, one lost one's turn. Players, when blocked, shouted "*Zara!*" A good moment to add an oath or two! Another favorite sedentary game, *morra*, required no equipment. Much like our "rock, paper, and scissors," it required the players to guess how many fingers would be extended. At the inn, drinkers played *morra* to see who had to pay for the next round.

Men and women of all ages and classes were addicted to betting. They wagered on dice and cards and *morra*, and also on future events: who would be elected pope or what sex a child would have. Some operators made a living off this appetite, making book, renting out dice and tables, or, like the Florentine diplomat Buonaccorso Pitti, playing for high stakes. This love of gambling horrified moralists, both clerical and lay. To them, betting was the ruin of fortunes, the calamity of heirs; it gave rise to fights and provoked blasphemy. At the same time, gambling appealed to the taste for risk and to the sense of strategy and calculation so central to Italian culture. Furthermore, although it made for quarreling, it also sometimes bolstered alliances. There can be solidarity in sustained rivalry; in many societies, internal foes often lock ranks swiftly against outside enemies. This fact could hold for partners at dice, as it did for the squalling fistfight factions of Pisa, Venice, and Siena, fierce patriots all. Gambling also spun webs of debt, and debt, though fractious, also sustained solidarities. (See Chapter 7.)

As with prostitution, rather than strive in vain to banish vice, regimes often sought to curtail and channel gambling. Campaigns to abolish betting met dogged popular resistance. The captain of a Maltese privateer, according to the memoirs of the Spanish buccaneer Contreras, to avoid the usual ructions tossed overboard all dice and cards. Undaunted, the crew of many nations carved concentric circles on the deck; then each man rummaged in hair and clothes, caught his racing louse, placed it in the center, and, at the signal, cheered its progress to the finish line. Winner took all. The captain just gave up.[21] Unlike the thwarted captain, many governments tried compromise. Some authorities permitted gambling only on certain days or in certain places. They preferred to keep the danger out in the open. Others, to profit from what they could not quench, auctioned off the rights to run a gaming house.

---

### A CROOKED GAMBLER

Ascanio Giustini, the son of a prominent Roman lawyer, disgraced his family as a notorious cheat. (We met Ascanio in Chapter 6, in a slanging match and sword fight with his brothers.) Below, from a trial of 1555, is testimony against him by a noble partner at *primiera*, a cousin of poker where one bets from a four-card hand. He was asked if he had ever seen Ascanio cheat:

> Your Lordship, yes, I have seen him cheat. For once he was playing with me, and I had a 49. Ascanio showed me a 51. He had a card, slipped under another, so you could not see it. But Asdrubale Sanguigni made me a sign that he [Ascanio] had another card hidden underneath, so I pulled out the cards that he had in his hand and discovered the other card, and found that there were five of them. I got furious, and he returned my money. Another time, I saw him do the same thing when he was playing with messer Pier Nicola, that when the cards came into his hand, and he was dealing, sometimes he took five, but in such a way that Vincenzo and the others weren't aware of it, but I, who was watching, saw it. And I am sure he did this on purpose, for he never showed his cards [at the hand's end]. . . . He also brought loaded dice, and he settled down to play with me, with Giulio Girone, Antonio di Gallesio, Pier Nicola and others. And when I and the other men saw that he always made things go his way with these dice, we sent out to purchase other dice. And when he played, he would always let the dice fall onto the floor, and when he went to look for them, he would fetch his own [instead], in such a way that nobody noticed. And we kept playing with those dice of his, and we thought we were playing with our own, the ones we had sent out for. And at the end of the game, Giulio Girone wanted to keep the dice, and Ascanio replied that they were his. When Giulio said that they were his, Ascanio left and took his dice. And that time he won a lot of *scudi*.[22]

---

## CONCLUSION

Sociability and theatricality pervaded almost all the activities we have seen. They ran through Carnival and other spectacles, through fighting, hunting, and gambling. They also shaped gardens, villas, palaces, and churches—spaces crafted as backdrops to events. Theatricality even touched ordinary conversations, learned and rough. A dissenter might object: there was always reading! Point well taken! But the quiet, solitary novel reader had not yet been invented, nor had the companionable novel. In the Renaissance, very often one read aloud, often to others. The learned did sometimes retreat to the privacy of the *studio*, there to ponder, alone—as did Machiavelli, fallen from his job, in his tedious rural exile from Florence and politics. Nevertheless, even in his solitude, Machiavelli did not shrug drama off. At the climax of what is probably the Renaissance's most famous private letter, he describes to his friend Francesco Vettori how, after a day of country trivia, he returns to his true friends, his books:

> When evening comes, I return home and go into my study. On the threshold I strip off the muddy, sweaty clothes of everyday, and put on the robes of court and palace, and in this graver dress I enter the antique courts of the ancients where, being welcomed by them, I taste the food that alone is mine, for which I was born. And there I make bold to speak to them and ask the motives of their actions. And they, in their humanity, reply to me.[23]

Machiavelli's robes of court and palace may have been ironic metaphors, not real, but his idea illustrates a feature of his culture. Even reading, that most reclusive entertainment, as he pictured it to self and friend, was a form of play, a conversation, a social moment for the spirit. One had to dress the part, as always.

## NOTES

1. Archivio di Stato di Roma (ASR), Governatore, Tribunale Criminale, Atti 22, 484v (1557).

2. Robert Davis, "The Trouble with Bulls," *Social History/Histoire Sociale* 29: 58 (1996), 288.

3. On the races in Rome, M. Boiteux, "Carnaval annexé," *Annales: Economies, Sociétés, Civilisations*, 32: 2 (1977), 356–377. The Italian buffalo is not a bison but a cousin of the Asian water buffalo.

4. For the frozen Arno, see Robert Davidsohn, *Storia di Firenze*, v. 7 (Florence: Sansoni, 1965), 552; on games, see 541–619.

5. Michel de Montaigne, "Travel Journal," in *Complete Works*, trans. D. Frame (Stanford: Stanford University Press, 1958) 983–1002, 1012–1013, 1016–1021.

6. On the *vigna*, see David R. Coffin, *The Villa in the Life of Renaissance Rome* (Princeton: Princeton University Press, 1979), 16–22.

7. ASR, Governatore, Tribunale Criminale, Processi sixteenth century, b. 85, case 9 (1563).

8. On jousts and *palla maglia*, see David R. Coffin, *Gardens and Gardening in*

*Papal Rome* (Princeton: Princeton University Press, 1991), 227–229, and for enter-tainment in general, 227–243.

9. Montaigne, "Travel Journal," 960, cited with discussion in Coffin, *Gardens and Gardening*, 248.

10. For villa fountains, see Coffin, *Gardens and Gardening*, 28–57 and for the birds, 54. For Tivoli, see Coffin, *The Villa*, 311–340, and for the squirts and oozing benches, 327.

11. For taverns, see a superb article by Giovanni Cherubini, "La taverna nel basso Medioevo," in *Il lavoro, la taverna, la strada: scorci di Medioevo* (Naples: Liguori editore, 1997), 191–224.

12. William J. Connell and Giles Constable, "Sacrilege and Redemption in Renaissance Florence: The Case of Antonio Rinaldeschi," *Journal of the Warburg and Courtauld Institutes* 61 (1998), 53–92 and especially 59, for the picture.

13. ASR, Governatore, Tribunale Criminale, Atti 22, 51r-v (1557).

14. Ibid., Costituti 526, 167v-71r (1603).

15. "Rules for Dancing," in *Nobiltà di Dame. Fabritio Caroso*, ed. J. Sutton (New York: Oxford University Press), 97. On dancing, see also Guglielmo Ebreo of Pesaro, *De Pratica seu Arte Tripudii. On the Art and Practice of Dancing*, ed. B. Sparti (Oxford: Oxford University Press, 1993).

16. On Venetian sallies, see Davis, "Bulls," 288, and Robert Davis, *The War of the Fists: Popular Culture and Public Violence in Late Renaissance Venice* (New York: Oxford University Press, 1994), 59.

17. ASR, Governatore, Tribunale Criminale, Costituti 52, 34r (1557).

18. Coffin, *Gardens and Gardening*, 228.

19. ASR, Governatore, Tribunale Criminale, Processi sixteenth century, b. 85, case 14, 492r-v (1563).

20. Thomas Coryate, *Coryat's Crudities*, v. 1 (Glasgow: James MacLehose and Sons, 1905), 385.

21. Alonso de Contreras, *The Adventures of Captain Alonso de Contreras*, trans. P. Dallas (New York: Paragon House, 1989), 23–24. This translation is very loose.

22. ASR, Governatore, Tribunale Criminale, Processi sixteenth century, b. 20, case 4, 376v-79v (1555).

23. J. R. Hale, *Machiavelli and Renaissance Italy* (Harmondsworth: Penguin, 1961), 112.

# 17

# Last Words

Daily life anywhere is an almost endless topic. Yet, for past times, our access is often hard; we usually know better how princes mustered armies than how people cleaned their teeth. Still, Renaissance Italy has left many traces, so that we may know it richly. The combined legacy of prolific writing, naturalistic arts, religious and secular buildings with their assorted furnishings, and much loving, expert preservation has left historians with wonderful materials for research and speculation. At the same time, as this book shows, our picture is still half smudge and shadow. Italy's regions and people were highly diverse. And some, much more than others, have claimed the historian's eye. Vibrant Florence, Venice, and Rome bedazzle those looking backward; it is less easy to see other lively urban centers and hard indeed the varied countryside, where most people lived. Similarly, the wealthy and educated elites loom far larger than numbers warrant. Their ways, though colorful and engaging, scarcely typify the experience of the vast majority: peasants, carters, weavers, washerwomen, beggars, prostitutes, and gypsies. It takes inference and detective work to piece together an image of the past; much still remains clouded.

At the same time, the abundance of materials at hand, and their relative transparency, lets anyone interested explore at will. Bountiful museums on both sides of the Atlantic display not only paintings and statuary, but also ceramics, metalwork, and furniture; some great collections are now only a few mouse clicks away. Renaissance music is alive, in concert and, more widely, on disk. Dance, opera, and drama appear on stage. And there still are books on paper: the Renaissance's own writings, modern scholars' studies, and historical fiction, some of it, including the stories noted in our bibliography, alert to the plausible feel of everyday experience. But some historical novels and most movies set in Renaissance Italy should be consumed with a goodly pinch of salt.

When exploring, keep in mind that daily life embraced many things: material goods, activities, social exchanges, beliefs, and values. In the broadest sense, daily life was the experience of culture. It involved tastes, habits of vision and understanding, rhythms of sensation and emotion. It was a zone of agency. That is, people, even if poor and disadvantaged, made choices, seeking to survive and to make the best of things. At the same time, for everyone—high and low alike—choice was never free. Some of the will's impediments were material, others far less tangible. Any fully rounded history of daily life keeps at center stage both tangible things and mental culture, and traces their myriad connections.

One Renaissance theme, and barrier, was danger. The prosperity and safety of persons, families, and larger communities was always precarious. Scarcity, disease, and loss to natural catastrophe, theft, or war lurked and haunted. By historical measures, Renaissance Italy was only middling rich, wealthier in general than in the Middle Ages or the three centuries after 1600, though far poorer than today. Goods were very precious, not only as social markers but also as sources of modest security. As for insecurity itself, it at once repelled and fascinated Renaissance people. It awakened fear and anxious prayer and supplication. But, at the same time, it also appealed to a widespread yen for taking chances. Commerce, politics, and play itself all awakened a gambler's taste for calculated wagering in hopes of profit in the face of uncertainty.

Another Renaissance theme was solidarity, danger's antidote. Social ties were at once useful and costly; one made sacrifices to keep them strong. Alliances with one's fellows, as with God and other supernatural partisans, were precious in the face of dangers. Yet many risks themselves were of human origin. As a consequence, all sorts of dealings, at work and play, were shot through with urgency as Italians strove to reinforce bonds and stave off betrayal. Thus, shared pleasure, though a good in itself, was not only end but means. Play, feasting, carousing, singing, dancing, and sharing the kaleidoscopic spectacle of life shored up friendships and coalitions. Not that Italians were cynics, endlessly conniving. Their calculations were often subtle and instinctive, even barely self-aware. Nonetheless, the urge to ally was alert and active.

Danger's second great remedy, alongside sociability, was worship. Renaissance religion took its energy from its links to safety, of soul and body, of self and of community. Persons, singly or in family, guild and confraternity, or in whole villages and towns, paid respects to divinity in hopes of shelter from all possible ills. Spilling across much of daily life, religion intermingled with magic and medicine. It also marked time and shaped the life cycle.

One place where things and culture met was in the calculation of prestige, Italy's great yardstick of worth and worthiness. Money mattered, especially for those who lacked it. For the rich, wealth and goods counted, more than for their own sake, as a main means to acquire and enact honor. The Renaissance itself was, among other things, an exercise in cultivating status through refined taste and uncommon knowledge; it stimulated connoisseurship. The production, consumption, and display of material goods thus served a double purpose: satisfying bodily needs and marking position in the world. There is nothing new in this for us today, but what distinguished Italy from now was how formalized was the hierarchy and how sharply agonistic were the contests. Food, dress, architecture, furnishings, and even games all entered into rituals of status rivalry and social definition.

Renaissance life was shot through with drama. Acting and spectating gave pleasure and served useful ends. Italians forever improvised on well-known roles. By choice and reflex, they played themselves on great and little stages, before audiences as big as a piazza crowd or packed cathedral or as small as a solitary enemy, friend, or lover. In these theatrics, convention and invention mingled. As often in art, the tension between the expected and the unexpected gave piquancy, and drew and held a crowd of watchers. Daily life, then, was full of dramas on every scale. Humdrum was also there, but well punctuated with lively moments.

Renaissance Italy differed from our twenty-first-century world in physical environment and in institutional and cultural responses to it. Renaissance Italians had their own sense of time and space and of the human order they could build in these dimensions. True, they shared with us all a basic humanity and held religious beliefs akin to those of some of us. Nevertheless, Renaissance Italians experienced themselves and lived their daily lives inside a web of circumstances and understandings that together made them very distinct. To know them well, we must recognize and respect both their closeness to us and their real remoteness. To do so takes a leap of historical imagination, a rich adventure of the mind.

# Resources and Bibliography

## FURTHER READING

Bedini, Silvio. 1997. *The Pope's Elephant*. Harmondsworth: Penguin.

Bell, Rudolph. 1999. *How to Do It: Guides to Good Living for Renaissance Italians*. Chicago: University of Chicago Press.

Brown, Judith C. and Robert C. Davis, eds. 1998. *Gender and Society in Renaissance Italy*. London: Longman.

Brucker, Gene. 1986. *Giovanni and Lusanna*. Berkeley: University of California Press.

———. 1998. *Florence: The Golden Age, 1138–1737*. Berkeley: University of California Press.

Cipolla, Carlo. 1992. *Miasmas and Disease: Public Health and the Environment in the Pre-Industrial Age*. New Haven: Yale University Press.

Cohen, Thomas, and Elizabeth Cohen. 1993. *Words and Deeds in Renaissance Rome: Trials before the Papal Magistrates*. Toronto: University of Toronto Press.

Ginzburg, Carlo. 1980. *The Cheese and the Worms: The Cosmos of a Sixteenth-Century Miller*. Baltimore: Johns Hopkins University Press.

Hale, J. R. 1961. *Machiavelli and Renaissance Italy*. Harmondsworth: Penguin.

———. 1990. *Artists and Warfare in the Renaissance*. New Haven: Yale University Press.

La Roncière, Charles de. 1988. "Tuscan Notables on the Eve of the Renaissance." In *A History of Private Life*, v. 2, *Revelations of the Medieval World*, ed. G. Duby, 157–309. Cambridge, MA: Harvard University Press.

Masson, Georgina. 1975. *Courtesans of the Italian Renaissance*. New York: St. Martin's Press.

Origo, Iris. 1963. *The Merchant of Prato*. Harmondsworth: Penguin.

Riley, Gillian. 1993. *Renaissance Recipes: Painters and Food*. San Francisco: Pomegranate Artbooks.

Ruggiero, Guido. 1993. *Binding Passions: Tales of Magic, Marriage and Power at the End of the Renaissance*. New York: Oxford University Press.

Thornton, Peter. 1991. *The Italian Renaissance Interior, 1400–1600*. New York: Abrams.

Welch, Evelyn. 1997. *Art and Society in Italy, 1350–1500*. New York: Oxford University Press.


## PRIMARY SOURCES, IN ENGLISH TRANSLATION

Alberti, Leon Battista. 1969. *The Family in Renaissance Florence*. Trans. R. Watkins. Columbia: University of South Carolina Press.

Arano, Luisa. 1976. *The Medieval Health Handbook: Tacuinum Sanitatis*. New York: George Braziller.

Aretino, Pietro. 1973. *Aretino's Dialogues*. Trans. R. Rosenthal. New York: Ballantine Books.

Brucker, Gene. 1971; reissue 1992. *The Society of Renaissance Florence: A Documentary Study*. Berkeley: University of California Press.

———, ed. 1967; reissue 1991. *Two Memoirs of Renaissance Florence: The Diaries of Buonaccorso Pitti and Gregorio Dati*. Prospect Heights, IL: Waveland Press.

Castiglione, Baldesar. 1967. *Book of the Courtier*. Trans. G. Bull. Harmondsworth: Penguin Books.

Cellini, Benvenuto. 1998. *Autobiography*. Trans. G. Bull. Rev. ed. Harmondsworth: Penguin Books.

Coryate, Thomas. 1905. *Coryat's Crudities*. 2 vols. Glasgow: James MacLehose and Sons.

Della Casa, Giovanni. 1986. *Galateo*. Trans. K. Eisenbichler and K. Bartlett. Toronto: Centre for Reformation and Renaissance Studies.

Firenzuola, Agnolo. 1992. *On the Beauty of Women*. Trans. K. Eisenbichler and J. Murray. Philadelphia: University of Pennsylvania Press.

Landucci, Luca. 1927. *A Florentine Diary from 1450 to 1516*. Trans. A. Jervis. London: J. M. Dent and Sons.

Michelangelo. 1987. *Michelangelo, Life, Letters, and Poetry*. Trans. George Bull. New York: Oxford University Press.

Montaigne, Michel de. 1958. "Travel Journal." In *Complete Works: Essays, Travel Journal, Letters*, trans D. Frame, 912–1036. Stanford: Stanford University Press.

Moryson, Fynes. 1903; reprint 1967. *Shakespeare's Europe: A Survey of the Condition of Europe at the End of the 16th Century, Being Unpublished Chapters of Fynes Moryson's Itinerary (1617)*. 2d ed. New York: Benjamin Blom.

Pius II. 1962. *Memoirs of a Renaissance Pope: The Commentaries of Pius II. An Abridgment*. Trans. F. A. Gragg. New York: Capricorn.

Platina. 1998. *On Right Pleasure and Good Health*. Trans. M. E. Milham. Tempe: Medieval and Renaissance Texts and Studies.

Pulci, Antonia. 1996. *Florentine Drama for Convent and Festival: Seven Sacred Plays*. Trans. J. W. Cook. Chicago: University of Chicago Press.

Strozzi, Alessandra. 1997. *Selected Letters: A Bilingual Edition*. Trans. H. Gregory. Berkeley: University of California Press.
Vecellio, Cesare. 1977. *Vecellio's Renaissance Costume Book*. New York: Dover Publications.

## NOVELS

Haasse, Hella S., 1990. *The Scarlet City: A Novel of 16th-Century Italy*. Chicago: Academy Chicago Publishers.
Park, Jacqueline. 1997. *The Secret Book of Grazia dei Rossi*. New York: Simon & Schuster.

## SOUND RECORDINGS

*Dolcissima et Amorosa: Early Italian Renaissance Lute Music*. Paul Odette. Harmonia Mundi (France) 907043.
*English and Italian Renaissance Madrigals*. Hillyard Ensemble. Virgin Classics 61671.
*Music for the Florentine Intermedii of 1589*. Taverner Players. EMI/Reflexe CDC 7 47998 2. Music for a Medici celebration.
*Renaissance Music*. Ensemble Ca. 1500. Chandos 524.

## MUSEUMS

Many museums on both sides of the Atlantic have excellent Renaissance collections. Some have rapidly expanding Web sites.

### Collections of Furnishings and Objects

In Italy: Florence, Palazzo Davanzati (a furnished Renaissance house); Milan, municipal museums at the Castello Sforzesco; Naples: Galleria Nazionale di Capodimonte.

### Painting and Sculpture

In Italy: Milan, Pinacoteca di Brera; Venice, Galleria dell'Accademia; Florence, Galleria degli Uffizi; Rome, Musei Vaticani.

In the United States: Washington, DC, National Gallery of Art; New York, Metropolitan Museum of Art; Boston, Isabella Gardiner Museum; Los Angeles, J. Paul Getty Museum.

## SELECTED SCHOLARLY WORKS

Ago, Renata. 1998. *Economia barocca: Mercato e istituzioni nella Roma del Seicento*. Rome: Donizelli.
Baxandall, Michael. 1972. *Painting and Experience in Fifteenth-Century Italy*. Oxford: Oxford University Press.
Burke, Peter. 1987. *Historical Anthropology of Early Modern Italy*. Cambridge: Cambridge University Press.

Capatti, Alberto, and Massimo Montanari. 2000. *La cucina italiana*. Rome: Laterza.

Chambers, David, and Trevor Dean. 1997. *Clean Hands and Rough Justice: An Investigating Magistrate in Renaissance Italy*. Ann Arbor: University of Michigan Press.

Cherubini, Giovanni. 1984. *L'Italia rurale del Basso Medioevo*. Rome: Laterza.

Chojnacki, Stanley. 2000. *Women and Men in Renaissance Venice*. Baltimore: Johns Hopkins University Press.

Cohn, Samuel K., Jr. 1996. *Women in the Streets: Essays on Sex and Power in Renaissance Italy*. Baltimore: Johns Hopkins University Press.

Davidsohn, Robert. 1965. *Storia di Firenze*. V. 7. Florence: Sansoni.

Davis, Robert C. 1991. *Shipbuilders of the Venetian Arsenal: Workers and the Workplace in the Preindustrial City*. Baltimore: Johns Hopkins University Press.

De Giorgio, Michela, and Christiane Klapisch-Zuber, eds. 1996. *Storia del Matrimonio*. Rome: Laterza.

Frugoni, Arsenio, and Chiara Frugoni. 1997. *Storia di un giorno in una città medievale*. Rome: Laterza.

Gentilcore, David. 1992. *From Bishop to Witch: The System of the Sacred in the Early Modern Terra d'Otranto*. Manchester: Manchester University Press.

Goldthwaite, Richard. 1980. *The Building of Renaissance Florence: An Economic and Social History*. Baltimore: Johns Hopkins University Press.

———. 1993. *Wealth and the Demand for Art in Italy, 1300–1600*. Baltimore: Johns Hopkins University Press.

Grendler, Paul. 1989. *Schooling in Renaissance Italy: Literacy and Learning, 1300–1600*. Baltimore: Johns Hopkins University Press.

Groppi, Angela, ed. 1996. *Il lavoro delle donne*. Rome: Laterza.

Grubb, James S. 1996. *Provincial Families of the Renaissance: Private and Public Life in the Veneto*. Baltimore: Johns Hopkins University Press.

Hay, Denys, and John Law. 1989. *Italy in the Age of the Renaissance, 1380–1530*. London: Longman.

Herlihy, David, and Christiane Klapisch-Zuber. 1985. *Tuscans and Their Families*. New Haven: Yale University Press.

King, Catherine. 1998. *Renaissance Women Patrons: Wives and Widows in Italy, c. 1300–1550*. Manchester: Manchester University Press.

Klapisch-Zuber, Christiane. 1985. *Women, Family, and Ritual in Renaissance Italy*. Chicago: University of Chicago Press.

Muir, Edward. 1981. *Civic Ritual in Renaissance Venice*. Princeton: Princeton University Press.

———. 1993. *Mad Blood Stirring: Vendetta and Factions in Friuli during the Renaissance*. Baltimore: Johns Hopkins University Press.

Ortalli, Gherardo, ed. *Gioco e giustizia nell'Italia di Comune*. Rome: Viella.

Pullan, Brian. 1971. *Rich and Poor in Renaissance Venice: Social Institutions of a Catholic State to 1620*. Oxford: Blackwell.

Rocke, Michael. 1996. *Forbidden Friendships: Homosexuality and Male Culture in Renaissance Florence*. New York: Oxford University Press.

Romano, Dennis. 1987. *Patricians and Popolani: The Social Foundations of the Venetian Renaissance State*. Baltimore: Johns Hopkins University Press.

———. 1996. *Housecraft and Statecraft: Domestic Service in Renaissance Venice, 1400–1600*. Baltimore: Johns Hopkins University Press.

Ruggiero, Guido. 1980. *Violence in Early Renaissance Venice.* New Brunswick, NJ: Rutgers University Press.

———. 1985. *The Boundaries of Eros: Sex Crime and Sexuality in Renaissance Venice.* New York: Oxford University Press.

Scaraffia, Lucetta, and Gabriella Zarri, eds. 1999. *Women and Faith: Catholic Religious Life in Italy from Late Antiquity to the Present.* Cambridge, MA: Harvard University Press.

Sereni, Emilio. 1997. *History of the Italian Agricultural Landscape.* Trans. R. Burr Litchfield. Princeton: Princeton University Press.

Trexler, Richard C. 1980. *Public Life in Renaissance Florence.* New York: Academic Press.

———. 1993. *Power and Dependence in Renaissance Florence.* 3 v. Binghamton: Medieval and Renaissance Texts and Studies.

Weissman, Ronald. 1982. *Ritual Brotherhood in Renaissance Florence.* New York: Academic Press.

# Index

Academies, 83

Accounting, 29, 139, 141, 144, 266–67

Adolescents, 193–97; illnesses, 242; work, 268–70

Adultery, 34, 207, 209

Age and status, 75, 191–95, 208. *See also* Life cycle

Agency, social concept, 2, 14–15, 89, 247

Agonism: defined, 79–80; honor and, 95–97. *See also* Competition

Agriculture: fertility festivals, 174; organization, 21, 24–26, 151–52, 254, 268–70; seasonal rhythm, 169, 171, 174–75

Alberini, Marcello, author, 144

Alberti, Leon Battista, humanist, 61, 147–48, 206, 260

Alum, 26

Amalfi, 150, 152

Americas, 225–26, 228, 246

Ancient world, as model, 3, 166, 172, 221; for city layout, 157; for ideas on the life cycle, 193, 208; for literary culture, 134–35, 138, 143, 293;

for medical theory, 240, 244. *See also* Humanism

Animals: as carriers of disease, 242–44; hunted, 151, 288; snakes, 249; wolves, 151

Animals (domestic): bulls, 173, 288; in Carnival, 173, 277; donkeys, 25, 151, 268; as energy source, 261–62; milk of, for human consumption, 185; oxen, 269–70; pets, 289–90; quartered with humans, 217; sheep, 150, 256 (illus.); straying, 116, 269; tormented for sport 48, 289 (illus.); watched by children, 192. *See also* Birds; Dogs; Horses; Pigs

Anticlericalism, 19

Apulia, 6, 150, 151, 174, 229

Aquinas, Thomas, saint, 194

Architecture: domestic, 86, 158–61, 217–21, 224; military, 148–49, 158; rural, 151–52; urban, public, 152–55

Ariès, Philippe, historian, 179

Aristocratization, 27, 76; architecture and, 285; chivalry and, 286–87; culture and, 28; humanism and, 140;

**About the Authors**

ELIZABETH S. COHEN is Assistant Professor of History at York University in Ontario. She is co-author, with Thomas Cohen, of *Words and Deeds in Renaissance Italy*.

THOMAS V. COHEN is Associate Professor of History at York University in Ontario. He is co-author, with Elizabeth Cohen, of *Words and Deeds in Renaissance Italy*.